Africa in Translation

Social History, Popular Culture, and Politics in Germany
Kathleen Canning, Series Editor

Recent Titles

African Students in East Germany, 1949-1975
Sara Pugach

The Arts of Democratization: Styling Political Sensibilities in Postwar West Germany
Jennifer M. Kapczynski and Caroline A. Kita, Editors

Decolonizing German and European History at the Museum
Katrin Sieg

Spaces of Honor: Making German Civil Society, 1700–1914
Heikki Lempa

Bankruptcy and Debt Collection in Liberal Capitalism: Switzerland, 1800–1900
Mischa Suter

Marking Modern Movement: Dance and Gender in the Visual Imagery of the Weimar Republic
Susan Funkenstein

Anti-Heimat Cinema: The Jewish Invention of the German Landscape
Ofer Ashkenazi

Dispossession: Plundering German Jewry, 1933–1953
Christoph Kreutzmüller and Jonathan R. Zatlin, Editors

Sex between Body and Mind: Psychoanalysis and Sexology in the German-speaking World, 1890s–1930s
Katie Sutton

Imperial Fictions: German Literature Before and Beyond the Nation-State
Todd Kontje

White Rebels in Black: German Appropriation of Black Popular Culture
Priscilla Layne

Not Straight from Germany: Sexual Publics and Sexual Citizenship since Magnus Hirschfeld
Michael Thomas Taylor, Annette F. Timm, and Rainer Herrn, Editors

Passing Illusions: Jewish Visibility in Weimar Germany
Kerry Wallach

Cosmopolitanisms and the Jews
Cathy S. Gelbin and Sander L. Gilman

Bodies and Ruins: Imagining the Bombing of Germany, 1945 to the Present
David Crew

The Jazz Republic: Music, Race, and American Culture in Weimar Germany
Jonathan Wipplinger

The War in Their Minds: German Soldiers and Their Violent Pasts in West Germany
Svenja Goltermann

Three-Way Street: Jews, Germans, and the Transnational
Jay Howard Geller and Leslie Morris, Editors

For a complete list of titles, please see www.press.umich.edu

Africa in Translation

A History of Colonial Linguistics in Germany and Beyond, 1814–1945

SARA PUGACH

THE UNIVERSITY OF MICHIGAN PRESS
Ann Arbor

First paperback edition 2022

Published in the United States of America by the
University of Michigan Press
Manufactured in the United States of America
Printed on acid-free paper

First published in paperback August 2022

A CIP catalog record for this book is available from the British Library.

Library of Congress Cataloging-in-Publication Data

Pugach, Sara Elizabeth Berg.
Africa in translation : a history of colonial linguistics in Germany and beyond, 1814–1945 / Sara Pugach.
p. cm. — (Social history, popular culture, and politics in Germany)
Includes bibliographical references and index.
ISBN 978-0-472-11782-6 (cloth : alk. paper) — ISBN 978-0-472-02777-4 (e-book)
1. Translating and interpreting—Africa. 2. Translating and interpreting—Germany. 3. Multilingualism—Africa. 4. Intercultural comunication—Africa. 5. Sociolinguistics—Africa. 6. Sociolinguistics—Germany. I. Title.
P306.8.A35P84 2011
496.07'043—dc22 2011014829

ISBN: 978-0-472-03907-4 (pbk : alk paper)

To my parents
Eleanor Heumann-Pugach
and
Joseph Pugach
and to the memory of my grandmother
Carrie C. Berg

Acknowledgments

Many people and organizations have helped me over the years that I have worked on this book. Bill Bravman and the late B. Marie Perinbam were the first to encourage me to study German colonialism in Africa. At Chicago, Ralph Austen, Michael Geyer, George Stocking, and Jan Goldstein proved excellent advisers. From 1997 to 1999 a German Academic Exchange Service (DAAD) fellowship enabled me to pursue dissertation research in Hamburg. Once in Hamburg, Ludwig Gerhardt and Mechthild Reh of the *Institut für Afrikanistik und Äthiopistik* were invaluable guides to the history of their own institution. The Institute's librarian, Carmen Geisenheyner, cheerfully helped me locate rare books in its collection. Employees of the Staatsarchiv in Hamburg, including Rainer Hering and Heidelies Wittig-Sorg, guided me through their impressive collection of documents relating to Hamburg's colonial history.

A Mellon summer research fellowship in 1998 allowed me to travel to Cape Town, Johannesburg, and Pretoria. I am grateful to my South African colleagues Patrick Harries, Cynthia Kros, and John Noyes, all of whom exhibited keen interest in my topic and provided excellent advice on where to find South African sources. The staffs at the libraries of the Universities of Cape Town, Stellenbosch, Pretoria, and the Witwatersrand helped me locate documents concerning the German linguist Carl Meinhof's many South African students.

I am also grateful to the Mellon Foundation for granting me the fellowship that enabled me to finish my dissertation. A postdoctoral fellowship graciously funded by the Social Science Research Council's Berlin Program for Advanced German and European Studies for the academic year 2001 to 2002 allowed me to further my studies. In Berlin, the late Albert Wirz was a constant inspiration to delve more deeply into my subject, challenging me to go beyond what I already knew and explore new avenues of research. He is greatly missed. Also in Berlin, Holger Stoecker and I shared many long conversations about *Afrikanistik,* in addition to reading and critiquing each other's work. Karin Goihl, administrator of the Berlin Program, made me feel at home in the city. Andreas Eckhert, Caroline Jeannerat, Ulrich van den Heyden, Kathrin Roller, Susann Baller, Michael Pesek, Robbie Aitken, and Christine Stelzig all read or heard parts of this project during my time in Berlin, and contributed perceptive feedback. The staffs of the Bundesarchiv, Geheimes Staatsarchiv Preußischer Kulturbesitz, and Archive of the Berlin Mission Society were crucial in assisting me on my quest for information about such institutions as the *Seminar für Orientalische Sprachen.*

The Berlin Program provided an opportunity to visit archives elsewhere in Germany and Europe, and I am grateful to the staffs at the Archives of the Basel Mission, Archives and Museum Foundation of the United Evangelical Mission, Cambridge University Library, London School of Economics Library, and School of Oriental and African Studies Library for their assistance. I would especially like to acknowledge Paul Jenkins from Basel, an indefatigable researcher and archivist whose knowledge of the Basel collection, as well as of mission history in general, is unparalleled. His colleague, Guy Thomas, has been a worthy successor and aided this project in its final stages. In Wuppertal, home of the United Evangelical Mission, the late Bettina Golz helped me navigate the mission's archive.

In 2005, a Bernadotte E. Schmitt Grant for Research in European, African, or Asian History from the American Historical Association allowed me to return to Berlin and further explore linkages between Germany and South Africa. The Brenthurst Library in Johannesburg granted me a Harry Oppenheimer Fellowship in 2006, which enabled exploration of pre-1870 publications on African languages and cultures. The staff of the library provided outstanding service during my stay, and I would especially like to thank its director, Marcelle Graham, for her kind welcome.

During four years at The Ohio State University in both Lima and Columbus, I received both financial and moral support for my project. Nina Berman welcomed me to Ohio, read my work, discussed it with me in detail, and helped me become a better scholar. OSU historians Alice Conklin and Robin Judd were also excellent readers and critics. Stephanie Patton and Rebecca Nutt were both superior students and good friends. At California State University, Los Angeles, I have found another community of scholars whose wisdom has proven invaluable. I would especially like to thank my history department colleagues Cheryl Koos, Chris Endy, and Choi Chatterjee, who read and made astute comments on some of my final drafts. My History 533 graduate seminar at Cal State LA read one chapter of the book and helped me think through some last-minute issues; among my Cal State LA students, I would particularly like to thank Lucy Tambara, Lori Wilson, and Daniela Avola. The Los Angeles German Studies Workshop read a full draft of chapter 1 and helped me rethink how to work through it. Over the years Daniel Becker, Tuska Benes, Jeff Bowersox, Suzanne Brown-Fleming, Elizabeth Drummond, Kirsten Fermaglich, Debbie Gaitskell, Robert Gordon, Cora Granata, Patrick Harries, David L. Hoyt, Adam Jones, Paul Lerner, Deb Neill, Shula Marks, Laura Mitchell, Bradley Naranch, K. Molly O'Donnell, Karen Oslund, David Pizzo, H. Glenn Penny, Derek R. Peterson, Diana Snigurowicz, Helen Tilley, Daniel Walther, and Andrew Zimmermann have read or listened to parts of this manuscript, and I am grateful for their many outstanding insights.

Special thanks are due to Sara Lennox, who encouraged me to submit this manuscript to the University of Michigan Press, and to Geoff Eley for believing in it. Thanks also go to the two anonymous reviewers who provided the critical feedback that allowed me to revise and improve the manuscript. My editors at Michigan, Chris Hebert, Ellen Bauerle, and Alexa Ducsay, have done an outstanding job shepherding the book through the publication process. Jake Short not only read the entire book, he also suggested its title.

Jane Calvert, Alice Segal, Sophie Panossian, and Nancy Polutan have been excellent friends and made the sometimes lonely process of writing this book much more enjoyable. My husband, Scott Frey, has been more than a friend; he has been a conference "groupie," a reader of drafts at every stage of comprehension, a driver to airports, a visitor to far-flung corners of the world, a four-in-the-morning companion to Kinko's when seven copies of my dissertation needed to be printed out and bound—in other words, he has been a true partner, and I thank him for his constant love and support. Our daughter, Catriona Emily, came along toward the end of this project and has made every aspect of life more joyous. Art Pugach is the best brother a person could have, bar none. I have also been extremely fortunate to have parents who have encouraged me in all of my pursuits, academic and otherwise, from the time I was very small. Eleanor Heumann-Pugach and Joseph Pugach have been there for me the entire way, and I dedicate this book to them, as well as to the memory of my grandmother, Carrie C. Berg. Oma Carrie grew up in Germany, near Baden-Baden, and left not long after the Nazis passed the Nuremberg

Laws in 1935. Her stories of Germany, good and bad, first awoke my interest in the country and in how ideas of race evolved there. She is no longer here but continues to inspire me every day.

All of these people have helped me as I researched, wrote, rewrote, and rewrote again. However, any errors or oversights in the manuscript are mine and mine alone.

Earlier versions of some of these chapters have been published previously. An early form of chapter 2 appeared as "Lost in Translation: Carl Büttner's Contribution to the Development of African Language Studies in Germany," in *The Study of Language and the Politics of Community in Global Context,* ed. David L. Hoyt and Karen Oslund (Lanham, MD: Lexington Books, 2006), 151–84; an early form of chapter 4 appeared as "Theories of Language and Race in German Studies of Africa," in *Jan Czekanowski: Africanist Ethnographer and Physical Anthropologist in Early Twentieth Century Germany and Poland,* ed. Adam Jones, University of Leipzig Papers on Africa, History, and Culture Series No. 10 (Leipzig: Institut für Afrikanistik, 2002), 50–71; an early form of chapter 6 appeared as "Of Conjunctions, Comportment, and Clothing: The Place of African Teaching Assistants in Berlin and Hamburg, 1889–1919," in *Anthropology, European Imperialism, and the Ordering of Africa,* ed. Robert Gordon and Helen Tilley (Manchester: Manchester University Press, 2007), 119–44; and the part of chapter 7 on Meinhof's relationship to his South African students appeared as "Carl Meinhof and the German Influence on Nicholas van Warmelo's Ethnological and Linguistic Writing, 1927–1935," *Journal of Southern African Studies* 30, no. 4 (December 2004): 825–45.

Contents

Abbreviations

AEM	Archiv der evangelischen Missionswerk, Basel
AIAÄ	Archive of the Institut für Afrikanistik und Äthiopistik
BAB	Bundesarchiv Berlin
BFBSA	British and Foreign Bible Society Archives
BMW	Berlin evangelisches Missionswerk Archive
GStaPKB	Geheimes Staatsarchiv Berlin
JSG	J. S. Gericke Library Archive, Stellenbosch
Stabi	Staatsbibliothek zu Berlin
StaH	Staatsarchiv Hamburg
UCTA	University of Cape Town Library Archive
VEM	Vereinigte Evangelisches Missionsarchiv, Wuppertal

Introduction: African Studies and the Classification of Humanity

In June 1946, four South African scholars published a joint article that paid tribute to their intellectual mentor, Carl Meinhof. Meinhof was a German expert in African linguistics and former pastor, and he had died in February 1944. Communications from Germany had been interrupted during World War II, and news of Meinhof's death had just reached Africa's southern tip. His South African colleagues were very upset when they heard that he was dead, and their obituary praised him in effusive and at times almost maudlin terms. Anthropologist G. P. Lestrade commented that "in [Meinhof's] work as a teacher and guide of others interested in African languages and allied subjects, he gathered round him, both in his own school in Hamburg, and in places geographically far removed from that Mecca of the African linguist, an ever-growing band of pupils and collaborators, whom he inspired, stimulated, and in every way aided in the quest for knowledge of the African and his tongues."[1] Another of the essay's authors, Werner W. M. Eiselen—who would eventually become the first Secretary of Native Affairs under the apartheid government, and is sometimes referred to as the "intellectual architect" of that system[2]—added that, "with his splendid silver-white beard, prominent nose, and robust stature Meinhof cut an impressive figure. . . . He is no more, but his name and his work shall live on, also here in South Africa."[3] The article's final two contributors, B. I. C. van Eeden and Walther Bourquin, were hardly less demonstrative, and all four agreed that Meinhof's contributions to the field of African linguistics in particular, and African studies in general, were practically unparalleled.

While Lestrade, Eiselen, van Eeden, and Bourquin saw Meinhof as a leader in the field of African linguistics and extolled his forays into anthropology, religious studies, and related disciplines, today Meinhof is not well known outside of a few academic circles. This is unsurprising. Many of Meinhof's theories on language and ethnicity were uncompromisingly racist, including his contention that the lightest-skinned African "tribes" were usually the ones whose members spoke the most sophisticated languages,[4] or his assertion that the more vowels a language had, the more primitive it was.[5] Joseph Greenberg, an American expert in African languages who led postwar transformations in the field, chastised Meinhof for his racist ideas as early as the 1950s.[6] Thereafter, Meinhof's importance to linguistics and African studies waned.[7]

The tale of Meinhof and his German colleagues, who shaped and founded the discipline of African language and culture studies—*Afrikanistik*—is nonetheless critical for understanding the history of racial thought in Germany and how that thought contributed to segregationist and apartheid ideology in South Africa.[8] The particular strand of German race theory that Meinhof represented—and the one that became most influential in South Africa—was *culturally* or *linguistically* defined. Beginning in the nineteenth century, forms of that theory were propounded by Protestant missionaries and those who, like Meinhof, had close ties to the Protestant missionary establishment. In many ways, this cultural and linguistic racism was distinct from biological racism. The practitioners of biological racism assumed that certain physical traits were inherently superior to others, and that some of these physical characteristics were peculiar to specific human races. Consequently, some races were deemed naturally superior. But cultural and linguistic racism also played a significant role in drawing imaginary boundaries among peoples. Cultural and linguistic racism classified humanity according to grammatical, lexical, social, and religious criteria. Proponents of this kind of racism rejected the idea that members of different races were irrevocably distinct, and that those belonging to the "lesser" races would remain eternally inferior. Rather, they believed that the "civilization" and Christianity that Europeans brought to Africa and other parts of the colonized world might one day nullify racial differences. However, these differences would disappear very slowly, deferring the moment of racial equality so far into the future that no one alive in the nineteenth or twentieth centuries would ever witness it.

The argument that Africans could not attain equal status with whites unless they were first "civilized" legitimated European colonization.[9] Further, while linguistic or cultural racism was different from its biological cousin, they also overlapped. Indeed, the similarities between cultural and biological racism grew increasingly apparent in the later nineteenth century and only continued to multiply thereafter. Yet language always remained the central focus of the German missionaries, and it was primarily the German linguistic discourse that so intrigued South African scholars and policymakers. Moreover, the intellectual connection between Germany and South Africa did not start with Meinhof. Instead, its roots are located with figures such as the philologist W. H. I. Bleek or missionaries like Jakob Döhne, Karl Endemann, J. G. Krönlein, and Albert Kropf, who came to South Africa during the mid- to late nineteenth century and quickly busied themselves with learning, transcribing, and codifying African languages.

In the pages that follow, I trace the history of *Afrikanistik* from its preinstitutional beginnings on the mission field through its entrenchment in metropolitan academia during and after Germany's brief colonial period. Three specific strands weave their way through this history; they include the tale of the racialization of linguistics, the story of the professionalization of African studies, and lastly, at the end of the book, the account of how *Afrikanistik* influenced the thought of scholars and policymakers such as Eiselen and N. J. van Warmelo, who themselves contributed to segregationist and ultimately apartheid philosophy. Missionaries remain front and center throughout, since they initiated the discourse on African languages and their relationship to culture, ethnicity, and race, and continued to shape the discipline even after Germany lost its colonies during World War I. Although the missionaries active earlier in the nineteenth century were not associated with a specific national tradition or empire, once Germany had developed into a colonial power they, too, became imperial agents. When missionaries began to work alongside colonial officials, African language studies, which had served missionary aims, were reconstituted to suit German colonial objectives. This shift was anxiety provoking, because previously missionaries had identified themselves in terms of religion, not nationality. Once the colonial moment arrived, there was fierce debate over whether missionary loyalty lay with universal Christendom or Germany. Ultimately, most missionaries moved toward affiliation with German imperium and away from ecumenism.[10] Both the racialization and professionalization of African studies progressed quickly in this framework, meaning that as the discipline developed, it also nationalized.

The racialization and professionalization of African studies also went hand in hand with an increasing objectification of Africa. Meinhof was consumed with producing a linguistic and ethnological map of Africa. He believed that such a map would allow him to identify the origins and subsequent movements of every African group or "tribe." The project would help clarify the murky ethnic situation in Africa and make the continent's myriad cultures more accessible to German colonists who knew little if anything about Africa before heading there. Meinhof's linguistic map would organize the complex jumble of African peoples into a neat classificatory hierarchy that was largely made up of three distinct language families: the Hamitic, the Bantu, and the Sudanic/Nigritic. There were some subcategories—including Nilotic and "Bushman"—but for the most part, these three were the overarching categories with which Meinhof worked. In this way, Africa became a clearly defined, rationalized object of study that could be easily broken down, digested, and then controlled through European knowledge. This linguistic map never went uncontested, however; prior to Meinhof's rise as the dominant figure in African studies at the end of the nineteenth century, other scholars, including Bleek, Richard Lepsius, A. W. Schleicher, and Robert Hartmann, were working out their own Africanist maps, which varied considerably from each other's as well as from Meinhof's. Further, even after Meinhof was established as a fixture in Africanist circles, his ideas were constantly challenged, both by outside observers such as Austrian linguist Ferdinand Hestermann and by his own students, including van Warmelo.[11]

The compartmentalization and "mapping" of Africa undertaken by Meinhof and his colleagues constituted a form of Saidian Orientalism or Mudimbean alterity.[12] German scholars imagined that Africans spoke and acted in a certain manner and were unlikely to deviate from a specific set of behaviors. The Africa of their imagination did not correlate with what they encountered on the ground, but that was of little consequence; colonizers steadfastly believed in the exotic, primitive Africa of their invention. European images of Africa—German or otherwise—also had clearly destructive repercussions, since white colonists encouraged ethnic separatism where it had sometimes not previously existed, with dramatic and horrific results not only in South Africa but in many other African nations, for example, Rwanda and Burundi.[13]

African studies in general—and the study of African languages in particular—thus became critical to the German colonial project, since their knowledge allowed a seemingly chaotic linguistic picture to resolve itself into a neatly ordered map. Gauri Viswanathan has written that the academic field of English in Great Britain first emerged in the colonial context of the Raj, and that "no serious account of its growth and development can afford to ignore the imperial mission of educating and civilizing colonial subjects in the literature and thought of England, a mission that in the long run served to strengthen Western cultural hegemony in enormously complex ways."[14] It is almost a truism to say that the same was so for *Afrikanistik*. Yet with *Afrikanistik*, it was not the language of the colonizer but of the colonized that was being put to use in the service of imperialism. Missionaries, lay scholars, and colonial officials all wanted to use African languages to extend European power.

German images of Africans and their languages were not, however, especially stable; they shifted over time, as biological race grew increasingly important to linguistic description.[15] Further, individual opinions on the colonies and how Germans could best relate with their inhabitants varied widely. Missionaries, professionally trained scholars, and government functionaries did not always share the same vision of Africa. If we are trying to define *Afrikanistik* as an Orientalist discourse, this difference of vision becomes problematic. Thomas Trautmann has argued that the concept of Orientalism as characterized by Edward Said was "badly underspecified."[16] Saidian Orientalism was too expansive, incorporating a wide range of Western cultural products, from art to literature to philology.[17] It was an all-encompassing system of knowledge, absorbing all European views on the Orient into one monolithic image of the Other. By contrast, the nineteenth-century concept of Orientalism was narrow and primarily philological, based on the close reading and interpretation of texts. When philologists became involved with colonial policy, they often came into conflict with political officials who had opposing beliefs about how best to implement colonial control. Philological and political forms of Orientalism were different and cannot be lumped together under the same totalizing label.

Trautmann's work concerned India and pinpointed a tension between British philologists and colonial officials. Africanist scholars and government officials in Germany had similarly differing ideas about what constituted practical colonial knowledge and often disagreed over how that knowledge should be dispersed. Academics sought "deep" understanding of African natives through close analysis of oral texts. Conversely, civil servants wanted simple, straightforward communication that required little comprehension of their African subjects. Even though they were supposedly moving toward the same goal, that of efficient and productive colonization, linguists like Meinhof continually quarreled with administrative personnel over how to get there.

The South African case was different, since many of Meinhof's students worked directly for their country's government. Meinhof's student N. J. van Warmelo was government ethnologist, as was Lestrade. After Eiselen acquired his degree in Hamburg, he left academe entirely and spent his life in politics, working under leaders like Hendrik Verwoerd.[18] Their work contributed more to policy than Meinhof's; nonetheless, the general disconnect between scholars and bureaucrats appears in various contexts and constitutes another theme that will thread its way through this book.

The discourse of *Afrikanistik* was not, moreover, the exclusive domain of white missionaries, bureaucrats, and academics. Rather, it was the product of a colonial encounter between Germans and Africans. Without African collaboration Germans could not have carried out their linguistic inquiries. They relied on native middlemen—interpreters and translators—for information on all aspects of African life. While most Africans were not credited for their work and remain anonymous, others appear by name in German texts on African languages or represented themselves personally in published articles or letters with German correspondents. In general, colonial societies were defined by their hybridity,[19] and the case of *Afrikanistik* shows that the German colonies were not exceptions, nor was the German metropole. *Afrikanistik* was not merely the product of European dominance and African submission but of an interplay between two or more cultures. The science emerged among German missionaries and African informants on the mission field and traveled back to the German metropoles of Berlin and Hamburg, where it was taught by both Germans and Africans. Then finally, the knowledge that *Afrikanistik* had produced was carried once again to Africa with those who had studied it.

Afrikanistik, Protestant Missionaries, and (German) Colonialism

Germany was not unified until 1871 and did not acquire its overseas empire in Africa and the Pacific until the 1880s. That empire—never large in comparison to the holdings of England or France—collapsed bit by bit over the course of World War I. Given the short duration of German colonialism and its seemingly marginal position with respect to other eras in German history, scholars have only recently begun to realize how profoundly that brief colonial interlude affected the country. Over the last two decades or so, this realization has led to a marked upswing in research and writing on German encounters with the non-Western world. This spate of publications has confirmed that while Germany's colonial heyday was short, the country's formal colonial experiences had a significant impact on its twentieth-century history.[20] Colonial enthusiasm well predated the acquisition of empire, too, as Susanne Zantop's seminal study on German colonial fantasies in the pre-1871 era attests. Germans were fascinated by colonialism even in the absence of physical empire. They yearned for overseas possessions long before unification or the "Scramble for Africa" of the 1880s, and developed a strong belief that they were the "ideal" European colonizers, who would treat their imaginary subjects with a benevolence that none of the "real" European colonizers—the Spaniards, Portuguese, Dutch, French, or English—ever had.[21]

Colonial dreams of the kind Zantop pinpointed were deeply bound to German national identity. Images of Germanness were constructed alongside of and in association with images of non-Western Others. Carefully crafted knowledge of the Oriental or African Other was as important to modern Germans as it was for their English or French counterparts. Yet in a glaring oversight, Said did not consider German scholarship in *Orientalism* because Germany had no formal Oriental empire. Kaushik Bagchi and others have provided a powerful corrective to Said in suggesting that Germans were in fact crucial to Orientalist scholarship; they generated authoritative statements about the Middle East, India, and the rest of the world that informed the texture of the German imagination.[22] Orientalist thought was not constrained by the political situation but transcended the presence of tangible links to the non-West.[23] "The set of attitudes" that went along with the growth of European hegemony, which included the idea of the unchanging Other, were as pervasive in Germany as they were elsewhere.

Nineteenth-century Germans were perhaps even *more* preoccupied with the Orient than their neighbors with a political stake in the region. The turn of that century was a time of foment across Europe, as Napoleon destroyed the preexisting social and political order and imposed his own framework in its stead. In 1806 Franz II, the last Holy Roman Emperor, abdicated his throne and dissolved the empire, which had encompassed most German-speaking lands. The German territory that came under Napoleon's purview was reorganized into the Federation of the Rhine. By the time of Napoleon's defeat and the convening of the Congress of Vienna in 1815, the question of what sort of political structure would surface in central Europe was open. What did emerge was a loose German Confederation, which did not come close to satisfying those Germans who longed for the creation of a truly unified German nation. In the absence of a political nation, some sought a linguistic or cultural alternative through the study of comparative philology. They hoped that by uncovering the roots of the German people, they would also uncover a cohesive German identity. Philologists turned in various directions during their search, including eastward—to Asia and the "Orient"—looking for Germanic origins. Indeed, Tuska Benes has noted that the Orientalist Heinrich Julius von Klaproth coined the term *indogermanisch* with specific reference to a language group that could be traced back to central Asia.[24]

The passionate quest for origins among groups such as those found in the Caucasus bears further witness to the depth of German engagement with the wider world, and it connects, too, with arguments about colonialism. Both Benes and George S. Williamson have explicated the intensity of German forays into research on India and central Asia, which philologists hoped would, in addition to helping unearth German origins, shed light on such trenchant issues as the essential character of the Bible and Christianity.[25] The quest for Germany's—and humanity's—beginnings led as well to fierce debates about the concept of race and how the different "races" stood with regard to each other. Scholars like Blumenbach, Kant, Herder, and Hegel were endlessly involved with questions on human nature and the unity of mankind. Kant, for instance, argued vehemently against the suppression, enslavement, or colonization of "inferior" peoples on the grounds that they deserved equal rights, and that Europe disgraced itself and negated its moral superiority when it denied those self-same rights.[26]

Asia was often considered a wellspring of European civilization in philological discourse, if a contested one. Africa, however, remained a dark, savage wasteland: It was civilization's antithesis. While Kant's views were generally anticolonial, he was deeply ambivalent about Africans and their abilities.[27] Hegel dismissed Africans by arguing that the climate in which they lived was not conducive to history or higher forms of culture.[28] The eighteenth- and early nineteenth-century search for German national, linguistic, and religious origins may have led many places, but it did not extend to Africa. Even so, Africa would later become as entwined with the quest for origins as Asia. Wilhelm Bleek, renowned for his studies of South African languages and folklore, argued as early as the 1860s that "Bushman" and "Hottentot" mentalities were similar to those of ancient Europeans.[29] Later, Meinhof and his contemporaries echoed Bleek in their belief that the African present reflected Europe's primordial state.[30] Germans had not emerged from Africa, but that did not mean they were disconnected from it; Africa was not a place to seek one's roots directly, but it did mirror them and provided a key to unlocking human prehistory. Moreover, even if Germans were not directly descended from Africans, they could still trace links among African languages and their Indogermanic cousins. Meinhof, for example, posited a relationship between the Hamitic and Indo-European language groups.[31]

Colonial fantasies inspired philosophy and literature, and encouraged scholars to ponder what a German version of colonialism might look like.[32] Academics and intellectuals were not, however, the only ones interested in Africa, Asia, or the Americas; the potential relevance of overseas territories to German well-being impinged on more practical debates about issues such as immigration and the "boundaries" of Germanness, as Bradley Naranch has pointed out.[33] Yet in the precolonial era—and even into the colonial age—few Germans actually journeyed to Africa. Missionaries, among them the earliest Africanist philologists, therefore belonged to the minority for whom colonialism was concrete reality, not just idle fantasy. Todd Kontje has argued that in the nineteenth century the British made the Orient or broader non-West into a career, while for Germans it was still largely just an idea; this may have been true for most, but it was not so for missionaries.[34] Along with explorers, scientists, mercenaries, and sundry travelers, missionaries journeyed beyond the familiar many years before the establishment of the German Empire.[35] German and Danish missionaries dominated English organizations such as the Society for Promoting Christian Knowledge and Church Missionary Society, which were founded at the turn of the eighteenth and turn of the nineteenth centuries, respectively.[36] Germans were heavily invested in the British and Foreign Bible Society[37] and were represented in the London Missionary Society.[38] Further, missionaries brought Africa home to Germany through festivals designed to encourage local interest in their work abroad and pamphlets concerning their progress in the field.[39]

H. Glenn Penny has contended that ethnologists in imperial Germany were less interested in using their discipline to support national colonial aims than they were in crafting museum displays that would telegraph an expansive, humanist understanding of world history to much more local audiences.[40] Missionary involvement in colonialism did not automatically equal longing for German imperium either, if for different reasons. For most of the nineteenth century German-speaking missionaries worked in non-German empires in places like Georgetown (Freetown), Sierra Leone, with the permission of their foreign—usually English—hosts. They were members of English missionary societies and labored in the field beside their English colleagues. Instead of imagining themselves as part of a nation with fixed political boundaries, these missionaries identified with a transnational Protestant community that especially included Britons.[41] When they compiled their grammars and dictionaries, they did so in English, and for a mainly English-speaking audience and market.[42] African language studies emerged in this expressly international context, and missionaries conducted their research in the service of an ecumenical church rather than a national institution. This is a significant point, one that suggests that nationalism was not as crucial to the emergence of African studies in Germany as it was for the birth of Orientalism. It also complicates the idea that colonialism as practiced by Germans was necessarily and always "German" colonialism; while German-born and German-speaking missionaries were certainly supportive of colonial expansion, in this early phase it was—perhaps ironically—mainly British imperialism that they were buttressing.[43]

Through their connections with foreign missionaries, as well as with their congregations in Africa, missionary linguists became enmeshed in global networks of exchange and communication. This "globalization" was critical in shaping their perceptions of colonialism, which, prior to the late nineteenth century, was for them a Protestant, Western enterprise, not a German one. Globalization in the nineteenth century was generally connected to the spread of industrialization, which allowed people to travel much more quickly over greater distances than ever before, enabling the rapid transfer of goods on an international market, as well as of technologies.[44] Improvements in the medical field further allowed for the penetration of areas that were previously deadly to Europeans, since they lacked immunity to tropical diseases. Missionaries were constantly advancing further inland as the possibilities to settle more widely grew, and their movements away from the coast coincided roughly with the rise of Germany's own empire.

The process of globalization did not, however, lead to the acceptance of universality in Germany after its unification in 1871. On the contrary, the limits of the nation grew ever more sharply defined. Sebastian Conrad has argued that globalization created an exclusionary German national identity that manifested itself in discussions on topics such as passport controls and sanitary regulations. Questions about how to maintain an orderly industrial society sounded very similar whether the subject being addressed was African workers in German East Africa or their German counterparts in Westphalia; discourses on how to encourage work among "lazy" individuals varied little. At the same time, new understandings of space and territoriality defined African and German workers differently, with the latter being able to participate as members of the German nation, whereas the former were explicitly left out.[45] Marcia Klotz has likewise demonstrated that global encounters were critical to German identity; such encounters encouraged dualistic thinking, as Germans divided the world into two halves—one occupied by superior Westerners, the other by primitives whose land was ripe for colonization. As the world grew closer and contact between cultures more common, identity came to be constructed in binary fashion that took "civilized" and "savage" peoples as its two poles.[46] In Klotz's interpretation as well as Conrad's, German nationalism did not so much predate globalization as it was forged by it.

Once Germany had assumed colonial control over territories in Africa, China, and the Pacific, debates on "Germanness" and who belonged to the nation certainly increased in metropole and colony alike, as well as beyond. German South West Africa is a case in point. In the metropole, organizations such as the *Deutsche Kolonialgesellschaft* defined the parameters of the ideal German colony that would emerge in the South West, one built on agrarian German values and infused with a specifically German morality.[47] Meanwhile, as Birthe Kundrus, Daniel Walther, and Robbie Aitken have shown, German settlers in the colony strictly policed the borders of what they called *Deutschtum,* deciding who would and would not belong in the new German community they were constructing, one that was beset with problems of miscegenation.[48] Moreover, the issue of defining who did and did not belong to this broadly conceptualized "Germany," whose boundaries stretched wherever there was German settlement, was not limited to the overseas colonies; the position of Germans living in Poland, Russia, and elsewhere in the "East" were also central to debates on national identity.[49]

The march of globalization and simultaneous sharpening of German national identity complicated missionary objectives, as from the late nineteenth century missionaries were increasingly pressed to reexamine their loyalties. Figures such as Friedrich Fabri and Carl Büttner called the ecumenical, evangelical project into question when they argued for a closer connection between Germany's Protestant missionaries and the newly emergent German Empire. Fabri was a longtime director of the Rhenish Missionary Society, which was centered in Barmen. In 1879 he wrote the influential tract "Does Germany Need Colonies?," a question that he answered with an emphatic yes. Fabri believed, along with members of pressure groups such as the *Deutsche Kolonialgesellschaft,* that with the nation's exploding population came a responsibility to find new opportunities for German settlement abroad. Fabri's pamphlet did not change the missionary stance on ecumenicalism overnight, and indeed the relationship between mission and nation was passionately debated for decades.[50]

Missionary attitudes toward nationalism were changing around the same time that another development, in the realm of racial thought, was occurring. Pascal Grosse has contended that idea of racial hierarchy that was so central to Nazi Germany first emerged in the colonial and immediately precolonial periods. Eugenicists—those who practiced "race" science—became absorbed in colonial debates that reflected a distinct revision of earlier, liberal principles. The concept of meritocracy governing liberal beliefs in how the state should be structured in a post-Enlightenment world was mediated by a biologism that stressed the importance of racial descent to individual and societal success.[51] Moreover, Andrew Zimmerman has shown that the imperial period was one of transition from a humanistic perspective on society to one that was biologically driven. The "antihumanism" of anthropology, which had a broad appeal across Germany, rejected older ideas of linguistic nationhood in favor of an ethnic identity grounded in biological characteristics.[52]

New theories about racial order had a direct impact on missionary discourse about Africans. That this was so is discernible not only in their discussions on language but in missionary reactions to and confusion over the question of *Rassenmischung.* Kathrin Roller and Ursula Trüper have shown that marriages between German missionaries and native women were accepted in the early nineteenth century. For instance, Johan Hinrich Schmelen, a German member of the London Missionary Society, was married to a Nama woman named Zara, and they became patriarch and matriarch of a sizable clan.[53] As the century progressed, general acceptance of relationships such as that of the Schmelens declined among Germans, and those who were "half-caste" or *Mischlinge* were shunned.[54] By the early twentieth century the colonial government in South West Africa had reclassified two of Schmelen's descendants—who were once considered white—as natives.[55]

Whatever their claims to belief in a universal humanity that could be united in Christendom, missionaries were not immune to overarching political and intellectual trends, and by the early twentieth century were severely conflicted about the issue of race. In 1909, at the twelfth annual conference for German-speaking Protestant missionaries in Bremen, participants debated the mission's position on the "race question." They upheld the belief that mankind was essentially one—as opposed to the polygenists of the previous century, who had assumed that each race had a different origin[56]—but also agreed that the various races embodied their own peculiar qualities, and that at present they were both separate and unequal. P. Hausleiter, who gave the keynote address, argued that what separated the "Indogermanic" race from the other two major races, the "Mongolian" and the "African," was its monotheism. Religion and culture were still the main determinants of racial difference, not biology or genetics. Nonetheless, even as missionaries emphasized cultural divides, the language they used could recall that of biological race; at the same conference in Bremen, even missionaries who agreed that they would not forbid "mixed" marriages and hoped that the "Neger" (Negro) would become a brother in Christ were revolted by the idea that he might also become a "Schwager" (in-law).[57]

At the beginning of the nineteenth century, and for much of the precolonial era, German-speaking, Protestant missionaries did not see themselves as envoys of Germandom but, instead, as soldiers for an international Christianity. By the end of the same century and for the start of the next they worked alongside government officials and saw their efforts as contributing to an explicitly German colonialism. Along the way they created a distinct discourse on the interplay among language, culture, and race, which was influenced by linguistic nationalism but never defined by it. Protestant missionaries also represent a category of colonial agents and knowledge producers whom English-speaking scholars of German imperialism have not yet sufficiently addressed.[58] This book serves as a corrective by reintegrating the missionaries into the history of German colonialism and demonstrating how vital they were to the development and maintenance of empire, both German and otherwise.

South African Concerns

The German Protestant missionary debate on race was a vexed one. It was complicated by a conflicting desire to convert Africans and simultaneously keep them at arm's length. Moreover, missionary concerns about miscegenation were echoed in the German articles and books on African languages, which expressed ambivalence not about *Rassenmischung* per se but rather about the fixity of linguistic/racial groups and which peoples belonged in various, European-constructed, categories. However, whether it was confused or not, German missionary rhetoric on language and culture proved extremely appealing in late nineteenth- and early twentieth-century South Africa. German ideas concerning racial separation, both in theory and practice, resonated in a country where questions of human classification took on more immediacy, as African and European populations were coming into increasing contact with each other, and whites, especially Afrikaners, began to fear for their national survival.[59]

During the early twentieth century, when *Rassenmischung* was being debated in the German senate,[60] and the imaginary lines that German academics and missionaries were drawing among groups were growing ever more rigid, South Africa was going through its own state of flux. The South African (Anglo-Boer) War had ended in 1902. Thereafter the victorious British and defeated Afrikaners had worked together toward reconciliation, hoping to achieve a unified white-run government in South Africa that would deny all political participation to blacks. After the establishment of the Union of South Africa in 1910, which at least in theory solidified bonds between the British and Afrikaners,[61] government officials began to draft laws that would legally segregate Africans from whites. The Natives Land Act of 1913 expressly forbid African ownership of land outside of specially designated reserves, while the Native Urban Areas Act of 1923 extended segregation in cities. Both aimed at forcibly separating blacks from whites.

Meinhof dreamt of using his linguistic classificatory models to shape policy in the German colonies, dictating how various linguistic groups were to be treated based on a series of cultural traits that were supposedly associated with each language family;[62] yet evidence suggests that on the whole scholarly theories never were applied in Germany's territories, which were in any event lost during World War I.[63] Reserves of the kind that came to exist in South Africa did appear in German South West Africa following the Herero War of 1904–7, but they were not carved up based on academic information supplied by metropolitan scholars but were instead parceled out according to the loyalty that certain groups had displayed to the Germans.[64]

In South Africa, however, the white interest in defining and categorizing Africans continued well beyond World War I. Industrialization and labor migration had changed population dynamics, as increasing numbers of blacks move from countryside to city. Whites sought to regulate black traffic, while also ensuring that a large labor pool remained for the mines and other industrial complexes. The Afrikaner scholars who journeyed to Germany or demonstrated interest in German linguistic theories on Africa were intrigued with them precisely because the German methodology for determining group origins offered a solution to the question of where each "tribe" had geographically emerged, and thus where it "belonged." Van Warmelo, a Meinhof student and South Africa's government ethnologist from 1930 to 1969, discussed the problem of African displacement as one of the most significant facing the country in his 1935 *Preliminary Survey of the Bantu Tribes of South Africa.*[65] That book, which was used as a template for South Africa's homeland system under apartheid,[66] drew on the classificatory models that Meinhof and his colleagues had proposed. Like Meinhof, van Warmelo argued that the Bantu living in South Africa had experienced too much upheaval to confirm each group's primordial location, but he nonetheless proceeded to approximate the boundaries of the areas in which each lived.[67]

German arguments may also have proved compelling because there were already so many intellectual ties between Germany and South Africa. In the early nineteenth century, members of the Berlin Missionary Society established stations in the Transvaal and elsewhere,[68] and began to proselytize among people such as the Zulu, Xhosa, Venda, and Sotho.[69] Other German missionary societies, such as the Hermannsburgers and Moravians, also settled in South Africa.[70] The Rhenish Missionary Society was mainly in South West Africa, not South Africa proper, but some of its missionaries moved to South Africa instead of returning to Germany after their retirements.[71] Some of the German missionaries were active linguists, including Kropf, Döhne, and Endemann from Berlin, and F. W. Kolbe and Carl Hugo Hahn from Wuppertal;[72] others were relatives of individuals who would later become scholars and administrators for the South African government, such as Gustav Eiselen, father of Werner Eiselen. These missionary societies embodied the paternalistic attitude toward Africans that was so prevalent in linguistic discourse, since they believed in eventual equality for the races but did not think it existed in the present.

In addition to the missionaries, one other nineteenth-century German traveler to South Africa had a strong and lasting impact on all of the linguists who followed him, both German and South African. This was Bleek, who was among the first European scholars to write a dissertation on African languages. Bleek coined the term *Bantu* to describe that language family, and he also presented an early version of the Hamitic theory later espoused by Meinhof and his contemporaries. Bleek was best known, however, as the librarian for Cape governor Sir George Grey, and he ultimately immigrated to South Africa, where he settled. Bleek was not a missionary and in this sense does not fit into the general pattern laid out in this book. Nonetheless, his position in the field of African studies was so vital that he needs to be discussed in any study of the subject. Moreover, he was linked not only to South African scientific circles but German ones as well through his cousin, zoologist and race theorist Ernst Haeckel; Bleek therefore personifies the strong connection that existed between intellectual communities in the two countries.[73]

The German–South African association did not end with the nineteenth century, as the examples of van Warmelo and Eiselen show. Scholars from both regions were also united by a continuing fealty to diachronic theories of anthropology even after the British, for instance, had turned to synchronic explanations for cultural phenomena.[74] Indeed, South African *volkekunde,* which was predominantly practiced by Afrikaners and not those of English descent, bore a strong resemblance to German *Völkerkunde.*[75] Both suggested that cultural characteristics were diffused among far-flung societies over a period of time, instead of developing independently in different areas. A particular type of spear might manifest itself across cultures, and adherents of *volkekunde* or *Völkerkunde* would imagine that its origins lay with one society but that it had been transmitted to or borrowed by others. British social anthropology as represented by figures such as A. R. Radcliffe-Brown and Bronislaw Malinowski, by contrast, looked within a society itself to determine how cultural traits had emerged. In Germany, diffusionism was represented by what was known as the *Kulturkreis* school, whose most prominent members included museum workers Bernhard Ankermann and Fritz Graebner, the priest Wilhelm Schmidt, and the adventurer-collector Leo Frobenius. Carl Meinhof and his linguist colleagues were not technically part of the *Kulturkreis* school. Yet Meinhof's belief that languages spread as populations moved was extremely similar to diffusionism, and demonstrates that he and his South African colleagues were drawn to *Kulturkreis* philosophy.

The German racial theories that van Warmelo, Eiselen, and their colleagues espoused cannot be directly equated with the biological, eugenic understanding of race most commonly associated with the Nazis. Instead, like Meinhof their ideology was much more in line with the linguistic and cultural racism of the missionaries. While there were definite connections between Nazism and Afrikaner nationalism in South Africa,[76] the intellectual origins of apartheid and preapartheid thought were exceptionally diverse.[77] Eiselen's insistence on separate development and the potential of Africans to reach the same civilizational pinnacle as whites, but in their own culturally unique way,[78] echoed that of Meinhof and missionary linguists such as Diedrich Westermann. Although Eiselen, in his capacity as secretary for Native Affairs in Verwoerd's government, was the Meinhof student most strongly tied to the apartheid regime and its brutal practices, he viewed race through a cultural lens, not a biological one. This is a significant point, since it draws attention to the general disjuncture between Nazi and missionary racism. Biological or eugenic and cultural hypotheses on race could and did overlap, as chapter 4 will demonstrate. Nonetheless, Africanists drew mainly on cultural and linguistic terms in their writings and were often ambivalent toward overtly physical descriptions of their subjects. Linguistic racism shared ideas with its biological counterpart but was not the same.

Organization of the Book

Many missionary or missionary-linked linguists were caught between the pragmatic and the academic, since they started to research African languages for the practical purpose of evangelization but found themselves increasingly drawn to studies of human origins and interrelationships among far-flung peoples. The first chapter of the book examines these missionary linguists in the earliest, practical stage, before academic questions or problems with a colonial government became as much a matter for concern. It focuses on the missionaries' pietist heritage and how it influenced their work in Africa. I argue that the missionaries who became linguists at this stage were also universalists, ones who were not actively involved with political upheavals in Germany or nationalist struggles. Instead, they identified themselves primarily with the church and its members, irrelevant of whether they were German-speaking or not. Racism was certainly not absent from the dialogues of missionaries before German unification in 1871 and German colonization in the 1880s, but there were few efforts to codify difference or express German patriotism. This chapter also looks at some of the early German missionaries in southern Africa, as well as at Wilhelm Bleek, the linguist who became Cape Colony governor Sir George Grey's librarian and who coined the terms *Bantu* and *Hamitic* to describe African language families.

The second chapter, by contrast, focuses on the missionary shift from embracing universalism to eschewing it in favor of nationalism. It covers what happened when Germany became a colonial power in Africa and the amateur discipline of African studies moved from the mission field to metropoles like Berlin and Hamburg. In the late 1880s African language studies were institutionalized at Berlin's Seminar for Oriental Languages, where courses on Africa and its peoples were instituted for the first time in "newly colonial" Germany. The mission connection remained; Carl Büttner, the former Rhenish society missionary in South and South West Africa, was the first African language instructor at the seminar, where he also taught courses in "The Geography and Ethnography of Central Africa, with a special emphasis on German Colonial History."[79] Büttner is an enigmatic and transitional figure in the history of African studies, a new kind of missionary whose loyalty to the German state was unwavering. Büttner could neither stand his life in the mission field nor tolerate the Africans to whom he preached,[80] and he ultimately left the mission and began to work for the German government. He assisted them in procuring South West Africa as a colony. Throughout his brief colonial career—which ended with his early death in 1892—Büttner always kept up his language studies and was a major champion of the nationalization of both the mission and its African language research. He blended his practical and theoretical responsibilities quite efficiently and seemingly without effort, not seeing any conflicts of interest between the two. This chapter charts Büttner's involvement with the colonial cause, as well as the foundation and early growth of the seminar to which he belonged.

While Büttner did briefly struggle to make the importance of African languages known to the German colonial establishment,[81] his protégé, Carl Meinhof, became much more caught up in the practical-theoretical bind. Meinhof, who posited himself as a champion of both Protestant missionaries and German nationalism, is the third chapter's subject. In some ways the mission did embrace Meinhof's theories about African languages and cultures, but it also resisted his ideas and held him at arm's length. For instance, Meinhof's suggestion that students of African languages acquire comprehensive training not only in individual languages but also in the basic grammatical and morphological structures of the Bantu language family met with mixed results. Discussing whether Meinhof's research might have a positive influence on "native" African morality, Barmen mission inspector A. W. Schreiber disdainfully noted that to expect this was tantamount to belief that "the German people would receive similarly salutary benefits from German studies."[82] Moreover, other missionaries told Meinhof that while they admired his scholarship, they could not commit themselves to sending him students once he began to teach out of his rural Pomeranian parsonage.[83]

Because he was the most important early twentieth-century scholar of African studies, Meinhof continues to figure prominently in the chapters that follow. The fourth chapter is about his relationship with Felix von Luschan, their formulation of the Hamitic hypothesis, and their tendency to conflate physical with linguistic traits when classifying African peoples.

In the fifth chapter, I examine the channels through which linguistic and other ideas about Africa were transmitted to those who pursued "colonial" studies in Hamburg or had occasion to read about them in the journals published there. Specifically, the chapter addresses the establishment of a phonetics laboratory to supplement the classroom learning of African languages. The laboratory was significant because it highlighted the fact that African studies was now also considered a physical science, and that the sounds Africans made were deemed more significant than their cultures or societies. The antihumanist conception of a society where physical differences trumped cultural concerns exerted a considerable impact on African linguistics,[84] though older beliefs in the value of culture and civilization never disappeared.

The seminar and the laboratory later added to it were instrumental in shaping Africanist discourse in early twentieth-century Germany and were conduits for disseminating the theories that Meinhof and his colleagues had proposed. Germans founded and maintained these institutions, leaving the impression that it was only Germans who had a role in molding *Afrikanistik.* However, nothing could be further from the truth, and in chapter 6 I look at the non-Germans who contributed to disciplinary formation, specifically the African lecturers and teaching assistants who worked in the classrooms of Berlin and Hamburg. From the institutionalized beginnings of the Seminar for Oriental Languages, "native" speakers were indispensable to the language-learning process. In 1908, Berlin seminar director Sachau recalled that at its inception in 1887, the goal was to have "teaching [that was] organized around joint instruction by a German scholar and one or more indigenous *Lektoren* [lecturers]."[85] The idea was that only native speakers would possess the capability to instruct others in the proper accent and mode of expression for their languages. Yet these native speakers were not parrots; some, such as the Togolese Victor Toso, became actively involved in discussions on the grammar and morphology of

African languages. More important is the fact that African assistants both rebelled against and complied with the images of their languages and people that the Germans presented. The *Lektoren* therefore both subverted and confirmed European notions of race; they questioned their placement in racial hierarchies but also, in some instances, reasserted those same positions for personal political or economic gain.

In the seventh chapter, the focus is on the relationship between the German Africanists and their South African colleagues in the post–World War I era. When Germany was stripped of its colonies, Africanists felt stripped of their purpose. There no longer seemed to be practical reasons for their studies. Some, especially Westermann, did continue with their practical functions in the service of mission societies and educational institutions in other European countries, but many Africanists and missionaries felt cheated by the allies and were more reluctant to collaborate with them. Ultimately, some turned to the Nazis, since they believed that Hitler was interested in returning Germany to its formal colonial glory. From the start South Africans were, however, considered different, and a sense of camaraderie developed between Afrikaners and Germans. Indeed, the German discourse on Africa was co-opted and extended in South Africa. While Africanist work continued apace in Germany throughout the interwar years and World War II, much of this chapter will still concentrate on the evolving relationship between Germans and South Africans, and how German missionary ideas of "race" and language may have been put to practical effect in South Africa in the years leading up to apartheid and beyond.

The book concludes with a look at what has happened to *Afrikanistik* since World War II and reconsiders its legacy in both Germany and South Africa. Africanist concerns were not of immediate interest to Germans, but in South Africa increasing emphasis was placed on ethnic separation. In Germany, African language studies were largely confined to the university, although they were surely pertinent to the humanitarian workers who followed in the colonialists' wake.[86] Those same studies took on urgency in South Africa, where white anxieties led to a fanatic desire to police the borders between races. The German Africanists were certainly not the only contributors to the apartheid discourse of the postwar era. However, the nineteenth- and early twentieth-century Africanist missionaries and scholars did feed the discussion on language and race that factored into its production.

CHAPTER 1

Before the Fact: The Beginnings of African Studies on the Mission Field, 1814–87

In 1806 Gustavus Reinhold Nyländer, then twenty-nine, arrived in Georgetown, Sierra Leone, to begin work for the Church Missionary Society (CMS).[1] Prior to joining the London-based CMS, Nyländer, who was an ethnic German from Lithuania, had studied at a Berlin seminary.[2] He started his missionary career in Georgetown but by 1812 had moved to an area called the Bullom Shore, on the opposite bank from the city, and founded his own mission station. While there, he learned the local Bullom language, transcribing its vocabulary and noting its grammatical structure. What resulted was the *Grammar and Vocabulary of the Bullom Language,* which appeared in 1814.[3] Nyländer also compiled a spelling book with scriptural exercises for the students he taught in the mission field,[4] and he translated parts of the New Testament into Bullom.[5] Despite his linguistic and evangelical efforts, Nyländer was pessimistic about his assignment. He did not believe that his proselytization had much effect on the Bullom speakers. "I have sown tears," he said, "labouring in hope—encouraging myself with this, that God's word would never return void."[6] Nonetheless, Nyländer remained in Sierra Leone for almost nineteen years, until he died from an illness that swept through the missionaries in the village of Kissy, where he had ultimately relocated to evangelize among freed slaves.[7]

Nyländer's work on Bullom is notable because it was the first African-language grammar and dictionary published by a German Protestant missionary in the nineteenth century. Other German missionaries soon followed Nyländer's example, accumulating vocabulary from African languages across the continent. Nyländer's insistence on the centrality of God's word to his vocation echoed through the pages of his successors and was similar as well to that of eminent German philologists such as

J. G. Hamann and J. G. Herder, who likewise focused on the significance of the word in divine revelation.[8] Missionary linguistics was, indeed, tied to academic philology through a similar pietist heritage that stressed the significance of a deep, personal affiliation with Christ over rigid adherence to strict theological doctrine.[9]

This chapter will trace the history of those nineteenth-century German missionaries who, like Nyländer, became involved in linguistic transcription and laid the foundation for the discipline of *Afrikanistik*. These missionaries straddled two worlds. On the one hand, they were Germans who came from loosely affiliated states that were struggling to unify but still very much politically divided. They belonged as well to a German *Kulturnation* defined not by geography or politics but by cultural, intellectual, and linguistic commonalities. In the nineteenth century, comparative philology, which had such a marked influence on missionary work, was largely a German enterprise and therefore an important facet of the *Kulturnation*. Since the *Kulturnation* extended everywhere Germans were present, reflecting their sophistication and *Bildung*, German-speaking missionaries literally became its first envoys in sub-Saharan Africa.[10] Most of the early to mid-nineteenth-century linguists also came from either Prussia or Württemburg, which were the main seats of German Pietism.[11] Although the missionaries lived after the apogee of the pietist movement in the late seventeenth and early eighteenth centuries,[12] they lived through the age of Germany's early nineteenth-century *Erweckungsbewegung* (awakening) and the "new" pietism.[13] The expressly German pietist milieu was thus formative.

On the other hand, however, missionary linguists were deeply religious Christians who identified themselves with an ecumenical church that transcended national boundaries, including those of the *Kulturnation*. They worked primarily for English missionary societies, not German ones, and spent much of their lives overseas; many died there. Their pietism was cultivated in a German setting but, as Andrew F. Walls has argued, also had a critical impact on the Great Awakening in Britain,[14] which meant that German and British missionaries shared a similar belief system. Where the Germans were imperial representatives, it was for the British Empire in territories such as Sierra Leone, which was founded in 1787 by English abolitionists as a safe haven for 400 freed slaves, and became a crown colony in 1808.[15] When Prussia suffered humiliating defeat by Napoleon and the Holy Roman Empire collapsed in 1806, Nyländer had already been in London for over a year and was preparing for his trip to Georgetown.[16] Later, as revolution swept across Europe in 1848 and Germany attempted unification at the Frankfurt Parliament, Nyländer's successors were still in Africa, far removed from the tumult of that year, the Parliament's ultimate failure, and the reassertion of conservative dominance. Instead, they inhabited a pluralistic world where it was their Christianity and not their Germanness that mattered; while academics with university appointments such as Herder, Wilhelm von Humboldt, and J. G. Fichte debated the significance that German language had to the unique spirit and essence of the German people,[17] the missionaries labored on remote stations in West and East Africa, sometimes as the only German speakers for miles.

German Missionaries, British Missionary Societies

It is not a coincidence that Nyländer, the first CMS missionary to publish an African dictionary, was German.[18] The German predominance in African language scholarship was part and parcel of a larger German monopoly in the newly burgeoning field of comparative philology, as well as of a German longing to explore and understand the wider world. Although Germany had no official colonies in Africa or elsewhere until the 1880s, Germans were very receptive to the world around them in their "precolonial" phase. Zantop and others have amply demonstrated that German fantasies of colonialism and otherness expressed themselves in literary and philosophical publications throughout the eighteenth and nineteenth centuries, and indeed even before.[19] Such fantasies also made their way into philological scholarship, where they emerged in weighty discussions on the relationship among different languages and peoples. German intellectual concern for the "Orient"—the Middle East, but also the Indian subcontinent—was especially keen. The Western discovery that Sanskrit belonged to the Indo-European language family, and was indeed the parent of that family, drew substantial attention in Germany. Although an Englishman, Sir William Jones, first observed the relationship between Sanskrit and its cousins,[20] from early on it was Germans like Herder who were the most actively engaged in its interpretation and classification.[21]

Africa, too, attracted increasing German attention in the nineteenth century, both in philology and elsewhere. Scholars with a focus on Africa included Wilhelm Bleek, the first "professional" Africanist linguist and immigrant to South Africa,[22] and renowned ethnologist Adolf Bastian, who first voyaged to the continent in 1873.[23] *Völkerkunde* museums—museums of ethnology—proliferated later in the nineteenth century, offering the public a glimpse of African culture. These were complemented by *Völkerschauen,* or "people" exhibitions, in which members of so-called exotic ethnic groups or races—African and otherwise—were ushered from city to city and paraded around for the amusement of European visitors.[24]

The general focus on Africa reflected in museums and at *Völkerschauen* was primarily a phenomenon of the postunification era. Missionary engagements with Africa, however, well predated more general public awareness of ethnological artifacts and tribal displays. Nyländer may have been the first German to publish on African languages, but he was not the first Berlin-trained candidate to arrive in Sierra Leone. Seventeen of the first twenty-four missionaries that the CMS sent to Africa had studied in Berlin.[25] Once in Sierra Leone Nyländer was, moreover, surrounded by other fledgling missionary philologists. C. F. C. Wenzel, a missionary from Breslau who joined the CMS the year after Nyländer, had begun work on an "English-Susoo dictionary," which he had "completed . . . to letter U" by 1809.[26] Indeed, most of the early CMS German missionaries in Sierra Leone were involved in some form of linguistic transcription and translation.[27]

The CMS recruited many of its best missionary linguists from Germany; Walls has remarked that Henry Venn, secretary of the CMS from 1841 to 1873, "got his commercial advice from Manchester but his linguistic counsel from Germany."[28] From 1804 through around 1860, the CMS sent Germans to most of its primary African fields. In West Africa this included not only Sierra Leone but also Nigeria, while in East Africa the main CMS mission was in Kenya.[29] By midcentury august scholars such as Egyptologist Richard Lepsius and Max Müller were also advising the CMS on linguistic issues.[30] Nonetheless, missionaries were in the field meeting Africans and transcribing African languages earlier than almost anyone else. Moreover, the missionary rationale for pursuing linguistics only occasionally corresponded with that of their academic counterparts. The German interest in language has often been associated with the German quest for independence and a stable, unified national identity. George Mosse and Leon Poliakov have argued that Germans took such an interest in linguistics largely because of the early nineteenth-century Romanticism that connected a *Volk*—a people—to the soil on which it lived as well as to the tongue that it spoke.[31] For intellectuals such as Herder, language represented the spirit, or soul, of a nation.[32] Jakob Grimm's fascination not only with the German language but with German literature shows that he too came to associate culture with language and see the two as inseparable.[33]

To a certain extent, missionaries and philologists did share common concerns about language. Both were inheritors of the seventeenth-century German pietist tradition that stressed a personal bond with Christ. Pietism was a movement emphasizing reflection, inner spirituality, and Christian rebirth. Born in the late seventeenth and early eighteenth centuries, pietism arose to counter what was seen as the rigid nature of orthodoxy and to downplay doctrinal differences between Lutherans and Calvinists.[34] Walls indeed suggests that it was this pietist spirit, born in continental Europe in general and Germany in particular, that sparked the Protestant missionary movement and the Great Awakening. Halle and Herrnhut—the former the base of pietist progenitor August Hermann Francke, the latter the home of the Moravians—were the first two poles of pietist missionary action.[35] The missionary belief in the deeply mystical, revelatory power of language stemmed as much from pietism as did that of individuals like Herder and Hamann. As Williamson has remarked, some of the most significant German intellectuals of the nineteenth century, including David Friedrich Strauss, Friedrich W. J. Schelling, Georg W. F. Hegel, and Friedrich Hölderlin grew up in the same Swabian milieu, and with a similar pietist upbringing, as the CMS missionaries.[36]

For pietists, the Bible also played a critical role. The biblical translations that German pietists produced led to a profoundly new way of envisioning the book itself, as Jonathan Sheehan has suggested. Pietists saw the Bible as a text for general consumption, and not the personal provenance of the learned elite.[37] Consequently, the Bible was the crux around which pietist life turned for all believers, regardless of social or class status. For instance, in the formulation of Philipp Jakob Spener, another father of pietism and Francke's teacher, family time was to be spent in contemplation, reading and reflecting on the Bible.[38] In addition, even prior to the birth of comparative philology in the late eighteenth and early nineteenth centuries—generated by Jones's announcement that Sanskrit was the parent of all Indo-European languages—philology was central to pietist scholarship. Textual analysis was an integral part of university study for Francke and Spener, and was the raison d'être of the former's *Collegium Orientale theologicum* at Halle, where theology students learned a wide range of languages and engaged in critical biblical translations, including ones into Ethiopian.[39]

The kind of profound affiliation with God that the Pietists advocated could, moreover, only be achieved if the Word touched a person's heart in his or her native language. No other language would truly be able to provide the same flash of insight and lay the foundations for belief; only an individual's native tongue could communicate the essence of the Christian message. This concept—that only a person's first language was suitable for conveying Christian truths—is similar to the nationalist idea that each language was unique to a specific ethnic group. The reasoning behind the missionary belief that the native language alone could engender conversion also shared common attributes with the conviction that language was an external projection of the nation. Native languages were so effective at transmitting the Christian message precisely because it was the mother language that structured a person's mental patterns and thought. In a foreign language, Christianity would appear foreign; in a native language it would be trusted, known.

The objective of missionary language study in the earlier nineteenth century was nonetheless not principally the creation of discrete ethnic communities or nationalist sentiment; rather, it was to usher potential converts into an international Christian community. On the face of it, this missionary ideal was universalist. Most of the German Protestant missionaries who were active from approximately 1800 to 1870 did not assume a particularly "German" identity. Missionary identity was instead tied to either an individual missionary's home region, such as Württemburg, or to a supranational Christianity. This meant that German-speaking missionaries joined English societies such as the CMS or London Missionary Society (LMS), whose primary field was in South Africa.[40] They wrote mainly in English and often published with English imprints such as the British and Foreign Bible Society (BFBS).[41]

In their capacity as employees of the CMS, German missionaries also represented the British empire and on occasion even identified themselves with the British. Adrian Hastings has pointed out that J. L. Krapf, a German missionary for the CMS, proposed in 1841 that British political authority be established in Ethiopia to help secure the country for Christ when missionary endeavors were failing, very specifically tying the success of Christianity to that of British colonialism.[42] In an 1862 Hausa grammar, Krapf's CMS colleague J. F. Schön went a step further, quoting English abolitionist T. F. Buxton's assertion that "from the slave trade itself, a nation has been reclaimed, and now enjoys, in comparison with Africa, a blaze of light, liberty, religion, and happiness. That nation is Great Britain."[43]

The largest concentration of missionary linguists in the early nineteenth century belonged to the CMS. Yet there were some linguists in German-speaking missionary societies during this era. Jakob Ludwig Döhne, a Zulu specialist, and Albert Kropf, whose focus was Xhosa, were both members of the Berlin Missionary Society (BMS), which was founded in 1824 and had its first field in South Africa.[44] As late as 1846, however, the BMS was still considered more of a supplier for other missions than an independently functioning society.[45] The Rhenish Missionary Society (RMS), founded in 1828 and headquartered in Wuppertal, produced F. W. Kolbe, J. G. Krönlein, Carl Hugo Hahn, and, most significantly, Carl Büttner.[46] Since the main fields of the RMS were in South Africa and Namibia they mainly specialized in languages of the region. The Seminary of the Basel Mission was established in 1815 and sent many of its candidates to the CMS, LMS, and other Dutch and German missionary societies. In 1828, however, the Baselers opened their own station on the Gold Coast, in what is modern-day Ghana.[47] J. G. Christaller was their most prominent missionary linguist. The most famous representative of the North German Missionary Society, Diedrich Westermann, was only born in 1875 and not really active until the turn of the twentieth century, but the NGMS itself was founded in 1836. Originally the NGMS did not send missionaries to Africa, but in the late 1840s it opened a station in Eweland, in what is now Togo.[48] Like their peers in the BMS most NGMS missionaries came from Württemburg and were steeped in the pietist tradition.[49]

Those missionaries who did belong to German societies were not above forsaking them when it was convenient. This was the case with Kolbe, who was born in Gütersloh in 1821. Kolbe, who would become a specialist in Bantu linguistics, abandoned his first career as a typesetter to study at the seminar of the RMS from 1841 to 1844. The RMS then sent him to Worcester, in the Cape Colony, where he resided from 1844 to 1847. From 1848 to 1852, Kolbe preached among the Herero in Namibia and was still in the service of the RMS.[50] In 1853, however, Kolbe left his post in Damaraland and traveled to George in South Africa. Once there, he wrote a letter to the deputation of the RMS explaining that he had decided to leave them for the LMS because he did not like how the administration of the RMS treated its missionaries.[51]

Döhne was another missionary who left a German society for an English-speaking one. He was born in Zierenberg, a suburb of Kassel, in 1811 and joined the BMS in 1832.[52] In 1836, the society sent him to South Africa, where he worked with the Xhosa and Zulu. After a disagreement over the best strategy for proselytizing to the Xhosa, however, he shifted allegiance to the American Board of Missionaries[53] and remained in its service while compiling his most influential linguistic work, *A Zulu-Kafir Dictionary.* Döhne claimed that it was the American Board that had first asked him to create the dictionary, and that the English colonial government in Natal had later seconded the Americans' request.[54] Both Döhne and Krönlein of the RMS accepted support for their linguistic work from an English imperial authority: Sir George Grey, governor of the Cape Colony from 1854 to 1861, was their patron and funded their research.[55] Indeed, when neither the Americans nor the Natal government ultimately came through with financial assistance, Döhne turned to Gray for support and even dedicated his dictionary to the governor.[56]

These cases demonstrate that the arena in which Germans like Kolbe, Döhne, and Krönlein worked was fluid and not yet defined by national allegiances. German missionaries were not harbingers of German Empire and maintained an ambivalent relationship to imperialism. For the British context, Norman Etherington and Andrew Porter have argued that it is a mistake to conflate missionary and imperial expansion. In the late eighteenth and early nineteenth centuries, British missionaries were interested in providence and God's divine plan to spread Christianity to all corners of the globe, not the entrenchment of English rule.[57] They attached themselves to empire where it was convenient but were not national enthusiasts until the later nineteenth and early twentieth centuries.[58] The same held true for the Germans, who were deeply conflicted over how far they should support empire even after 1871. For the most part, they eventually did champion the imperial project and defended German political and business interests.[59] Yet their backing was certainly not a given; their historical connections to the British and Protestant ecumenicalism were simply too strong.

The communities that nineteenth-century missionaries inhabited were also multicultural. This was particularly apparent among the Germans who labored for the CMS in Sierra Leone or on the various mission fields in South Africa. Ex-slaves, who spoke a pastiche of languages, were chief among the inhabitants of Sierra Leone's Freetown, and they mixed with German and British missionaries alike. This did not mean that ethnolinguistic classifications did not occur. The vernacular in Sierra Leone might have been English, but that did not prevent missionaries such as S. W. Koelle from quizzing as many Africans as possible on their native languages; the result was his early classification of west African languages, the *Polyglotta Africana.*[60] Koelle, who was originally from Cleebronn, a suburb of Heibronn in Württemberg, studied at the Seminary in Basel from 1841 to 1845 and then joined the CMS. He studied Arabic in Tübingen and then left for Sierra Leone, where in addition to his general missionary duties, he took on the role of chief linguist at the Fourah Bay Institute.[61] Koelle traveled widely in Sierra Leone, and A. B. C. Sibthorpe, a contemporary of his in the 1840s, said that Koelle "was always in spectacles, with a large folio of foolscap size in his hand, going from village to village, translating the various languages, and collecting specimens of languages from the natives of different countries of Africa who have been brought into the colony of Sierra Leone."[62] Sibthorpe pointed out that Koelle did this in the name of preparing the way for evangelization of the west African interior; nonetheless, his work also led to an early European categorization of African languages and peoples.[63]

Koelle was not the only missionary trying to make sense of or map the wide range of languages he encountered. Rachael Gilmour has shown that by the 1830s missionaries were actively trying to delimit the boundaries of the Zulu Kingdom through studies of its language, which standardized and codified the Zulu language and determined the extent of Zulu geography.[64] While the achievement of universality through Christ was a goal on the one hand, on the other, elevation of native language acquisition emphasized difference over unity. Moreover, it was the classification and the definition of ethnic particularity through language that would come to characterize the direction that African Studies took. In this sense, Africanist scholarship was part of a broader current in German comparative philology, which also sought to classify the world's peoples according to the languages that they spoke.

Comparative Philology and African Studies

Before Otto von Bismarck unified Germany after the Franco-Prussian War of 1871, the country had little political fixity. The German-speaking states of central Europe that had been part of the Holy Roman Empire until Napoleon ravaged the Continent were reorganized into a loose confederation at the Congress of Vienna in 1815. This German confederation had no overarching political structure and did not provide its citizens with a firm sense of national identity.[65] After Vienna, pro-unification German liberals dared to believe that there was a real possibility for the creation of a German nation-state. However, conservative forces assured that the foundation of a German nation would have to wait.[66] The liberals saw a brief opportunity to take command during the revolutions of 1848 and seemed on the verge of finally forming a politically centralized Germany. Indeed, the Germanist and folklorist Grimm was among the representatives at the Frankfurt Parliament who struggled to forge a constitution that would establish Germany as a political entity.[67] But the revolutionary interlude soon ended, and conservatives once again ensured that Germany would not be united. Lacking the certainty of political union, Germans turned to language as something that bound them together and made them part of a cultural and linguistic nation, even if they did not yet belong to a political one.

The general German interest in language gave rise to an active community of philologists intent on locating German origins and proving the inherent value of German language and culture. These philologists were also inspired by a revolution in the study of language itself, one that dramatically changed the way Europeans thought not only about language but about history and their place in it. It was in the late eighteenth century that the Englishman Sir William Jones, a British administrator in India, announced that the Indogermanic languages were related to the ancient Indian language of Sanskrit. Even more, Jones maintained that Sanskrit was in fact the *parent* of the Indogermanic language family, and that all of the family's modern branches had evolved from it.[68]

Jones's revelation—that an Indian language had given birth to the modern tongues of Europe—laid the foundation for the new academic discipline of comparative philology.[69] Jones's realization that Sanskrit was related to the languages of Europe, and that it was "more perfect than the *Greek,* more copious than the *Latin,* more exquisitely refined than either, yet bearing to both of them a stronger affinity, both in the roots of verbs and in the forms of grammar, than could possibly have been produced by accident" opened new vistas for linguistic and historical research.[70] Jones's pronouncement marked the start of the "Indo-European century," when philologists discovered that a wide range of languages spoken in far-flung geographical regions had a common ancestor.[71] Jones did not take Sanskrit to be the Indo-European protolanguage, as did the German Friedrich Schlegel.[72] Rather, Jones saw it as a descendant of the protolanguage, but one that was closer to it than any European language.[73] Comparisons of grammatical structure, vocabulary, and morphology thus indicated—as odd as it may have seemed to contemporaries at the turn of the nineteenth century—that Indians shared a common heritage with Europeans. Many decades later in 1871, Kolbe—who at the time had resettled in Cape Town—remarked that while the relationship between "Hindoo" and Indo-European was something that "every schoolboy is now taught to accept as an undisputed fact," in the past it had likely made the "French savants smile," because such a philological connection would have appeared ludicrous.[74]

For the era, Jones's theory was radical on several levels. First, early modern philologists thought that ancient Hebrew—the language in which the Bible had been written—was the oldest, "original" human language.[75] Second, Europeans saw Indians as dark-skinned primitives who could not share the same cultural heritage as the more cultivated Europeans. Yet India's modern inhabitants were descendants of those who had spoken the noble, highly intellectual Sanskrit. Third, in comparison to Hebrew, Latin, or ancient Greek, Germanic cultures and Germanic languages had themselves appeared coarse and unworthy of scholarly consideration [76] Relating German to Sanskrit put it in a whole new light. If German was derived from Sanskrit, it must have retained some of its parent's sophisticated properties.

The idea of Sanskrit as a protolanguage was also threatening. Edwin Bryant has noted that as European empires expanded and encountered peoples with civilizations as ancient as their own, the historicity of the biblical narrative was increasingly called into question. Since the Middle Ages, Europeans had generally believed that the Old Testament was an accurate reflection of historical events. If Brahmin texts predated these events, however, biblical chronology would collapse, and the whole edifice of Christianity would crumble. The descent of all languages from one common parent was also in doubt, as was the position of Hebrew as that parent.[77] Jones was personally concerned enough with the challenge to biblical authority that he concluded his studies with the assertion that Sanskrit literature did not upend the biblical account but rather confirmed it, as Trautmann has suggested. Nothing in Indian history, Jones maintained, came before biblical creation.[78]

Philology tested the biblical narrative in other ways as well. Benes has argued that biblical criticism as practiced by German Orientalists located the Bible in a specific historical context and demonstrated that it was the by-product of a unique culture.[79] Orientalists hoped to use language to organize the peoples of the world into a classificatory hierarchy, which would determine their relatedness to each other but also illuminate biblical historicity. Because Hebrew had long held the place of the oldest and most august language in the academy, contesting its position was a perilous business. In order to combat the threat to Hebrew, conservative Protestant scholars such as Wilhelm Gesenius and Heinrich Ewald attempted to prove a closer affiliation between Indo-European and Semitic language families through analysis of similarities among "root words." They did so in an effort to refute attacks on monogenism that questioned the unity of mankind and its emergence from a common origin.[80] Orientalists of this mind-set also directly influenced missionaries like Koelle and Kolbe, who tried to establish affinities between Indo-European and African languages. Indeed, Koelle studied Arabic under Ewald in Tübingen,[81] while Kolbe read widely in Gesenius's *Hebrew Grammar.*[82]

Jones's theories on the relationship between Sanskrit and the Indo-European languages transformed the field of language studies and its allied discipline, biblical criticism, throughout Europe. Nowhere, however, did Jones's ideas reverberate more loudly than in Germany. The early to mid-nineteenth century saw a preponderance of German scholars enter the discipline of comparative philology, including Herder, Fichte, the Schlegel brothers August and Friedrich, Humboldt, Franz Bopp, August Pott, and Grimm. They were all intent on sketching the interrelationship among languages, focusing primarily on Europe and Asia but sometimes attempting to encompass other parts of the world. They were also interested in how the German language mirrored the soul of the German *Volk.* Grimm's famous fairy tales were not simply quaint stories compiled for the amusement of children; instead, they recaptured and revived the significance of a distinctly German culture embodied in its heritage and its language. Although Grimm is most widely known for the fairy tales, his *Deutsche Grammatik,* published in four volumes between 1819 and 1837, was what he considered his magnum opus.[83] The *Grammatik* made clear that the German language was just as important as the classical languages that were more widely seen as acceptable objects of academic analysis.[84]

From the beginning of the nineteenth century, German philologists even imagined their own mother tongue as the connecting bridge between east and west, between Asia and Europe. Far from being a coarse, unsophisticated language, German was the true inheritor of Sanskrit. This belief affected how German scholars envisioned the language family of which both were a part. While other European scholars preferred to describe the Euro-Asian linguistic complex as "Indo-European," in 1823 philologist Julius Klaproth proposed the alternate description of "Indo-German." He used this label to describe those peoples who had originated from the same Asian *Urheimat,* as Benes has shown.[85] Even today, German linguists continue to employ the term *Indo-German* while most others opt for *Indo-European.*[86] Moreover as Bryant points out, Klaproth believed that Indic and German represented the limits of the language family's boundaries to the west and east.[87] The designation *Indo-German* elevated the German language and *Volk* to a rarefied position as descendants of no less a place than the Garden of Eden, which was thought to be in Asia.[88]

Since German interest in language and its relation to national identity and origins was so keen, Germans took the lead in defining the new field of comparative philology. By the beginning of the nineteenth century, both Wilhelm von Humboldt and August Schlegel had identified certain grammatical "types" that would act as a guide to linguistic classification. These types were critical for the analyses of nationalist scholars and would become essential to the work of missionary linguists in Africa. According to Humboldt, all languages could be divided into four basic groups: the isolating, the agglutinating, the inflecting, and the polysynthetic.[89] The last of these, the polysynthetic, was applied mainly to native American languages, and Africanists ignored it. The other three were crucial to African classifications.

Words in isolating languages did not have the ability to combine together and form new concepts.[90] Instead, sentences were made up of strings of roots that could be combined in infinite ways, with even the plural and reflexive being expressed through separate terms.[91] Such languages could convey meaning but not relatedness, because they had no prefixes, suffixes, or other grammatical markers to demonstrate connections among different concepts. The most well-known example of an isolating language was Chinese, but this category also included the "Sudanic" or "Nigritic" languages of western Africa.[92]

By contrast, agglutinative languages contained the grammatical markers that isolating ones lacked. These markers could be attached to word stems as prefixes or suffixes to form new ideas. However, fully new word stems were not created this way, as they were at the final, inflectional stage. The agglutinative class encompassed the massive Bantu language family, which dominated two-thirds of the sub-Saharan African continent.

In inflectional languages, meaning and relatedness fused to make new, freestanding words, whose component parts sometimes disappeared in the union. Moreover, whereas the roots of words in isolating or agglutinative languages did not change internally—as for example in shifts of tense—inflectional languages exhibited this kind of phonetic alteration.[93] Languages with inflection were also the only ones that displayed grammatical gender, which meant that they divided nouns into classes on the basis of gender. This point became especially salient for Africanists like Bleek and

Meinhof, who equated grammatical gender with the linguistic and cultural sophistication of groups such as the Hamites. Hamitic languages were thus considered inflecting, which put them in the same category as the Indo-European and Semitic language families.

Similar form was not always enough to ensure that languages were related. Languages also followed certain rules and laws, much as physical, chemical, or biological systems did. The most famous such laws were the sound shifts that Grimm posited for the Indo-European languages. He proved that a set of sounds in one language could appear as an entirely different set in another, regularly and completely, without meaning that the languages were unrelated. On the contrary, this only indicated that over time the one sound had mutated into the other. Such shifts were not random and followed an internal logic of their own. Belief in such laws and their immutability would later be embraced by an entire school of linguists, the neogrammarians.[94] Moreover, the concepts of sound shift and sound law had application well beyond the Indo-European arena. In the 1840s Bleek used the same concepts to establish similarity among the agglutinating Bantu languages in southern Africa.[95] Subsequently, Meinhof and those who worked with him continued to try to determine the validity of sound shifts in Bantu and other African language families.[96]

The discipline of comparative philology changed substantially over the century. Especially after Darwin's theory of evolution, the field began to cloak itself in the language of biology, as Stephen Alter has shown.[97] August Schleicher, who was active from the 1840s until his death in 1868, is often credited with creating the most Darwinian theory of language evolution.[98] Schleicher demonstrated how different Indo-European languages had branched out from a common protolanguage, just as several related living species might have evolved from an extinct parent. Schleicher also reconstructed this protolanguage and even wrote a fairy tale in it. Indeed, the grammatical categories that scholars such as Humboldt and Schlegel had delineated had taken on significant pre-Darwinian evolutionary implications by Schleicher's time, as the lowest form, the isolating, was said to give way to the agglutinative middle stage, which would eventually cede to the highest level, the inflectional.[99] In Schleicher's estimation this meant that languages, like species, evolved through different stages.

The evolutionary aspects of linguistic theory would come to have certain connotations for the study of African languages. The majority of African languages were Bantu and assigned to the agglutinative group, placing them at the center of the developmental cycle. Bleek took the earliest active role in fitting African languages into the classificatory hierarchy that earlier comparative philologists had constructed. Bleek had been born into a bourgeois family in Berlin in 1827 and baptized by the prominent theologian Friedrich Schleiermacher. He originally studied theology at the university in Bonn, following the example of his father, Friedrich, who was also a theologian.[100] The younger Bleek's studies of biblical criticism were crucial to his later involvement with comparative philology and ultimately led him to that field, as Andrew Bank and Robert J. Thornton have noted. Bleek was also captivated by the Orientalist concept that it was possible to determine historical connections among various peoples through the study of their language.[101]

Bleek's 1851 Bonn dissertation, "De Nominum Generibus Linguarum Africae, Australis, Copticae, Semiticarum aliarumquae Sexualium," reflected his interest in classification. In the work, he focused on what he termed the "sex-denoting" languages, those that expressed grammatical gender. After settling in South Africa, Bleek continued delving into the differences between sex-denoting and non-sex-denoting languages. He believed that most African languages were non-sex-denoting, but that there were some exceptions, such as Nama. Bleek suggested that the languages of the Nama—or "Hottentot," as they were often referred to at the time—were not of the same origin as those of their neighbors, the San or "Bushmen," a theory that German linguists and anthropologists of the next generation would embrace. He speculated that the Nama's ancestors had migrated from northern to southern Africa, but that the grammatical form of their languages had not changed much over time. Bleek therefore grouped Nama languages with the northern, sex-denoting African languages that were considered relatives of the languages of the Semitic and Indo-Germanic language families. He then became the first to name Nama and related sub-Saharan African languages "Hamitic," after the biblical story of Ham.[102]

The linguistic categories that Bleek used were never value-neutral. The word *Hamitic* was itself a loaded term. Contemporaries would have recognized it as a reference to the "Hamitic hypothesis," which held that the Hamites, mysterious, light-skinned nomads from the Caucasus or Middle East, had introduced everything that was culturally or linguistically sophisticated to Africa. Meinhof later became an avid proponent of the hypothesis, as we shall see in chapter 4. Whether your mother tongue was sex-denoting or non-sex-denoting also determined how you thought, as well as how sophisticated your thought was. Bleek, like non-Africanist philologists before him, believed that sex-denoting languages represented the height of linguistic complexity, whereas non-sex-denoting languages languished at an earlier stage of linguistic development. In volume 1 of *A Comparative Grammar of South African Languages* (1864), Bleek maintained that "the forms of language may be said to constitute in some degree the skeleton frame of the human mind whose thoughts they express."[103] He continued to state that "the nations speaking Sex-denoting languages are distinguished by a higher poetical conception, by which human agency is transferred to other beings, and even to inanimate things, in consequence of which their personification takes place, forming the origin of almost all mythological legends."[104] Bleek's insistence that sex-denoting languages allowed for more advanced thinking was coupled with a belief that non-sex-denoting languages were incapable of certain forms of expression. He argued that non-sex-denoting languages could produce neither their own mythologies nor their own fables, because they could not conceive of how to transfer human qualities to animals or inanimate objects.[105] While Bantu literature could be historical or legendary, even encompassing "horrible ghost stories and tales of witchcraft," it would never be mythological because its form was agglutinative and non-sex-denoting.[106]

By contrast, Nama mythological literature excited Bleek. He believed that it mirrored early European literary endeavors in form and, sometimes, in substance. Bleek had a keen interest in demonstrating how Nama and European fables were related, and in comparing Nama stories to those of Germany's "Reynard the Fox" tales. Different animals may have populated Nama and German fables—jackals, hyenas, leopards, tortoises, baboons, and lions instead of foxes, rabbits, and hedgehogs—but the themes they suggested were remarkably similar. In *Reynard the Fox in South Africa* (1864), Bleek raved that Nama "literary activity has been employed almost in the same direction as that which had been taken by our own earliest literature" and claimed that this meant there was "a much greater congeniality between the Hottentot and European mind than we find between the latter and any of the black races of Africa."[107] Bleek did not go so far as to propose that correlations between the Nama and Europeans indicated a common origin, though he did hint at it. His attempts to establish connections between Nama and European were similar to the efforts of Herder and Schlegel to prove a genetic relationship between German and Sanskrit.

Over the course of the nineteenth century scholars slowly recognized that African languages were legitimate objects of study. Still, they were often considered uncivilized forms of expression and on occasion even likened to animal speech. Ernst Haeckel, the famous zoologist who also happened to be Bleek's cousin, disparagingly compared Africans to apes, insisting that even their languages were more akin to the noises made by monkeys than to the work of a "Goethe or Schiller."[108] Since African languages were not the primary focus of any philological studies until Bleek, misconceptions about their animal nature were not easily dispelled. Meinhof claimed that even in the early twentieth century, it was commonly believed that African languages had no fixed grammar rules and that African vocabulary could be strung together in any order and still retain meaning.[109] Even before Bleek, however, missionary linguists were challenging this myth. They did so mainly to spread the word of God, as their pietist upbringing demanded. Simultaneously, they were aware of comparative philology and its significance in their native Germany, borrowing categories such as "Semitic" and "Indo-German" from the discipline. As they worked at bringing Christianity to Africa through their grammars, dictionaries, translations, and primers, they also developed ideas on where African languages fit within an ever-expanding linguistic hierarchy.

Practical, Theological, and Academic Concerns

Above all else, nineteenth-century Protestant missionaries considered language the most practical means of disseminating the gospel.[110] Religious concerns therefore guided them to philology. In 1857 J. B. Schlegel, a North German missionary stationed among the Ewe in Togo who was unrelated to the Schlegel brothers, published a grammar of their language. In it he made clear that he hoped the book would find its way into the hands of those who followed in his footsteps, as "language is the first and only lever through which the spirit and the word of God can prepare even the most decadent and deeply sunken people of Africa for the Kingdom of Jesus."[111] In other words, language was first and foremost a tool. At the same time, Schlegel echoed a theme that would thread its way through most nineteenth-century missionary philology: The idea that a native language, not a foreign one, was the only tongue suitable for expressing the gospel to Africans.[112]

Schlegel's comments were far from the only ones of this sort. The introductions or forewords to dictionaries and grammars usually included statements of the authors' hopes that their work would be blessed by God and contribute to missionary work in Africa.[113] They also stressed that learning African languages was part of a missionary's basic responsibilities, whether in the active sense of gathering and transcribing, or the passive one of learning from what had already been gathered and transcribed. In 1861, for instance, J. F. Schön of the CMS remarked that "while we would never make the Missionary a mere linguistic inquirer, we would still recommend to him to devote some time to the collection of a native *literature* [emphasis in original], to think no story told by a native in his own way and manner too unmeaning or unimportant to deserve committing to paper."[114] Schön was one of the most prolific missionary linguists of the nineteenth century, since he worked on the West African languages of Hausa, Igbo, and Mende. Born in 1803 in Baden, Schön studied in Basel and at the CMS college in Islington. The CMS sent Schön to Sierra Leone in 1832, and in 1841 he accompanied the future African bishop, Samuel Crowther, on what was known as the Niger expedition.[115] The expedition was an antislavery crusade funded by the British government and was also meant to open up new fields for evangelization.[116]

For Schön, linguistic knowledge was crucial to the dissemination of Christianity, and his career was dedicated to its acquisition. He believed it was a missionary's duty to copy out African languages and even suggested that, if too many European and native missionaries were uninterested in linguistic work, the CMS should "appoint, in every new Mission, one European and one Native, to be devoted exclusively to linguistic labours, for at least some years."[117] His conviction that missionaries needed to devote at least some attention to linguistic and cultural pursuits was echoed by most of his missionary linguist colleagues and became dogma for Meinhof and his followers.[118]

There was also a more strictly theological reason for missionary interest in African languages. According to Birgit Meyer, missionary philology was motivated by "reference to a myth connecting the Old Testament narrative about the building of the Tower of Babel and the New Testament account of the outpouring of the Holy Spirit of Pentecost." In the first of these allegories, the well-known story of Babel, humanity was united through one language. After men started to build a tower with the express purpose of reaching heaven, though, God knocked mankind back to earth and, as punishment for its misdeed, shattered the one language and condemned humanity to speak myriad, mutually unintelligible tongues. The Hamites come into play here: They had originally orchestrated the plot to build the tower and thus were situated the furthest away from God after the disaster. At this point, the second allegory, that of the Pentecost, takes over. At Pentecost, the Holy Spirit was sent to Jesus's disciples, who were imbued with the power to "communicate in all languages once only." The meaning behind this story is that God was instructing his followers to learn all the world's languages in order to bring the lost peoples of the earth back into his fold.[119]

Most German missionaries had a pietist upbringing, and it was this pietism that informed their conduct in the field.[120] The allegories of the Tower of Babel and the Pentecost, stressing the significance of language to man's fall and redemption, must have resonated very loudly with them. Krapf, the CMS missionary who is best known for being one of the first Europeans to reach Mount Kilimanjaro and Mount Kenya, is a good example of a pietist who took the appeal to preach in native languages to heart. He was reared in pietist Württemburg, trained in Basel, and believed strongly in the transformative powers of language. This led him, as M. Louise Pirouet points out, to misunderstand Christianity as it manifested itself in other cultures, particularly the Ethiopian.[121] Krapf was a missionary in Ethiopia for five years, from 1837 to 1842, before he and his partner, C. W. Isenberg, were expelled from the country.[122] During that time, Krapf's main goal was to produce a Bible that would contain both Ge'ez, Ethiopia's ancient church language, and Amharic, the modern vernacular.[123] Yet he was frustrated by the Ethiopian response to his work, and commented that "the (Ethiopian) people of Shoa . . . do not like very much the Amharic. They like the Ethiopic (Ge'ez) more. We endeavour to prove that as the Amharic is the language of the country and the Ethiopic requires a long study, the Amharic is much more preferable to an unknown language. We refer to 1 Corinthians XIV, where Paul is speaking about the uselessness of speaking in an unknown tongue."[124] Because Krapf was so thoroughly committed to the idea of native-language proselytization, he could not comprehend the Ethiopian preference for their church language, Ge'ez.

Since native-language studies were of such profound importance, biblical translations were central to missionary work. Whether he was speaking of Amharic, Ge'ez, or any other language, Krapf believed that "a correct translation of the Bible is the most difficult, important, and responsible matter that any mortal man can take upon himself."[125] Krapf was deeply concerned with the power of the written word and fearful of making mistakes in his translations. Making translations as literal as possible was crucial, but so difficult that the missionaries' work often hardly outlived them. After Krapf's death Leo Reinisch, an Africanist scholar at the University of Vienna, complained that new translations of the Amharic Bible were needed, since Krapf's translations were *too* literal. Krapf had hewed too closely to the original Hebrew, making his translations unintelligible to native speakers.[126]

Krapf recognized, too, that there were instances when the Bible would have to be distributed in languages not native to the people who would receive them, irrespective of the biblical decree to preach the gospel in every known language. He likened the necessity for Ge'ez among nonnative speakers such as the Oromo (Galla) to that of other European languages in Germany, remarking that "there are many Galla, who read Amharic. . . . Again there are many Abyssinians who understand the Galla language very well, and who would rather like to read the word of God in a foreign language, as many unconverted people with us like to read the Bible in French, English, & Italian rather than in German."[127] In order to "soften" people for the use of their own language, Krapf would have them start reading in a foreign one and hope that, after appropriate training, they would acknowledge the importance of switching to their own tongue. It was also why he advocated side-by-side translations in "high" church language and the vernacular; if Ge'ez and Amharic were viewed on the same page, congregants "would find, that the text in Amharic is not at hostility with the Ethiopic as they always presuppose."[128] Krapf's ultimate goal was for Ethiopians to employ the same language in church as they did on the street and to bring a revitalization of their form of Christianity with it.

Krapf worried further that sole focus on native language transmission, while vital to pietist principles, could stymie evangelization. Many Ethiopian and nearby dialects had not been committed to writing, and before they were, their speakers had no access to native language scriptures. In some instances, missionaries made conscious choices to transcribe certain languages and "vernacularize" them at the expense of others. This is what Christaller argued for in 1864, when he tried to decide which of the Akan languages spoken in Ghana should be committed to writing.[129] In the case of Ethiopia, Krapf intoned, "now I would ask, shall these Christians remain without any medium, by which to learn and hear the will of God, until they receive a translation of the Scriptures in their respective dialects?"[130] Krapf feared that sticking too closely to the pietist dictum that native languages be the only means of communication would alienate potential converts, and he claimed that it had already done so in parts of Ethiopia.[131]

As important as the practical and theological benefits of linguistic work were, missionaries rarely ignored the intellectual aspects of their studies and were aware of their significance to philology. Döhne discussed the dual nature of grammatical analysis in 1857, saying that "in the study of languages in general, and of barbarian languages in particular, two objects are to be aimed at—a philosophical and a practical." He continued to explain that "the philosophical object is the attainment of an insight into the character of a people, by means of an accurate acquaintance with the form into which its thoughts are moulded,—and which is invariably the true expression of the national spirit. . . . The immediate practical object, as far as barbarous tribes are concerned, is that a literature should be created for the propagation of Christian truth and the extension of civilization."[132] In addition to creating a body of written knowledge to help in the dissemination of Christianity, missionaries were bidden to delve into the "nature" of African peoples. Döhne saw no contradiction between theory and practice; one enriched the other, so that while "the Christian missionary always devotes the first place in his zeal and labours to the Gospel" he could also contribute to science. Science would function to speed the "redemption of a fallen world" by aggrandizing "the sphere of human knowledge."[133]

Krapf also had very "scholarly" tendencies. He came from a farming family, as did most of the Württemburg missionaries. After his family decided that he would enter the service of the church, Krapf went to grammar school and then continued his education at the Missionary Seminary in Basel and, finally, the University of Tübingen, where he received a degree in theology.[134] In later years he became an intellectual force and was received by such famed German scholars as geographer Carl Ritter and naturalist Alexander von Humboldt.[135] Krapf's research was expansive and not limited to language; he also introduced readers to his version of African history, for example, chronicling the Swahili past in a grammar of 1850.[136] Further, Krapf's CMS colleagues Koelle and Schön were both bestowed with the prestigious Volney prize for comparative philology for their work on West African languages, as was Christaller.[137] There is little doubt, therefore, that these missionary scholars had powerful connections to the academy.

Missionaries moved in an academic world and were avid students of comparative philology. Simultaneously, they had to prioritize their practical and theological duties. One of the biggest challenges missionary linguists faced was to express meaning as they thought God had intended, but still couch it in a way that remained true to the essence of each individual language. They also hoped one day to make biblical texts available in as many African languages and dialects as possible, even if it was not realistic in the mid-nineteenth century. In order to approach this goal, the missionaries required African aid. The employment of local assistants, both in the field and later, once a missionary had returned to Germany, was already common in the mid-nineteenth century. The school at Saint Chrischona had Ethiopians working on translations of local languages throughout the period. Some even visited Krapf in Korntal after he had returned from Africa, as we will see in chapter 6.[138]

In this era, missionaries often spoke of their African colleagues as being more responsible for Bible translations than they were. Christaller claimed that he had "not produced anything of my own, but simply what was provided for me by the Sacred Authors on the one hand, and on the other what was placed at my disposal by our Native Assistants and by the language of the country," and he called himself "merely an instrument in the matter."[139] Schön spoke of having supervised the Reverend J. C. Taylor, an Igbo, as he translated the gospel of Matthew into his native tongue. Schön said that the translation had been made "under his roof," but he maintained that the resultant text was Taylor's, not his.[140] His colleague C. A. Gollmer, a missionary to the Yoruba, commented that his society, the CMS, actively discouraged Europeans from translating the Bible into Nigerian languages, since "natives could do it so much better."[141]

Africans employed as translators, interpreters, and scribes were omnipresent on mission stations. Yet German missionaries always monitored their movements, and it was the missionaries who had the final say on issues such as which words to include in a text. There was also an active drive to make African stories fit pietist molds. In 1863 Krapf related the tale of a young Oromo woman who had been taken from Egypt to Germany twelve years earlier. She had arrived in Korntal and was educated there. The woman, whose name was Pauline Fathme, converted to Christianity and moved to Basel to be with her godfather, Christian Friedrich Spittler, founder of the Basel Bible Society and a charter member of the Basel Missionary Society. Fathme died in Basel, but not before "lift[ing] up her hands and in the most solemn and suppliant manner entreat[ing] [Spittler] to remember the Galla, her countrymen, by sending Missionaries & the Bible to them." Her dying words became a clarion call to establish mission stations among the Oromo. For Krapf, it was in addition an appeal to translate the Bible *into* Oromo. He believed Oromo was key to conversion for all the peoples of central and southern Africa, since he claimed that the Oromo would set up their own missions and ultimately have a chain of stations extending from north to south. Fathme's prayers would be answered through the work that could be done for and by the Oromo with their newly translated Bible.[142] Krapf grafted his own understanding of conversion onto Fathme. Her deathbed plea became an invitation to native language proselytization.

During the mid-nineteenth century, German missionaries were active on a discursive and physical field that people of various ethnicities, both European and African, traversed. That field was relatively open, as Germans, English, converted members of several African groups, and other Europeans mixed companionably, all with the goal of bringing those who were not yet Christian into the fold. They were not considered much in terms of biological race, as they would be in the later nineteenth and early twentieth centuries. The word *race,* which occurred periodically in missionary texts, was used in the broad sense of "nation," referencing a cultural and linguistic category.[143]

As multicultural as the missionary world appeared, the playing field was not level. European Protestants were of similar status, but Africans were a different matter. European missionaries, whether German, British, or otherwise, regarded Africans as *civilizationally* inferior. Africans were often described as savage, heathenish, or barbarous. Of the Oromo, Krapf said he believed them the most intelligent people in East Africa, capable of becoming a beacon on their continent just as the "Germanic race"—and here he referred to the Germans *and* the English—was for Europe. Yet in 1860 he also considered their current state to be one of "barbarism," which could only be lifted with their conversion to Christianity.[144]

Missionary reliance on civilizational, not racial, tropes to describe the fallen states of Africans corresponded well with the antiracist theories of mid- to late nineteenth-century German anthropology. Benoit Massin has contended that under the direction of Rudolf Virchow, the discipline assumed a decidedly liberal, antiracist stance. Liberal anthropologists such as Virchow and his student Felix von Luschan censured racism but also had an ambiguous position toward it, sometimes formulating their arguments about issues such as the ability to acclimate to various environments in racially suggestive language.[145] They were, however, still committed monogenists, who believed that all people came from the same origin, in contrast to polygenists, who held that different races had separate origins. This put the anthropologists in the same camp as the earlier Orientalist philologists Benes discusses, and with the missionaries as well. The position of the missionaries on race was thus liberal but ambivalent, since missionaries accepted the unity of mankind as a given but considered Africans to be hopelessly behind in their civilizational and cultural development.

Classification and Civilization

Throughout the entire period under consideration, from 1814 to 1945, missionaries and the linguists who followed them insisted that civilizational status and language were vital for understanding African difference. They used language and "culture," broadly defined, to group the peoples of the world. Eventually, the Afrikaners who studied in Germany during the 1920s also looked to language as an ethnic determinative. The missionary emphasis on native languages fed into a variety of later conversations on the need to maintain a "separate but equal" policy in countries like South Africa.

In the early to mid-nineteenth century, however, the classificatory system that would later fall into place was fluid, and not fully codified. Missionaries who spoke about African groups did so much more loosely than their successors would; for instance, Krapf's theory that the Oromo were the most intellectual people in East Africa was only marginally connected with their belonging to any broader linguistic or racial category. In an 1840 book on Oromo, he speculated that the Oromo language "has something in common with the Semitic, as well as with the Japhetitic [*sic*] (i.e., Indo-European)."[146] Yet Krapf was even uncertain of the extent to which Semitic and Indo-European were connected and therefore of the strength of their relationship to Oromo and other African languages. Later, in 1854, Krapf did make a tentative attempt at classification in a vocabulary of Masai or "Wakuafi." He posited that there were four loose language families on the continent, which he termed Semitic-Arabic, Cushitic-Arabic, Nigro-Cushitic, and Orphno-Cushitic. This specific mode of classification was never adopted by the wider academic establishment and was itself quite flexible and subject to constant change.[147]

There were attempts at stricter classifications. Koelle's 1854 *Polyglotta Africana* is the most prominent example. The *Polyglotta* compared vocabulary from 100 West African languages and identified some linguistic groupings that are still valid today.[148] This classification was made by a man who was a monogenist committed to proving the unity of mankind, in the mold of Gesenius or Ewald. In an 1851 study of Sierra Leone's Vei language, Koelle maintained that, when it came to a comparison of

African and European languages, "the sameness or affinity of sounds . . . cannot be accidental, but must have a broader and surer basis . . . what else can that basis be, but the common humanity which the Negro shares with the Caucasian."[149] Koelle's 1854 grammar of the West African Kanuri language, which was spoken in the sizable empire of Bornu, upheld his commitment to monogenism; in the text, he disparaged those "who have observed that the Negro race is not a genuine branch of the human family" and argued that "the genuine humanity of the Negroes can be proved in a variety of ways; and one of them is the *philological* [emphasis in original]."[150] Koelle then provided a list of Kanuri root words that he considered cognates of their Indo-European and Semitic cousins.[151] Strenuously opposing polygenism, Koelle's philological research reaffirmed the unity of mankind.[152]

The general missionary focus on where African languages fit within the comparative philological hierarchy in itself defied polygenism. Missionaries were eager to prove that African languages were related to Semitic and Indo-European ones, and part of the broader family of man rather than separate from it. Time and again, missionaries pondered African connections to European and Asian languages. They made these links to languages from across the continent, encompassing tongues spoken from Ethiopia to Kenya to Sierra Leone to Nigeria. Schön's 1862 grammar of Hausa, the most widely spoken language in western Africa, posited it as a Semitic language. He made this claim based on comparisons between Hausa and Hebrew root words, and on the observation that Hausa was sex-denoting.[153] In a 1864 grammar of Temne, a Sierra Leonean language, CMS missionary C. F. Schlenker did not propose outright that Temne belonged to the Semitic family, but did comment that "philology will find ample materials to bring forward some striking analogies between the Temne and other, not only African but Semitic and European languages."[154] Krapf, moreover, tentatively classified both the Oromo and the Masai of Kenya as Semitic.[155] The suggestion that these languages might belong to the Semitic or even Indo-European families established their association with the civilized peoples of the world and their capacity to join them through Christianity.

The CMS missionaries did not suggest that any of the languages that would later be classified as Bantu were linked to the Semitic or Indo-European families. Kolbe, of the RMS and later LMS, did make this claim. He wrote copiously on language history in general and the relationship between the Bantu family and other language families in particular, hypothesizing about such issues as the progression of language from simple, "primeval" vowels and roots through more complex, polysyllabic, forms.[156] In his studies on Bantu and linguistic origins, Kolbe referred to the Indo-European languages as Aryan[157] and concluded that the parallels between these and Bantu were too striking to be coincidental. Drawing on the idea of comparison between root words, which scholars like Klaproth also employed,[158] Kolbe attempted to demonstrate roots common to Indo-European and Bantu languages. For example, he held that the words *hug* and *huge* were "words that can easily be identified in Herero . . . in the roots *hunga* and *honga.*"[159] Much of Kolbe's work on Bantu was thus dedicated to uncovering how it fit with the more well-known Indo-European and Semitic families.

Missionary linguists incorporated African languages into broader classificatory structures and hoped to establish their relatedness to Indo-European and Semitic. However, they did not regard all African speech—or all African peoples—as equal, and the missionaries' relationship to the languages they studied was often ambiguous. Krapf refused to write his Oromo grammar using Ethiopic script for two reasons: First because he believed Oromo was related to Indo-European and therefore required Roman characters, and second because he considered the Oromo more capable of evangelization than the neighboring Abyssinians, who employed Ethiopic script to write Amharic and Ge'ez. Krapf declared himself "convinced that the light of the Gospel and Science will be kindled first amongst the Gallas, and then proceed to the Abyssinians, who have nothing but the name of Christ."[160] Their Ethiopic script was thus unfit for explaining the Christian religion. In part, Krapf denigrated the Abyssinians because they practiced a different form of Christianity—and a much older one—than the CMS. Yet his remarks about the difference between the Abyssinians and the Oromo reflected a deeper belief in the civilizational rift among various African peoples, and their adaptability to Christianity and Western culture.

Although the missionaries agreed that African languages belonged on the same family tree as Indo-European and Semitic, and were not wholly separate from them, it is also clear that they thought African tongues fit at the bottom of that hierarchy. Kolbe believed that "Bantu [was] destined to shed light on the Aryan family and on the origin of language universally" precisely because of its extreme primitivity. Bantu languished at an "earlier stage of development" than Indo-European and thus offered the philologist the chance to "*discover the very first laws by which language was formed* [emphasis in original], and to restore the original concord between language and nature, words and things."[161] The concept that African languages had retained their original, primitive form more so than any others was not singular to Kolbe, either; the idea was central to Meinhof's later conviction that the study of African languages was crucial to understanding human origins.

Conclusion

In 1862 the first installment of Bleek's *A Comparative Grammar of South African Languages* was published. It was followed by a second installment in 1869. Bleek's descriptions of southern African phonological and grammatical forms were ultimately codified into a classificatory hierarchy, which unsurprisingly assigned Nama or Hottentot languages to the same overarching, sex-denoting category as Indo-Germanic and Semitic, and Bantu to a different, agglutinative category. While grammatical gender was central to his method of classification, Bleek asserted that pronomial prefixes and suffixes were also key. Bantu languages were marked by their use of prefixes; Nama and other sex-denoting idioms commonly employed suffixes. These prefixes and suffixes were crucial, Bleek believed, for determining a language's age. The older a language, the more likely that words that would one day evolve into prefixes or suffixes had not yet done so; as an example, he took the English suffix -dom, which in contemporary times expressed itself only in words such as *freedom* and *fiefdom,* but in the past had maintained a separate meaning and existence.[162]

As significant as they were to the study of Africa in Bleek's nineteenth century, the Bantu and Nama languages were not the only categories into which sub-Saharan African languages could fall. Bleek posited an essentially tripartite classification, and conjectured that the languages of the San or Bushmen belonged to another group entirely, a theory Meinhof would echo. Since Bleek believed that scholars had neglected Bushman languages, he devoted most of his time in the years leading up to his 1875 death studying those languages, along with Bushman customs, habits, and literature. He even delayed the completion of additional volumes for the *Comparative Grammar* until he had thoroughly researched Bushman, by which point it was too late.[163]

Bleek's work in the 1860s initiated a new phase in the categorization of African languages, inasmuch as it introduced this specific framework for classification based on the relationship among languages in the Bantu family. His labors did not, however, signal the end of missionary participation in African philology. Bleek maintained close contacts to missionaries in South Africa, including Döhne, Krönlein, and the latter's RMS colleagues Carl Hugo Hahn, J. Rath, and F. H. Vollmer.[164] These missionaries did send Bleek information from afar in the tradition of missionary fieldworkers supplying data to armchair scholars. Yet they also did much more. They analyzed the linguistic material they had collected, and published their own works on it. As representatives of both evangelical pietism and comparative philology, they considered it their duty to record and teach the languages they learned. After Germany unified and became a colonial power, the center of linguistic research shifted from their stations in Africa to cities like Berlin and Hamburg. Still, missionaries remained central to the discipline through at least the first half of the twentieth century, intertwining themselves ever more closely with the academic establishment as *Afrikanistik* became institutionalized.

CHAPTER 2

Beyond the Missionary Field: The Development of African Studies at the *Seminar für Orientalische Sprachen* in Berlin

In the late 1870s, missionary attitudes toward German nationalism began to shift. Friedrich Fabri's 1879 pamphlet "Does Germany Need Colonies?" was representative of this new era in the relationship of Protestant missionaries to nationalism. The essay, written by the onetime Rhenish Mission inspector who had become Bismarck's main colonial adviser, went into great detail about Germany's need to become more internationally competitive. One of its main arguments concerned the relationship of science to nation-state and empire, and Fabri was insistent that German research on Africa and other parts of the non-Western world serve German interests. "Are we to be and remain only theoreticians in this field too, merely collecting and researching for the benefit of the world at large?" Fabri asked. "Are we to continue sitting in our studies and making ourselves familiar with all the quarters of the globe, without finding a second national home anywhere overseas? Is this a situation which can in the long run be reconciled, we will not say with our national honour (sic), but with urgent national requirements?"[1] Fabri was doubtless aware of missionary contributions to colonial science. However, since they worked in foreign mission fields, he saw their labors enriching the empires of others. He desperately wanted that to change and for them to participate in enriching German colonialism instead.

For most of the nineteenth century, German missionaries did not support a specifically German colonialism and often worked in the service of the British. With German unification and, later, German imperialism, the issue of whether to support German overseas endeavors became an issue of contention. Germany obtained most of its African empire, which encompassed territory in the southern, eastern, and western reaches of the continent, in 1883 and 1884.[2] Bismarck was never particularly interested in colonial ventures but turned to them in the 1880s because of multiple concerns both foreign and domestic, which various historians have detailed and disputed. Colonialism was part of German competition against Great Britain, but it also factored into social equations at home in different ways. Conservative elites hoped to buttress the hierarchical social system that afforded them so many privileges against countervailing social forces, such as rapid industrialization and urbanization, by offering colonialism up as a sop to the bourgeoisie and working class.[3] One of the conservative tactics, in this formulation, was to incite an already nascent Anglophobia and solve domestic and foreign policy problems with one fell swoop. As David Blackbourn and Geoff Eley have shown, though, the aristocracy was not as firmly in control as historians once believed.[4] The middle class also played a substantial role in advancing colonial aims through support of the various pressure groups—including the Pan-German League, Naval League, Society for the Eastern Marches, and Colonial Society—that arose to lobby for colonialism in the late nineteenth century.[5] Interest in protecting the rights of Germans overseas, and in finding new outlets for emigrants that would allow them to remain under German hegemony, also entered into arguments for colonization.[6]

All of the divergent domestic and social forces at play in the 1880s culminated in Bismarck's convening the Berlin West Africa Conference from 1884 to 1885. The conference, which effectively recognized the sovereignty of European powers in specific African regions, divided the continent among them. The decisions made in Berlin were significant for missionaries, since they meant that German missionary societies could now work in German-controlled territories. German missionary societies had generally been moving closer together since 1846, when they began to hold joint mission conferences. In 1866, their meetings became more formal, coalescing into an annual "continental" Mission Conference that was held in Bremen. Finally in 1885 a German Protestant Missionary Board was established, loosely uniting German-speaking societies such as the Basel Missionary Society, the Berlin Missionary Society, the Rhenish Missionary Society, the North German Missionary Society, and the Leipzig Missionary Society.[7]

Neither the conferences held earlier in the century nor the board's creation spelled the end of ecumenicalism. Gustav Warneck, the theologian who was the guiding force behind *Missionswissenschaft*—missiology—

was, for one, staunchly opposed to the amalgamation of national and missionary interests. As publisher and founder of the *Allgemeine Missionszeitschrift,* the leading German language journal of missionary scholarship, Warneck was influential across German missionary societies. Contending that the *Reich* on earth was separate from the *Reich* of God, he argued stridently against missionary involvement in German imperial affairs, although he did recognize the need for limited collaboration.[8]

At the same time, as of 1884–85 countervailing social and political pressures were pushing missionaries toward ever closer involvement with the German Empire. As Altena has observed, Fabri had been an imperial enthusiast since the late 1860s, when he called on Prussia to intervene in ethnic clashes in South West Africa and protect the Rhenish Missionary Society's investment in the region. In contrast to Warneck, Fabri contended that missionaries were essential not only to the dissemination of Christianity but to an elevated culture that was anchored in Germandom.[9] The Bremen Continental Conference of 1885 provided something of a victory to Fabri and his supporters, among them Alexander Merensky, a prominent Berlin Missionary Society inspector who also created a workbook for the transcription of Bantu languages.[10] The German Protestant Missionary Board was also called into existence at this conference. Representatives of both pro- and anticolonial viewpoints sat on the board, including Warneck and Fabri. The Foreign Office sent its own delegate to the conference, which, as Altena comments, demonstrated an obvious governmental show of interest in missionary affairs.[11] Missionaries remained riven by the issue of national affinity, as the vehement anticolonial rhetoric of missionary officials such as Friedrich Michael Zahn, director of the North German Missionary Society, attests.[12] Nevertheless, the new political climate exerted a powerful influence on the mission. Even those who advocated against cooperation were now part of an overarching colonial complex and, once they worked inside a German colony, became, if not exactly the handmaidens of German colonialism, then at least ambivalent participants in the spread of German Empire.[13]

As the political situation under the missionaries' feet quickly shifted, they continued to be as involved in linguistics as ever, if not more so. In 1886 Reinhold Grundemann, a missiologist and cartographer who was affiliated with Warneck,[14] reported that over 220 German Protestant missionaries were involved in African language research.[15] Many leading figures in the procolonial movement were particularly interested in language, and the new move toward nationalism had a significant impact on

African studies. Fabri is not usually associated with philology, but in 1859 he did publish a series of essays that included a piece on the origin of language and how it might be connected to the earliest forms of heathenism, a tract that echoed pietist views about the need to proselytize in all languages.[16] Moreover, in the 1860s Fabri was not only looking for Prussian military intervention in South West Africa; he was also looking to collaborate with non-German Bible societies on various translation projects. He had worked with the Dutch Bible Society to ensure that one of his Rhenish missionaries was able to translate the Bible into the Pacific language of Dayak, and "lent" the services of another one of his missionaries to the British and Foreign Bible Society so that he could complete a translation into another Pacific language, Nias.[17] Fabri also corresponded with the BFBS concerning Nama, specifically regarding funding for Krönlein's New Testament translation. He even apologized to the BFBS for Krönlein's unwarranted addition of a "German preface for linguists" and assured the society that it would be removed.[18] This example shows that even Fabri, who was later known as the "Father of the German Colonial Movement,"[19] understood the need for cross-national cooperation in some areas.

While Fabri was obviously interested in linguistic issues, his role in the history of *Afrikanistik* is still relatively minor. However, Carl Büttner, Fabri's Rhenish ally, was seminal both to the intellectual development of the discipline as well as to its nationalization. Next to Fabri, Büttner was also the most important procolonial missionary. Büttner's route to southwest Africa and his position as a leader in African language and culture studies was a circuitous one. Born in Königsberg in 1848, he would later study theology and non-Western languages in his hometown.[20] During his years at university, Büttner decided on a missionary career and applied to go to China with a Berlin Missionary Society. He was rejected and instead spent the years 1870 to 1872 at the mission house in Barmen (Wuppertal), seat of the Rhenish Missionary Society, which had built a network of mission stations in southern Africa.[21] Büttner embarked for South West Africa in 1872 as one of the most highly educated members of the society and was handpicked to be its linguist at the Otjimbingue mission station. In Otjimbingue Büttner studied Herero and was soon recognized as one of the most prominent Africanist linguists of his time.

Büttner was an ardent nationalist. Like Fabri, he also realized that his work in Africa made collaboration with non-Germans necessary. Although his early years in South West Africa coincided with the beginnings of German imperium, Büttner actively sought aid and protection from the

British and was not overtly concerned about turning to a foreign source. Yet he later became the Kaiser's special ambassador to South West Africa and helped procure it for Germany. In his eventual capacity as professor of African languages at the Berlin *Seminar für Orientalische Sprachen,* Büttner was also a zealous promoter of German-language materials on African languages. He lamented that "the best books on African languages have appeared in English, but have German authors," and tried to rectify this situation through the publication of a German journal of African languages, the *Zeitschrift für afrikanische Sprachen.*[22] Büttner is therefore a transitional figure in the history of *Afrikanistik,* since he originally labored in an international sphere but came to advocate for an expressly German colonialism and an African studies discipline that would be dominated not by German scholars writing in English but by Germans using their mother tongue.

Carl Büttner the Missionary

Büttner's Africanist career began, ironically, in London. Before setting sail for Cape Town, from which he would proceed to South West Africa, Büttner met with British missionary officials to discuss questions concerning the translation of certain religious texts and tracts into Herero.[23] The visit to England was not an especially happy one. Büttner expressed mixed feelings toward the British. On the one hand, he had a propitious meeting with English explorer and anthropologist Francis Galton. Büttner remarked that "it is clear to me that the general level of education [in England] is higher than that of Germany, owing to the freedom of the press and the frequency of newspaper reading." But he also made snide comments about the behavior of English missionaries. He commented that once they were in attendance at a meeting, "the scandal that these good Britons make with their cheers and 'hear, hears' is hardly imaginable in Germany." Büttner admired the British but was unnerved by their behavior.[24] He may also have been jealous of their imperial successes, as his later efforts to displace English as the main language of African studies suggest.

Büttner's ambivalence toward the English was matched by his ambivalence toward Africans. On the positive side, Büttner's first impression of the Herero was good. He was optimistic about their conversion and about translating and transcribing their language. In a letter to the leadership of the RMS, he explained, "I have to admit that I have the same favorable impression of the Herero that the other brothers had when they came here."[25] Büttner added that it was not much more difficult to approach and communicate with the Herero than with Europeans.[26] The first students he taught in Otjimbingue were not remarkably different from those he had worked with in Germany.[27] All in all, he found that the Herero were not what he had expected based on the portrayals of "negroes in books." For a "race that was supposed to stand nearest to the apes," he was impressed that the Herero took such an interest in politics and self-governance.[28]

Büttner's general acceptance of Africans influenced his assessment of race relations in the colonies. He was not concerned with socialization among whites and blacks or "coloureds,"[29] implying that communities that did not encourage interaction between the "races" were weaker than those that did. On a visit to the town of Saron in South Africa, Büttner happily reported that "it was especially good to see that while in many other places the difference between whites and coloreds seems almost like a caste difference, in Saron everything is a jumble."[30] Büttner was even in favor of interracial marriage, as Lora Wildenthal has shown. Worried that converted African women and biracial children could be driven to destitution if abandoned by profligate German men, he argued in 1887 that marriage would offer protection against such neglect.[31]

Büttner's early opinions on Africans diverged dramatically from those of racial theorists like Joseph Arthur de Comte Gobineau. Whereas Büttner believed that race mixing could enhance the population of South West Africa and pointed to families like the Schmelens as proof,[32] Gobineau feared the results of interracial union. His infamous essay *The Inequality of Human Races* attributed social degeneration to the mixture of unlike blood. The "degenerate man" of Gobineau's nightmares bore little relation to his pure ancestors, and his procreation with those of other races had doomed his very existence. Gobineau maintained that this degenerate "and his civilization with him, will certainly die on the day when the primordial race-unit is so broken up and swamped by the influx of foreign elements, that its effective qualities have no longer a sufficient freedom of action."[33] Gobineau's work, written in the 1850s, had a strong influence on German racism. Massin has shown that, while Gobineau's writings found few audiences in the 1860s and 1870s, in the 1880s they began to come into fashion. They were embraced by racial thinkers such as the composer Richard Wagner and the archaeologist Gustaf Kossinna, the latter of whom located the original Indo-European or "Aryan" race in Germany and believed that race mixing had been the downfall of those who had migrated away from the German cradle.[34]

Protestant missionaries tended to reject these extreme racist arguments, since they contradicted the idea that all people could be saved through God's grace. Nonetheless, while missionaries like Büttner theoretically espoused liberal beliefs about Africans, in reality they were often less sanguine. The longer Büttner stayed in South West Africa, the more his opinions of the Herero began to dim, and he began to sound more like Gobineau or Kossinna. By December 1873, hardly a year after his arrival, Buttner saw the Herero as an unsalvageable *Volk*. He referred to both the people and land around him as "empty" and "leeched" of spirit.[35] In 1874, his outlook grew yet bleaker. Trying to make the Herero understand his sermons was "torture," and his parishioners constantly frustrated him. Büttner maintained that only one had been able to interpret his message, and that one incorrectly.[36] Eventually, Büttner commented that "in Europe, you really cannot imagine what it means to have a whole people made up of nothing but whores, thieves, liars, and misers, in which even the most honest of men deserves to be put in jail at least once each weekend."[37] For Büttner, the entire Herero nation was depraved, and he felt drained of all optimism and vitality.

It was in this context of despair that language became a site of colonial contestation for Büttner. Likewise, the discipline of linguistics became an arena for determining Africa's future as either a Europeanized, Christianized domain or an eternally backward, savage place. Büttner was convinced that he was fighting a war between civilization and its opposite; molding Herero and other African languages to convey Christian ideas was therefore critical to gaining Africa for Europe and for Christ. These aims were complicated by what Büttner considered the inferior nature of Herero and other Namibian languages. The poverty of the Herero language reflected lacks in moral character and intellectual development, which only true belief in Christianity could fill. However, the exiguity of the language itself made conveying Christian beliefs in ways the Herero could understand them difficult. Because the Herero were herders and much of their life revolved around cattle, for instance, their religious ceremonies centered on the slaughter and consumption of cows. This focus complicated Büttner's efforts to search out suitable vocabulary.[38] Without words to make the Herero comprehend key Christian images, they could not advance. They would remain morally and mentally backward, unable to enter the polite, refined society that Europeans enjoyed as their birthright. Since Büttner's critiques of language were embedded in this much broader cultural context—a context that language supposedly mirrored—his more general attitudes toward the Herero and other African groups were profoundly intertwined with his assessment of their language and its potential for growth and transformation.

Before leaving for South West Africa, Büttner believed he had the power of God on his side and that his future converts would be subject to that power. After spending time among the Herero, however, he realized that they were the powerful ones. They did not conform to his expectations of compliant, innocent heathens, and he interpreted their lack of conformity as representative of a debased moral character. Büttner was constantly confounded by the Herero ability either to reject Christianity entirely or to assimilate Christian practice to their own culture without losing their identity. As with the Malagasy Christian converts that Pier M. Larson has described, who saw cross and Bible as tools for warding off local dangers such as crocodiles,[39] the Herero interpreted the Christian message to suit their own needs. Büttner staunchly maintained that "Christians should wear European clothing, live in European houses, produce European craftwork, live in the European manner, not just from milk, grasshoppers, and wild onions, but also from corn, and bury their dead in coffins." Adapting Africans to European mores such as these proved difficult, though, not least because there was often insufficient land on which to grow the corn that Büttner considered a staple of a good European, Christian diet, or the right material to build coffins.[40]

Herero appropriations of Christianity were mutable, and expanded beyond the framework that missionaries provided. One man, for example, spoke of the Christian God as being a "playmate" of his chief, whom he also considered a god This, Büttner explained, was how the Herero understood the concept of the Christian God; not as almighty, but as on a par with their chiefs and ancestors.[41] Thus, while Büttner had hoped to impose a Foucauldian order on the Herero through the learning of the Bible and Christian constraint, he was thwarted because Herero and German religious terminology could not be made identical.[42]

None of Büttner's antipathy toward the Herero made him exactly like Kosinna or Gobineau; his continued commitment to missionary principles distanced him from their attitudes toward the prizing of pure blood, as did his belief that mixed peoples exhibited the best of both races, not the worst. In this respect, he remained more similar to liberal anthropologists like Rudolf Virchow, the physician and social reformer who was central to the establishment of the anthropology discipline in Germany. Virchow recognized strict differences among the races but also believed in an underlying human unity that had changed over time as peoples migrated to dissimilar geographic regions.[43] Like Büttner, Virchow was not opposed to racial mixing and saw it as having potentially positive effects.[44] The intellectual influences shaping Büttner's beliefs were complex, since he had affinities both with a committed anti-Darwinist like Virchow and a Darwinian enthusiast like Galton, who coined the term *eugenics* and was well-known for his studies of "hereditary genius."[45] Büttner was an ambivalent figure and grappled for most of his life with his antipathy for Africans and concomitant desire to Christianize them.

As Büttner's disenchantment with the Herero grew, his woes with the English also increased. Büttner was originally eager for the British in the Cape Colony to annex large swaths of South West Africa and provide protection and more formal political organization to the region. The British did not, however, make any moves to do so, with the exception of annexing the area around Walvis (*Walfisch*) Bay in 1878.[46] What irked Büttner even more was the behavior of one of the English representatives, W. C. Palgrave. Palgrave arrived in Namibia in 1875 as an emissary of the Cape government and was intent on expanding its protection to the chief of the Herero, Samuel Maharero. Büttner described Palgrave as barging into local affairs as though he were "Alexander the Great" preparing to conquer "half the world."[47]

Palgrave's arrogance so outraged Büttner, in fact, that he began to see German intervention and political domination as the only acceptable solution to the question of Namibia's future. He was convinced—despite his negative assessment of the Herero—that German colonization, coupled with continued missionary endeavors, would lead to their successful conversion and introduction to "civilization." The pessimism and racist outlook that he had developed in Namibia led him to two conclusions: that the region required German overlordship to bring it under control, and that language study and comparative philology would play a major role in such a project, since it was only through command of the language that the Herero would finally be brought to heel and the battle between civilization and heathenism won for the West. For Büttner, linguistic concerns still trumped biological ones, since it was language that would reincorporate Africans into the family of civilized man.

Büttner's early experiences in precolonial southern Africa had a marked influence on the rest of his life, which illness ended early: He died in 1893, when he was only forty-two. Büttner engaged eagerly in the German colonial cause both before and after it moved into the mainstream, and he believed that German control in Africa would bring order to chaos. Yet Büttner would not be such a remarkable figure had he not actively contributed to colonization on a political level and to the nascent discipline of African studies as a scholar. While he originally returned to Germany to become pastor for the small East Prussian community of Wormditt,[48] he ultimately went on to make a name for himself in politics and academia. As one of the chief negotiators between Namibian and German interests in the mid-1880s, as well as the first German lecturer specifically hired to teach African languages, ethnology, and geography at Berlin's *Seminar für Orientalische Sprachen,* Büttner's influence on German attitudes toward Africans stretched well beyond the end of his own life.

Büttner's political involvement circled around his position as *Bevollmächtiger* (plenipotentiary) of the German emperor in Namibia. Büttner was sent, along with Heinrich Göring—father of the infamous Nazi Hermann—to finalize contracts between African chiefs and the German *Reich.* It was these contracts that would make the region Germany's first official colony. The contract negotiations did not have an auspicious beginning; businessman Adolf Lüderitz had tricked Nama chief Joseph Fredericks, whose domain surrounded the Rhenish mission station at Bethany in southern Namibia, into signing over an enormous tract of land. Büttner was ordered to expand the original purchase through agreements with other local chiefs, who had been leery of dealing with Göring after the debacle with Lüderitz. Whatever Büttner's opinions of the Herero during his tenure as a missionary he had evidently engendered trust among the population and was able to secure the necessary contracts to turn the entire region over to Germany.[49] His linguistic skills were certainly beneficial to the negotiations, since he was one of the few Germans who could communicate with Namibians in their mother tongues.

By the time that Büttner journeyed back to South West Africa in 1885, while he still professed missionary sentiments, he had separated himself from the RMS. The RMS had also undergone changes in the intervening years; it was no longer under the leadership of the nationalist Fabri. Instead, the RMS advocated a policy of nonintervention in political affairs for its missionaries, although this stance was ambivalent, and the mission was always to some extent beholden to German colonial governance.[50] After leaving the RMS, from 1886 to 1889 Büttner became a mission inspector for explorer Carl Peters's extremely procolonial Evangelical Missionary Society for German East Africa (*Evangelische Missions-Gesellschaft für Deutsch-Ostafrika*) (EMGDO). Frustrated with missionary ecumenicalism, colonialists such as Peters called for the creation of a new mission society that would be firmly linked with German imperialism, and that would cater to both new German emigrants to East Africa and African natives alike. Peters used the society, which was also known as Berlin III, to serve his own interests, and it was unavoidably entangled with the aims of his probusiness *Deutsche-Ostafrikanische Gesellschaft.*[51] New missionary societies such as Peters's were formed expressly to promote German colonial aims, leaving older ones to consider where their loyalties lay and to argue the merits of supporting Germany.[52] Büttner's procolonial, pro-German stance seemed to make him an ideal candidate for the EMGDO. However, Büttner never reentered the mission field as a member of Peters's society and ultimately cut ties with it as well; EMGDO officials wanted Büttner to limit his linguistic work, which he refused to do.[53] His career as a linguist had evidently grown more appealing than missionary work.

When Büttner arrived at the Seminar for Oriental Languages in 1887, he was as passionate in his support of German imperialism as any civil servant or military officer. He represented a new brand of missionary linguist, one who was extremely nationalistic and dedicated to the goal of German expansion. Many of the missionary linguists of the new generation were, like Büttner, nationalistically minded, and this was reflected at their conferences and in their books and essays. They wrote for a largely German audience, a shift from the norm during the early to mid-nineteenth century. They belonged to German mission societies and often worked in German colonies. The German Protestant Mission continued to struggle with how to balance a supposedly universalist Christianity with increased demands to defend Germany's colonial governments. If not all mission societies offered unconditional backing for their country's imperial aims, few actively protested them, either.[54] While nonmissionaries with direct ties to the *Reichskolonialamt* certainly entered the African studies field in greater numbers from the 1880s onward, there were still many missionaries working beside them, and most of them had the shared goal of advancing German expansionism. Büttner was one of the first to start this trend, and it continued while he was at the seminar and for years after his death.

The Creation of a Seminar for Oriental Languages in Berlin

The final years of Büttner's career were intimately tied to the Seminar for Oriental Languages. The seminar opened its doors in 1887, only three years after Germany became a formal colonial power. It was an academic department at Berlin's Friedrich-Wilhelms University and the first institution in Germany to offer regular instruction in African languages and cultures. Berlin thus became Germany's first center for African studies, and the seminar's establishment signaled an important shift in the primary location of "colonial" knowledge production from the missionary field of the African periphery to the metropolitan core. Within several years, the seminar had become a key player in the development of information on the colonies. It allowed future German colonists to examine Africans and other non-Europeans away from their "natural" habitats and in the comfort of a sanitized, safe, and orderly classroom.[55]

The creation of the seminar and the slow institutionalization of African studies in Germany also heralded a shift away from the earlier, international roots of the discipline embodied in the Protestant Mission. In its early stages, the seminar was essentially a branch of the Foreign Office, and most of its students were Germans preparing for colonial careers. Accordingly, the seminar emphasized those African languages spoken in the German colonies or languages that could prove economically beneficial to German traders. Missionaries had transcribed languages from across the continent, often in English-run territories; from the 1880s, they were encouraged to concentrate on the major German "colonial" languages. This is unsurprising, considering that the seminar was government-funded and had connections with nationalist pressure organizations such as the Colonial Society. The Colonial Society formed in 1887, the same year as the seminar, and was an amalgum of two preexisting organizations: the Colonial Association and the Society for German Colonization, the latter of which Peters had established in 1884.[56] Early on, Peters expressed a lively interest in the seminar's curriculum. He believed that Berlin needed to offer courses in Bantu languages and wrote a memo arguing as much to Bismarck in March 1887. Peters explained that as the German population in the colonies would soon be expanding, there would be an increased need for Bantu language knowledge that the seminar should be ready to fill. He speculated further that German business ventures in Africa would soon flourish, and the businessmen conducting them would require a rudimentary knowledge of Bantu languages as well.[57]

Peters's confidence that legions of German immigrants would soon flood the African colonies was misplaced, as was his faith that German businesses would reap unimaginable riches from expeditions in Africa; the colonies never drew many settlers, and profits from Germany's overseas empire were marginal at best.[58] Inspired by Germany's putative colonial successes of the 1880s, and excited by the potential of its new possessions, however, colonial fantasies thrived as never before in this era of increasing national agitation and reformulation of the German political, social, and economic landscape. Germany had industrialized later than its main foes, England and France. Once the process of industrialization had started, though, Germany quickly began to challenge and then outstrip its neighbors in terms of production. As Germany's industrial might grew, so did its imperial ambitions. Competition among Europe's great powers had a global reach, and each tried to amass as large an empire as possible. Germany had a particular interest in displacing England as the world's preeminent maritime power, and it strove to create a navy that could best the British, creating pomp and pageantry to sell the fleet to the German people, as Jan Rüger has shown.[59] This sort of international rivalry was hardly inconsequential for a school like the seminar, since most of its students attended in order to pursue careers that would advance German concerns abroad, whether in military, political, or economic venues.[60]

The seminar also had its own nationalist mythology. According to legend, the original inspiration for the seminar came from a specific incident involving China, one that conveniently involved the colonially apathetic Bismarck. Eduard Sachau, the seminar's director from its founding through 1918, related that Bismarck believed more young Germans needed to be trained in non-Western languages after having difficulties locating a German who could interpret Chinese for him.[61] Other evidence suggests that it may not have been Bismarck, but Wilhelm Grube, a lecturer at Friedrichs-Wilhelm University, who first advocated the foundation of an institution like the seminar. Grube made his recommendation in 1884, after his personal Chinese teacher quit teaching him. He believed that the Chinese who worked at the embassy in Berlin were generally unwilling to have Germans learn their language. If a German who planned to go to China hoped to study Chinese beforehand, Grube argued that it would be best to find him tutors not affiliated with diplomatic circles.[62]

Both of these stories show that at the outset, the seminar was envisioned as a school for interpreters, who were in short supply during the early to mid-1880s, just as German interactions with the extra-European world were growing more frequent, and official German colonization was intensifying. There was some exigency connected with the German interest in founding an interpreter's academy, because of a belief that Germans were not as knowledgeable about foreign peoples and languages as their main European competitors. Bismarck was supposedly aware of this lack and proposed that Germany create an institution along the lines of the Austrian Oriental Academy in Vienna.[63]

There was also a fear that if Germans in the colonies remained reliant on native "middlemen"—interpreters with a command of both European and non-European languages—they ran the risk of being fed false data by persons who wanted to deny colonists certain knowledge. Grube, for instance, had qualms about how much the Chinese really wanted Germans to learn their language. Africanists did not trust their subjects either. In 1898 August Seidel, the secretary of the Colonial Society, voiced a suspicion that African interpreters did not have the best interests of German colonizers at heart when advocating for the publication of his grammars on Swahili and Duala.[64] If Germans bypassed the middlemen and learned Asian and African languages themselves, Grube and Seidel suggested, they would no longer have to worry about being deceived and would be more confident in their knowledge of foreign situations.

By 1898, when Seidel was worrying about African interpreters, African languages were well ensconced in the seminar's curriculum. Yet according to Sachau, when plans were first made to incorporate the seminar into Friedrich-Wilhelms University, sub-Saharan African languages were not even mentioned.[65] Early reports on the feasibility of creating a foreign language academy always mentioned its relevance for both "Asien" and "Afrika," but the former always took top billing, and North African Arabic was the lone African representative.[66] This omission was, Sachau later admitted, a glaring error, which in a memorandum of 1886 included only "theoretical lectures and practical exercises in the six main living languages of the Orient and East Asia," these being Turkish, Arabic, Persian, Japanese, Chinese, and something called "Jewish Idioms."[67]

Africa was as significant, if not more, to German colonial goals as Asia was, even in the 1880s. Why then were African languages omitted from the seminar's plans? Sachau claimed that the exclusion of the "leading East African lingua franca, Swahili" could be easily explained by the "embryonic conditions of [German] colonial relations in 1886." Despite his connection to Fabri and worry that Germans were falling behind their European competitors on the colonial front, Bismarck's general disinterest in

Africa may also have played a role. He simply did not consider the country's African possessions pertinent to international relations.[68] However, Sachau also pointed out that although Swahili was not explicitly mentioned in the 1886 memorandum, Africa was *implicitly* included in the seminar's program.[69] He was probably telling the truth, since when Gustav von Goßler, then minister of the Department of Education and Health, wrote Bismarck to discuss Grube's request, he mentioned that the study of both Asian *and* African languages in Germany had been neglected, and were more richly cultivated in France and England.[70] The seminar's name might have indicated otherwise, but as Sachau insisted it was still considered both an "Oriental" *and* a "colonial" Academy.[71] This dual purpose was later confirmed when both Swahili and a course in southern African geography were incorporated into the seminar's first course catalog.[72]

Even so, in the seminar's first years academic emphasis was decidedly on Asia. Swahili was the only sub-Saharan language taught until 1897.[73] Enrollment by either future members of the foreign service or military officers, who dominated the student body, was generally low, with only eleven pupils attending in the first semester, the fall of 1887. All of them were signed up for Asian language classes, with the greatest number, six, taking Chinese. Over the next few years military and civil servant participation remained paltry, with usually either no students or only a handful listed for any class. The first German military official studying an African language did not arrive until the spring of 1889, when an army lieutenant registered for Swahili.[74]

The priority accorded to Asian languages during the seminar's early years had something to do with the greater theoretical knowledge of Asian tongues, which was actually considered a stumbling block to opening greater trade relations with Asia. An 1885 memo concerning the potential foundation of the seminar complained that, in comparison to foreign institutions, "at German universities there are either no chairs for the [Asian] languages in question, or they essentially are limited to a theoretical course in the centuries-old languages of the scholars, literature, and tradition, which is quite removed from the living languages of the people." Throughout the nineteenth century, the memo continued, where Asian languages were taught it was within a philological framework that only "trained scholars" would understand.[75] As relationships between Germany and Asia deepened, financial considerations were coming to the fore and necessitated a different kind of linguistic knowledge, a practical one as yet unrecognized at German universities.

The shift to emphasizing practical over academic knowledge that occurred in Asian philology was not unique. The purpose of the university itself began to change in the nineteenth century, when more and more students—the so-called *Brotstudenten*—received educations not for academic purposes but to learn a profession. Their rise was connected with a similar growth in the number of "practical" training academies in Germany, institutions that explicitly shunned intellectual pursuits in favor of pragmatic ones.[76] At the same time, the nineteenth century had changed philology in other ways. Interest in "living languages" increased, while excitement for their ancient cousins waned. There was a move toward reforming philological and literary studies, turning away from the focus on classical languages such as Latin and Greek and giving more weight to *Neusprachen* like German, French, and English. This fed into a desire to raise the respectability of national languages and literatures.[77] German itself was recast in terms of its importance for national identity and the creation of the *Volk*,[78] receiving special attention and gaining new prominence in the curriculum of German universities.[79]

The increasing value given to practical education, coupled with the renewed intellectual focus on living languages, meant that how Asian languages were taught at the seminar differed from how they were addressed at more traditional universities. In the case of Asian languages, there was also a solid academic literature to build on, even if the emphasis on what was significant about it had changed. There was much less literature on Africa, most of it produced by missionaries. However, the newfound emphasis on the pragmatic value of linguistics and the increased significance of living languages were pivotal to African studies. Their primitivity and "purity" were in this respect attractive, since according to experts like Büttner many African peoples had remained isolated for eons, their languages unsullied by encounters with other groups. Büttner made as much clear when he said that "Africa doubtless had unique conditions for the formation of modern languages. . . . in many areas the desert almost completely disrupted communication among tribes and it is not impossible that some languages may have had no contact with any outside influences for eons." He went on to add that, for this reason, "research into African languages will lead us to new discoveries about the development of our own European languages; it is not impossible that with more intensive study in comparative philology we will come to learn more about that time when humanity was not yet divided into great ethnic and linguistic families."[80] Africans and their languages, trapped in the historical present, would allow German scholars to plumb the depths of the European past not through crumbling texts but through living people. The idea that the antiquity of African languages was what made them so vital to philology became a hallmark of arguments for their importance to the German colonial project. Years later in 1910, Meinhof would similarly argue that the lack of a written literature in most African languages made them the ideal object of inquiry for scholars interested in living speech, since there was no static from ancient literature to disrupt the examination of contemporary grammar, morphology, and phonetics.[81] The lack of a long intellectual tradition in African linguistics was thus formulated as an advantage in a transforming academic environment that emphasized practicality over pedantry.

Early to mid-nineteenth-century missionary philology had always enjoined the practical and the scholarly; the main reason for all the translations, grammars, and dictionaries produced was evangelization, but issues of classification and the confrontation with polygenism were also critical. The missionary ability to combine the practical with the theoretical may have appealed to Sachau when he was looking for an African specialist in 1887, though it is more likely that Büttner was appointed to his position because there were few other options. Missionaries were still the main experts in African languages, and Büttner was living in Berlin and still closely affiliated with Peters and Fabri. He could also double as an adviser on mission affairs.[82] In the five years Büttner spent at the seminar, he therefore assumed a variety of roles. His area of specialty was southern Africa, but as Swahili was the only language on the seminar's books for its first ten years, he taught no other, although African history and geography also fell under his purview.

In addition to teaching, Büttner was chief publisher of the *Zeitschrift für afrikanische Sprachen*. He began to petition for its publication in 1886, before his appointment to the seminar. The *Zeitschrift* as he envisioned it would be both an intellectual platform for German missionaries and scholars to write about Africa and its languages in their own mother tongue, as well as a manual for businessmen and colonists with no linguistic experience. Prior to the *Zeitschrift,* Büttner claimed that Germans, himself included, were forced to write in English because they lacked a forum where they could publish in German. Büttner believed that Germans had contributed more to African language studies than anyone else, and he found it a disgrace that the formal academy in Germany had paid so little attention to them. He talked about African philology as a "branch of science that we (in Germany) have rather neglected."[83] For decades German missionaries had labored for an English-speaking audience without recognition. With his journal, Büttner announced that the German academy would finally notice the missionaries who researched Africa, and hoped that the scholarship produced therein would demonstrate German superiority in the study of non-Western languages.

Büttner's journal, like the seminar itself, was thus a nationalist project. While languages from outside the German colonies did receive some attention, the journal's emphasis was on languages within German-controlled borders.[84] The *Zeitschrift* published a German-Kikamba dictionary that Büttner had acquired from Krapf, who had died in 1881.[85] Since Kikamba was spoken in German East Africa, the dictionary would have practical application. The dictionary also highlighted Krapf's German origins, unquestionably demonstrating that one of the world's most famous Africanist philologists, who had usually written in English during his lifetime, was indeed a proud German. Other journal authors had more directly nationalist ties, including Merensky, the procolonial mission inspector from Berlin, and Captain Curt von François. In 1887 François was a military officer stationed in Togo, where he collected vocabulary from four local languages.[86] He would go on to become commissioner of German South West Africa from 1891 to 1894 and was intimately involved in the extension of German control in the region. After Büttner's death the journal became even more closely tied to nationalist movements, since Seidel, secretary of the Colonial Society, took over as editor. In addition to government funding, under Seidel's stewardship the Colonial Society provided some of the journal's financial backing, as did the German East Africa Company, another Peters vehicle.[87]

Missionaries remained leaders in the field of *Afrikanistik* until after World War II. Nevertheless, once Germany became a colonial power, they were joined by civil servants, military officers, and businessmen, who were now publishing linguistic material and teaching at the seminar. After Büttner's death, the position of German-speaking Swahili lecturer remained vacant for about two years but was temporarily filled by a Dr. G. Neuhaus, in 1895.[88] Carl Velten, a former interpreter (Dragoman) in German East Africa, began teaching Swahili on a more permanent basis in 1897, and Julius Lippert, who would teach Hausa, assumed his academic post in the same year. Both Neuhaus and Velten were also graduates of the seminar.

Unlike Büttner, his successors Neuhaus, Velten, and Lippert were not missionaries. They were drawn instead from the growing corps of colonial civil servants, secular Africa enthusiasts, and philologists interested in African languages. Neuhaus was a lawyer, Velten an interpreter, and Lippert a librarian with a doctorate in classical philology. The networks they belonged to were different from those of the nineteenth-century missionary linguists, who worked in British circles. Take the case of Velten. After studying Swahili, Arabic, and Herero in Berlin, in 1893 Velten went to Dar es Salaam to assume a position as *Hauslehrer,* or private tutor, for the family of East African governor Friedrich von Schele.[89] During his tenure in East Africa, Velten taught Swahili to military officers and other interested German parties,[90] and collected linguistic and literary information from members of various ethnic groups, chief among them several Hehe prisoners whom Schele "supplied."[91] Velten benefited from his relationship to the colonial government in various ways; when the *Schutztruppe* suppressed a rebellion in the south of the colony, they confiscated "1500 documents of all sorts," along with the diary of the captured revolt leader, Hassan bin Omaro.[92] Because Velten was the one who could translate and interpret them, he became the recipient of these "spoils" of war.

Training in African languages now focused on political and economic ends. Lippert, an expert in Greek, Latin, and Arabic, was sent to Tunis and Tripoli from 1897 to 1898 to learn Hausa, which was spoken in both Cameroon and Togo. While there, Lippert assessed the political situation and reported back to the seminar. He discussed the rising dominance of the French in North Africa and the competition they faced from the Italians. He spoke of the gap between the increasing prosperity of the colonial state and the mounting destitution among Arab families. He commented, too, that the Arab population held the Germans in high regard, and that he had been heartily welcomed during his forays into the Arab and Jewish quarters of Tunis.

The seminar itself had strong political interests; it may have been an academic unit at Friedrich-Wilhelms University, but its entire purpose was to support German imperialism. Its staff was dedicated to preparing their students for the careers awaiting them in the German colonies and elsewhere in the non-Western world. Yet beginning with Büttner, missionaries always played a role in supporting German colonialism in general and the seminar in particular. Among the seminar's other early employees were Adam Mischlich, a Hausa expert who had attended the missionary seminar in Basel but eventually became a regional overseer for the German colonial government in Togo;[93] Westermann, who as a member of the NGMS proselytized among the Ewe in Togo and became the Western world's leading expert in their language; and Meinhof. The positions that missionaries and missionary devotees like Meinhof assumed at the seminar were part of the overall sea change in the way that African studies were imagined. For much of the nineteenth century, African language research was conducted to aid in the spread of Christianity and European civilization writ large. From the 1870s and 1880s, such research was no longer employed only or even primarily in the service of Christ, but in that of the German colonial state.

Conclusion

During the 1890s, African languages grew in popularity at the seminar.[94] Enrollment numbers climbed steadily as the twentieth century dawned, and they peaked during years of political and military crisis. The Herero uprising against German colonial rule began in January 1904; in the fall semester of 1903, twelve military officers had registered for African language training.[95] As the Maji Maji rebellion raged in German East Africa from 1905 to 1906, the number of pupils in the seminar's Africa-themed classes also rose.[96] Germany's commitment to the colonies was increasing, and so was interest in the seminar. Prominent figures such as *Reichskolonialamt* secretary Friedrich von Lindequist, East African governors Adolf von Götzen and Heinrich Schnee, and Togo governor Julius von Zech auf Neuenhofen passed through the seminar's doors, as did those with the more humble position of forest warden, land surveyor, or customs inspector.[97] Language proficiency had become necessary for anyone heading to the colonies in an official capacity.

There was little interest at the seminar in cultivating knowledge of all the African languages in the German colonies. The concentration was instead on a few key tongues, namely, Herero, Swahili, and Hausa. The first was significant during the German-Herero War, while the latter two were key as tools of business and governmental transactions. Swahili was especially privileged, since it had become the preferred mode of communication for Germans in East Africa. Other East African languages were deemed impractical and unnecessary. When Catholic missionary J. M. M. van der Burgt attempted to procure funding for a Kirundi dictionary from the *Reichskolonialamt* in 1902, Götzen recommended against financing the project, arguing instead for the broader dispersal of Swahili.[98] Burundi, which would later become a Belgian colony, was at the time part of German East Africa. As of 2008, it is spoken by approximately six million people, while Swahili is spoken by five million. However, Swahili also has a second-language population of fifty million.[99] In a revealing study of the rise of Shaba Swahili, a dialect originally spoken by only a few hundred that grew to be the lingua franca of Africans across Katanga province in the Belgian Congo, Johannes Fabian convincingly demonstrated that colonial control was extended through colonial policy that favored the language for workers in the region.[100]

As Charles Pike has shown, some colonizers hoped that their own language, German, would become the official language of the colonies. In reality though, only a handful of East Africans ever learned German. Ironically, this meant that Swahili became the primary colonial language in the region. German officials wanted to use the language, which had been spreading from inland as a vehicle of trade well before their arrival, to consolidate German rule. They also saw it as a bulwark against English, which was in use throughout the colony and which they wanted to "drive" out of it.[101] Eventually, Germans became so enamored with Swahili that they even envisioned transplanting it to Cameroon and also making it the *Verkehrsprache* in West Africa.[102] Research into other vernaculars or study of them at the seminar could only hamper the German objective of making Swahili their main colonial language, and so it was actively discouraged.

Missionaries were interested in this same kind of linguistic consolidation, as pointed out in the previous chapter. The languages the missionaries promoted as potential vernaculars were, moreover, usually the same ones that the seminar recognized as critical for German political and economic expansion in Africa. Missionaries had introduced these languages to the German academy and colonial bureaucracy, which took notice of their centrality for international trade and international affairs. Hausa, for instance, became an instrument in the struggle with Britain and France for imperial hegemony in West Africa. Sachau noted that the British and French had been in contact with the business-savvy Hausa much longer than the Germans, and credited English missionaries with having established the small cache of Hausa literature that existed.[103] British businessmen had worked among the Hausa for decades more than their German counterparts, which had led to the founding of a course in the Hausa language and institution of a scholarship for students of Hausa at Christ's College, Cambridge.[104] As a corrective, Sachau urged that the seminar draft pamphlets describing the "products of German industry" in Hausa—complete with illustrations—for distribution in Togo and

Cameroon.[105] This would not only support Germany's ongoing competition with its European rivals but ensure access to many other African peoples through the spiderweb-like contacts that the Hausa maintained with a variety of ethnic groups in the region.

Both the early nineteenth-century missionaries and the colonial officials who followed them sought to employ languages such as Swahili and Hausa to their own benefit, whether for the aim of expanding European authority under the aegis of Christianity or for strengthening the rule of one nation-state. Once the seminar had emerged as the main locus of African language research and study, the idea that linguistic knowledge was to be used specifically in the German imperial service was solidified, and the quest for the origins of language and the unraveling of their interrelationships were marginalized. The cultural implications of linguistic knowledge were never exactly ignored, but practical considerations became paramount. For Carl Meinhof, though, intellectual questions remained vital, and he tried to impress their significance upon a colonial establishment and missionary community that had grown increasingly indifferent to academic issues such as linguistic classification and hierarchicalization. Büttner was his mentor, and Meinhof tried to build upon his tradition while forging his own school of African language studies.

CHAPTER 3

The Making of a "Great Africanist": Carl Meinhof in Zizow and Berlin, 1886–1909

Carl Meinhof's Early Career

After Büttner's death it was Meinhof, his student, who became the central figure in African studies. Unlike Büttner, Meinhof was never a missionary. Yet he grew up in a world where the mission was all-important, and it played a dominant role in shaping his ideas and beliefs. Carl Friedrich Michael Meinhof was born on July 23, 1857, in Barzwitz (Barzowice), which was in the Pomeranian county of Schlawe. He was descended from a long line of Swabian pastors, including his father, Friedrich.[1] Friedrich was deeply involved in Protestant mission causes and passed his love of the mission on to his son. On his mother Clara's side, the younger Meinhof had a very strong intellectual pedigree: His grandfather, Karl Ludwig Giesebrecht, was a poet, teacher, and director of the *Grauen Kloster Gymnasium* in Berlin; his great-uncle Ludwig Giesebrecht was a widely known nineteenth-century poet and lyricist;[2] and his uncle, Wilhelm Giesebrecht, was a historian of the Holy Roman Empire.[3]

Considering the history of his father's family, it comes as no surprise that Meinhof became a pastor himself. Nor is it remarkable that he became a scholar, not only because of his maternal relatives, but since he was well trained in a variety of subjects from the earliest age. Growing up, his first teachers were Clara, a local sexton named Völkner, and two of his eleven siblings, his older brothers Otto and Max. In 1868 he left them and relocated to Halle to live and study with his mother's brother-in-law, Theodor Ader. Ader was a director at both a *Gymnasium* and the *Frankische Stiftung,* an institution that was founded in 1698 by the pietist theologian Francke.[4] Meinhof attended Ader's *Gymnasium* from the third year on and began to study at the University of Halle in the spring of 1875. Once there, he concentrated on theology with Luther expert and biographer Julius Köstlin.[5] Meinhof had ample occasion to consort with various unnamed academic luminaries during this period, many of whom he met at his uncle Wilhelm's house in Munich.

Despite the intellectual stimulation of Halle, Meinhof transferred to Erlangen later in 1875 because the "direction of theology" at that university was more appealing to him. This made sense in terms of the links that Erlangen had with the pietist circles that fueled the missionary movement. In the early nineteenth century Erlangen developed its own school of theology, which was neopietist in nature and harkened back to the original precepts of Luther. The school was deeply conservative, confessionalist, and romantic, and it rejected the rationalism of the Enlightenment.[6] For early to mid-nineteenth-century Erlangen theologians such as Adolf von Harless, Johannes C. K. Hofmann, and Gottfried Thomasius, the idea of experience, in particular the experience of sin and rebirth in Christ, was central to Protestantism.[7] According to Paul Tillich, this experience transcended questions about the historicity of the Bible, and the difficulties of proving that events that had occurred two thousand years prior had actually transpired. The fact that you had faith, and had come to that faith through your own personal experience of redemption, was proof enough; your connection to the divine affirmed the reality of the Bible.[8] While not a missionary, Meinhof shared the missionary conviction that the Christian message had to touch the soul to affect conversion, and that a personal encounter with Christ would lead to a lifetime of belief. For this reason, he certainly would have found Erlangen's teachings attractive.

By the time Meinhof arrived at Erlangen, the founding generation embodied by Harless, Hofmann, and Thomasius had gone, but the tradition they represented exerted a powerful pull. Even so, Meinhof admitted that he never developed a "correct inner relationship" to theology. He therefore started to focus on *Germanistik* alongside it. He worked briefly but intensely with philologist Rudolf von Räumer, an expert on the theories of August Schleicher. Von Räumer was particularly concerned with issues such as standard orthography, phonetic change, and language origins, all of which were later critical to Meinhof.[9] Like both Meinhof and the missionary scholars who proceeded him, von Räumer was interested in proving ancestral affiliations between languages that appeared, at first glance, quite different from each other. He tried to demonstrate that there was a connection between Indo-European and Semitic—the two inflecting language families that both Bleek and Meinhof linked to Hamitic.[10]

After concluding his studies in Erlangen in 1877, Meinhof moved to Greifswald to work with religious and linguistic scholar Hermann Cremer.[11] Cremer was head of the Greifswald school of theology, which had intellectual roots similar to those of Erlangen.[12] Meinhof confessed that he still did not like theology but was nonetheless sufficiently inspired to sit through a series of theological examinations in Greifswald in 1878 and 1879. In the meantime, in 1879 he found work as a *Gymnasium* teacher in the Pomeranian town of Wolgast. However, as Meinhof "saw that [he] could not live without scholarly work," in 1881 he also took an examination *pro facultate docendi,* along with yet another theological test.

After leaving Wolgast Meinhof moved to Stettin, where he assumed a position teaching religion at a local *Gymnasium.* He stayed in Stettin until he became pastor in Zizow in 1886. In Stettin Meinhof married his first wife, Elly Heyer, who passed away in 1894; he was remarried to Anna Kloss in 1895, and between the two women he had twelve children. Despite his manifold religious and familial obligations, he always found time to pursue linguistic research. Before he began to study African languages, he concentrated on Assyrian, Aramaic, Arabic, and an advanced course in Hebrew. To that end, he wrote an article on Hebrew pronunciation and reviewed a Hebrew grammar.[13] He was further engrossed in his own German dialect *Plattdeutsch*—low German—and wrote a few essays on the topic in his early twenties. In the article "Orthographische Briefe an Eine Dame," written under the pen name "Mai," Meinhof published a series of letters addressed to an inquisitive woman interested in learning more about *Plattdeutsch.* He described what orthography the language might take were the dialect written instead of oral, asking questions such as, "Accepted that *Plattdeutsch* is struggling to become a self-sufficient literary language, what would be the most purposeful orthography for this new literary language?"[14] Meinhof did not continue to write much about German or other Indo-European languages. Yet this article foreshadowed his later concern for topics as diverse as African oral literature and standard orthographies for African languages. Orthography indeed became one of Meinhof's central foci in the 1920s, when he battled with Westermann and members of the International Institute for African Languages and Cultures in London over which orthographic system to standardize for use in transcribing African languages.[15]

Over the course of the 1880s Meinhof slowly turned his attention to African languages. He was spurred to action by Germany's colonial acquisitions, which convinced him that he should learn more about the continent and its languages. Meinhof also received encouragement to study African languages from Protestant mission societies in general and his good friend Büttner in particular. Meinhof's original interest was in west and central African Bantu languages. This was situationally defined, because the first African that Meinhof met, Njo Dibone, was from Cameroon and taught Meinhof his native language, Duala. Quickly though, Meinhof began to expand his horizons beyond Duala and develop a rapport with Büttner. Meinhof credited Büttner with having given him his first major linguistic "assignment," the completion of a list of African root words. Büttner had begun work on the list, but since he was overburdened with other duties in Berlin, he passed the project off to Meinhof. The initial result was Meinhof's "Preliminary Remarks to a Comparative Dictionary of Bantu" (1895), which attempted to establish a clear method for constructing such a dictionary.[16] Only a few years later, in 1899, Meinhof completed the much longer, more detailed and comprehensive *Grundriss einer Lautlehre der Bantusprachen,* or *Bantu Phonology,* which included not only instructions for how to transcribe "known or unknown" Bantu languages but also a description of *Urbantu,* the hypothetical parent to all contemporary Bantu languages.[17] *Ur*-Bantu was similar to August Schleicher's *Ur*-Indo-German. Like von Räumer, Meinhof was beginning to draw connections between individual languages, proving their relationships to one another.

Establishing a Center for Africanist Research in Zizow

The *Grundriss* was the work that launched Meinhof's academic career. It was well received by scholars such as experimental psychologist Wilhelm Wundt, Berlin anthropologist Felix von Luschan, and Halle Germanist and phonetician Otto Bremer. Eventually, the *Grundriss* helped Meinhof position himself as one of the most prominent colonial scholars in Germany. Yet even before the book appeared, Meinhof was not a complete unknown. For at least a decade preceding its publication, he worked closely with Protestant missionaries who visited and studied with him in Zizow. Meinhof had already begun to establish this metropolitan site for the study of Africa long before he left his country parish for Berlin and Hamburg.

His research space was not nearly as extensive as the ones that were created in those cities. Nonetheless, the parsonage in Zizow contributed to and extended discourse on the classification of Africa in particular and of humanity in general. It helped solidify the metropole, as opposed to the colony, as the most important locus of linguistic and ethnographic knowledge production by drawing students not only from Germany but from Africa itself. By the 1940s Lestrade might have only recalled Hamburg as the mecca for African linguistics, but for his predecessors in the 1880s and 1890s, it was Zizow.

Zizow was not a school in the traditional sense. Meinhof held no formal classes. His students came to him either alone or in pairs, and there were never very many of them. Unlike the pupils in Berlin, who were primarily Germans pursuing careers in the colonial service, most of Meinhof's students were missionaries. These students were demographically distinct from pupils who went to the seminar in other ways as well. Some were "geborene Afrikaner," men of German ancestry who had been born to missionaries in the field and raised in South Africa; they included C. Schumann, Karl Nauhaus, and the brothers Theodor and Paul Schwellnus.[18] They were not wide-eyed neophytes without background knowledge of Africa or its inhabitants. They had grown up on mission stations and learned to speak African languages fluently as children. Black Africans like Dibone occasionally visited Zizow too, although their exact number is unknown. Meinhof sometimes talked of the sustained contact he had kept with his African pupils, but it is unclear whether this contact mostly took place in Zizow or elsewhere, since Meinhof did make work-related trips to Berlin and its environs in the 1880s and 1890s.[19] These Africans did not work with the missionaries who studied under Meinhof but with him alone.

Zizow's importance was closely linked to its reputation, and that of Meinhof, among the missionaries. Even though Germany was now a colonial power and there were more lay linguists, missionaries remained the most dedicated to African philology. Meinhof soon became their main linguistic authority; he attended countless missionary conferences and published myriad articles in journals such as Warneck's *Allgemeine Missions-Zeitschrift*.[20] In Berlin missionary Karl Endemann's words, Meinhof was a "linguistic genius." In 1901—before Meinhof had joined the seminar or set foot on the African continent—Endemann called his friend "*the most important of all Bantu scholars* [emphasis in original], regardless of the fact that he is a Pomeranian country parson who has never been to Africa."[21]

Missionaries like Endemann, who had spent most of their lives in Africa or in some cases been born there, deferred to a man who did not travel there until 1902, when he was already forty-four. Meinhof's students gratefully absorbed his knowledge, which had been attained in a classroom, library, or study, believing it would enrich their personal understanding of Africa.[22]

What did Meinhof offer his missionary pupils? What metropolitan paradigm would help them answer long-undetermined questions about African languages? Essentially, Meinhof gave them a systematic method for transcribing and producing detailed phonologies of each and every Bantu language.[23] He crafted a step-by-step program for assessing which sounds appeared in a given language, what they meant in that language, and how much it deviated from a hypothetical *Ur*-Bantu.[24] Meinhof supplied missionaries with a concise comparative methodology that, if followed correctly, promised no Bantu language would remain a mystery. Walther Trittelvitz, a Berlin mission inspector, said it best when he told a story about how one of his society's missionaries, who had lived among the East African Shambala for six years and spoke their language "quite well," had spent his vacation with Meinhof in Germany. In a matter of hours with Meinhof the man was able to "solve a whole host of problems that the missionaries of Usambara had worked on in vain."[25] Although Meinhof never enjoyed sustained contact with the Shambala, Trittelvitz was certain that he had more insight into the construction of their language than anyone else.

For some of his missionary colleagues, Meinhof's work had other, deeper implications. They were convinced that Meinhof's research had a distinct *moral* component. In 1901, Meinhof applied to the *Reichskolonialamt* for state funds that would allow him to make his first research trip to Africa. When deciding whether to approve his request, the colonial office sent letters to various missionaries and asked for their opinion of Meinhof. The questions posed were not all related to Meinhof's linguistic ability. Rather, the *Reichskolonialamt* asked about the intrinsic "value" that his travels might have, and whether they would contribute to the "moral uplifting of the native population."[26]

The answers that the *Reichskolonialamt* received were not uniformly positive. A. W. Schreiber of Barmen disdained the idea that Meinhof's work would have any impact on the natives. He remarked that to believe Meinhof's work would influence native morality was as ludicrous as thinking that Germanic studies might have a similarly salutary effect on the

German people.[27] Yet Schreiber's stance was not representative. On the contrary, Berlin mission inspector Johannes Wendland said, "It is probably without doubt that Meinhof's linguistic work, which is highly esteemed by our missionaries, is of substantial importance to the colonial development of the African protectorates. It may be recognized as a fact of experience that the cultural betterment of peoples continues to evolve as their language is reduced to writing. . . . The complete deciphering of their language is therefore indispensable to the moral advancement of the natives, because it is . . . the main means through which a new mental landscape can be constructed."[28] For Wendland, transcribing a language on the printed page was tantamount to etching a new, Christian and European value system on the African heart. Once a language was decoded, it would be possible to create a literature that reflected both Christian and Western ideals. Trittelvitz, too, believed that Meinhof's work had moral relevance, and that without it native education would be severely compromised. Trittelvitz likened Meinhof's "national education" contributions to the colonial railroad and its worth for economic progress; the economy would still function without the railroad, and *Volksbildung* would continue whether or not Meinhof's linguistic methodology was incorporated into missionary plans to expand and quicken the pace of African language transcription. However, neither the economy nor the education system would function *very well.* Trittelvitz was indeed so certain of Meinhof's importance that he suggested his society would delay printing new primers for African students until the linguist had visited East Africa.[29]

The *Reichskolonialamt* found the missionary recommendations persuasive, and Meinhof was granted funding. The Prussian minister of culture, Konrad von Studt, said, "I . . . have newly become convinced that the realization of the trip will not only profit Pastor Meinhof . . . but that also the missionary societies, which send their candidates to him for training, continue to take considerable interest in the trip, as well as in its results from a general linguistic perspective."[30] Since the 1880s, missionaries had become ever more closely linked to the colonial state, regardless of their ambivalence, to the point that they sometimes even relied on a state-sponsored *Kolonialrat* for extra financing and were increasingly present at colonial congresses and exhibitions.[31] At the same time, the state wanted the missionaries to support its authority and the laws it enforced in the colonies; von Studt backed Meinhof because he hoped to keep the missionaries happy and assure them of their critical importance to the German colonial project.

Originally, Meinhof had planned to visit both East and South Africa. Meinhof wanted to see South Africa not out of any direct concern for the British colony or Boer Republics, which at the time were concluding the bloody South African War (1899–1902), but because of a keen concern for one particular language, Northern Sotho/Pedi. In the *Grundriss* Meinhof speculated that Sotho provided the best example of regular sound shifts away from *Ur*-Bantu, and that it would be easiest to demonstrate how modern Bantu differed from its parent using Pedi as a test case. Indeed, Meinhof had developed his hypothetical *Ur*-Bantu from observations of Pedi.[32] On the trip, Meinhof expected to examine the linguistic and ethnological relationships between the Bantu "Kaffirs" (Xhosa), Hamitic "Hottentots" (Nama), and Sudanic/Nigritic "Bushmen" (San). Deciphering these relationships later became Meinhof's obsession, as he struggled to prove how language demonstrated links among seemingly disparate groups.[33] This early attention to South African languages foreshadowed an abiding enthusiasm for the region that would continue for the rest of Meinhof's life.

German authorities prohibited Meinhof from visiting South Africa because of the war, however. Officials from the *Reichskolonialamt* and state treasury came close to deciding that if Meinhof could not make both halves of his proposed trip, it might be better for him to postpone the entire journey indefinitely.[34] Since he did not want to lose financial backing for East Africa, Meinhof restructured his research proposal to emphasize the primary significance of East African languages. Now he argued that "the Languages of East Africa stand phonetically much closer to the hypothetical [*Ur*-Bantu] than Sesotho [*sic,* Pedi or Northern Sotho]" and appended a table demonstrating sound differentiations among *Ur*-Bantu, Sotho, and an amalgam of East African languages. Meinhof claimed that he did not use as many East African Bantu languages as examples in the *Grundriss* because they had been improperly transcribed and aurally misunderstood, containing tones that were difficult "for the European ear to distinguish or even recognize." His work in the German colony would, Meinhof explained, lead to a better comprehension of slight variations in tone and allow him to construct a clear orthography that would finally end the confusion over pronunciation and ease communication. It would produce primers that would help both the missionaries in their instruction and African students in learning to read their native languages. Moreover, to complete this work Meinhof would use research on the more fully studied South African languages to develop phonetic theories about their East

African cousins.[35] Meinhof crafted his new proposal expressly to serve German colonial interests. While the state had ancillary concerns for South Africa, it was obviously not as significant as East Africa; thus East Africa became the potential Bantu cradle for political reasons—because it was part of the German Empire, and South Africa was not.

For the Protestant mission, the importance of Meinhof's travels to East Africa rested on the continuing development of his comparative technique, which Meinhof said would teach missionaries to learn not from memory but from "deep understanding," and from the uniform system of orthography that he would institute.[36] While the trip was significant to his missionary colleagues, however, it was not the only issue that interested them; his research at home in Zizow was obviously also of concern. His work gave them the necessary tools to learn Bantu languages more efficiently, and it also allowed for the construction of native literatures that would buttress their goal of civilizing and "Christianizing" Africans. They considered his endeavors preeminently practical, since they would promote evangelization. Meinhof also understood the pragmatic value of his research. He firmly believed that if students of Bantu were introduced to the comparative method it would be easier for them to gain access to the hearts and minds of a broad range of different African groups.[37] In the foreword to the revised edition of his *Grundriss* he said, after discussing the scientific benefits of the book, that "the practical uses of such a work are also not narrow. The existing, empirically determined dictionaries and grammars can be checked. Above all, though, knowledge of the structure of Bantu words is completely indispensable for the recording of hitherto unknown Bantu languages, and it is this practical goal that [the material] which follows will first and foremost serve."[38] As he sat at home in Zizow sifting through old books on various Bantu languages, most of which he had received either from Protestant missionaries or the German government,[39] Meinhof believed he was creating something as significant as the seminar to the enforcement of German control: a guide to the proper analysis of Bantu that would, ultimately, give his countrymen leverage in understanding native peoples.

Meinhof's paradigm for deciphering and classifying African languages was quintessentially metropolitan. The Africans he met in Germany did influence him, but because most of his knowledge came from either European texts or Protestant missionaries, his methods and sources were rooted in German understandings of Otherness, ones that placed Africans on a low civilizational level. Yet Meinhof himself would not have seen it this way. He would have argued that his descriptions of Bantu were steeped not in European but African knowledge. In a later book, the 1911 *Die Christianisierung der Sprachen Afrikas,* Meinhof chastised those who treated African grammatical categories as though they were the same as European ones. He took French Catholic missionary Petrus Maria Le Berre to task for describing the Mpongwe language of Gabon as though it were French,[40] labeling its component parts with "imparfait, passé défini, [and] passé antérieur."[41] Meinhof urged Protestant missionaries to reject Le Berre's example and asked them to think back to when they first began learning Indo-European or Semitic languages. With each new language, he suggested, they had entered new worlds with new mental landscapes. Because African languages usually differed much more from German than did Indo-European or Semitic tongues, missionaries who learned them would have to try even harder to imagine themselves into a new mental universe.[42] At the same time, Meinhof was not entirely different from Le Berre. Because it employed similar methods of reconstruction, Meinhof's Urbantu was reminiscent of August Schleicher's *Ur*-Indogerman.[43] Meinhof strove to escape European models and evaluate African languages on their own terms, but he was so deeply enmeshed in the European academic context that this was all but impossible.

Meinhof's Slow Move to Berlin

While missionaries wrote most of the African language dictionaries and grammars that appeared in the nineteenth century, only a few had academic backgrounds in philology. Traditionally, missionary candidates received most of their schooling at special seminaries associated with individual societies. J. Haller, a pastor who had taught for the Basel Missionary Society, explained that before candidates went overseas they usually had six or so years of training in a variety of subjects, including theology and ancient languages.[44] Languages were, indeed, among the most important components of this formative missionary education; when discussing the seminary of the Berlin *Gesellschaft zur Beförderung der evangelischen Missionen unter den Heiden* in 1833, an unnamed pastor commented that "what [our] pupils are in a position to learn from the *confused* languages of mankind is that which may give them a glimpse into the word of God, or to open up for them the way to become closer to and understand the hearts of those with whose care they will soon be entrusted."[45]

Missionaries could also be expelled from the seminary for lack of linguistic aptitude, as an unfortunate man named Heinrich Kittlaus discovered in 1890.[46] However, with the notable exceptions of the Leipzig Mission and the *Brüdergemeine* (Moravians) of Herrnhut, for most of the nineteenth century missionary candidates first encountered "native" African languages only when they were already abroad.[47] Haller did not believe this sufficed. He felt that when missionaries were already in the colonies, they would lack inspiration for further learning. "It is not seldom that young missionaries sigh about the language exercises and language study they must attend to after they leave," he commented. "They come to the mission field in order finally to begin their mission work after many stressful years of preparation, and now they find that they once again must deal with spelling, sounding out words and syllables, declination, conjugation, construction . . ." In addition, Haller noted that the often inhospitable climate of the field had a negative impact on the missionary desire and ability to learn.[48]

Haller's complaints about missionary education were not novel. Both Meinhof and Endemann bemoaned the lack of missionary commitment to language. Endemann was particularly distressed by the level of linguistic knowledge among his fellow Germans in South Africa. In 1875 he argued that his colleagues made the "fight in the interest of African languages pointless," because the orthographies they used to transcribe Northern Sotho created "linguistic confusion."[49] Meinhof's later lectures show that there was in fact no standard orthography for Northern Sotho, and that many missionaries followed no particular rules when recording African languages.[50] Endemann suggested that missionaries adopt a universal system of spelling based on Lepsius's 1863 phonetic alphabet to standardize Pedi script,[51] but his advice was largely rejected.

The dearth of language training options in the late nineteenth century motivated some missionary societies to send their pupils to Meinhof or enroll them at the seminar. There were similarities between the two institutions. Both Meinhof and his seminar colleagues believed that Germans would receive the best language training in the metropole, not the colony. Sachau helped found the Seminar for Oriental Languages precisely so that civil servants and businesspeople could acquire knowledge of Asia and Africa before leaving home. As for Meinhof, he questioned the validity of throwing students pell-mell into the field before they acquired a basic knowledge of African languages. In a speech that he gave at the World Missionary Conference in Edinburgh, Meinhof made an impassioned plea to those who were unconvinced that the metropole was a better location for language study than the colony. He did not disregard the value of *continued* education in the colony but still insisted that it was "in the home country" that "the foundation (of philological learning) must be laid."[52]

While both Sachau and Meinhof agreed that metropolitan training was necessary for their students, they differed on how that training should occur. Meinhof championed the comparative method above all else. He maintained that it was only by understanding the structure of Bantu languages, how they were morphologically and grammatically composed, that a European could grasp their inner logic. If one followed Meinhof's approach, he would not only memorize a language but become intimately acquainted with its structure. Meinhof's students would recognize that each language was a separate universe, with its own rules and standards.

The directors of the seminar were not interested in the unique makeup of each language or what it said about the mentality of a given people. Seminar teachers had only a few months to train their students, and understanding Bantu or other African languages at a high level of complexity would take too long. The seminar focused on ensuring that its students would be able to communicate sufficiently with natives. This was probably the reason why, when Meinhof first asked that the seminar hire him in 1898, 1899, and 1900, he was rebuffed.[53] Sachau was particularly unhappy with Meinhof's methodology. His rationale for rejecting Meinhof was thus that "the teaching responsibility of the Oriental Seminar is a purely practical one: Instruction for the imperial service, especially with regard to language. . . . There is no room for scientific, comparative, grammar in Seminar instruction."[54] The study of individual languages and not language families would fulfill the government's need for impeccably trained interpreters. Moreover, it was too early for Meinhof's extensive, comparative endeavors. Bantu languages were so numerous, with "new sources" being discovered each year, that Sachau and his colleagues, Lippert and Velten, feared a comparative grammar or phonology would already be "fully antiquated" soon after its creation.[55]

Sachau's refusal to vet Meinhof's application to the seminar highlights tremendous variation in how the "practical" was defined. On the one hand, the entire purpose of African languages for the seminar was to allow communication between civil servants and natives on a basic level. There was little governmental interest in publishing more complex linguistic texts or grammars on more obscure languages.[56] On the other hand, Meinhof and his missionary colleagues were concerned with developing an understanding of as many African languages as possible, so that native literatures could be created and the "souls," not just the bodies, of Germany's colonial population could be conquered. The value of language acquisition thus differed in Berlin and Zizow, and this difference was intimately related to the issue of practicality. The missionaries who visited Pomerania to learn from Meinhof prepared for Africa in a particular way, one that they believed would effect the smoother transmission of Christianity.

Nonetheless, in June 1902 Sachau abruptly changed his mind about Meinhof and what he could contribute to Berlin. Where Sachau had once considered Meinhof and his *Grundriss einer Lautlehre der Bantusprachen* detrimental to African studies, he now welcomed the idea of having Meinhof at the seminar. In 1899 and 1900, Sachau had called Swahili the most significant African language and the most important to cultivate. He saw African languages other than Swahili and Hausa as unnecessary and judged Meinhof's methodology to be useless. By 1902, however, Sachau was concerned that Swahili and Hausa were not enough for a growing curriculum and felt that Meinhof would allow more flexibility because he could also teach Duala, Herero, and Ewe, all languages spoken in the German colonies.[57] Sachau also expressed interest in incorporating a course on Bantu phonology, something he had been dead-set against earlier.[58]

The reasons why Sachau changed his mind are not clear, but there are several possible explanations. First, many missionaries were choosing to study with Meinhof, not the seminar, and if he went to Berlin, they were likely to follow.[59] Second, governmental funding for Meinhof's African travels had been approved, demonstrating political interest in his research. Finally, the academic community was giving Meinhof increased recognition. Throughout the 1890s, while campaigning for financial support for the *Grundriss,* Meinhof repeatedly called attention to the praise he had received from Viennese scholar Friedrich Müller, a man he would later criticize severely for his close coupling of language and race.[60] In this early part of his career, however, Meinhof relied heavily on Müller's statement that his work was "of the highest quality," raising it time and again in correspondence with the *Reichskolonialamt.*[61] In the same decade, he continued to receive positive responses to his work from other quarters, namely, the psychologist Wundt,[62] the anthropologist Luschan, the Germanist Bremer, and the phonetician Eduard Sievers. It may have been impossible for Sachau to ignore Meinhof's rising acclaim and to recognize that he would contribute to, not detract from, the seminar's reputation. Consequently, the seminar finally hired Meinhof in 1903.

While things did not change immediately after Meinhof arrived in Berlin, there would be a slow but steady shift from emphasis on the individual language to the language family, if not necessarily in teaching, then at least in research. With Meinhof's relocation from the metropolitan periphery of Zizow to the core of Berlin, practical African studies in the capital began to take on a new form, one that was also more scientific. What mattered was no longer the single, isolated language or people but the family, the ethnic group, with all the predetermined traits that were supposedly attached to it. The movement had begun with Büttner, who originally began work on the comparative vocabulary of Bantu.[63] It played itself out with Meinhof and the seminar's next new African studies teacher, the Meinhof-recommended Diedrich Westermann, who also wrote a comparative grammar, this one of Sudanic/Nigritic languages.[64]

Meinhof and Race

As an academic, Meinhof distinguished himself through Africanist research that contributed both to colonial and Christian causes, as well as with the advancement of a specific classificatory hierarchy that ordered the peoples of African according to the languages that they spoke. Along with Westermann, Meinhof founded *Afrikanistik* as a modern, university discipline. What, however, of Meinhof as a person? From the available sources, the first thing that is striking is Meinhof's large ego. This was coupled with a stubbornness that often led to confrontation with his peers. He was very convinced of his intellectual positions and not afraid to express them, whether in arguments with Sachau when he was at the seminar in Berlin, with his colleague and student Martin Heepe in the early 1920s, or with Westermann, his onetime friend-turned-adversary, at the end of the same decade. Meinhof butted heads with Sachau over the practicality of establishing a phonetics laboratory in Berlin or establishing a new African languages journal and when he did not get what he wanted grew disgruntled and left for Hamburg in 1909.

Meinhof's tangles with Heepe were more extreme and brought him into direct confrontation with the administration of the University of Hamburg during the early 1920s. Meinhof had commissioned Heepe to create a dictionary of the Cameroonian Ewondo language but was not satisfied with the results and refused to approve it for publication in the *Abhandlungen des Hamburgischen Kolonialinstituts* (Papers of the Hamburg

Colonial Institute), a series of books edited by Meinhof on various scientific topics related to the colonies. Partly on the recommendation of Westermann, the university rejected Meinhof's request to stop publication and went ahead with the printing.[65] Meinhof was incensed, complaining bitterly to the rest of the faculty that he was the only one at the University of Hamburg competent to decide whether a manuscript in his field should be published or not.[66] His objections to the committee investigating the situation were so vociferous that W. Schubring, an Indologist at the university, said, "I am extremely skeptical about whether Mr. Meinhof should appear in front of a meeting of the faculty senate. I can only warn against every oral negotiation with him and must strongly advise to at the very most allow him to express himself in writing."[67] Schubring's earlier dealings with Meinhof had obviously been so unpleasant that he did not wish to repeat them.

Meinhof's headstrong—even ornery—personality certainly made him enemies inside the academy. Disagreeing with him could also be dangerous, as Heepe's later career demonstrates; after his run-in with Meinhof Heepe never rose to the top of the field of *Afrikanistik* and long after his death maintained a reputation as a "difficult" colleague.[68] Moreover, even more established colleagues such as Westermann were not immune from Meinhof's wrath. Meinhof and Westermann had been good friends from the early twentieth century through the late 1920s, addressing each other in the familiar *Du* and bolstering each other's work. In the tense atmosphere of Germany's "postcolonial" phase in the 1920s and 1930s, however, the pair squared off over a variety of issues. Meinhof opposed Westermann's contention that the Sudanic/Nigritic languages of West Africa were related to the Bantu languages spoken further south.[69] The pair also squabbled over the creation of a proper orthography for transcribing all African languages.[70] Westermann's method won out and was applied by the International Institute in London,[71] and he and Meinhof communicated only rarely thereafter.

These stories suggest that Meinhof was opinionated and intolerant. He was willing to do whatever was needed to ensure that his ideas prevailed. When it came to relationships with Africans, however, Meinhof was relatively advanced for his era. He was paternalistic and did not in any way consider Africans on the same civilizational level as Europeans; he shared the general missionary belief that all humans were essentially equal, but that some had not yet reached their civilizational pinnacle and needed others to guide them in the proper—Christian, Western—direction. Even so, it is hard to lump Meinhof together with more virulently racist Africanist scholars such as Bernhard Struck, a colleague who wrote on how the inferiority of African languages corresponded to a similar physical inferiority.[72] From the 1880s Meinhof accepted Africans like Dibone into his home and was as open to learning Duala from Dibone as he was to teaching him German. His willingness to support his African assistants in the face of racist pressure was sometimes even remarkable. After Meinhof started working for the seminar in 1903, one of the African *Lektoren* who worked there, Mtoro bin Mwinyi Bakari, was fired for marrying a German woman named Bertha Hilske. Sachau and Velten condemned Bakari's behavior and demanded that he be let go.[73] By contrast, Meinhof stated that as long as Bakari's work was satisfactory—which he thought it was—he saw no reason to fire him.[74] Bakari's case demonstrates that while Meinhof held specific theoretical ideas about racial and linguistic classification, they did not necessarily carry over into his assessment of individual Africans or their intellectual capabilities. His refusal to condemn Bakari for marrying a white woman also puts his views in line with those of Büttner, who condoned interracial marriage, and against those of Gobineau or Kossinna, who feared that race "mixing" would lead to the degeneration and ultimate destruction of "pure" racial types.

Meinhof also stressed what he considered positive African traits in his academic work. "By the word African a European understands above all someone who is dark-skinned, a *negro* [emphasis in original]. The actual negroes are industrious people, who have been esteemed as workers since time immemorial. They have proven that they are open to new ideas by their incorporation of American plants, such as corn and tobacco."[75] Blackness did not make Africans inhuman. On the contrary, they were as well-equipped to develop as anyone else, provided they did so within a Western, Christian framework. Meinhof's opinions were quite close to those of his Protestant missionary colleagues, with whom he shared a comparable upbringing and common belief about the perfectability of all humanity through Christianity. His views of Africans were stereotypically paternalistic; as Ludger Wimmelbücker has recently noted, Meinhof finally turned against Bakari when he thought the lecturer was being disrespectful of his German colleagues and students. Meinhof did think that Africans had to show proper deference to Europeans and affirm a racial "order" in which they did not speak back to or contradict whites.[76] Meinhof did not see Africans as *biologically* inferior or without potential;

nonetheless, his ambivalence toward them was evident in his inability to accept them as complete equals and recognize that they had the same inalienable rights.

Meinhof was a host of contradictions and decidedly ambivalent in his relationship to race and race theory. He was adroit at advancing his own intellectual objectives and not shy about criticizing others. He defended Africans against his colleagues' racist attitudes but did not consider them equals. Even more confusingly, Meinhof joined the Nazi Party after it came to power in 1933 because of a belief that Hitler would restore the German colonies. As a Nazi, Meinhof worked alongside colleagues at the newly named "Hanseatic" University of Hamburg on a committee dedicated to reinvigorating colonial knowledge under the new regime.[77] Meinhof's paternalism was racially charged, and his Nazi allegiance will be discussed more fully in the final chapter. To label Meinhof simply as "racist" is, however, to remove him from historical context and judge him by contemporary standards. As Thorsten Althena has argued for Protestant missionaries in general, it is difficult to measure their racism on a modern scale. They lived in a world where certain racial differences were assumed, yet they often rejected the overt scientific racism that the Nazis extolled. They considered Africans benighted, but not necessarily biologically Other. Instead, it was their distance from Christianity that was a disadvantage.[78]

The contradictions that defined Meinhof were reflected in an increasing inability to distinguish between linguistic and biological traits. The Hamitic hypothesis, the subject of chapter 4, was what provided Meinhof with the overarching framework for his classificatory schema. Based on Bleek's early formulations of linguistic difference in Africa, Meinhof claimed there were three main sub-Saharan African language families: the Hamitic, Bantu, and Nigritic/Sudanic.[79] These were supposedly divided according to purely linguistic criteria, but in fact biology also played a role. Hamites were understood as "white" Africans, while Sudanic and Bantu speakers were viewed as "black" or "mixed." Anthropologist Luschan's afterword to Meinhof's 1912 *Sprachen der Hamiten* was accompanied by a series of photographs that emphasized the different appearances of Hamites and other African peoples.[80] The images suggested a very direct link between the languages being discussed in the main body of the book and the skin color and facial attributes of the men and women pictured. For Meinhof, the pietist focus on language as a conduit to Christianity and civilization became intertwined with Darwinian evolutionary theory and scientific racism. The centrality of language never disappeared, but it was now embedded in a new set of meanings that posited difference according to physical characteristics in addition to cultural ones.

Meinhof's ambivalence toward race is understandable, given that he came of age academically during a period in which theories about it were generally in flux. He perfected his system of linguistic classification around the fin de siècle, when eugenics and biologically based racism were becoming increasingly popular throughout Europe. The liberal notion that the races were inherently similar—if not all advanced to the same level of civilization—was giving way to a belief that there were immutable, unbrookable differences among them. Grosse had noted that the German bourgeoisie—to which Meinhof belonged—was particularly captivated by the idea that race was a necessary component of social organization.[81] While most of Africa had fallen to Europe and its military and technological superiority in the 1880s and 1890s, Africans were unhappy with colonial rule and often resisted it; Germany had experienced a number of military confrontations even before the Herero War and Maji Maji uprisings broke out in the early twentieth century.[82] This frightened both the small number of colonizers actually living in Africa and the middle class in the metropole, who felt threatened not only by the distant specter of racial hybridization but with the much closer fear of socialism and workers' calls for reform. Race provided a means of reordering a world gone topsy-turvy, and of reasserting bourgeois, German, and white dominance.

Sciences like medicine, eugenics, and anthropology were instrumental in "proving" white preeminence. Linguistics, with its emphasis on the superiority of inflecting languages spoken mainly by light-skinned groups, contributed as well to bolstering European authority. Moreover, the discipline reinforced the overall hardening of ethnic and racial boundaries in the colonies, a hardening that did not take into account the shifting, mutable state of most African groups. Language studies "mapped" an imaginary racial hierarchy onto the colonized, which was static—when conditions on the ground were not. This had important political connotations. Meinhof's belief that language could determine ethnic affiliation and point of origin was especially appealing to early twentieth-century white South Africans struggling with what they called the "native question." After the Anglo-Boer War ended in 1902, the victorious English and defeated Afrikaners moved toward rapprochement. Both sides worried about African urbanization and the threat of increased African involvement in local politics and the economy, and were beset with a continual anxiety over race mixing. Afrikaners and British alike wanted to ensure a plentiful black labor supply through migrancy but did not want Africans to settle in "white cities." With the Natives Land Act of 1913 and the Natives Urban Areas Act of 1923, segregation was legalized as the Union of South Africa forbade blacks to purchase property outside of specially designated reserves and regulated their presence in large towns.[83] One justification for relegating Africans to specific districts was their supposedly long histories in those areas, which could be determined through grammatical and lexical comparison. The protolanguage of a group could be traced to its source, and that would be considered the group's "ancestral" homeland.

Germans and white South Africans shared similar concerns at the turn of the twentieth century: They grappled with how to control "undesirable" populations whose labor was also central to the industrial economy, as well as with issues of intermarriage, miscegenation, and how to prevent racial "bastardization" and the degeneration of the white race. Just as white South Africans tried to create vast black labor reserves in their territory, so did Germans in Namibia implement laws and restrictions designed to impoverish the Herero and Nama and make them economically useful to the settlers in the colony. In both Germany and South Africa, race, too, was used to justify the abominable treatment of Africans and to exclude those who were of "mixed" racial ancestry.[84] Philology was important because it could both demonstrate the natural inferiority of Africans inherent in their more "primitive" isolating and agglutinative languages and find spaces for them geographically removed from European communities but close enough to provide the manpower needed to keep the colonies running.

Even with the rise of biologism and its reorganization of social and racial hierarchies, the older belief that it was culture and not biology that determined difference never entirely disappeared, at least not among Meinhof and his missionary colleagues. The persistence of culture as an explanatory device is best reflected in Meinhof's work on the deterioration of African society in the face of European encroachment. His argument that African languages and cultures had to be preserved as the unique reflection of African mentality was rooted in the earlier, pietistic conviction that each *Volk* had to accept Christianity in its own particular language. It was a position that, ironically, dovetailed well with white South African concerns about the native question. In the wake of a visit to South Africa, in 1927–28, Meinhof lamented the loss of African traditions and blamed it on a common disregard for the significance of native languages.

> African culture, language, custom, and clothing have been decaying, as has everything African, since contact with European culture. In South Africa we see people dressed in European, Asian, and Arabic clothing, but no one in Negro costume. The Hottentots have almost entirely lost their language, the Bushmen have become completely extinct; some tribes are able to hold on to their language and integrity better with the help of the mission, which through the introduction of script gives them the possibility to maintain their language. People are beginning, sporadically, to recognize that it is language which contains the soul, blessing, and honor of a *Volk,* as a Bushman has already so elegantly put it. For each language there is a dictionary, we seek an orthography for it, attempt to transcribe fairy tales in it, but it is perhaps already too late; the Negroes are the victims of European education. They should not have been taught English or Afrikaans, but have had a sense of their own culture kept alive through their mother tongue; (instead) this has been irretrievably neglected.[85]

Meinhof's comments in 1928 were similar to those of his student Werner Eiselen in 1950, when he made a speech to open a meeting of the Ciskeian General Council.[86] Admonishing Africans who disapproved of the Group Areas Act, which assigned races to different city neighborhoods, Eiselen said that, along with an act called the Native Builders' Bill, it would "bring with it not only an enormous expansion of potential employment for qualified Bantu men and women, but . . . also be to the great advantage of the Bantu public in general who will be served by people of their own race."[87] While this specific statement does not address language, it points to a shared belief that people would benefit most from interaction with others of their own race, not members of a different one. Moreover, Eiselen was well known as advocate of mother-tongue education and argued that educating Africans in European languages was a mistake.[88] Eiselen, like Meinhof, did not champion biological racism; instead, he argued that all human beings had the same civilizational potential, and that individual cultures were to be cherished and preserved in relative isolation, lest a stronger culture destroy a weaker one. This led inexorably to an endorsement of segregation and "separate development" based on cultural, not physical, ideals.[89]

Meinhof and Eiselen shared a deep-seated belief in cultural particularism, as well as the conviction that Africans would only reach the same civilizational plane as Europeans with guidance from the Christian West.

This conviction was firmly entrenched in the same German Protestant context that impelled missionaries to transform and "modernize" African societies while simultaneously safeguarding their traditions and "unique" cultural attributes.[90] Language, again, was as much a means of reinforcing *Volk* identity as it was of fostering change. The inconsistencies inherent in Meinhof's theories, which praised human unity but also stressed difference, shaped *Afrikanistik* in its foundational stages, as they did South African "applied" linguistics. As time progressed, and Meinhof became the doyen of African studies, known not only in Germany and South Africa but also far beyond, his ideas on ethnicity and language dominated the field and came to determine how African groups were classified. This classification would be grounded in both racial *and* cultural precepts, reflecting Meinhof's position as both a missionary acolyte and a firm supporter of bourgeois German imperialism.

Chapter 4

Anthropology and Linguistics United? Carl Meinhof, Felix von Luschan, and the Hamitic Hypothesis

Connections between Nineteenth-Century German Anthropology and Linguistics

Carl Meinhof was the consummate networker. From the time he was training missionaries in Zizow, he was constantly visible both in the world of the mission as well as in that of the "colonial" sciences, dominating debates and forcing his opinions on others. This made him some enemies but also accorded him a commanding position in the field of African studies and the academic world beyond. Meinhof cultivated his friendships carefully, from the early days of his career as Büttner's colleague through his twenty-year correspondence with *Völkerpsychologie* authority Wundt. None of his intellectual relationships were, however, as intricate or profound as the one he maintained with anthropologist Felix von Luschan. Meinhof and Luschan exchanged letters for decades, visited each other on several occasions, and were occasional scholarly collaborators.[1] It was in his studies with Luschan that Meinhof worked out some of his most complicated ideas about the intersection between language and race. Meinhof's partnership with Luschan also produced enormous theoretical contradictions, as the pair continually conflated evidence from linguistics, physical anthropology, and ethnology to fit their arguments about classifying Africans.[2]

Meinhof's and Luschan's very different academic backgrounds—Luschan's in medicine and anthropology, Meinhof's in theology and linguistics—contributed to the inherent inconsistencies in their work.[3] While experts from disciplines such as anthropology and linguistics strove to reinforce each other's theoretical positions, they did not always produce results that neatly overlapped. Cooperation between practitioners from separate fields could prove difficult. On an intellectual level, the process of defining or classifying Africans was compromised by the fact that linguistic and anthropological knowledge or data often could not be reconciled. This dislocation made it difficult for scholars to combine the results of their separate investigations and fit them into tidy conceptual boxes.

In the nineteenth century, the theoretical precepts undergirding linguistics and liberal German anthropology were somewhat different. At the time missionary research on language demonstrated that Europeans and Africans shared a bond that separated them, as it did all of humanity, from animals. Proving that African languages were cousins of the Indo-European and Semitic families was about much more than demonstrating similarity between sounds or vocabulary; it showed that Africans were incontrovertibly part of the same species of mankind, not removed from it as the polygenists would have had people believe. This did not mean that all peoples were exactly the same, or on a similar civilizational level. Nations were above all linguistic constructs, with grammar shaping each people's mental universe and giving it a unique ethnic identity; this was what made it so important to preach the Gospel in each individual's native tongue. To gain such insight into African minds, missionary Africanists adapted the methodology of Orientalist and Indogermanic philology with its focus on texts, carefully transcribing oral literature in addition to grammar and vocabulary in order to acquire the fullest possible picture of each specific universe.

The discourse surrounding African philology changed as the nineteenth century neared its close and as the racial divides separating language families became ever more sharply drawn. The new discipline of phonetics, which will be discussed in the next chapter, also recast linguistics as a natural science, distancing it from the humanistic pursuit of philology by refocusing attention on bodies and the sounds they produced instead of written texts. Nevertheless, for missionary linguists a core belief in the undeniable humanity of all people remained, even as it was overlaid with biologistic features. As Zimmerman has shown, however, by the mid- to late nineteenth-century anthropologists had already rejected humanistic pursuits such as philology and indeed disdained them.[4] Like Africanist linguistics, anthropology did have some missionary origins.[5] However, in the mid- to late nineteenth century many of its main practitioners were also doctors or those trained in the natural sciences.[6] Anthropologists did not have the same interest in proselytizing as did the missionary linguists; they were intent on collecting physical data, not converting souls. Their concentration on objects removed from cultural context was also ahistorical, whereas philology was intimately involved with tracing humanity's history through linguistic evidence.

Anthropology and linguistics did share some traits. Both were originally grounded in institutions external to the university, Africanist linguistics in the mission, anthropology in scientific societies and museums.[7] In addition, ethnologists such as Adolf Bastian concurred with the belief that there was a certain genius present in all peoples, and that each exhibited progress through individual invention.[8] Even craniology—the physical anthropological practice of measuring skulls in order to compare them across "races"—did not necessarily imply that blacks and whites were irrevocably Other; as Massin has contended, such practices often served to reinforce a discourse of sameness, not one of difference. Craniometric indices measured in order to prove the existence of pure racial types had in fact done the opposite: They had shown that Europeans were so mixed that determining racial type was both impossible and undesirable.[9] German physical anthropology at this stage was monogenist, too, which meant that many of its practitioners believed all mankind stemmed from the same source, rather than from separate beginnings.[10] In this way nineteenth-century German anthropology dovetailed well with missionary linguistics, since both rejected the idea that Africans belonged not only to another race but to another species.

In the late nineteenth and early twentieth centuries, however, discourses and impressions of Otherness also began to shift. Ethnology, for example, was moving away from Bastian's idea of individual invention and toward geographer Friedrich Ratzel's concept of diffusion, which held that cultural products were not innovative to each society, but instead were carried—diffused—from one to the other.[11] As anthropology transformed from an object-oriented approach to one that incorporated historical analysis, it rebuffed the ahistorical tactics of scholars like Bastian and Luschan's mentor, Rudolf Virchow. This new historicism did not lead to the flattening-out of cultural difference but to its sharpening, as the universality of human thought and production was replaced with attention to individual cultural peculiarities.[12]

While diffusionism or the *Kulturkreislehre* (theory of cultural circles) that it helped produce—which considered cultures to belong to certain "circles" from which they acquired knowledge of tools, religion, and so forth—is not explicitly present in linguistic theories such as Meinhof's and Westermann's, it is not absent, either. Meinhof openly disparaged some of the main *Kulturkreis* theorists, in particular Leo Frobenius and Father Wilhelm

Schmidt. On the one hand Meinhof praised Frobenius for having brought the significance of African research to the public's attention, while on the other he dismissed Frobenius's work as amateurish and lacking in "scientific accuracy."[13] As for Schmidt, he and Meinhof were competitors on the "African studies" market, since each established his own journal, Schmidt *Anthropos* and Meinhof the *Zeitschrift für Kolonialsprachen.* In 1912, an *Anthropos* article written by Schmidt's colleague and confidant, Ferdinand Hestermann, commended Meinhof for his hypothesis that the Bantu languages had emerged as a result of clashes between proto-Hamitic and Nigritic peoples. Hestermann explained and endorsed Meinhof's view that Bantu languages often retained Nigritic features, such as isolating roots, despite their more advanced nature.[14] Not long afterward, however, Hestermann changed his mind about Meinhof and heavily critiqued his work in *Anthropos,* especially targeting his research on experimental phonetics.[15]

Because of their religious affiliations and rivalry not only for journal articles but for African souls, there was little love lost between the Catholic Schmidt and his followers and the Protestant Meinhof and his. It is thus possible that Hestermann's criticisms were grounded in arguments that had as much to do with Meinhof's rivalry with Schmidt as they did with academic differences.[16] Regardless of Meinhof's contempt for Frobenius, Schmidt, or Hestermann, and an almost complete lack of references to the *Kulturkreislehre* in Meinhof's works, there were many similarities between his theory and theirs. Culture-historical anthropology was grounded in the notion that all peoples had culture and history, regardless of how "primitive" they seemed. The trend toward including historical analysis in German anthropology, which was steadily growing in popularity around the turn of the twentieth century, contradicted previous assumptions about *Naturvölker.* Virchow, Bastian, and their associates believed that all societies developed uniformly, and that their internal consistency accounted for the similarities across humanity. The study of historical processes would complicate anthropological research instead of illuminating it, because interactions among societies over time concealed man's true, original nature.[17] Diffusionism turned anthropology on its head by rejecting the idea of universal human genius and arguing that some cultures borrowed while others innovated.

Meinhof's form of diffusionism, as we shall see in more detail as the chapter progresses, concerned the spread of linguistic traits across African societies. His version of the Hamitic hypothesis, in which the Hamites merged with Africa's original "Nigritic" inhabitants to create the Bantu languages and peoples, is diffusionist and historical in nature. Meinhof's work was much more in line with that of *Kulturkreis* Africanist Ankermann or Frobenius than it was with Bastian's. A diffusionist paradigm would, moreover, have made sense politically, since Meinhof's research was largely informed by German nationalism and imperialism. In general, the infant country's colonial endeavors pushed both anthropology and African linguistics rightward. Massin has remarked that the onset of colonialism in Germany had a marked effect on the "racial liberalism" of physical anthropologists. While decrying those who, like Ernst Haeckel, would classify Africans as "apes" or call them "animalistic," anthropologists nonetheless assumed a Darwinian evolutionary hierarchy that placed "savage" Africans near the bottom of the ladder, at first culturally, and then by association racially and biologically. Despite their assertion that all people were related and stemmed from the same source, even well-known progressives such as Virchow categorized Africans and other colonized people into vastly dissimilar racial groups. These groups were not classified as different species but were wholly separate in terms of their position on a developmental scale.[18] Further, even though Meinhof's friend Luschan was deemed Virchow's "spiritual" successor, he had close affiliations to colonial societies and organizations, endorsing their goals and acknowledging mental and physical "difference" among blacks and whites.[19]

At the turn of the twentieth century, both linguistics and anthropology were turning away from earlier, inclusionary conceptions of humanity and increasingly using race as a marker to divide "civilized" societies from their "savage" cousins. The two disciplines were also now working in the service of German imperialism; this was something else they shared. The early nineteenth-century missionary commitment to ecumenicalism had faded in favor of support for the colonial state. Meanwhile, canonically anthropology has been considered the colonial science par excellence, born along with imperialism even if, as George Stocking has noted, much of what was said about the pragmatics of the discipline was posturing and rhetoric, and there was little indication that it had much concrete benefit.[20] However, as Penny and Matti Bunzl have suggested, the roots of *German* anthropology may be less linked to those of colonialism than those of their British or French counterparts. Steeped in a tradition that emphasized *Bildung* and a liberal belief in the universality of mankind, anthropologists championed pluralism and international cooperation among scientists over racism or nationalism.[21]

German disinterest in colonialism made sense not only from an intellectual position but from a political one. While the English and French had long been involved in nationalist imperialism in places like the West African coast, the Caribbean, and South Asia, Germans had no such lengthy colonial tradition.[22] It was also the late nineteenth-century emergence of Germany as a nation-state and imperial power that pushed anthropology ever further rightward, to the point that by the interwar era, racist ideas had saturated the discipline. Anthropologists became preoccupied not with the diversity of the world's peoples but with the need to control and understand specific populations in the German colonies. They also had to cater to public demands for imperial entertainment and products. Displays in ethnographic museums, for example, could not be limited to a sliver of the intellectual elite but should appeal on a mass level.[23] These could, moreover, be linked with a wider movement to incorporate Germans of all classes into the imperial project and to make Germany's position as a world power essential to national identity and national pride as a whole.[24]

By the turn of the twentieth century, though, both anthropology and Africanist linguistics were reforming in a way that stressed racial difference over human universality. Even in this new era, however, the disciplinary boundaries dividing various aspects of African studies—anthropological and linguistic—were still quite malleable. There were few experts in any single subject, even though "professionalization" had begun at institutions such as the Berlin Seminar for Oriental Languages, and some scholars had started to specialize in given areas. This meant that Africanist linguistics, physical anthropology, ethnology, and geography were all what Meinhof referred to in 1910 as *Hilfswissenschaften,* "Auxiliary Sciences"; when information collected in one discipline left gaps in understanding, scholars would contribute data from other fields. As Meinhof noted with particular respect to Africanist philology, "in our time of increasingly more particularized studies it is completely impossible for a researcher to master several sciences. . . . This has led to an endeavor to see specialists in various areas mutually helping each other wherever possible. And it is so that African linguistics has also been called upon to act as an 'auxiliary science for all manner of other disciplines' . . ."[25] And act as an auxiliary science it did, as linguists strove jointly with anthropologists to unravel the "mysteries" of African origins.

Especially when issues concerning race were involved, however, disciplinary lacunae were not easily filled, and there was a tendency to conflate anthropological and linguistic knowledge. The colonial context complicated the problem of classifying Africans even further, as the exigencies of colonialism compelled scholars such as Meinhof to produce totalizing, simplistic images of the indigenous populations in Germany's protectorates, much as anthropologists now created museum exhibits for public, not "academic," consumption. Africans were slotted into well-defined categories such as "Hamitic," "Bantu," or "Nigritic/Sudanic." In this schema, the Hamitic languages were considered the most culturally advanced, the Bantu came second, and the Sudanic were last, seen as the most "primitive" people in Africa.

These labels carried both linguistic and anthropological connotations, as well as racial ones. But they also claimed immense practical value for Germany's imperial project; once German colonists came to understand the differences among these linguistic families, which were being recast in terms of race, it would be easier for them to acquire a very precise understanding of their social structures. This could be the case even when colonizers were encountering specific African groups for the first time. Once a colonist knew that a certain people was "Bantu," for instance, he or she would have a good idea of what to expect from both its language and its culture. As Meinhof continually insisted, linguists were in the constant process of "mapping" all Africa through its languages. When they had finished, he believed Germans would "know" the inhabitants of their colonies effectively enough to control them, maintaining that "the surprising amount of new discoveries about the native mind is not only important because it generally teaches us to have a higher regard of (African) culture, but also because it helps us to recognize the different nature of various people. What is correct for one group might be wrong for another."[26] Coming to "set" conclusions about the ways in which African languages, cultures, and physical characteristics were to be ordered was not easy, since Meinhof believed that African groups had "mixed" over time. Regardless, Meinhof was still confident that German scholarship could uncover the original condition of Africa's races, because experts in linguistics and anthropology would be able to determine overlapping conjunctions between the grammatical and physical data that they had separately collected.[27]

The remainder of this chapter will explore the problems associated with Meinhof's and Luschan's interdisciplinary efforts. I will show that contemporary scholars were cognizant of the perils of transposing arguments made in one context into another, even while they still insisted on doing so. As the colonial sciences continued to develop in Germany and assume places in schools such as the Berlin Seminar and Hamburg Colonial Institute, there was an increasing temptation to create master theories of racial development, both in Africa and elsewhere. Meinhof indeed believed that reaching conclusions about African origins would help Europeans find their own roots, since certain African groups might provide "links" or "bridges" to European prehistory. When there was not enough evidence in his own subject, African linguistics, his connections to the colonial educational establishment would allow him to support his claims by using data that had been mined elsewhere and using other scientific methodologies, such as those of anthropology.

Interdisciplinarity and Africanist Research

The methodological approach of combining data from different academic fields to reach conclusions concerning African history is not necessarily problematic. More contemporary scholars of Africa, such as archaeologist David Philippson and linguist Kay Williamson,[28] have emphasized the importance of drawing on information from their own academic fields when reconstructing early African history. They have also acknowledged that there are difficulties with retracing the exact footsteps of the African past. The written sources available are often simply not as extensive as they are for other areas of the world, and so Africanist historians must sometimes rely on linguistic, oral, archaeological, or even botanical data; as historian David Lee Schoenbrun has demonstrated, linguistic, ethnographic, and other sources can play a role in the historical reconstruction of precolonial African history. He has asserted that, in the area of Africa's Great Lakes, "ancient history not only undergirds the modern, but still lives, today, in the laying out of a banana garden, the pounding of barkcloth, the social therapy given to an AIDS sufferer, even in the importance of the crested crane in Uganda's coat of arms."[29] The principle of using interconnected *Hilfswissenschaften* to explore African history where literary sources are lacking is therefore still current and can be used to elucidate sections of a chronicle that would otherwise remain unattainable.

Meinhof and Luschan had already identified the need to use information from disparate disciplines in their studies of Africa around 1900 and started to discuss issues surrounding the conjunction of linguistics and anthropology in a correspondence that began in this period and continued through Luschan's death in 1924. At the beginning of their letter exchange, Luschan was already a relatively well-established anthropologist in Berlin, whereas Meinhof largely stood outside academic circles. Despite their differences in academic rank, which closed significantly once Meinhof arrived in Berlin in 1903, Luschan showed a marked interest in Meinhof's work, and the pair shared many of the same intellectual curiosities. Both were concerned with identifying similarities and differences across African ethnic groups and defining what made someone "Bantu," "Hamitic," or "Sudanic." Time and again when Meinhof was writing to Luschan, he drew attention to his research on these three language families. He often mused not only about how they were connected to each other but also about their possible relationships to more far-flung languages, such as Old Syrian or Mongolian, for example, questioning whether a "mixture of blacks with the Mongolian race" had influenced racial "types" in the Near East.[30]

Over the course of their long relationship, Meinhof and Luschan also collaborated more concretely on three different occasions, in 1905, 1906, and 1912. The subjects they covered were the "Hottentots" (Nama) of German South West Africa (Namibia); a troop of traveling "pygmies" from Central Africa; and, finally, the languages of the "Hamites," the ethnic category that Meinhof and Luschan considered most civilizationally "advanced" in comparison to that of other African groups, and which they felt would present them with the most problems when it came to reconciling language and "race."

While the methodological approaches that Meinhof and Luschan employed resemble those of later scholars in some ways, there is a difference between their research and more current studies. Present-day intellectuals are interested in reconstructing historical processes, such as the movements of people across the African continent, in order to uncover sequences of past events and explore how various groups arrived at their present locations. The research of contemporary Africanist linguists, anthropologists, archaeologists, and historians is certainly not without its own political and social agendas. However, more recent research is still fostered under very different historical circumstances from the work produced by Meinhof and Luschan, whose scholarly projects were consumed not only with tracing historical processes but with issues of race and racial classification related to Germany's imperial project. Greenberg, the American who became the most prominent Africanist linguist in the field during the 1950s, lambasted Meinhof for his reliance on racial categories to support linguistic classifications. After proposing a new way to organize African languages in 1966, Greenberg went on to discuss the Hamitic theory.

> The vagueness of the use of the term Hamite and its extension as a racial term for a type viewed primarily as Caucasoid, has led to a racial theory in which the majority of the population of Negro Africa is considered to be the result of mixture between Hamites and Negroes. . . . The speakers of "Nilo-Hamitic" languages are called racially half-Hamites. The Bantu are considered to be another type of Hamiticized Negro on the basis of speculations by Meinhof (for which he never produced proof, nor is any proof possible).[31]

Greenberg considered Meinhof largely responsible for the confusion of language with race that had led to the false categorization of African groups. Through his influence on British anthropologists such as C. G. Seligmann, who contributed to Meinhof's *Zeitschrift für Kolonialsprachen* and used his schema for organizing Africans into racial groups, Meinhof's impact on contemporary understandings not only of language but also biological race had been considerable.[32]

In the wake of Greenberg's recasting of African linguistic classification, many of the old terms and groupings were set aside and replaced with new categorizations and terms. Therefore, while today Bantu languages are still viewed as an important linguistic category, they are no longer seen as a separate family but, rather, ordered with the Niger-Congo branch, which also includes the Mande, Kwa, and Atlantic groups.[33] Meanwhile, the so-called Hamitic languages have been reclassified as Nilo-Saharan, and many of them renamed Cushitic.[34] These groupings demonstrate that many of the relationships between languages that Meinhof and others of his generation posited were false, based more on what they wanted to see than on solid evidence.

Meinhof, Luschan: Linguistics, Anthropology

The tension arising from Meinhof's and Luschan's use of anthropological and linguistic data dovetailed with an inability to reconcile classifications based on language with classifications based on physical characteristics. Meinhof and Luschan struggled with how to define who was Hamitic, who was Bantu, and who was Negrito.[35] The Hamites were the most difficult to categorize. In 1929 Leipzig ethnologist Günther Spannaus wrote an essay that looked back over almost a century of research into the use of the word *Hamitic* in academic discourse. He maintained that Hamites could be described in at least three ways—in terms of linguistics, physical anthropology, and ethnology—and argued that this was the greatest impediment to scientists attempting to classify Africans.

> One of the most interesting and important questions that has confronted African ethnology in the last decades is the so-called "Hamitic question," i.e. the question of the origin of the Hamites and their significance for the cultural and social history of Africa. The difficulties of the problem are grounded in the multiplicity of the concept "Hamite," which shows different faces depending on whether you look at it from a linguistic, physical, or cultural perspective.[36]

Spannaus explained that Hamitic languages were usually—but not always—the more sophisticated, inflecting languages spoken by lighter-skinned North Africans, whereas physical or "racial" Hamites comprised the "non-Negro element of the North African population," and cultural Hamites were mostly cattle herders and raisers.[37]

In many ways, Spannaus summarized the parameters of a debate that had perplexed linguists and anthropologists alike from the nineteenth century. The divisions among the linguistic, physical anthropological and ethnological "Hamites" that Spannaus outlined are evocative of Meinhof's and Luschan's descriptions of Hamites and other African racial or ethnic categories. Before discussing the Hamites as they appeared in Meinhof's and Luschan's work, however, it is important to understand the roots and antecedents of what is commonly known as the "Hamitic hypothesis." The idea of a "Hamitic" race or class of people has a long history. During the middle ages Christians saw all Africans as Hamites and considered them accursed because of their ancestor Ham's failure to cover up the nakedness of his father, Noah, while he slept. In the Bible, Noah punished Ham's arrogance by condemning his descendants to slavery at the hands of his brothers' progeny, since Shem and Japheth had covered Noah when Ham failed to do so. Although the Bible does not mention the skin color or outward appearance of Ham and his siblings, medieval interpretation held that Ham's progeny—the Hamites—were African, whereas the children of Shem were the Middle Eastern Semites and those of Japheth were the Indo-Europeans.[38]

With Napoleon's late eighteenth-century discovery that the "Hamitic" Egyptians were heirs to a complex and sophisticated culture, the story of the Hamites shifted. In its new retelling, only one branch of Ham's family, the Canaanites, had been cursed; the rest had developed the kind of advanced civilization found in Egypt. Hamites were now redefined as the *Herren,* or masters, of Africa, light-skinned and lordly.[39] This was the definition of *Hamite* that later scholars such as Meinhof, Luschan, and Spannaus followed.

For Meinhof—as well as for Luschan, Spannaus, and their contemporaries—the original biblical explanation of the Hamitic theory was relatively unimportant to scholarly classifications of Africans. In Meinhof's version of the Hamitic hypothesis, the word *Hamite* denoted a scientific category, not a religious one. This may seem odd for a man who both was a pastor and maintained strong ties with the Protestant mission. Moreover in Meinhof's 1912 *Sprachen der Hamiten* (Languages of the Hamites), his most extensive work on Hamitic languages and peoples, he claimed to accept the biblical interpretation that the children of Shem were Asian, those of Japheth Caucasian, and those of Ham African, at least on some level.[40]

Yet the Hamites Meinhof identified in his linguistic and cultural treatises were not the same as the Hamites of the Bible. Biblical Hamites were black, while linguistic ones were white, or at the very least "mixed."[41] Why would Meinhof have continued to apply a word with such an arguable meaning? Essentially, he believed that because the term *Hamitic* had already been accepted in academic circles, it would be impossible to expunge it from the scientific vocabulary. But how did he explain the fact that the word had come into such widespread use? In the *Sprachen der Hamiten,* Meinhof traced the popularity of the name back to what he perceived as a more general nineteenth-century scholarly or philological prejudice.

> If someone were to ask what the origins of this false terminology are, it is to be answered that, until recently, the educated world occupied itself almost exclusively with inflectional languages, thus essentially with the languages of the Caucasian race. Therefore this race, which was regarded as actual humanity, was divided into three large groups: the Indogermans (Japheth), the Semites, and the Hamites. Today, when we know that most human languages are not included in this division, we can no longer be satisfied with it. The small admixture of Nigritic blood which the "Hamites" possess has therefore induced people to lump them together with the Negroes, from whom they are somatically and linguistically divergent.[42]

Meinhof's argument was a subtle critique of polygenism, which had excluded the greater part of humanity from studies of language and culture. It was also a jab at those philologists who had not recognized the number of complex forms that languages could take.

Meinhof was uncomfortable with the term *Hamites,* a word that was in itself unstable and subject to rapid redefinition—but used it anyway, since he claimed there was no better alternative. Classifying the Hamites, Bantu, or Negritoes was, indeed, central to the three projects on which Meinhof and Luschan collaborated. The first of these, Luschan's "On the Racial Affinities of the Hottentots," which was coupled with Meinhof's "The Language of the Hottentots," attempted to answer the already well-worn question of whether the so-called Hottentots (Nama or Khoi) were racially and linguistically closer to the Hamites, who were mainly located in northern or eastern Africa, or the Bushmen (San or !Kung) who were their neighbors in southern Africa. The second, Luschan's 1906 "Sechs Pygmäen aus Ituri" (Six Pygmies from Ituri) and Meinhof's "Untersuchung der Pygmäensprachen" (An Investigation of Pygmy Languages), did not directly address the Hamitic problem. Nonetheless, the article took issue with the relationship between racial and linguistic categories, this time by exploring the possible makeup of the Sudanic-speaking Negritoes. Last, Meinhof's 1912 book *Die Sprachen der Hamiten,* to which Luschan appended a lengthy afterword, tried to put all the pieces of the puzzle together to assess how closely Hamitic languages and races were affiliated and at what points they diverged. The book and essays all highlight Meinhof's and Luschan's conviction that the Hamites were inextricably connected to both Bantu and Sudanic speakers. Their Hamitic hypothesis could not have existed without reference to other African populations. In a sense, it was therefore more aptly a "Hamitic-Bantu-Sudanic hypothesis" than a strictly Hamitic hypothesis.

In all three texts, Meinhof and Luschan conflated their data and its results. They saw their respective disciplines, African linguistics and physical anthropology, as *Hilfswissenschaften* that could assist each other in solving problems about the complex nature of African ethnicity and race. This was so even though Luschan had originally rejected the entire notion of "Hamitentum" and believed—following the lead of ethnologist Robert Hartmann—that all Africans shared an *Urverwandschaft* (original relationship). Early in his career, Luschan claimed that there were no differences among the Hamites, Bantu, and Negritoes. Later, however, Luschan admitted that the linguistic evidence pointing to disparities among the groups had won him over. By 1906, when he reported on a trip he had made to South Africa for the Berlin Society of Anthropology, Ethnology, and Prehistory, he declared that he was now convinced that language represented a "kind of index fossil, and one of our most important signposts in the still so murky terrain of African ethnology."[43] Accordingly, Luschan had become a firm and enthusiastic proponent of the Hamitic hypothesis, which held, in opposition to Hartmann or French linguist Lilias Homburger, that Africa was made up of several distinct cultural and "racial" groups.[44]

Meinhof was the one who presented Luschan with the linguistic evidence that compelled him to change his mind about the Hamitic hypothesis. While Meinhof had achieved most of his early academic recognition for his work on Bantu languages like Duala, he was also always interested in examining the Hamitic and Sudanic/Nigritic families. Meinhof wanted to investigate the puzzle of Hamitic languages already presented by German scholars such as Bleek, Viennese linguist Friedrich Müller, and Lepsius, who had written a Nubian grammar and created a standard system of orthography for the transcription of languages not written in Roman script.[45] Meinhof hoped to extend their research and finally determine the answers to questions such as how to categorize the northwest African Fulbe (Fulani), whose language he believed represented a developmental stage between Bantu and Hamitic, or where the East African Masai had first originated and the extent to which they might actually be Semites.

Although Meinhof and Luschan were good friends who enjoyed rich intellectual exchanges, Meinhof also insisted that mixing linguistic with anthropological evidence could be risky. He strove to avoid the traps that had snared some of his predecessors and held that his analyses of African relationships were based purely on linguistic—not physical anthropological or ethnological—proof. For example, Meinhof was extremely skeptical of Müller's linguistic categories. He considered them grounded more in biological than linguistic criteria. In Müller's multivolume *Grundriss der Sprachwissenschaft* (Outlines of Linguistics), he classified African languages according to hair type, devoting one volume to the languages of straight-haired peoples, one to the languages of curly-haired peoples, and one to the languages of "woolly" haired peoples.[46] Meinhof negated Müller's proposed classificatory schema at the 1905 German Colonial Congress, where he held that "linguists can receive much stimulation from physical and cultural anthropology and vice versa—but there is no doubt that there must be a methodological error when anthropological points of view are prematurely approached in linguistic investigations."[47] As a possible corrective to Müller, Meinhof suggested that purely linguistic phenomena—such as the existence of grammatical gender in noun classification, inflection, or the appearance of clicks—be compared to determine whether or not two languages were related, and that physical traits be discounted in the early stages of philological research.

Yet undergirding Meinhof's work—not to mention Luschan's—was still the belief that Hamites were in some way originally white. Through intense racial mixing over hundreds of years some, like the Hottentots or Nama, might have taken on the physical characteristics of the neighboring Bushmen or San. This did not, however, detract from their original position as racial "Hamites." In the essay "On the Racial Affinities of the Hottentots" Luschan explained that whenever two groups met and intermingled, their languages and "somatic" types were never equally influenced. He held, "As a matter of fact, we see the somatic type depending on the numeric relation between the old native population and the newcomers."[48] This effectively meant that members of an "attacking" tribe would lose most of their distinguishing physical characteristics, since the attackers were usually outnumbered by those they had conquered. Further, the invaders would likely have brought few women on their travels. Therefore, they would have had no choice but to marry the subjugated women and produce offspring with them. After several generations, a bastardized race would then be born. Even so, Luschan argued that a people's original status as Hamites could never be completely obscured.

> We see the mental culture develop independent of all numeric relation, and the superior language, the superior religion, and (if there is any) the superior writing, survive. In a few cases we might see the old language persist with women and children; but generally the language, or at least the grammar, of the superior invaders survives, and very often is actually adopted by the native race.[49]

The best way to ascertain whether a group had been Hamitic was to study its language and to look for Hamitic traits in its structure. The "tribes" whose languages possessed a specific morphology and usually exhibited grammatical gender were thus likely descended from "racially pure" Hamites.

Despite Luschan's belief that the Hamites' "white" biological characteristics had faded when they came into contact with their numerically superior black victims, his arguments did not agree with those of Gobineau or Kossinna. Elsewhere, Luschan contended that "we all know that a certain mixture of blood has always been of great advantage to a nation. England, France, and Germany are equally distinguished for the great variety of their racial elements." Nonetheless, while he did not reject the benefits of intermarriage outright, Luschan also thought that the jury was still out with regard to the question of its positive or negative impact on future generations. Anthropologists were "especially ignorant as to the moral and intellectual qualities of half-castes."[50] Luschan's ideas were certainly more in line with those of Meinhof, Büttner, and the missionaries than the hard-line antimiscegenationsts. Still, the problem was not that Luschan renounced race mixing but that he valued some biological and intellectual characteristics over others, and those tended to be ones possessed by whites.

Luschan began his paper on the Hottentots with the assumption that all sub-Saharan African languages could be parceled out into the Hamitic, Sudanic, or Bantu categories, except for those of "the Arabs, the Portuguese, the Boers, and other people immigrated recently . . . [and] the Bushmen, the Hottentots, and the various pigmy [*sic*] tribes of tropical Africa."[51] However, he quickly moved toward "proving" Hottentot affiliation with Hamites, using Meinhof's linguistic findings to bolster his arguments. In his essay "The Language of the Hottentots," Meinhof rounded out Luschan's anthropological argument with technical linguistic details. He asserted that because Hottentot languages exhibited grammatical gender—the division of nouns into separate classes according to whether they were male or female—they had to be grouped among the inflecting languages, the only ones that Meinhof believed showed this trait. At the time, the sole African languages that scholars believed displayed grammatical gender were Semitic and Hamitic. Meinhof did not question whether the Hottentots were Semites but concluded that, on the basis of the type of language they spoke, they had to be Hamites. This furthermore indicated that their languages were related to those of the Indo-Europeans, since they were also inflecting. Meinhof's implication was that far from being a "prehistoric" people, the Hottentots were connected to the highly sophisticated and advanced Indo-Europeans. As Luschan had suggested, they had lost their "racial" attributes as they mixed with the Bushmen, but their "superior" language remained.[52]

Linguistic arguments also supplemented anthropological ones in Meinhof's and Luschan's discussion of a group of central African Ituri "pygmies" (Twa) who visited Germany as part of a *Völkerschau,* or people exhibition, in 1906. Once the pygmies arrived in Berlin, Luschan and Meinhof submitted them to a battery of tests. They wanted to determine the pygmies' origins and their degree of relation to other African races, including the Bushmen. Working together, Luschan and Meinhof tried to categorize the pygmies on both philological and physical grounds. Luschan, for example, reported that the pygmies' language was one of the factors that had convinced him they were truly from the rainforest region, and thus "authentic" pygmies, not the "fakes" who had been paraded around Europe in the past.[53] He made this claim despite his own admission that information on pygmy languages—not excluding the speech that he had learned from listening to and speaking with the Ituri group—was scant at best and difficult to pin down. Luschan only mentioned the "Hamites" in passing, conjecturing that one of the pygmy women "had some Hamitic blood," since she was lighter-skinned than her companions and had a "strikingly small nose."[54] Nonetheless, his effort to classify the pygmies was still an attempt to order a piece of the African racial and linguistic map according to the organizing principle of the Hamitic hypothesis, which dictated that Africans could be identified by specific grammatical and biological traits.

Where Luschan's remarks on pygmy language were introductory and probably designed to make his audience aware of the important relationship between anthropology and "colonial" linguistics, in his part of the essay Meinhof turned to a more complex and detailed analysis of pygmy speech. He noted that the so-called pygmy language was similar to the West African languages that, on the basis of their primitive, isolating structures, had recently been classified as Sudanic. In sharp contrast to the inflecting Hamitic and Indo-European languages, Sudanic languages were considered simple in terms of grammatical structure, made up of strings of roots that were "isolated" from each other and could not be combined to create new words and meanings. Like Ewe, which was widely spoken in the German colony of Togo, Meinhof held that Pygmy was isolating, and that both languages, Ewe and Pygmy, also made "rich use" of musical tone. The pygmy language, he admitted, had obviously adopted a lot of Bantu vocabulary; for instance, the numbers one through five in "pygmy" were all of Bantu origin. This did not, however, detract from the language's obvious Sudanic structure, one that Bushman also shared. Meinhof did not say whether he assumed a genetic relationship between the pygmies and the Bushmen. Pygmy language had no clicks, which were a fundamental element of Bushman. Yet they did contain velarlabials ("sounds which are produced by a narrowing of the soft palate and a simultaneous occlusion of the lips"),[55] which Meinhof surmised were either related to clicks or could develop into them.[56]

A combination of anthropological and linguistic information was thus mustered to support Luschan's and Meinhof's conclusions that the pygmies were both Sudanic speakers, and likely related to the Bushmen. The correlation between anthropological and linguistic data also moved them a step closer to "proving" pygmy primitivity, since it allowed them to fit the pygmies into a certain developmental slot. Pygmies were sorted into the least advanced category of Africans, along with those other Sudanic speakers whom the Hamites had conquered.

There was little critique of either Meinhof's and Luschan's piece on the Ituri pygmies or their work on the Hottentots, even though each used racial evidence to make claims about linguistic classification. However, the overarching problems with their collaborative methodology became apparent even to contemporaries in their final joint enterprise, the *Sprachen der Hamiten.* Most of the book was devoted specifically to solving linguistic questions, and Meinhof was its actual author, with Luschan adding anthropological material only in an afterword. In the text, Meinhof analyzed the languages of a variety of African groups from across the continent in order to ascertain their position as Hamitic. Among the peoples studied were the Hausa, Masai, Nama, Somali, and Fulbe (whose language is commonly referred to as Fulfulde). Not all of these languages were universally accepted as part of the Hamitic language "family"; the year before the *Sprachen der Hamiten* was published Meinhof wrote an article about Fulfulde that posited it as a *pre-Hamitic* language on the cusp of blossoming into a Hamitic one.[57] Yet in the book Fulfulde was included among the Hamitic languages and, whatever Meinhof's protestations that his analyses were not racial or cultural, evidently also included the Fulbe in the Hamitic "race." He referred to them as a "herding and ruling folk among the Negroes" that travelers had described as "proud, manly, and warlike."[58]

The Fulbe—and, for that matter, the neighboring Hausa—were, in general, a classic instance of a group where "race and language" did not match, which presented scholars such as Meinhof and Luschan with a predicament. Physically, the Fulbe were considered "light-skinned Hamites," but nonetheless they spoke a language that in many ways seemed closer to that of the darker-skinned Bantu. Meinhof explained this surprising, confusing contradiction by maintaining that a nomadic group speaking a language similar to that of the Fulbe had conquered a pastoral,

"Nigritic" people, and that this resulted in a "mixed" ethnicity that was neither entirely Hamitic nor entirely Sudanic. Meinhof argued further that the very geographic proximity of groups like the Fulbe to true "Negroes" made them so hard to identify as Hamites, and led some to type them—erroneously—as Sudanic.[59]

The Fulbe were not the only group that problematized the classificatory scheme outlined by Meinhof in the *Sprachen der Hamiten.* The East African Masai were also difficult to order. In 1904, Meinhof wrote a review of a book called *The Masai* (*Die Masai*) that was written by Moritz Merker, an officer in the German *Schutztruppen.* Drawing on linguistic, anthropological, and quasi-historical information, Merker argued that the Masai were in fact not originally Hamitic or any other kind of African—they were instead Semitic, and very likely related to the Arabs of the Middle East.[60] While Merker did not have any specific linguistic training or background, he clearly suggested that the Masai language was Semitic, though more on anthropological than philological grounds.

In his critique, Meinhof attacked and dismantled Merker's contention that Masai was Semitic. Instead, he questioned Merker's understanding of Masai and the importance he had placed on the language in his analysis.

> Even if the author does not want to give linguistics the first word in deciding this question, we will, if we have to talk about Semites at all, not be able to dispense with it. The label "Semitic" is in scientific circles first applied to linguistic observation. The Phoenicians are counted as "Semites" because they speak a Semitic language, even though biblical reports place them among the Hamites; Arabs are called "Semites" for similar reasons, even though "Hamitic" admixture has here been maintained since ancient times. Jews are also considered Semites, despite their, as the author knows, strong mixing with alarodic [an outmoded, racially charged term for Caucasian] blood. If one wants to use the term "Semites" in this sense, then, the Masai do not belong, as one does not require much time studying their language to see that they are not, in this sense, Semitic. Linguistically the Masai are Hamites and there can seriously be no question of their belonging to the Semites.[61]

Meinhof challenged Merker on the grounds that his linguistic analysis was not precise, and that this imprecision had led him to make an incorrect categorization on the basis of faulty ethnological data.

In his discussion of Merker, Meinhof pointed out a serious rupture between linguistic and anthropological classifications of ethnic or racial groups. Linguistic and anthropological Hamites—as well as Sudanic or Bantu speakers—did not correlate on a one-to-one basis. The Phoenicians were not racially Semitic, even if they spoke a Semitic language; the same held true for some Arabs and Jews. Further, while Meinhof completely rejected Merker's assertion that the Masai language was Semitic, he was evidently not so sure about their "race" or "culture." For Meinhof, Merker's problem rested in the inability to disentangle ethnological, anthropological, and linguistic data. He was able to find some merit in Merker's argument, insofar as there was little doubt in his mind that Hamites and Semites were ethnologically and anthropologically related and shared an *Urverwandschaft* (originary relationship).[62] They also had some linguistic traits in common, as both the Hamitic and Semitic language families were inflecting and exhibited grammatical gender. Moreover, there were plenty of Semitic "loan words" in Hamitic languages, not to mention Hamitic loan words in Semitic languages.[63]

The Rwandan Hima, Tutsi, and Hutu were also difficult to categorize. In his afterword to Meinhof's *Sprachen der Hamiten,* which was titled "Hamitische Typen," Luschan addressed the issue of "typical" Hamitic biological and racial features. Unsurprisingly, these included light skin, small noses, and tall, thin physiques. Even as Luschan maintained that it was often the dissimilar pair of "negroid" body type and "Hamitic" language that prevailed after culture contact, the Hima and Tutsi obviously presented him with a dilemma. The Tutsi were, he believed, far more "white" than the Masai, and loath to mate with their Bantu *Untertanen.* Still, puzzlingly, they had evidently assumed the latter's language. "We currently have no satisfactory explanation for this actually very surprising deviation from the norm," Luschan mused, "and it is not yet out of the question that, in the case of individual Hima tribes, we might still succeed in discovering the remnants of their own old languages." At the time, though, it appeared to Luschan as if these phantom languages had permanently evaporated and "sunk into the ocean of the forgotten."[64] However, Meinhof and Luschan also glided over this caesura, not giving it primary importance or allowing it to detract from their shared conviction that Hamites were white rulers and Sudanic or Negrito blacks their underlings.

The inclination to conflate language with race—and linguistic data with physical evidence—was strong in publications such as Meinhof's and Luschan's. Even during their own time there were, moreover, those who criticized and decried such conflation. Shortly after the 1912 publication of the *Sprachen der Hamiten,* Hugo Schuchardt, a prominent and sometimes controversial linguist from the Austrian University of Graz,[65] criticized Meinhof for failing to recognize the difference between linguistic and racial phenomena. Schuchardt believed that racialist thinking permeated the book—which, it will be remembered, Meinhof claimed was based entirely on linguistic principles—and that such thinking condemned both Meinhof and Luschan to remain caught in a trap of circular logic.

> Both the questions "What are Hamitic languages" and "What are Hamites" are clearly dependent on one another, and the answer must either be "Hamitic languages are those that are spoken by Hamites" or "Hamites are those who speak Hamitic languages." The one is an anthropological explanation, the other a linguistic. Meinhof would admit to the wording of the first when he says "Languages of the Hamites" instead of "Hamitic languages"; but in fact, here he can only want to express one wish, that of seeing the tribes which speak Hamitic languages as a unified group not only in language but also in physical constitution. To this end, he reaches his hand out to his anthropologist friend Felix von Luschan; but he decidedly supports himself on [Meinhof's] shoulder, and cannot escape the linguistic explanation of "Hamites," and thus we go around in circles.[66]

American anthropologist Edward Sapir similarly challenged the book's use of anthropological and linguistic definitions.[67] Finally, at the German Colonial Congress of 1910, amateur anthropologist and entomologist Paul Staudinger verbally chastised Meinhof for a speech he had held on the current situation of African linguistic research. Staudinger maintained that "with all the previous research and knowledge, we can speak of a Hamitic language group. However, to classify all of the different people who speak a Hamitic idiom as somatically and anthropologically the same—as 'Hamites,' and thus as a 'race'—is simply not possible."[68] Meinhof did not directly answer Staudinger's criticism; rather, he evaded it by stating that "the difference between anthropological and linguistic modes of observation is obvious, but does not hinder the mutual support of these sciences."[69] The fact that the fusion of anthropological and linguistic classificatory criteria raised a number of questions was outweighed by the benefits of interdisciplinary methodology. Meinhof admitted that knowledge of a group's language would not allow scholars to determine its race conclusively—there had been too much "intermingling" for that. However, Meinhof still felt it was possible to speak of Hamitic *types,* which was why he had asked Luschan to write the afterword to his book on their physical attributes.

Even while Meinhof glossed over Staudinger's comment at the Colonial Congress, he and Luschan were painfully aware of the difficulties inherent in using both anthropological and linguistic criteria in their classifications. Meinhof's inability to classify groups such as the Fulbe and Masai in itself testifies to a certain amount of confusion. Further, the issue of whether—and to what extent—racial typologies factored into linguistic ones, and vice versa, emerged in their correspondence. In a 1907 letter to Luschan, Meinhof commented that however much people might complain that Luschan "mixed up" or "confused" linguistics and anthropology, he knew that his colleague fully understood the differences between the fields. Meinhof remarked that Luschan "wanted to know the disciplines separately" but, at the same time, did not simply want to "exclude the possibility that language is at least a very important ethnographic feature."[70] Meinhof never stated that language and race had a one-to-one correspondence either; in another letter, he said that the Bantu—whom he described as a "mixture of Hamitic and Nigritic," with very variegated "somatic" qualities—proved that they were two distinct subjects.[71] Their languages might put them into one category, but their racial features would land them in another.

The classification of certain groups among the Hamites in spite of evidence to the contrary had explicitly colonial overtones. As Sachau pointed out in his memos about the Hausa at the Berlin Seminar, those groups were critical to German economic and political competitiveness in western Africa.[72] The Hausa and Fulbe have a closely intertwined history and are sometimes referred to jointly as the "Hausa-Fulani."[73] Both groups are Muslim, live throughout West Africa, and were well known among Europeans for their business dealings by the late nineteenth and early twentieth centuries. Sachau first agitated for the inclusion of Hausa in the seminar's curriculum. By 1909, however, finding a Hausa lecturer to teach in Berlin had become increasingly difficult, and he pondered whether Fulbe might be more appropriate. Reports from Cameroon indicated that the Fulbe language was more widespread in the colony than Hausa, and Sachau indicated that the colonial "authorities" were pressing for him to hire someone who could speak Fulfulde.[74] Meinhof left Berlin that same year, but his successor, Westermann, met a Fulbe man named Abdallah Adam during a research trip in Egypt and the Sudan. Considering that Adam could speak not only Fulbe, but Hausa and Arabic, the seminar was extremely eager to procure his services. He was hired in 1910.[75]

Meinhof may have no longer been at the seminar when Adam arrived, but he was certainly aware of how important both the Fulbe and Hausa were to German colonial success.[76] Their perceived position as cultural overlords in western Africa was critical to the Hausa being classfied among the Hamites, as well as to the Fulbe's status as either a "proto-Hamitic" or Hamitic people. As possessors of an advanced culture whose members were devout Muslims and had languages that had already been reduced to Arabic script,[77] the Fulbe and Hausa stood closer to the European colonizers than their Bantu or Sudanic neighbors. It was difficult for linguists, anthropologists, or colonial administrators to conceive of peoples who had developed their own complex civilizations as originally African; consequently, they used both racial and linguistic evidence to classify them as at least partially white.[78] More recent scholarship has placed Fulfulde among the West Atlantic languages, which includes Wolof, a language that Meinhof classified with the Sudanic/Nigritic family.[79]

Conclusion

The question of how linguistic and anthropological methods could be jointly applied in the evolving discipline of African studies continued after Germany lost its colonies. In 1930, when the University of Leipzig was searching for a scholar to head its Institute for African languages, two of the four contenders for the position were dismissed out of hand because one of them had too little ethnological background and the other too much. All the candidates had some training in both Bantu and Hamitic languages, which was crucial for the job. According to Walter Gotz, the dean of Leipzig's philosophical faculty, the university recognized that "Africa's linguistic world is quite extensive and varied" and that "Semitic, Hamitic, and Bantu languages have to be equally considered."[80] From further correspondence and discussion concerning the hire, however, it also seemed that the faculty required something more: first, that a candidate have actual "field" experience, and second, that he be recognized as a pedigreed linguist or philologist. This meant that Martin Heepe—who had worked with Meinhof but also criticized him—was excluded on grounds that he "work[ed] in a purely philological realm, without consideration of the circumstances, or the realization that language is not a self-sufficient life-form but, rather, only a part of the entire culture and . . ."[81] Meanwhile, Bernhard Struck was refused because he was, even by his own previous admission, more an ethnologist and physical anthropologist than a linguist.[82]

Both rejections were motivated by personal factors; neither Heepe nor Struck was popular among their colleagues, and Heepe was considered particularly abrasive. This may, indeed, even have been the reason behind his characterization as not ethnologically minded, since his supporters pointed out that he had more field experience than August Klingenheben, the university's top candidate and eventual hire, and that some of his detractors had quarreled with him precisely over anthropological, and not linguistic, matters. Struck's case is more difficult to unravel, and tied more directly to the problem of conflating linguistic and anthropological evidence. His proponents—several unnamed members of related disciplines including ethnology, geography, and colonial agriculture—considered Struck especially well suited to the linguistic position because his "ethnological works concern themselves exclusively with problems that appear important for the solution of linguistic problems." Struck's detractors were just as convinced that he was more of a dilettante than anything else; instead of focusing on a single discipline, he had studied ethnology, physical anthropology, geography, and linguistics.

Struck's mixed academic background was apparent in his philological work, where he often drew concrete connections between biological race and language. His 1921 "Somatische Typen und Sprachgruppen in Kordofan," for instance, was culled from linguistic evidence that Meinhof had collected during a 1914 trip to the Anglo-Egyptian Sudan, but went beyond it in linking biological traits, including skin color and head size, to Meinhof's data.[83] Personally, Meinhof was more befuddled by the article than anything else. After Struck sent it to him for evaluation, Meinhof thanked him briefly but admitted that he had not understood the bulk of it.[84] In rejecting the proposal that Struck be considered as an "Orientalist" or "philologist," Leipzig's philosophical faculty obliquely mentioned the essay, as well as the entire "Hamitic" debate and Struck's position in it. They maintained that "in ignorance of the incorrectness of the idea that there is a direct connection between language and race, which has long been the recognized position and scholarly standpoint of linguistics, he searches to unite ambiguous calculations of the mathematical relations of skull bones to morphology."[85] It was Struck's insistence on equating racial and linguistic evidence that, in the end, forestalled and eventually thwarted his candidacy. Struck was unable to avoid the trap of conflation, and his career suffered for it. This was ironic, considering that Meinhof, the field's top scholar, had also often been accused of conflation.

When the discipline of *Afrikanistik* was first forming, it was highly fluid. Its practitioners saw their science as one that would answer difficult questions about Africans in conjunction with physical anthropology and ethnology. As time went on, however, it became increasingly evident that linguistics and anthropology were separate domains that did not always produce results that dovetailed. When they were used together, the conclusions that ensued often concurred with a specifically colonialist and racialist ideology that distorted the complex relationship among African peoples and turned it into a straightforward tale of white conquest in black Africa.

Chapter 5

Experimenting in the Metropole: The Theory and Practice of African Studies, 1908–19

Carl Meinhof joined the Hamburg Colonial Institute in 1909. The new position afforded him considerable control over the growing discipline of African studies. Meinhof was chair of his own Department of Colonial Languages and assembled a sizable staff of European lecturers and African assistants. He founded the *Zeitschrift für Kolonialsprachen* and established a phonetics laboratory. In addition, Meinhof reached a broad segment of the German public through a well-attended series of general lectures on African religion, law, and poetry, all of which were linked to his more general concern with language.[1] With these extra resources, Meinhof became a towering figure in the field, largely determining its direction in the pre–World War I era.

The only constraint on Meinhof during his Hamburg years was the Colonial Institute itself, an establishment dedicated not only to Germany's imperial interests but to the business concerns of the local Hamburg elite. The institute continued to employ the practical approach to colonial science favored at the seminar. Knowledge was based on a synthesis of information received directly from the colonies and experimentation with colonial "objects," human or otherwise. Germans attending classes at the institute could acquaint themselves with the foreign nature of far-off lands before ever leaving home. Even more so than the Seminar for Oriental Languages or Meinhof's parsonage in Zizow, the institute presented itself as "better" than the colony for the study of Africa. The institute fabricated a sterilized image of Africa in an almost hypermetropolitan setting, where the colonial "field" was reinvented in the German laboratory. The main goal of the institute was to introduce pupils to the "lived reality" of Africa and Germany's other colonies by offering them a complete education in all aspects of colonial life, from plants to animals to soil to people. The theory was that colonial education was best conducted from afar, in a place where various aspects of Africa could be recreated without the messy complications of illness, death, or miscegenation that might occur in the colonies themselves.

This "hypermetropolitan" space did not go uncontested. All branches of the institute were arenas of tension between the scholarly and the practical. The institute was Hamburg's first degree-granting academic establishment,[2] and the city's scholarly community began to discuss turning it into a full-fledged university even before it had opened.[3] Meanwhile, imperial and business interests wanted to offer the best practical training possible, one that limited philosophical or theoretical inquiry. For example, in 1912 Hans Zache, a civil servant who had been stationed in East Africa, taught a course called "Swahili Exercises Concerning the Treatment of Natives and Native Rights." He refused to use Bakari, who was Meinhof's regular Swahili assistant, in his class. Zache deemed Bakari "unsuitable" because he was too much of a "scholar" and spoke "grammatical Swahili." Zache much preferred the services of his personal "Suaheliboy," whom he claimed spoke the language precisely "as the Negroes" did.[4]

There was a distinct gap between what Meinhof, a trained theologist and linguist, and Zache, a career colonial official, thought their students needed to know. Meinhof wanted to teach "pure" coastal Swahili (*kipwani*), while Zache preferred that his charges learn the inland lingua franca, a dialect that he believed was patently "ungrammatical." What Meinhof and Zache taught differed on other levels as well. Meinhof aimed first for his students to communicate more efficiently with Africans, since this would facilitate conversion to Christianity. Second, he encouraged them to gather data on both well-known and "dying" languages, so that Germany would have a more complete picture of Africa's linguistic and ethnic map. This was a relatively subtle way of extending colonial power through knowledge. Zache was interested in more immediate presentations of authority. His language classrooms were mock courtrooms, where students and Africans played the roles of judge and accused, respectively.[5] By employing both Meinhof and Zache, the institute demonstrated that there was a deep divide in how colonial knowledge was imparted, as well as in what was considered important about it.

Constructing a Colonial Institute in Hamburg

The Seminar for Oriental Languages was originally conceived as an academy for interpreters and translators, and thus it had language as its main object from the beginning. The Colonial Institute had loftier goals. It opened on October 20, 1908, as a training facility specifically designed to suit the needs of Germans preparing for all manner of colonial careers.[6] Hamburg was given permission to launch a central bureau (*Zentralstelle*) for gathering and processing all academic and practical written material pertaining to overseas colonies, both Germany's and others'. The bureau was to help cultivate relations between the Colonial Institute and those living in the colonies by supplying them with scientific information, in effect acting as a clearinghouse for its collection, storage, and dissemination.[7]

That the institute was founded in Hamburg is itself significant. As a member of the Hanseatic League, Hamburg had been involved with business enterprises beyond the German-speaking realm since the Middle Ages. Hamburg's colonial activity only intensified in the nineteenth century, when it played a crucial role in transatlantic shipping with the foundation of businesses such as the Hamburg-America Company. Two dominant Hamburg families, the O'swalds and the Woermanns, were major traders in Africa; the O'swalds were active in East Africa and the Woermanns in Cameroon well before official German colonization had begun.[8] In the 1850s Hamburg and the other Hanse towns formed a pact with Zanzibar's sultan, which gave them preferential trading rights on the island.[9] Hamburg's international connections were extensive, covering not only Africa but the Middle East, the Americas, and the Pacific.[10] Indeed, when the Hamburg-America Company was established in 1847 its motto, *Mein Feld ist die Welt* (the world is my field), aptly illustrated the city's global aspirations.[11]

The city of Hamburg was a privileged metropolitan space in much the same way as the institute would be. Even in the mid-nineteenth century, when most of Germany was still agricultural, the city was supported by commercial and business interests that integrated it into the wider world.[12] By the time the institute opened in 1908, Hamburg was so deeply embedded in the global economy that it was simply unthinkable without empire.[13] Like Birmingham, England, which Catherine Hall argues was a colonial metropolis whose inhabitants were daily confronted with the material and intellectual presence of imperialism, Hamburg was a crossroads for the dissemination of colonial manufactures and ideas.[14] City pride was heavily vested in the bustling port and in grandiose naval displays of its maritime might, as Rüger has illustrated; Hamburg delineated its own particular, local identity in the German Empire through emphasis on its seafaring history, which was intertwined with its position as an international trading hub.[15] Hypermetropolitan spaces like Hamburg were by definition also hybrid ones, heavily influenced by the products and people continually arriving from the colonies and elsewhere. This meant that categories of "self" and "Other" were more apt to become blurred in cities such as Hamburg, where the Other was ever-present.[16] As the institute grew, the need to define Africans and other non-Westerners as different from Germans became increasingly pressing, with foreigners being relegated to particular spaces and excluded from others.[17]

Bernhard Dernburg, secretary of the *Reichskolonialamt* from late 1906 to 1910, was quickly convinced that Hamburg was the ideal setting for a Colonial Institute. When he visited the city with future East African governor Heinrich Schnee in 1907, they took a tour of the city to assess its suitability. Guided by former Hamburg mayor Werner von Melle, who was the city's chief negotiator for the institute, they strolled along the docks and warehouses at the port. Upon arriving at one of the warehouses, Alfred Voight, a botanist who had accompanied them, was approached by a man wanting to show him a new shipment of rice. The man was concerned that his goods had been damaged in transport. However, all was not lost because, as von Melle described, "Professor Voight explained the situation to him botanically, and was able to reassure him of the unchanged value of the product. This unstaged, natural episode much pleased [Dernburg]. 'That is,' he said, 'the kind of combination of theory and business practice that I value. And, in the end, it can only happen here, with you in Hamburg.'"[18] The passage of colonial products through the harbor on a daily basis, offering academics immediate opportunities for analysis and research, persuaded Dernburg that Hamburg was indeed the starting point through which foreign products—and peoples—daily entered the rest of Germany.

Hamburg also appealed to Dernburg and the *Reichskolonialamt* on a political level. The first conversations about opening a Colonial Institute took place at a time of great ambivalence toward colonialism. Dernburg, a banker who was one of the nation's most successful business leaders, was chosen secretary of the *Reichskolonialamt* expressly to revitalize sagging colonial interests in the wake of the Herero and Nama Wars of 1904 to 1907.[19] During this period, the German military committed genocide against the Herero and Nama peoples in South West Africa, moving to violent excess as they slaughtered their opponents.[20] Further, there was a more general view that the *Reichskolonialamt* was financially irresponsible, and that its officers were wanton profligates who caroused with natives when they were not abusing them.[21] If big business could step up its colonial activity, public pride in the colonies might be restored. Dernburg and his associates therefore believed that Hamburg, the nation's business capital, was the ideal location to repair German colonialism's damaged reputation.[22]

Once established, the authors of the institute's first annual report argued that the primary difference between the institute and Germany's other colonial academies lay in the purpose it was to serve. They claimed that neither the Berlin Seminar, with its emphasis on language, nor the *Kolonialschule* in Witzenhausen, with the more vocational goal of training farmers, offered a comprehensive program in all aspects of colonial society.[23] While the Colonial Institute also trained colonial officers, it was intended to fill a more exclusive niche. The institute would combine intellectual rigor with the practical knowledge that Dernburg so valued, and produce well-rounded alumni conversant in a variety of colonial subjects.[24] Before 1908, Germany had sorely neglected its responsibility to understand the foreign cultures it conquered. "Everywhere the European turns," the report suggested, "he encounters cultures that, from his point of view, are unquestionably inferior. . . . These are . . . cultures whose ideologies and thoughts differ fundamentally from our own. The necessity of somehow explaining or coming to terms with these cultures has been misunderstood and underestimated for a long time, the longest in Germany."[25] The report's writers suggested that Germans knew little about the wider world and that this needed to change for German colonialism to be successful. By offering a broad range of courses that would introduce pupils to all aspects of colonial life, the Colonial Institute would rectify this glaring gap in German education and produce well-rounded students to serve the empire. The institute's faculty hoped to achieve what Protestant missionaries had attempted through their decades of linguistic and anthropological research: They wanted to convey enough knowledge of a culture to their students so that the latter could effectively administer and change it.

African Languages at the Colonial Institute

The Colonial Institute's main objective was creating well-rounded civil servants expressly suited to administering colonized peoples. Surprisingly, however, African languages were largely ignored in the institute's first course catalog.[26] African language study was limited to beginning and advanced Swahili, both of which were taught by Carl Becker, an Islamicist who also gave instruction in Arabic. Von Melle attributed this oversight to the need to appease Berlin, where people were upset that the Colonial Institute had been founded in Hamburg instead of the capital.[27] The institute's first annual report also subtly criticized the seminar's concentration on language, arguing that while language study was fundamental for understanding other cultures, it did not suffice. "Knowledge of a language is certainly, as an indispensable tool of comprehension, a prerequisite for the study of a foreign culture. . . . It is likewise the case that language alone can only communicate one part of culture."[28] Although language training had its place, the report maintained, it was neither the most important instrument for colonists nor the primary function of the institute.

Behind the scenes, though, language study was a point of contention. While von Melle had agreed to postpone the issue of teaching colonial languages at the institute, his colleagues complained that this would mean students would have to go to Berlin to supplement their education. The Hamburg business community allowed that it would be unwise to anger Berlin but thought there should still be a search for a Bantu language professor, to be conducted as "unobtrusively" as possible.[29] Members of the new institute's faculty also hoped that whoever assumed the position would teach not only Swahili but also colonial administration. The ideal candidate would have had some colonial experience, preferably in East Africa.[30]

The matter came to a head when Schnee, the East African governor, and Hamburg senator Justus Strandes, who had long personal experience in East Africa and especially Zanzibar with his company, Hansing & Co.,[31] recommended candidates to fill the language post. Among these, the most prominent were a government official, Ludwig Meyer, and the headmaster of the government school in Tanga, P. Blank, who also published the Swahili newspaper *Kiongozi* (The Guide).[32] Neither of them had the linguistic experience of missionaries like Krapf, Koelle, or Büttner. Both Meyer and Blank had simply happened to serve in German East Africa and learned Swahili while there. In this way they had gotten their own training "backwards," since they had picked up whatever knowledge of Africa they had in the colonies, not the metropole.[33]

In a different vein, *Völkerkunde Museum* director Georg Thilenius suggested that whoever was chosen to teach Swahili should also be an Orientalist, competent to discuss the rapid spread of Islam in Africa and make sense of the Muslim role in the German colonies. Essentially, Thilenius advocated the appointment of an Orientalist who fit the nineteenth-century model Trautmann has described, someone who was expert in philology and literature, and was interested in links between Africa and the Middle East.[34] Thilenius argued that, while Swahili was structurally a Bantu language, it had at the same time already been "infiltrated with Arabic elements," thereby necessitating an instructor competent in Islamic studies and Arabic.[35] Orientalist scholarship had a long tradition in the German academy. African studies, by contrast, had yet to establish its foothold in the university and remained largely the province of missionaries and their supporters. The divergent opinions on who to hire reflected a general ambiguity about the shape the discipline would take, and whether it would be an applied science or a more scholarly pursuit. The faculty approached the possibility of hiring Meinhof away from Berlin only after Blank and Meyer declined to join the institute. Both Becker and Franz Stuhlmann, a zoologist renowned for his travels with Emin Pasha in East Africa, saw Meinhof as their only serious candidate and felt that acquiring him would constitute a major coup.[36]

Because he had more experience with African languages than anyone else on the faculty, Becker prepared detailed reports for the *Professorenrat* on both the general exigencies of African linguistics and Meinhof's importance to the field. Becker explained why the rapidly expanding Colonial Institute could no longer dispense with a permanent professor for African languages.[37] Most of the students attending the institute in its first year had planned to work in Germany's West African colonies, where no indigenous language had asserted itself as a lingua franca and the main mode of communication between Africans and Germans was Pidgin English.[38] This state of affairs could not continue indefinitely; Pidgin English was itself considered an incursion by a foreign colonial power into German territory, and there was even a brief and failed attempt to replace it with something called *Kolonial-Deutsch.*[39] The institution of west African linguae francae was thus necessary explicitly for *German* colonial development, making it inevitable that civil servants in Togo and Cameroon would have to acquire west African languages like Ewe, Duala, and Ewondo.[40] Moreover, additional courses in Swahili, as well as in other related Bantu languages, would have to be introduced to accommodate those students planning to work in East Africa.

In the report, Becker also contemplated whether a professional linguist or civil servant should be chosen for the position. He decided that the former would be better, since he believed that the Colonial Institute would "scarcely be able to find someone equally a master of both eastern and western languages" in a career colonial officer. Becker continued, "Under the circumstances, the appointment of a man who is knowledgeable about the entire area is without doubt preferable." The Colonial Institute had indeed been founded to meet practical goals, but its faculty had a duty to solve theoretical problems, and the emergent *Afrikanistik* was primed to do so. Becker concluded his remarks to the *Professorenrat* by mentioning that Hamburg was now ready to take over the primary role of collecting and transmitting linguistic data that missionaries had once played. The city would be able to create a center for the analysis and dissemination of knowledge about African languages to rival any in the world.[41]

The language Becker used in this and other reports reflected a keen desire to professionalize African studies.[42] He disparagingly described the discipline as consisting half of Egyptologists and half of missionaries. However, since "African philology" was a relatively new field, it had few active professionals. Becker did acknowledge the significance of missionary scholarship, because he thought that some missionaries had extensive scientific knowledge and might have been able to fill the Hamburg position. But Becker doubted whether any would really want to give up life in the colonies any more than the civil servants had. Besides, missionaries usually lacked the university education that Becker saw as an essential precondition for a professorial post at the Colonial Institute.[43]

Meinhof, by contrast, was both practically and theoretically inclined. He was trained not as a missionary but as a theologian and teacher, and had already received the title of professor in Berlin. However, even though Becker promoted Meinhof as the "only truly scientific Africanist philologist" in Germany,[44] his appointment did not go unchallenged, particularly in the business community. Indeed, Becker's enthusiastic posturing on Meinhof's behalf may have been related to a letter that Strandes had written. Strandes sent Becker the letter because of "new doubts" about Meinhof's suitability.[45] Someone had shown Strandes an article of Meinhof's that dealt with the issue of how to enlist lay support for the mission, and Strandes was unsure whether a man with such close missionary ties would be able to conduct his duties at the Colonial Institute in an objective manner.[46] He pointed out that, in addition to his various speaking engagements at missionary events, Meinhof had written an open letter to the business community asking that it support the Protestant mission financially and even suggesting that its members join the Berlin Missionary Society in some capacity.[47] For Strandes, this was proof that Meinhof was involved in unacademic activities not befitting the institute. Like most of northern Germany, Hamburg was largely Protestant. However, the city was also known for its secularism and a relatively low level of church attendance.[48] Even early in the nineteenth century a writer for the *Evangelical Magazine and Missionary Chronicle* had lamented that Hamburg was an "irreligious" city, whose inhabitants thought "of nothing, in general, but business and pleasure."[49] This may have been an exaggeration, but Hamburg's merchant community was still not thrilled with the idea of employing a professor of African philology so dedicated to the Protestant missionary cause.

Becker tried to assuage Strandes, assuring him that Meinhof was equally tolerant of both Catholics and Protestants, and would not let his religious biases influence his teaching.[50] However, Becker was not quite accurate in his assessment of Meinhof's attitude toward Catholicism. Meinhof did contribute to Catholic journals, including Schmidt's *Anthropos,* but was convinced that Protestant missionaries had made and would continue to make more contributions to African studies than their Catholic counterparts; he even expressed annoyance with those who believed that Catholics, not Protestants, had contributed more to African philology in the nineteenth and early twentieth centuries.[51] The Colonial Institute hoped to draw students from all walks of life and religions, and the *Professorenrat* held meetings to discuss offering a program in colonial training to Catholic missionaries before Meinhof's arrival.[52] Someone as clearly partisan as Meinhof could detract from the institute's secular and universalist leanings. The roots of *Afrikanistik* were extrainstitutional and located with the Protestant missionaries. Yet as the discipline professionalized, there were attempts to unmoor the discipline from its missionary origins and secularize it.

At least in 1909, however, this unmooring would not occur. While concern for Meinhof's religious background lingered, his myriad publications and ample experience won out.[53] Strandes and other Hamburg businessmen remained unsure of whether a practical colonial man would not "suffice" for teaching Swahili, but said they understood the *Professorenrat*'s preference for an academic.[54] Their anxiety about Meinhof's missionary involvement was also offset by the reality that the Colonial Institute would eventually need to hire someone to teach *Missionswissenschaft.* The businessmen thought that Meinhof would be able to teach courses in missiology alongside his other classes,[55] provided that a Catholic lecturer was found to counteract the favoritism this could potentially create.[56] With Strandes's objections aside, there were no reasons to reject Meinhof's appointment. He was invited to come to the *Kolonialinstitut* in fall 1909, and he accepted almost immediately.[57]

The Organization of the Department of Colonial Languages

Once in Hamburg, Meinhof moved quickly to found a phonetics laboratory and start publication of a new journal for African languages. The first provided students and scholars with hands-on contact with Africans; the second gave a voice to missionaries and others outside Hamburg. Of course, to have either, Meinhof needed his own department of "colonial" languages. At first, this *Seminar für Kolonialsprachen* was to be squeezed together with Otto Franke's department of East Asian languages and cultures in the same small set of rooms in order to save space. The *Professorenrat,* however, soon decided this would not do, since "the difference between these [academic] areas, which scarcely have anything to do with each other and consequently use completely different teaching methods and equipment, have . . . made spatial separation desirable."[58] This is indicative of the perception, at the Colonial Institute as elsewhere, that African and Pacific languages were unlike other foreign languages, the so-called *Kultursprachen* of Europe and Asia. The "colonial" languages sometimes possessed no written literature, and so there were few textbooks available in them. Thus these languages had to be explored, fixed, and made accessible before they could be taught as the *Kultursprachen* could. The resources required for instruction in African languages were very different from those used to teach East Asian ones and necessitated an area that could accommodate bulky phonetic equipment.

During his first year in Hamburg, Meinhof was both director and primary lecturer at the *Seminar für Kolonialsprachen.* He taught Swahili and Duala, and a course in comparative Bantu and phonetics with special consideration for African languages.[59] This last class, which Meinhof had also offered in Berlin, was his most important. The content of his lectures was likely based on the 1899 *Grundriß einer Lautlehre der Bantusprachen* and its successor, the 1906 *Grundzüge einer Vergleichenden Grammatik der Bantusprachen.* No institute could offer classes in all the languages of Africa—or even want to, considering that one of the goals of linguistic transcription and the creation of new literatures was to create linguae francae and allow some neighboring dialects to become "naturally" extinct.[60] Nevertheless, Meinhof hoped to make his students capable of quickly absorbing the Bantu languages they encountered in the field, whether already known or newly "discovered." If they knew the grammatical, morphological, and phonological structure of Bantu in general, they would be better prepared for this task.

Bantu languages only represented one family, however, and the institute soon felt the need to expand its curriculum and incorporate African languages from other groups. Thilenius commented that the "professorship for colonial languages is only a euphemism as long as it remains limited to Bantu." When Becker first addressed the *Professorenrat* about finding an African linguist, he had placed the bulk of his emphasis on the importance of Bantu. Even so, he had also mentioned West Africa's linguae francae—which fell into all three language families, Hamitic, Sudanic/Nigritic, and Bantu. Before the institute's actual foundation, Becker had believed that they were slightly less important than, say, Swahili, because of the status of Pidgin English in Cameroon and Togo. Nevertheless, since Germans did not want another European tongue dominating one or more of their colonies, these linguae francae would eventually have to be offered. When they finally were incorporated, it was for expressly practical reasons. The *Reichskolonialamt* was planning to send a number of military doctors to the Colonial Institute, where they would take classes at the *Institut für Schiffs- und Tropenkrankheiten.* Because the doctors were mostly being sent to Western or Southwestern Africa, officials in Berlin hoped they would also be able to study the languages of these areas, which included the Bantu Herero and Duala, but also the Hamitic Hausa and Fulani. Furthermore, Meinhof expected that some missionary candidates from the *Norddeutsche Missionsgesellschaft* would be attending the institute prior to decamping for Togo, and they needed instruction in the Sudanic/Nigritic Ewe language.[61]

Adding these new languages meant hiring a new instructor. On Meinhof's advice, the *Professorenrat* invited the former missionary Westermann, who had been a colleague of Meinhof's in Berlin, to assume the post. Next to Meinhof, Westermann was the most significant Africanist scholar of the early twentieth century. A North German missionary trained in Basel, Westermann spent only a few years in Togo before ill health forced him to return to Germany. He has been identified with the practical side of language studies and Meinhof with the theoretical, but this division is not strictly correct.[62] While Westermann was concerned with finding the best way to teach African languages to German missionaries and colonists, so was Meinhof. In addition, just as Meinhof had developed templates for scrutinizing the structure of the Bantu and Hamitic language groups, Westermann crafted a framework for studying their Nigritic or Sudanic neighbors. In his comparative book *Sudansprachen,* published in 1911, Westermann chose a different language family as his object of investigation but imitated Meinhof's methodology. He too believed that the future of linguistic research lay not in deep analysis of single languages but in broad understanding of an entire group.[63]

When Meinhof was in Berlin he convinced Sachau to bring Westermann to the seminar;[64] in Hamburg, he tried to compel his colleagues to do the same. The report he presented them on Westermann was glowing, outlining all of his achievements and calling him a genius in the field of African studies. "Westermann," Meinhof said, "has deep insight not only into the grammar, morphology, and sound laws of languages, but also possesses an astounding degree of linguistic competence. Time and again I have been convinced that he is fluent, and completely able to converse with natives. This means that he can keep his eyes peeled for other practical and scientific questions." Instead of struggling to speak with Africans and devoting all his efforts to the act of simple communication, Westermann was able to collaborate with experts in other scientific disciplines and go well beyond what the average missionary might accomplish in a dictionary or grammar; for instance, Meinhof held that Westermann had gathered an astounding amount of botanical vocabulary, which he published as a guide to plant life in the German colonies.[65] This book, *Die Nutzplflanzen unserer Kolonien und ihre wirtschaftliche Bedeutung für das Mutterland* (*The Useful Plants of Our Colonies and Their Economic Significance to the Motherland*), was designed for the explicit benefit of German overseas business.[66] In the pre–World War I era Westermann was certainly a missionary in Büttner's mold, supportive of the aims of German Empire.

Considering Westermann's experience with African languages—which was demonstrative of the power that missionary linguistics and ethnography continued to exert—and his ability to handle issues beyond the linguistic, Meinhof saw him as the only choice for Hamburg's new position. Even Strandes, who had been so reluctant to accept Meinhof's appointment, was enthusiastic about Westermann. This was a definite sea change, insofar as Strandes had worried earlier about the adverse effects of missionary influence on the institute. However, Strandes was willing to abandon his trepidation about Westermann's missionary links because of the more immediate concern that the institute find a *Togo-Kenner* to help advance German economic interests. As a former missionary with the kind of "practical" experience that the business community valued, an acknowledged expert not only in languages but in all aspects of Togolese life, Westermann was very attractive.[67]

Westermann, however, proved more loyal to the *Seminar für Orientalische Sprachen* than Meinhof had been, and would not break his contract with Berlin.[68] This was a major loss for the Colonial Institute, since the two primary figures in early African studies—Meinhof and Westermann—remained divided between Hamburg and Berlin. The institute still acquired a *Dozent* for West Africa, the twenty-five-year-old August Klingenheben who lectured in Hausa and Fulani, but he did not have as much experience as the North German missionary—or the same missionary background. Klingenheben was born in Barmen, the seat of the Rhenish Missionary Society, but spent his entire life in academe; he did study theology alongside philology and *Semitistik,* but was never in the ministry. He was representative of the new generation of Africanist scholar, one whose career began at the university, not on the mission field.[69]

Despite not getting Westermann, the department's curriculum continued to swell and incorporated Ewe, Hausa, Ful, Herero, Nama, Ewondo, and Ndonga. Meinhof had the authority to hire a solid corps of assistants, both African and European. Still, Meinhof had little success attracting students to attend the new classes. Many of his pupils were missionaries, although the *Reichskolonialamt* did send some students.[70] The low enrollment at the department of Colonial Languages was typical of the entire institute, which did not appeal to the business community as Dernburg and Strandes had hoped.[71] Classes in Hamburg should have been filled to capacity with prospective businessmen and colonial officials, yet many of these were either not interested in the Colonial Institute or did not have the time to attend it. Kurt Redlich, one of the rare businessmen who was enthusiastic about the institute, complained that few of his colleagues understood the opportunity they had in Hamburg. Redlich remarked that in early 1914 only eight new students had signed up for courses, which was an embarrassment for the professors who had to lecture in cavernous, nearly empty halls. He found this all the more surprising because "a businessman without any theoretical economic knowledge is today no longer a true businessman."[72]

In spite of low enrollment, Meinhof's situation was not grim. Audiences for his special lecture series were large, as they were for other, similar series, indicating public interest in colonial subjects. Meinhof's lectures, which were eventually incorporated into books such as *Die Dichtung der Afrikaner* (1911), were popular because they were intended for a general audience instead of a professional one, and made a concrete effort to link Germans and Africans together in a common humanity. When speaking of myths and sagas, for instance, Meinhof drew on the fact that for Africans both were distinct combinations of history and fantasy, just as they were for Europeans.[73] Further, he told his audience that he saw evidence of possible Hamitic invasion in the same myths and sagas, sharing his ideas about linguistic, cultural, and racial difference with a broad cross-section of the Hamburg public.[74] It was thus in these open lectures and not in individual classes that Meinhof had the most success disseminating his theories on the linguistic, cultural, and racial makeup of Africa. If the practical aspects of *Afrikanistik* had not attracted as much attention as Meinhof had hoped, he could console himself with the fact that his academic output not only was prolific but had an extensive reach. Moreover, through the influence of the laboratory and journal, Meinhof eventually established Hamburg as a meeting point for Africanist scholars from around the world.

Pedagogy and Research in Meinhof's Department and Laboratory

Expressly political factors motivated the development of Meinhof's academic department in Hamburg. As the importance of West Africa heightened, for instance, the curriculum expanded to accommodate its languages. What, however, actually went on in African studies classrooms? How were courses taught, and what kinds of "scientific investigations" did Meinhof and his colleagues conduct?

To a great extent, Meinhof and his staff used techniques similar to those of Berlin. Labor was divided between Europeans—mostly Germans—and Africans. The Germans were the lecturers who "translated" African grammar and vocabulary into terms students could understand, whereas the Africans' main job was to demonstrate correct pronunciation and elocution. Meinhof believed that their roles could not be reversed. He found it unlikely that even the best European instructor would be able to mimic "exotic" African sounds on a consistent basis, unless he happened to be the son of a missionary and raised with an African language as his native tongue.[75] Therefore, very few Europeans could teach students to speak an African language correctly, at least on a purely mechanical level. At the same time, Meinhof said that Africans could not teach Europeans grammar in terms that Europeans could comprehend. He explained it this way at the 1910 World Missionary Conference in Edinburgh.

> The native . . . is doubtless master of his material in the fullest sense, but he does not understand European thought as it appears in the brain of the pupil. Thus he is totally unable to supply the connecting links between European and non-European ideas. . . . He who has ever interested himself in non-European languages knows . . . how great the gap is between these and our own. The discrepancy is based not only on the vocabulary or in a few deviations in the method of expression, but is founded on a complete differentiation in the whole construction of the language, or in other words on quite another method of thought. What is plain to the one is unintelligible to the other, and what appears difficult to one is natural to the other. So, in African dialects, it is quite frequently the case that what the European calls the front, the African calls the back.[76]

Thought was largely determined by grammatical structure. Europeans and Africans, who spoke languages belonging to different families that were on different levels of sophistication, would not fully be able to describe their languages to each other. This did not mean Germans were to take European grammatical categories and simply superimpose them on African ones; this could produce unreliable results and even hinder communication. Nor did it mean that Africans had no input into the construction of grammars, especially when they were being written for the first time. Without Africans, as will be further explored in chapter 6, German scholars had no means of deepening their knowledge of African languages on any level. Nonetheless, the actual mechanism of teaching the laws of African grammar to the untrained, nonacademic European could only be done by another European.

In the department's classrooms, African assistants worked mainly on helping European students with their pronunciation, while German lecturers and professors taught grammar. At the phonetics laboratory Africans and Europeans also served different functions, even if the line there was not so clear-cut. Here European students were encouraged not only to listen to Africans and repeat what they heard them say but also to examine them with their eyes. Depending on how close they were to the African "test subject" under observation, this would allow them to see the exact place where articulation occurred or how the African moved his speech organs while talking. This is significant. Meinhof was steadfast in his insistence that African languages had to be absorbed visually before any attempts were made to understand them aurally.

> First, the learner must be shown how he personally makes sounds. He is impelled to touch his own lips, to look in the mirror. Words are pronounced for him and he is required not to listen with his ear, but to observe the movement of the lips with his eyes. If he has understood how known sounds are produced, he can then be shown the way that unknown ones are, until he sees the difference (between them). Then he must try to mimic these, and when he finally can do so, he can also learn to hear.[77]

When W. H. T. Gairdner, a British clergyman who visited Meinhof's department in March 1912 to sit in on its classes, referred to the African teaching assistants as "living phonographs," because they stood "on the [European's] side" to be "cranked up" whenever there was need of demonstration, he was therefore only half right.[78] For Meinhof, the African assistants were obviously much more than phonographs. They were also, quite literally, Meinhof's "texts," to be "read" by students and studied by scholars.

Ironically, this method of learning had some of its roots in the training of *Taubstumme,* deaf-mutes who could neither speak nor hear. Those who were deaf and mute could not learn to speak by listening to and repeating what they heard. They had to rely on visual cues and in so doing demonstrated that language could be learned visually as well as aurally. Only when students were able to "think themselves into the position of a deaf-mute" would they be cognizant of the importance of phonetics to the study of African languages.[79] By extrapolating from the study of the abnormal, in other words, students would arrive at an understanding of why they had to observe the way sounds were formed before personally repeating them.

In contrast to the deaf-mutes, however, African difference had little to do with *physical* abnormality. Meinhof disparaged those Germans who maintained that "in spite of anatomy . . . the gums of the English are differently built,"[80] when they could not learn to speak English with the proper accent, and he felt likewise with respect to Africans and their languages. To Meinhof, African difference rested in psychology and culture. The missionary G. L. Cleve had made Meinhof aware of the ways in which custom could precipitate sound shift by demonstrating how sounds in some Bantu languages were transformed by the ritualistic wearing of lip pegs and mutilation of teeth.[81]

> With these mutilated organs, a person can, naturally, not articulate all sounds as he can with healthy ones. As a result of the mutilation, a type of articulation thus becomes general. Even after the custom has disappeared, the articulation remains. This theory can also apply to specific cases. So, for example, Yao women wear a big piece of wood in their upper lips. They can't speak the letter f, and because the children learn to speak from the women, the f has disappeared from the language. It has only recently returned with loan words.[82]

In a different vein, Meinhof's mentor Wundt claimed that in the transition from countryside to city, sound shifts of a kind that Meinhof had noted for Swahili often began to occur.

> Wundt has made us aware of a process that is surely worth noticing, namely that in the city, with increased contact, people speak more and more quickly than they do in the country with little contact. . . . Naturally, in quick speech sounds will be more fleetingly pronounced and then disappear entirely. Thus for example in Swahili, which as a coastal and trading language is spoken very quickly, the l after the stressed syllable has as a rule dropped away. Likewise the u after an m has mostly vanished, because both sounds, as lip sounds (bilabials) are very similar. People no longer say múti for tree, but rather m'ti, similar to how we still write "lesen" but actually say "lesn."[83]

Language change was thus related to cultural phenomena, and students would be wise to remember this.

Even so, neither Wundt's nor Cleve's explanation sufficed to explain all sound shifts. This was why Meinhof turned to the phonetics laboratory. In the laboratory African pronunciation was still considered the result of African psychology, but it was ultimately the body, and not the mind, that became the main object of investigation. Meinhof was convinced that the empirical observation of living beings would accord him the opportunity to train Germany's colonizers in proper pronunciation and uncover the sound laws so important to the exposition of African prehistory.[84] His gaze and that of his students rendered Africans objects. This kind of gaze is similar to what Mary Louise Pratt has described in terms of travel writing, where African Others almost disappeared into the landscapes surrounding them, leaving only vestigial traces or "scratches" to indicate their existence.[85] The difference was only that here the gaze was located not in the colonies themselves but, rather, in the midst of a familiar, scientific, and metropolitan laboratory environment.

Because of Meinhof's belief in the importance of phonetics for both the teaching and research of African languages, when the laboratory was finally founded it was expressly crafted to serve these purposes. This was made explicit in the text of the original regulations for the laboratory.

> 1. The laboratory for experimental phonetics is a department of the Seminar for Colonial Languages. Its primary purpose will thus be research on colonial, especially African, languages . . .
> 2. Therefore, apropos paragraph one, students who work on African languages will have priority of use . . .
> 9. All recordings made with the laboratory's investigative machinery are and will remain property of the Seminar for Colonial Languages.[86]

For the first year or two of the laboratory's existence, Meinhof made sure that these regulations were followed and that the laboratory was jealously guarded against too much use on the part of "outsiders," that is, members of the Colonial Institute and public who were not directly involved with African or Pacific language research.[87]

In order to ward off these potential interlopers, Meinhof argued that African and other colonial languages were better objects for scientific observation than their modern or ancient European cousins. This was also one of the reasons that, from the beginning of his career, Meinhof had described himself as a linguist, not a philologist. What did this mean? Anna Morpurgo Davies has shown that in the early nineteenth century, when linguistics or *Sprachwissenschaft* first began to assert itself as an independent, university-sponsored discipline, scholars like Grimm drew a clear distinction between the emergent field of linguistics or comparative philology and classical philology, which had a longer tradition. Linguistics was the study of language *für sich,* as an organism that had "fundamental laws and regularities."[88] It could be investigated without external reference to its written literature. Philology, by contrast, was more of a means to an end, that end being the explication of texts.

By the beginning of the twentieth century, the line separating philology from linguistics had hardened to such a degree that someone like Meinhof, who was classically educated in *Germanistik* and theology, could by dint of the discipline he practiced call himself a natural scientist, more similar to a physicist or chemist than a literary-minded philologist. Meinhof believed that linguistics and philology were completely different. The first was an energetic, modern discipline that focused on the physical production of language. The second was mostly concerned with the kind of musty, crumbling document that Meinhof disdainfully described as "a more or less shadowy fragment of life." The linguist had "the life of the language before him"; sadly, a philologist of, say, ancient Greece or Rome had only the silent remnants of what had once been a distinguished culture.[89]

African and other "colonial" languages made perfect linguistic subjects precisely because they often lacked the extensive written literatures of the *Kultursprachen.* They had to be recorded as they were, in their present, most up-to-date states. There were, in addition, simply so many of them. Ancient languages only offered hints of former depth in the textual artifacts of a few literate scribes, but Africa had hundreds of thriving, interrelated languages. Some were even in what Meinhof termed very "primitive" states of development and changing before European eyes under pressure from external forces, such as neighbors whose languages were more sophisticated.[90] Africa offered Europeans the rare opportunity to see languages metamorphose and, based purely on speculation, let them imagine how their own languages might once also have evolved.

> Natural science works mostly with the comparison of separate, distinct processes, and has in this manner discovered their laws. The linguist can do the same. The languages of primitive peoples are for the most part understood only by a few individuals, never by many millions, as is the case with civilized ones. The smaller this number of individuals is, the larger the number of languages. Thus we have not only some dozen, but hundreds of languages to deal with, and therefore a body of comparative material that in our wildest dreams could not be more extensive. No historical philologist has command of such riches. Now, just as the natural scientist reconstructs the developmental history of similar forms as they appear next to each other, so are we able to rebuild the history of language from closely related languages and dialects. And we are also in the happy position of being able to examine the validity of our constructions in the presence of living objects.[91]

If enough researchers could be mustered, at least some of these languages would be studied, recorded, and then compared to see how closely they corresponded to one another and whether they had similar origins. In this way linguists could determine which languages were oldest by measuring them against the theoretical *Ursprache* and then seeing how many of its forms they had retained. On the basis of what was known about general linguistic development and how languages went through evolutionary "stages," it would be possible to determine who were the oldest inhabitants of Africa, and who the newest.[92]

Meinhof knew that students of African languages had been aware of the importance of general phonology and sound shifts to the history of Africa, or at least to the categorization of its languages, since early in the nineteenth century. Comparative analyses had been undertaken in the *Mithridates* of J. C. Adelung and J. S. Vater in 1812, and the Orientalist Klaproth had produced a description of Kanuri vocabulary in 1826.[93] Koelle had prepared the *Polyglotta Africana* in 1854, and in 1863 Lepsius had created his standard phonetic script for representing all the languages of the world.[94] Yet because Meinhof and his predecessors had been "dependent on simple observation, without experiments,"[95] their findings had remained imprecise. However, thanks to experimental phonetics, a science that first began to take root in the late nineteenth century, linguists suddenly had the opportunity to conduct their research with more sophisticated methods that would, Meinhof hoped, prove useful to both practical and historical studies.

What was experimental phonetics? According to Giulio Panconcelli-Calzia, a naturalized German whom Meinhof appointed as the first director of the phonetics laboratory and one of the premier experimental phoneticians of his day, "the task of experimental phonetics" lay in "determining, dissecting, classifying, and researching the conditions of change in phonetic processes occurring in the present, independent of geographical location."[96] Experiment itself was best defined as "the intentional, arbitrary creation of a phenomenon under any simplification or change of factors."[97] Where untrained observers would "wait patiently"[98] for the appearance of such phenomena, the experimental phonetician would take the matter into his own hands, using either organic or mechanical methods to produce the desired effects in his subjects.

The "organic" methods that Panconcelli-Calzia mentioned were conducted simply, using hearing, sight, or touch.[99] Researchers would watch the faces and mouths of their test subjects to see what sorts of movements these made when certain sounds were being produced, or place their hands on their heads, noses, chests, or larynxes in order to ascertain how they vibrated during speech. One might imagine that Meinhof's students standing in front of their mirrors, assessing how they spoke, could have made use of such techniques. By contrast, the mechanical methods, which Panconcelli-Calzia also termed "non-organic," are more difficult to describe and, to some extent, remain obscure.[100] Nonetheless, it is clear that experimental phonetic machinery—some of it designed to "fix" the movement of speech pictorially in graphs, some of it producing more transitory results—supplemented the five senses in determining how language functioned. X-rays "supported the eye" by displaying "the movements of the diaphragm, if only momentarily and . . . through the shadow of the liver."[101] X-rays could show movement of the larynx, which could also be observed using a laryngoscope, a tool for peering down the throat.[102] Neither of these, however, produced fixed images that could be analyzed after the fact. Therefore, such devices were augmented by machines that captured the rise and fall of sound graphically, as exhibited by airflow.[103] Among these the most important was the kymograph, a motorized, rotating drum upon which a stylus charted the fundamental frequency of a speaker's voice in sinusoidal curves as the test subject spoke into a tube.[104] Sarah Barrows, an American who visited the Phonetics Laboratory in the 1910s, enthused that the kymograph represented what was "really a new and indirect way of writing, in which instead of words being transcribed by the hand in the conventional spelling, they are recorded by the instrument as they are formed by the organs of speech."[105]

These experiments, plainly, had to be conducted with living beings. Panconcelli-Calzia disparaged nineteenth-century efforts to study phonetic processes with dead material, though he did use cadavers himself in some instances.[106] Moreover, the experiments had to be "harmless." Any invasive procedures, for example tracheotomy, were not acceptable. They were not indicative of any "normal condition" and, besides, were unpleasant and painful for the person being tested.[107] In any event, experimental phonetics obviously demanded that test subjects be available; without them, the experiments could not go forward. Since colonialism demanded further investigation of African languages, Africans were indispensable to experimental phonetics.

Much to Meinhof's chagrin, however, Africans were not the only ones examined in the laboratory. Despite his protests, the laboratory was eventually opened up to other disciplines and the wider public. Indeed, not long after its foundation the laboratory was already being used for various other purposes, including music lessons, research on the deaf-mute, and investigation into sounds produced in other languages, among them *Kultursprachen.*[108] Even so, Barrows did refer to the Africans as the laboratory's premier *Experimentierkaninchen* (guinea pigs), evoking a particularly chilling image.[109] Further, the items that decorated the *Seminar für Kolonialsprachen* itself recalled the importance of physicality to its purpose at every turn; in 1912, the department held an exhibition, in which the "tools" of African studies were proudly on display. The exhibit emphasized the importance of bodies, as opposed to texts, for *Afrikanistik.* Shown were "anatomical preparations, models of speech organs, x-ray pictures, and plaques."[110] Everywhere the significance of physical science, of biology, of anatomy, predominated. At least at the beginning the department could not, realistically, have shared space with the East Asian Seminar. In terms of how their subjects were represented in the classroom, they were poles apart. In one case it was a written text that was investigated; in the other, the body.

The concern with physicality at the phonetics laboratory signaled a sharp turn away from missionary attention to language as an expression of culture and psychology. Biology supplanted spirit, and it was physical difference that mattered most. Still, all the efforts that were made to evaluate anatomical phenomena in the laboratory were done in the service of linguistic classification, so that once again it was language, rather than physical characteristics, that determined the categorization of mankind into discrete groups. In addition, when we remember that dissimilar physical attributes were considered the result of social praxis, as with the Yao women who wore lip-pegs, we begin to see that even when anatomy was the apparent object of investigation, culture was paramount.

The Department of Colonial Languages and the Phonetics Laboratory were the ultimate hypermetropolitan spaces. They offered students an opportunity to observe Africans in a controlled environment, which would allow their languages to be dissected better than they could have been in the colonies. The missionaries who had traditionally collected and transcribed African languages usually lacked the necessary preparation and training to make accurate phonetic transcriptions, thus unleashing the "wild" orthographies Meinhof often bemoaned. With the advanced technology in Hamburg that did not exist in Africa, it suddenly became much easier to extract linguistic and phonetic information. Languages could be recorded by phonograph in the laboratory and then played back repeatedly until a student was able to mimic the sounds it produced.

The true "field" was never completely devoid of technology either.

When Meinhof traveled to Kordofan in the Anglo-Egyptian Sudan in 1914, he was both shocked and pleased to find a phonograph warbling under a kiosk in a distant desert outpost far removed not only from Germany but from the Sudanese capital, Khartoum.[111] The supposed boundary separating metropole from colony had broken down here, too, with Western technology removed from center to periphery. While colonial power was still vested with European authorities, who controlled machines such as the phonograph and kymograph, they were also estranged from their original context in the highly ordered laboratory in their passage to souk or missionary station.

Once Germanists and music teachers had "infiltrated" the laboratory, the dichotomy between self and other that had been established in the seminar also began to break down, as the scientific gaze turned inward, from Africans to Europeans. This does not diminish the argument that Meinhof and his colleagues had originally constructed both seminar and laboratory as extracolonial arenas for the analysis of non-European peoples. Rather, it demonstrates the extent to which the line separating self from other had become blurred and confused. The laboratory was supposed to be the ideal setting in which to examine Africans. Yet the very fact that not only Africans but also "normal" and "abnormal" Europeans eventually came under scrutiny called the whole project into question, as the laboratory metamorphosed from a space specifically designed for the study of Africans to one more involved in cataloging an entire range of human phenomena.

Conclusion

The discipline of African studies changed considerably after its institutionalization in Berlin and Hamburg. Missionaries remained pivotal, but especially in Hamburg Meinhof reached out to new audiences, whether in his public lectures, through his laboratory, or with his journal, which included proverbs, sagas, and ethnographic descriptions alongside linguistic analyses. In addition the subject, whose preinstitutional origins were not linked with a specific national or imperial tradition, had become an appendage of German colonialism by the time that Meinhof joined the institute. Between his arrival in Hamburg in 1909 and the outbreak of World War I in 1914, most of the students he trained were German businesspeople, colonial officials, or missionaries going to Africa to work for or alongside the German Empire. Non-German scholars did write for Meinhof's

Zeitschrift in English, French, and Italian, but the majority of its authors wrote in German and were stationed in a German colony. Once Carl Büttner had bemoaned the fact that Germans, the best Africanist linguists, were forced to write in English. Under his student Meinhof's direction, however, the discipline of African philology was fully "Germanized."

Or was it? None of the German missionaries or professional linguists in Berlin, Hamburg, or Africa itself would have gotten very far without African assistance. In the field, Africans patiently taught missionaries their languages, providing them with the word lists, folk tales, and proverbs that later appeared in the pages of Büttner's *Zeitschrift für Afrikanische Sprachen* or Meinhof's *Zeitschrift für Kolonialsprachen.* Indeed, most of the grammars, dictionaries, and journal articles that German scholars produced were really coauthored with Africans, some of whom received mention in their publications, and many others who did not. The next chapter tells their story.

CHAPTER 6

Of Conjunctions, Comportment, and Clothing: African Teaching Assistants in Berlin and Hamburg, 1889–1919

In 1885 Njo Dibone traveled from Cameroon to Pomerania for the purpose of learning German from Meinhof. The specifics of Dibone's reason for coming to Germany, as well as why he wanted to learn the language, are obscure. He seems to have made the journey with an Admiral von Holtzendorff, the fiancé of one of Meinhof's relatives, who perhaps hoped that Dibone would learn German for business purposes.[1] Whatever Dibone's original aims, his travels marked the beginning of a connection that would grow to be more than a simple student-teacher relationship. While Meinhof was teaching Dibone German, Dibone began to instruct the then-minister in his native language, Duala. Since it was not long after their meeting that Meinhof embarked on his career in African linguistic and ethnographic research, there is little doubt that Dibone had a decided influence on Meinhof's later life.

Without Dibone, Meinhof would probably not have made as rapid progress in his early philological studies, because there were few Africans living in Germany who would have had cause to travel to Zizow to assist him. At the time, Meinhof knew no one else who was fluent in a Bantu language and willing to work with him on a consistent, daily basis. True, he was already friends with Büttner, but Büttner was living in Berlin and occupied with his responsibilities there. As an armchair scholar who did not often leave Germany, in the 1880s Meinhof was only beginning to acquaint himself with the network of missionary linguists who would later become his core group of students and admirers. Dibone was consequently the first to teach Meinhof an African language, accounting for his early preference to write about Duala and related dialects.[2]

Before he left Zizow, then, Meinhof sat reading in his armchair and was usually at the mercy of information supplied by others, both Africans like Dibone and missionaries who had more direct access to African languages in the field. Either way, neither Meinhof nor his missionary colleagues could have completed their work without African assistance; during an era when few Europeans understood African languages or knew much about African history and culture, they were beholden to African assistants and informants for most of their knowledge.

There is scant personal information regarding Dibone, who was a nephew of the Duala king Akwa and around twenty-eight years old in 1900, which means that he was a teenager when he first met Meinhof in the mid-1880s.[3] Nonetheless, while he was not a scholar per se and probably did not have any university training, Dibone had a lasting impact on the emergence and development of African studies in Germany. Dibone and others like him, who came to Germany to be teaching assistants and informants in Zizow, Berlin's Seminar for Oriental Languages, or Hamburg's Colonial Institute, therefore provided Germans with a powerful counterimage of the "African." These colonial subjects were quite different from what most Germans of the period might have imagined or, in some instances, even had occasion to see in encounters with the African men and women who appeared in touring "people exhibitions."[4] African teachers, who were commonly known either as *Lektoren* or *Sprachgehilfen,*[5] did not match the carefully cultivated stereotype of the purportedly "wild" natives who were so often put on display in Germany and elsewhere.[6] Rather, they quietly mixed with Germans in quotidian settings and had "normal" jobs that accorded them a specific niche in German society, if a problematic and contested one. African lecturers also had the opportunity to shape linguistic and anthropological discourses that were blossoming around the turn of the twentieth century, as they quite literally had the ears of some of the most well-respected Africanist scholars in Germany.

German academics thus needed African assistants, and they were central to the process of colonial knowledge production. Yet largely because of a dearth of evidence, little has been said about their contributions to ethnographic or linguistic scholarship, or about the pressures they faced living among a foreign people whose prevalent vision of Africa was still guided by notions of desolation and primitivity. *Lektoren* were not in Germany to entertain but rather to teach, and this assured a complex relationship; they may have been despised or looked down upon because of their "race," but it was difficult to deny their pedagogical importance.

In this chapter I will attempt to bring Germany's African teaching assistants back into German colonial history.[7] I hope to reinscribe the history of the *Lektoren* in the German "colonial library" and show how they understood their own position within the empire. Gaurav Desai has argued that such a "colonial library" needs to be redefined to incorporate texts produced by colonial Africans with attention to how their work not only mirrored but contributed to shaping colonial discourse.[8] In keeping with Desai, I will address both how *Lektoren* participated in the institutionalization of African studies in Germany and also how their movements—intellectual and otherwise—were limited by a society that assigned them very specific roles. While I will focus on the assistants' positions in the lecture hall and study, then, I will not restrict myself to their classroom experiences.

Although direct information concerning the *Lektoren* is scarce and usually comes from the German point of view, it still allows a glimpse into how African teaching assistants lived in cities like Berlin and Hamburg. Such information also demonstrates that Africans did not only confirm German stereotypes of African "civilization" and the levels it had reached; they also subverted those same stereotypes and, in some cases, used them to their own personal advantage. Moreover, through the assistants we get an idea of how much agency Africans actually had with respect to intellectual projects that have usually been assumed to be completely of European making.

On the German side, sources show how critical African—and other non-European—assistants were to the formation of a practical linguistic discipline, which was meant to supply its students not only with academic theories but also with the necessary tools for foreign conquest. Germans were caught in a double bind: Both those who gave instruction in African languages as well as the colonial civil servants, soldiers, and missionaries who were required to learn them needed African help but also feared giving Africans too much power. Protestant missionaries are again especially relevant to the story of the African assistants in Germany, since many of the *Lektoren* and *Sprachgehilfen* came to the country because of their association with the mission. African assistants such as the Ewe teacher Andreas Anno, who was a student of the North German Missionary Society in Accra, traveled to Berlin expressly to ingratiate themselves with the mission and try to find a role in it.[9] Both Meinhof and his missionary colleagues were grateful to the *Lektoren,* but the question of who was considered superior and who inferior always lurked at the edges of their relationships.

African *Lektoren* and *Sprachgehilfen* in Germany: Life at the Margins

The practice of bringing Africans to Germany started well before the foundation of either the Berlin Seminar for Oriental Languages or the Hamburg Colonial Institute. Throughout the nineteenth century, individual explorers in Africa took interpreters and guides that they met on the continent back to Germany.[10] In the late 1830s, for instance, Duke Maximilian of Bavaria brought four freed slaves from Ethiopia and the Sudan to Munich. Karl Tutschek, tutor to the duke's son, Prince Louis, also taught the Africans, who included Musallam Motekutu, a fourteen-year-old boy from Dar Fur who had been kidnapped and sold into slavery in Egypt. Tutschek worked with Motekutu and the others on a transcription of Oromo, the same language that Krapf would soon study.[11]

As for Krapf himself, in the 1850s and 1860s he repeatedly asked to have Ethiopians fluent in Oromo come to Württemburg and help him translate the Bible into that language.[12] An Ethiopian man named Martsha, who had received a Western education from the CMS in Bombay, also visited Krapf in his hometown of Korntal in 1868 and offered to translate the Bible into another language, Tigre, for the BFBS.[13] By the early 1870s, there were four Ethiopians employed as translators at Saint Chrischona, Basel's missionary training center. Krapf was adamant that the men work with him on his translations, commenting, "I am well-versed in Hebrew & read & speak the Amharic fluently, but it is absolutely necessary that a European who translates or revises the Bible in a foreign language, should be assisted by a native in order to issue a correct edition. It may be literally correct, but whether it is according to the genius of the foreign language is another question if the European has not any native at hand."[14] Well before the Berlin Seminar or indeed Carl Meinhof hired Africans to work with them, then, missionaries like Krapf were doing the same.[15]

As the century drew to a close and Germany became an imperial power, more Africans were making their way to the *Kaiserreich.* Some arrived with the increasingly popular *Völkerschauen,* while others, who belonged to wealthy African families like the Bells in Cameroon, traveled to the metropole for education.[16] The assistants arrived as part of this wave, some finding their way to Berlin because of connections with the colonial government, others because of ties to Protestant missionary societies or German businesses. Whatever their exact motivations for coming, *Lek-*

toren seem to have been drawn to Germany by a desire for social and financial mobility and a hope for the betterment of their own social standing.

All of the new visitors contributed to the development of a general image of Africa. Even so, not all Africans who lived in Germany were viewed the same way. While participants in the *Völkerschauen* were seen as rough and primitive, African *Lektoren* assumed a significantly higher status, if one that was always in question and under threat. Whereas members of people exhibitions were often treated with disdain, the discourse surrounding *Lektoren* was one of capability and the African potential for growth under European guidance. In this it appeared similar to the nineteenth-century missionary discourse on Africans, which also stressed African promise. Once in Germany, moreover, the assistants even bore the external "marks" of European respectability. On the whole they were better educated, with some, such as the Togolese Viktor Toso and the Ewondo chief Karl Atangana, having studied at Christian mission schools, and others, such as the early Swahili *Lektoren* Suleiman bin Said and Amir bin Nasur coming from traditional Islamic schools in Zanzibar or elsewhere in the Arab world.[17]

In addition, the assistants almost always donned Western dress. Here, though, the vexed position of Africans in Germany was brought into sharp relief, as clothing itself was somehow considered "un-African." Despite all of Meinhof's African acquaintances, he was still concerned that each new assistant might come to Germany naked, or in some state of undress.[18] On the one hand, Meinhof thought the *Sprachgehilfen* more "civilized" than other Africans because they had Western education and sustained his academic research. On the other hand, there was always fear that the assistants would revert to some prior stage of primitivity, shedding their European trappings and wreaking havoc in the streets of Berlin. It is telling that the one African assistant who was actually asked to put on "traditional" dress for his seminars was Hassan Taufik (Tewfink), a lecturer in Egyptian Arabic. One of the provisions in the contract that he signed with the Seminar for Oriental Languages in 1887 even stated that Taufik was to "wear his oriental costume when he is among professors or students of the department."[19] While it is unclear why Taufik was asked to wear his "oriental" costume and the sub-Saharan African teaching assistants were not, it may have been because German teachers thought they had no appropriate "native" outfits and were always nude or scantily clad. Arabs were plainly accorded a level of civilizational development that Africans were not. The general "image" of an Arab in Germany may have been of a man in "traditional dress," while that of an African was of a man wearing considerably less. *Völkerschauen* probably reaffirmed this image, since the Africans who worked for them typically performed in "authentic" traveling villages while wearing "traditional" garb.[20]

While *Lektoren* and *Sprachgehilfen* outwardly conformed to German standards of education, comportment, and dress, they were never placed on a par with white Germans. They occupied a middle space in which cultural signs jockeyed for position with racial ones.[21] African assistants were, however, undeniably integral to the learning process at the Berlin Seminar and Hamburg Institute. When discussions concerning the shape the seminar was to take were first initiated in the mid-1880s, the employment of "native-speaking" lecturers to work with German teachers was already a given. The principal methodology of the seminar rested on a division of labor between these two groups. Sachau held that this particular approach to language training was wholly unique to Germany.[22] Whether or not this was true is uncertain; the *École des langues orientales vivantes* in Paris did use what were termed *répetiteurs* to aid French professors in the classroom.[23] There is, however, no evidence of whether these were "natives" or not. Further, people throughout Europe did seem to admire the German system of "exotic" language training, which Sachau proudly acknowledged.[24]

Africans of course had to be recruited before the seminar's teaching program could be realized. In the beginning, it did not seem difficult to find people willing to make the journey to Berlin. The first *Lektoren* had connections with the German colonial government, and civil servants in the colonies sometimes arranged employment. This was the case with Suleiman bin Said, the first of the sub-Saharan African teachers in Berlin. He arrived in 1889, when he was seventeen. A former pupil of the seminar stationed in Dar-es-salaam, Karl Reinhardt, became acquainted with Said after Sachau asked him to find an assistant for Büttner.[25] Reinhardt knew Said's father, which likely smoothed the son's passage to Berlin.[26] The meetings between Reinhardt and Said went well, and soon the colonial officer was negotiating an agreement between Said and the seminar. In a written contract, Said acknowledged his intent to teach under Sachau's authority in Berlin. Said committed himself to three years' service and confirmed that he was to be paid 200 Marks a month.[27] This was comparatively less than what the Chinese *Lektoren* Au Fung Tschii and Hsüeh Tschen received in their respective contracts one year later, in 1890; Au Fung Tschii was offered 300 marks a month,[28] and Hsüeh Tschen was granted 350.[29]

Said's stay in Berlin was short, as he died of unknown causes after less than two years. Nonetheless, his case says a lot about German perceptions of Africans and what position they assumed in imperial society. Said's ethnicity and "race" were never as fixed as the founders of the seminar might have liked. Said had been hired to teach Swahili, but it is unclear if he actually considered himself Swahili.[30] His father was Arab and had emigrated from Oman to Zanzibar as a young man, where he met and married Said's mother.[31] From what can be pieced together, Said likely identified himself as much with the Arabs as with the Swahili. He compiled and published a list of "Sitten der Sansibarleute" (Customs of the Sansibari), which included discussions of both Arab and Swahili traditions. Further, soon after Said's departure from German East Africa, Reinhardt wrote to Sachau in exasperated dismay because "in Sleman's [*sic*] last letter to his father, he spoke very rudely of the situation with his salary . . . which leads me to the conclusion that Sleman [*sic*] has been treated as an Arab, and not as a Swahili, which he is, in other words he has been spoiled."[32] The implication was that as a Swahili Said had no right to complain about his wages—which were likely the main reason that he was in Germany, as he sent a portion of his salary home each month—but as an Arab, a member of a more "civilized" group, he might have.

Arabs—and other *Lektoren* not from sub-Saharan Africa—generally assumed a higher status at the Seminar for Oriental Languages. For example, Asian and North African teaching assistants were often older. Chinese teachers Hsüeh Tschen and Au Fung Tschii were thirty-seven and forty-two, respectively, whereas most of the Africans were only in their late teens or early twenties when they arrived in Berlin. Consequently, where the two Chinese *Lektoren* already had years of experience teaching and translating in China, the Africans usually had little training prior to their employment in Germany.

Non-African *Lektoren* were also given more responsibilities than African ones and had higher social standing. African teaching assistants had a variety of duties: They helped European instructors with their lectures, conducted speaking exercises with students, aided in the teaching of Arabic script, continued the work of informants in the colonies with linguistic transcription, submitted themselves to phonetic research, and related oral histories. On the face of it these responsibilities were not markedly different from those of their Asian and North African colleagues. At the same time, the work expected of Asians and North Africans was less regulated and monitored. They were more likely to have higher education and to have obligations outside the seminar. During his stay in Berlin, Taufik compiled a manuscript at the request of the Egyptian government and also produced several reports on life in Germany. Moreover, upon leaving the seminar Taufik was sent to London to work for Egypt there.[33] His successor, Mohammed Nassar, studied engineering and Egyptology in addition to teaching eighteen hours a week at the seminar, and he expressed hope of becoming the first indigenous Egyptologist of distinction.[34] Amin Ma'arbes, who taught Syrian Arabic for fifteen years, offered three independent courses on the subjects "1001 Nights," "Exercises in Reading and Explaining Arabic Script," and "Newspapers and Practice in Writing." He chose his own books for class, argued with one of the German instructors over what was the best text, and was married to a German woman, Ottilie Kaatz, apparently without any objections or repercussions.[35]

Sub-Saharan African *Lektoren* did not always assume responsibilities inferior to those of other *Lektoren.* Some translated and annotated texts, much as did North Africans and Asians. One might also contend that because they lacked the experience of their older colleagues, it was reasonable for the sub-Saharan African *Lektoren* not to do the same kind of work as the more well-trained Asians and North Africans. However, since some sub-Saharan African assistants remained in Germany for several years and had occasion to improve their teaching abilities, this argument is questionable. In addition, the African assistants' roles were often more subservient than those of *Lektoren* from China or the Middle East. The first, and most significant, of the Africans' duties involved standing next to a German coworker and mimicking difficult pronunciations. While this was not the same as leading a class, it was arguably of just as much significance. African *Lektoren* from the German colonies made themselves indispensable in this way, as few Germans, even those with advanced linguistic training, possessed perfect pronunciation in an African language. There was, however, a flip side to the relationship between African *Lektoren* and German teachers and students. *Lektoren* were considered invaluable but not because of their linguistic knowledge. Instead, they were prized for the purely physical ability to make certain sounds. Their worth to the developing science of phonetics in particular was assessed not on merit or personal skill but on the movement of vocal organs.

The African assistants' duties also extended outside the lecture hall, and in some situations they were able to exert more individual authority. After formal courses were over in the evening, *Lektoren* held speaking practice for their pupils, and here they were mostly in charge. In 1892, a list of how many students had sought out-of-class assistance from Amur bin Nasur, the man who succeeded Said as Swahili *Lektor,* was compiled. Nasur did not have many visitors; he usually had only two to three guests per day, out of ten students.[36] Even so, in a smaller, one-on-one environment, Nasur had occasion to shape his pupils' understanding of Swahili in much the same way that a contemporary graduate student might when teaching undergraduates a foreign language. At the same time, teaching freedom was not entirely open to the African assistants. The Colonial Institute did not allow its assistants to teach unsupervised, and while *Lektoren* did hold independent language exercises at the seminar in Berlin, they did not have their own courses in the way that Ma'arbes, the Arabic instructor, did.

The assistants' lives were proscribed in other ways that limited their movements in and outside of the classroom. Sexual politics, for example, were governed by the notion that Africans and Germans were not to form intimate relationships. When they did, it was at their own peril. In 1900, the Seminar for Oriental Languages decided to hire Mtoro bin Mwinyi Bakari, who was discussed in chapter 3, as a Swahili assistant. Bakari, who had been a tax collector in Bagamoyo, took the position in order to provide financial support for his wife and daughter in East Africa. While the first few years of his tenure passed without comment, by 1904 Bakari had caused a stir. Despite his wife in Bagamoyo, he had become engaged to a German woman named Bertha Hilske; not only that, another German woman had contacted the seminar to complain that Bakari had been engaged to her, and then left her. Bakari claimed that, as his Swahili wife had been unfaithful, he wanted a divorce and sent her a letter that said as much. Neither Velten nor the other authorities at the seminar believed that Bakari's proclamation of divorce was legal, however, and they saw him as still married.[37]

Bakari's situation deteriorated from this point. Although he had been looked upon favorably and considered an excellent instructor during his first three years at the seminar, Velten, his supervisor, now contended that this *Lektor*'s character was "weak," and that he was being blatantly manipulated by Hilske and her mother, whom Velten believed were only interested in Bakari's salary. The reasons for which Velten ascribed a weak character to Bakari are left largely unexplained, but there is the sense that, as an African, he was especially prone to being exploited by more intelligent and ingenious Germans, in particular women of "dubious" morals. Velten also contended that Bakari's work had suffered as a result of the liaison, as "it is well known that the Negro in love is, in his mindlessness

[*Stumpfsinn*], incapable of any work." The consequences of Bakari marrying Hilske could prove yet direr. The marriage, Velten intoned, had the potential to throw sexual—and racial—hierarchies into jeopardy in both colony and metropole. Bakari had already "sassed" a student by refusing to answer a question after the end of a class, showing "shocking" disrespect toward a white man.[38] Further, if he ended up bringing Hilske to East Africa, Bakari's actions would be

> of the greatest disadvantage for the reputation of Europeans in general and the few German women in the colonies in particular. Such a case has still not come to light in any of our African colonies, and hopefully will never come to pass. A German girl who is capable of marrying a black will surely sink even deeper in the colonies and bring shame to all Europeans. Even if the Europeans know just what to think of such a person, in the natives' eyes she will always remain the white woman, the German woman.[39]

Here Velten argued for a specific racial order, one that had to be maintained both within and beyond Germany. Fear that Bakari had and would continue to transgress the boundaries of this order led to his removal from the seminar and, although he briefly resurfaced later at the Colonial Institute, his marriage to Hilske ultimately excluded him from the company of "civilized" Africans who worked in the German academy. Having not complied with the hierarchical, racial order that set Africans apart from Germans, Bakari—and, for that matter, Hilske—lost their social standing and retreated to the margins of German society. Unlike the Moroccan Ma'arbes, whose marriage to Ottilie Kaatz was not questioned or challenged, Bakari's union with Hilske was viewed as too dangerous to allow.

Bakari's "sin" redounds through the history of African *Lektoren* in Germany. After he was cast out, the *Reichskolonialamt* decided that assistants should remain no longer than a year and a half in Berlin before being replaced, so that they would not have time to adapt to their surroundings or form intimate relationships. Furthermore, certain stipulations were added to the general contract between the seminar and the assistants, namely, that future Swahili *Lektoren* "reside with a suitable vocational school teacher" during their tenure in Berlin.[40]

Fear of rampant African sexuality also forestalled the employment of certain assistants. For instance, South West Africans were never allowed to teach in Germany. When Meinhof attempted to procure Nama and

Ovambo assistants for the Colonial Institute, the colonial government in German South West Africa expressed its "grave doubts" as to whether a native from the protectorate should be allowed to travel abroad.[41] Such a native, the government claimed, would "after the experience return completely spoiled for local conditions."[42] The inhabitants of South West Africa were depicted as tending more to depravity than those in Germany's other African colonies. Given the opportunity to leave, it was said they would drink, have untoward relationships with loose German women, and basically carouse about town in the most immoral of fashions. The governor of the colony at the time, Oskar Hintrager, intoned that "even with the sharpest supervision" the Ovambo people would be so overwhelmed by what they encountered in Hamburg that they would be unable to understand or digest it. Confrontations with the German working class—the "inferior male and female elements," as Hintrager put it—would hopelessly confuse them, and they would return to South West Africa believing they could treat its German settlers just as they had poor women in the metropole.[43]

There was thus anxiety that Africans, once exposed to German culture, would be unwilling to "stay in their place." After all, the government of German South West Africa maintained that it was three natives—Friedrich Maharero, Ferdinand Zemunja, and Titus Tjcamuhaha—who after participating in the Berlin Colonial Exhibition of 1896 returned to South West Africa and incited their countrymen to revolt in 1903.[44] This ultimately led to the disastrous Herero war. German settlers in South West Africa were especially concerned with issues of miscegenation; as Kundrus has argued, they wanted to create an ideal, ethnically pure society that would stand as a counterpoint to the immorality that was ravaging the metropole as it continued to modernize.[45] The idea of even more Africans getting ideas "above their station" in Berlin or Hamburg probably terrified them.

The realization that Europeans were not necessarily as intelligent or strong as Africans threatened German authority. African power subverted fixed racial hierarchies, which depicted blacks as inferior to whites, Asians, and Arabs. It also threw questions of citizenship and belongingness in the relatively new German state into doubt; as Wildenthal has shown, mixed marriages in the German colonies precipitated heated debate over who was German and who not. According to the citizenship laws of 1870 and 1913, citizenship was passed through the male line, so that even if a person's mother was non-European, he or she could still be considered German.

However, especially after the Herero war in South West Africa and Maji-Maji revolt in East Africa, citizenship of even those who had white fathers was called into question.[46] If mixed marriages between white men and black women were threatening, how much more so must have been unions of black men with white women, where the progeny would very decidedly not be German and the woman herself would forfeit her Germanness upon entering into the relationship.

African Ethnographies of Germany

The roles the assistants played were also academic ones, since they appeared in the classroom as masters of a particular knowledge who, while usually under European supervision, had some leverage in determining how their languages were portrayed. *Lektoren* worked within a German methodological framework that demanded the presence of a native assistant. They also moved within a German world, where they were only welcomed if they behaved in a certain manner and did not transgress racial boundaries. Even so, their very appearance in the classroom meant that they had some control over linguistic instruction. This was the most clear in instances when Africans aided German scholars with linguistic transcription.

One of the best examples of this kind of collaboration was Karl Atangana, Maria Biloa, Johannes Ngumu, and Paul Messi's contribution to Martin Heepe's *Jaunde-Texte* (Ewondo Texts). In order to complete a phonetic description of the Cameroonian language, Heepe, then a lecturer at the Colonial Institute, wanted to address problems concerning the nature of musical tone and sentence melody with the assistance of Atangana, an Ewondo chief who was also an assistant to Meinhof, Atangana's wife Biloa, his scribe Ngumu, and his nephew Messi. The group worked together for two years in the pre–World War I era, with Heepe recording the words and sounds that Atangana, Biloa, Ngumu, and Messi produced. The book that resulted was a joint effort.

Assistants occasionally received higher praise for individual contributions to linguistic study as well. When Sachau and Velten chastised Bakari for his relationship with Hilske, Meinhof defended him on the grounds that his personal life had not affected his performance in the classroom, and that he was ideally suited and prepared for linguistic work.[47] Meinhof was not the only one who had faith in Bakari; later he was briefly commissioned to give lessons to members of the Berlin Missionary Society.[48] Toso, too, was praised for his contributions to Meinhof's scholarship in Ewe, Toso's native language; indeed, Meinhof observed that, far from being unwilling to express his opinions, Toso sometimes argued fine points of grammar with him.[49]

There was, however, a shadow side to the significance of African participation in phonetic experiments: *Lektoren* were again described more as objects of study than academic contributors. In the section of Heepe's *Jaunde-Texte* devoted to phonetic analysis, there is a clear division between his tasks and those of the assistants. Heepe was the "scholar" whose project this ultimately was, while the others were there to "speak" into machines such as the kymograph.[50] They were necessary to the project for their physical capabilities, not their mental ones.

African *Lektoren* in Germany were trapped between two conflicting roles. In one sense they were academic peers. On other occasions, however, they were equated with pieces of technical equipment. Yet the assistants also fulfilled another function, which reinforced their intellectual significance and again demonstrated how much German researchers depended on them. From the earliest days of the seminar, assistants described their lives and traditions in various publications, and it was here that their voices came through most clearly, if often in translation. Said put together his list of Zanzibar customs for an anthology that Büttner compiled, and Amur bin Nasur contributed his life story for the same. Many other assistants—including Atangana, Messi, and Toso—wrote their own ethnographic texts or had them transcribed by Germans.

Early on Njo Dibone, Meinhof's teacher in Zizow, also assisted with literary and anthropological pursuits. While Dibone was living with Meinhof, he compiled a collection of *Märchen aus Kamerun* (*Fairy Tales from Cameroon*) with Elli Meinhof.[51] Moreover, Dibone negotiated the collection of West African idols for Luschan, Meinhof's friend and anthropologist colleague. Meinhof commented to Luschan that Dibone, in part owing to his position as King Akwa's nephew, had been able to supply Meinhof with local literature when no one else could. He therefore believed that Dibone would be able to procure the idols and create a catalog with the name and functional description of each.

Meinhof's assessment of Dibone's efforts was, unfortunately, not entirely positive. Meinhof complained that Dibone sometimes asked for financial compensation for his anthropological and linguistic work. The linguist presented Dibone's interest in payment in an unflattering, racist light, remarking to Luschan that "he has, as you know with negroes, his sensitive points, that is with money." It is difficult to assess what Dibone's actual position with regard to the work he did for Meinhof was. However, it is certainly possible that, as the main person in charge of business and trade for the Akwa family, Dibone had a vested interest in increasing its well-being, one that could be fulfilled by participating in academic research.[52]

There was also a different kind of economic impetus for *Lektoren* to provide information about their cultures. Said's "Customs of the Zanzibari" offered Germans a template for how to behave on the island, especially when conducting business deals. His text described how various inhabitants of the island interacted with each other, and what formulas Europeans should follow to facilitate relations with both the Swahili and the Arabs. If Germans wanted to be seen as polite, they would have to greet natives with the traditional *Hodi* and treat them with a certain degree of respect. Guests would have to use not only proper body language but also specific words and correct pronunciation. Said went out of his way to define certain terms in minute detail, such as *anzali,* which referred to a "rude" or "crass" person, and would likely apply to those individuals who were "uneducated" and "did not know how to speak." Said's writings on Zanzibar were not only descriptive but also prescriptive, offering a lesson to Germans who wanted to enter into economic or political partnerships in the area. By explaining exactly how those Germans should behave, Said was engaged in a "practical translation" between Swahili or Arab and German culture, one that supplied travelers with the information necessary to work in East Africa.[53]

While Said described only the Swahili and Arab customs of Zanzibar, Nasur compared the two cultures he knew best, the Swahili and the German. On the one hand, he translated Zanzibari culture for the Germans as Said had done, providing data on island life for German intellectual—and possibly economic—consumption. On the other, he became a positive critic of German culture, chronicling his interactions with "locals" in Berlin in a mostly optimistic fashion. Nasur depicted Germany as a neat, orderly place whose streets were "like silk" and that was "illuminated like a lamp, so that if there is moonlight you will not even notice it among the profusion of lamps." The houses, all of which had "at least three or four floors," compared with nothing he had seen before, and although poor Germans had to live in their cellars, these cellars were just like "the house of Taria," a rich Indian, in Zanzibar.[54]

In contrast to Berlin, Nasur's home city of Zanzibar was not clean or well ordered. He pictured it instead as a riot of color, sound, and confusion, filled with "cannibals" who, although they "admittedly did not eat flesh itself, consumed money" from unsuspecting tourists. Cheaters and thieves lurked all around, the implication being that if a German did not watch himself, he would be utterly lost.[55] Still, not everything in Zanzibar was unpalatable. German visitors could find quite friendly Arab and Swahili hosts, even if Nasur did warn them to "watch out" for inhabitants of the Comoros Islands, whom he characterized as particularly devious and untrustworthy.[56]

Nasur conducted a brief ethnography of Germany, describing its people as well as their surroundings. Germany was silent, empty, leeched of life, and this was a good thing, whereas Zanzibar was crowded and dangerous, and this was in part negative. However, even without knowing more about Nasur's background, we can surmise that his exultant opinions of Germany might have stemmed from the fact that he was writing for a German audience in general, and for Büttner in particular. He lavished praise upon the Swahili teacher in his text, lauding his hospitality and willingness to help the *Lektor* become acclimated to the unfamiliar surroundings of Berlin.[57]

Yet other evidence suggests that Nasur's German experience was not quite so rosy. In private correspondence, Nasur voiced dissatisfaction with Germany and its policies toward Africans, and he also expressed longing for Zanzibar. In an 1895 letter to Sachau, Nasur complained that, although he had been working for the seminar for four years, he had never been granted vacation. He noted that German colonial officials who were posted overseas were given six months of leave after only two years' service. Nasur found this unacceptable, explaining that "in my case you should take into consideration the fact that I am in a much worse position than are the German civil servants, because I have been completely removed from the habits of my homeland, my countrymen, and fellow religious believers, and been placed in a world that was originally wholly foreign to me."[58] Wistful for home, and especially upset about having lost several family members while in Berlin, Nasur both chastised his German employers and depicted a Zanzibar that, far from being a cheater's paradise, was a place to which he very much wanted to return.

While it remains difficult to assess the assistants' exact motives for writing ethnographic texts, it is clear that for Said and Nasur race was constructed very differently than it was for scholars like Meinhof. In many of the more than six hundred books and articles that he wrote in his lifetime, Meinhof struggled to define African racial hierarchies and where various groups fit within them. Theoretically, as a Bantu-speaking people he considered the Swahili at the "midpoint" of African development, between the less evolved Sudanic speakers and the more advanced Hamites.[59] Meinhof thus set up a hierarchy that organized people according to not only their languages but also the color of their skins and their cultural proclivities. Meanwhile in practice—that is, in Berlin and Hamburg—neither he nor his colleagues made much distinction between sub-Saharan Africans of separate "races"; in other words, they were all accorded the same treatment and placed on a level apart from Europeans, Asians, and Arabs.

In terms of this hierarchy, Said and Nasur were imagined as Africans, even though both had Arab fathers and Swahili mothers. As we have seen, Said saw himself as both Arab and Swahili, and this vexed Sachau. Nasur considered himself both Arab and Swahili as well. He came from a wealthy slave-owning family and had shuttled back and forth between Zanzibar, Oman, and the East African mainland during his youth.[60] In his contribution to Büttner's volume, Nasur also discusses the lives of both Arab and Swahili, and it is apparent that his identity was fluid, not exclusively defined in terms of either group. Theories like Gobineau's or Kossinna's, which imagined people of "mixed" descent as biologically inferior to individuals who were racially "pure," were alien to Said or Nasur. Instead, their status as part Arab and part Swahili was an elevated one, which gave them unique insight and access to both cultures.

The motivation behind African participation in linguistic or ethnographic ventures in the metropole may often be shrouded, and in some instances was based on monetary concerns; their translations and representations of African culture, too, may not have matched German expectations, since they were not divided into neat, bounded categories. However, in other cases it was in the self-interest of the *Lektoren* to please the Germans. Atangana, for instance, was intrigued with the power that a trip to Germany could bring. As an Ewondo colonial chief who had benefited from German rule, Atangana was able to bolster his reputation among the colonizers by going to the metropole and working with German scholars. In Heepe's *Jaunde-Texte*—which was not only a phonetic guide, but also a repository of Ewondo oral literature—Atangana lavished praise on Germany. From very early on, Atangana had a unique connection with the German colonial power. He had attended a mission school and thereafter been active as a government interpreter, paramedic, and secretary. Altogether, Atangana spent ten years in the service of the German colonial regime, and when this period elapsed, was installed as the "director and chief of all Kolo, from the East to the West."[61] Atangana's perception of Germany was colored by his position as a colonial chief who was favorably disposed toward German rule.[62] He complimented his German colleagues whenever he had the chance, claiming astonishment at the scholarship of men like Meinhof and Panconcelli-Calzia, and admiring the strength of European women.[63] He also recalled the great awe he felt when seeing the German Kaiser in person at the dedication of a new lecture hall in Hamburg, asserting that he was as exultant as any German at having the chance to meet his "ruler."[64]

Atangana was also interested in proving that Africans were capable of advanced civilization, and even that some had already achieved it. In a lecture at the Colonial Institute, Atangana explained that whatever "unusual" customs and traditions the Ewondo apparently had, both they and other ethnic groups in Cameroon now belonged to the German *Reich*. This had permanently changed their perspectives, in Atangana's estimation for the better. "Heathens" who had once married "200 wives" were now Christians with one mate, just like Europeans. The land was, Atangana maintained, becoming "civilized" under German influence, and his ethnography of it was accordingly one of progress and development.[65] Atangana stressed the idea of African transformation under the influence of Christian, German culture, echoing a theme often found in the Protestant missionary ethnography of the period.[66] Yet in other ways, Atangana's lecture actually ran counter to German narratives of colonial progress. Instead of emphasizing the *potential* of Africans to be "christianized" and "civilized," Atangana argued that many Africans were *already* civilized.[67] Again, he had a vested interest in demonstrating African ability, as the more competent Africans were considered in the eyes of his German audience, the better his chances of obtaining more power.

Atangana's nephew Messi, who lived out World War I in Germany, was also impressed with the country. Many of the texts Messi supplied to Heepe were reportage on German military superiority, filled with accounts of German heroism and paper-thin descriptions of the people the Germans were fighting.[68] Messi was also overwhelmed by the number of ethnic groups involved in the war with Germany, plaintively asking Atangana, "Can you even imagine how many [different] peoples they are battling?"[69] Just as Nasur was fascinated by the supposed orderliness of German society, so was Messi astonished by its largeness, the utter scale of World War I being unlike anything he had experienced in Cameroon.

Despite Messi's largely favorable opinion of Germany, there were undercurrents of tension in the texts he published with Heepe. While Messi was in Hamburg, Heepe was a prisoner of war in East Africa. One of Messi's texts, therefore, was a "Letter to Mr. Heepe," in which the *Lektor* poured out his feelings for the linguist. Messi, who knew few people and felt rather alone in Germany, had affection for Heepe and said he wanted "so much to be with" him. Yet when Heepe undertook his research trip among the Swahili in 1914, he did not even say goodbye to Messi, who judged him harshly as a result. "I said to myself: A European certainly does not know what love is. The European is namely so: You would like to have him, yes. You would like to give him everything that there is in the world, and he does not know how to estimate what you do for him."[70] Messi not only admonished Heepe, he also characterized his actions as "typical" for Europeans, and in that sense ironically made the leap of many *European* ethnographic texts of the period, which depicted Africans in stereotypical fashion as "primitive," "childlike," and so forth; just as Germans usually stereotyped Africans, so too had Messi developed his own stereotype of Germans.

The ethnographic and literary texts that African teaching assistants produced were, in sum, not necessarily what their German audience would have expected. They both reasserted German notions of racial and ethnic superiority and subtly undermined them by suggesting that Africans were more "advanced" than Germans might allow, or that African culture was hybrid and syncretic, and not confined to static categories such as "Bantu" or "Arab." Africans also used scholarship as a way of promoting their own goals, whether these included reaffirming loyalty to the colonial state or improving their own economic circumstances.

Conclusion

German colonial scientists were heavily reliant on African informants in the field and *Lektoren* in the metropole. Without them, German scholars would have had little access to the linguistic and anthropological information that shaped and determined ttheir careers. Indeed, as Sachau explained, "native" *Lektoren* were crucial to "exotic" language training in Germany and what, in his estimation, made it superior to similar instruction in other European countries. At the same time, life for Africans in Germany was heavily proscribed by racialized knowledge, which placed them in a developmental hierarchy and necessitated that they "stay in their place." When Africans transgressed preset boundaries, they were punished, and the higher status they had achieved as *Lektoren* suffered. While African teaching assistants in Berlin and Hamburg were technically seen as "more civilized" than the Africans who traveled with *Völkerschauen*—because of their social standing within the African community, or their missionary education—they were still subject to the same racial regulations, and not trusted.

Even so, that African *Lektoren* had substantial influence on the development of *Afrikanistik* cannot be denied. They contributed to the emergent science in the classroom and on the printed page, as well as behind the scenes, collecting data for German scholars. If there was not a sense of anthropological or linguistic "professionalism" among the assistants, there was still a feeling of educative responsibility. In *Jaunde-Texte,* for instance, Atangana described his work at the Colonial Institute in terms of his obligation to instruct Germans in Ewondo.[71] *Lektoren* were, furthermore, not just language instructors; they translated between cultures, describing their communities to German audiences that knew little or nothing about them. Although these translations were mediated by German scholars, there were still moments when Africans defied German categorizations and expressed their own ambitions. Said and Nasur were not just Swahili, they were also Arab; Atangana's countrymen were more civilized than the Germans thought. It is difficult to gain a sense of the texture of the lives of African *Lektoren* in Germany during the colonial period. The information we do have, however, presents us with a group of individuals who both met and subverted German ideas of what it meant to be African.

CHAPTER 7

After the Colonial Moment: German Influences on South African Linguistics and Ethnology, 1920–45

During World War I, German interest in African studies waned. With the exception of East Africa, Germany's African colonies fell to the allies early and were of minimal priority. Moreover, many of the field's most promising new scholars were young and military-eligible. August Klingenheben, later to become the first professor of African studies in Leipzig and ultimately Meinhof's successor in Hamburg, served mandatory military duty from 1912 to 1913, and in World War I he was stationed on the Eastern front and in Turkey.[1] Otto Dempwolff, who taught both African and Pacific languages, was an army doctor both before and during the war.[2] As Messi told us, Heepe was taken prisoner in East Africa and remained there for the duration of the war.[3]

With the discipline largely decimated by war, academic output slowed to a trickle. The previously thick *Zeitschrift für Kolonialsprachen* grew lean, with far fewer contributions appearing in its World War I–era volumes. Research that had been begun before the war was often not resumed until it had ended; Heepe was unable to publish *Jaunde-Texte* until his release in 1919. However, there were some positive developments for *Afrikanistik* during the war. Most important, one of the first prominent woman Africanists started her career. Maria von Tiling, an unemployed German, French, and history teacher living in Pomerania, was invited to work at the Colonial Institute in 1916 because of the lack of men. She knew no African languages when she arrived, but still taught Swahili in the winter of 1917–18. Von Tiling also studied Somali and distinguished herself as a scholar of Hamitic languages, earning her doctorate in 1924. Eventually, von Tiling married Klingenheben and gave up her own research when he moved to Leipzig.[4]

Von Tiling's work was, predictably, viewed through a gendered lens. The Viennese Africanist Wilhelm Czermak praised her dissertation on Somali texts because he claimed von Tiling had a uniquely "feminine ability" to look inside an individual language and gain "feeling" for it. According to Czermak, women had more of a talent for understanding the inner workings of "foreign psychic organism(s)."[5] Von Tiling's appointment was, moreover, never considered permanent. Like many women who went to work during World War I, her position was temporary, only meant to last until the war ended and her male colleagues could resume their employment. However, once the war was over, Meinhof advocated for von Tiling to remain on staff. She was involved in several projects that he wanted her to complete, and he found her work on Somali indispensable.[6]

Von Tiling was also part of a larger project to obtain linguistic and anthropological information from German prisoners of war held in camps throughout the country. These African POWs were mainly from French West Africa, although others came from the British colonies. Indeed, von Tiling's dissertation was largely based on conversations she had with Muhammad Nur, a Somali held in a camp at Ruhleben until Meinhof arranged for his release. Nur's autobiography was incorporated into von Tiling's dissertation.[7] Meinhof worked with the *Kriegsgefangenen* as well, visiting several POW camps and making recordings of Africans speaking—and singing—their languages while there.[8] Further, it was not only Germans who were bidden to work among the POWs; Eduard Sachau suggested that Subeiru bin Adamu, a Hausa lecturer who had been in Berlin since 1913, be dispatched to the nearby Halbmondlager in Wünsdorf to interpret for a group of Senegalese captives.[9]

The anthropological and linguistic information collected from foreign POWs had a substanial impact on the development of "race science" after World War I. As Andrew Evans has shown, studies of POWs were instrumental in casting off the last vestiges of nineteenth-century liberal anthropology and elevating the analysis of biological and genetic traits, making them central to the discipline.[10] For linguists, POW studies also offered a unique chance to investigate many more languages than they normally would have access to and, in addition, provided a way of staying relevant in a Germany devoid of colonies. This was important, since both during and after the war *Afrikanistik* constantly had to readjust itself and accommodate to changed political circumstances.

In the 1920s, when there were no more POW camps, Meinhof and his colleagues adjusted once again. They were compelled to turn outward, shifting their focus from strengthening the now-defunct German colonial empire to assisting other colonial powers, some of which they despised. In the 1930s and 1940s, by contrast, Africanists' hopes were renewed, as they came to believe that they could regain what they had lost in Africa. Consequently, many eagerly rallied to the National Socialist cause. One constant throughout the entire period, however—especially for Meinhof—was an increasing involvement with South Africa, where on some levels his ideas resonated more effectively than they had in Germany.

This final chapter will provide an overview of the history of *Afrikanistik* in the interwar years and World War II. I will examine the discipline's significance to South Africa in the era of segregation and also ask what impact it may have had later, under apartheid. German linguistics supplied the tools for categorizing Africans in southern Africa and elsewhere on the continent, while missionary philosophies that stressed the unique nature of each people contributed to discourses on separate development; together, they influenced a group of white South African scholars studying language and ethnology, or *volkekunde.*

In one sense, African studies as imagined by Meinhof were ineffective, not suiting Germany's colonial needs or contributing much to the implementation of its goals. The "classification of Africa" did not amount to very much in terms of practical German colonialism. Meinhof believed that his program for the transcription and dissemination of African languages was pragmatic. However, since neither the German colonial government nor all Protestant missionaries agreed, his methodologies and ideas did not have much concrete political effect. Yet in another way Meinhof and his associates assisted in developing a broad linguistic classificatory system that allowed for the evaluation and categorization of almost any ethnic group in Africa. This classification was never value-neutral; instead, it was permeated with racist and racialist sentiment. African studies were thus part of a much greater stream in German intellectual history, whereby people came to associate language with particular national types.[11]

On a larger scale, Meinhof's work and that of the missionaries and scholars who preceded him had wider reverberations. It helped lay the foundation for a particular way of thinking about Africans, in terms of linguistic, cultural, and racial hierarchies. The fact that language underpinned these hierarchies is important, because it was this fundamental human trait that, as Trautmann demonstrated for the case of British India, was frequently used as a gauge for determining other aspects of a nation's life. Whatever its practical connotations, *Afrikanistik* contributed to a growing discussion on the connection between language, discrete cultural and social analysis, and biology.

Despite Meinhof's ardent belief in the pragmatic efficacy of African studies, for Germans its real importance still rested in the realm of imagination, with the idea that Africans were divisible into separate, easily defined linguistic or racial categories and hierarchies. Yet these categories did achieve a "practical" effect in South Africa. Anthropologist W. D. Hammond-Tooke argued that Meinhof's impact on his students was insignificant and also mainly academic, not practical.[12] However, Hammond-Tooke's analysis does not stand up under scrutiny, since Meinhof's work was concerned with much more than the minutiae of grammar or phonology. It also encompassed studies of religion, literature, and race. Further, the German connection to South African race philosophy well predated Meinhof, as we have seen; from the nineteenth century, German Protestant missionaries—not to mention Wilhelm Bleek—were deeply involved in the construction of linguistic categories that would ultimately define and ossify ethnic boundaries in South Africa. Through German influence on South Africans such as Eiselen, van Warmelo, and their colleagues, the classification of languages became more than a scholastic exercise: It became a means of creating division and difference where little or none may have existed. Before looking more closely at the German–South African connection, though, I will first consider the role African studies played in interwar Germany.

Africanists under Weimar and the Great "Turn Outward"

To get at the root of the Africanists' turn outward and their eventual move toward Nazism, it is important to understand what happened to *Afrikanistik* between 1919 and 1933. Later Africanist support for the Nazis was fueled by a combination of two factors, the first being the preexistence of racialist sentiments that had been honed for decades, and the second a desire to gain back the territories their nation had lost and reverse the losses of the Treaty of Versailles. This was connected to a fierce national loyalty among both lay and missionary linguists.

Throughout the 1920s, German Africanists had to suppress this patriotism and quash their own imperial or nationalist aspirations. They concentrated on reorienting themselves and their discipline to a changed world, one in which they would have to assist and serve other countries—

among them former enemies—if they wanted their work to have further practical significance or a larger academic audience. This meant collaborating with British, French, and other foreign "colonial" scientists on projects such as the International Institute for African Languages and Cultures, which was founded in London in 1926.[13]

After World War I, Meinhof considered international collaboration distasteful. He felt deeply hurt not only by Germany's defeat in the war and its loss of the colonies but by how he believed the victors were treating his missionary colleagues. During the war most German mission societies—and some members of the Swiss-German Basel Mission—were expelled from Germany's conquered colonies. At the same time, their stations were appropriated by other, non-German mission societies.[14] Once the German missionaries were allowed to return, they complained bitterly of their experiences under the British. In 1926 Karl Roehl, a missionary in East Africa and noted Swahili scholar,[15] spoke indignantly about his life in the now-English colony.

> In spite of Locarno and Germany's entrance into the League of Nations, I do not believe in a German East Africa. . . . The English here also don't act as though they want to give us the land back. Indeed, I live here in our Mission house . . . but on the ground floor, where it gets very hot during the rainy season. By the way, five government officials also live here and, despite article 438 of the Versailles Treaty and the mission ordinance of the local government, no one is thinking about returning the house to us.[16]

Disgruntled by the British, Roehl bemoaned not only that German East Africa had ceased to exist but also the conditions under which he was forced to live. He was far from the only German missionary to express dismay with England and its colonial leadership. In 1920 Julius Richter, one of the more famous German *Missionswissenschaftlern* and a professor in Berlin, wrote a confidential, unpublished pamphlet entitled *Vor schweren Entscheidungen* (Facing Difficult Choices) and distributed it at a missionary gathering in Berlin. The content of the pamphlet addressed the question of "whether and to what extent the relationships with foreign, especially Anglo-Saxon, missions should and can be rekindled." This issue was pertinent because the German societies were deciding whether they should attend international mission conferences organized in "enemy" countries.[17] Although Richter contended that Germany should be represented, it was a difficult choice for him.[18] He was disappointed in the allies, and he characterized them as having a "shylock-like brutality."[19] Clearly, attitudes toward British and other foreign mission societies had changed dramatically from those of the nineteenth century, when German-speaking missionaries worked beside non-Germans and belonged to the same societies.

As a close confidant of many Protestant missionaries, Meinhof was well aware of their frustration with the restrictions placed on German missionary activity. The linguist's relationship with England had always been contentious anyway. Like Büttner he admired the British and their religious fervor.[20] Nonetheless, he was always annoyed by English reluctance to accept his ideas about linguistic pedagogy and begin language training at home in the metropole, and not first on the mission field.[21] After World War I, Meinhof grew increasingly concerned with the German role in a colonial world dominated by "foreigners." In a 1922 letter to a Dr. Abernethy in Washington, DC, Meinhof expressed outrage at the harsh measures taken against his missionary colleagues.

> The German mission societies were established with the object of preaching the Holy Bible far and wide and never aimed at political or commercial ends. For quite a century they have done their work under British government(s) without ever committing any act of disloyalty and even now all the accusations which were brought against them during the war have been proven to lack any source other than the ill will of our many enemies.[22]

Meinhof depicted the German Protestant Mission establishment as completely innocent and devoid of political guile—despite the somewhat conflicted position toward nationalism that many missionaries had held since Germany acquired its colonies.[23]

By the 1920s, Meinhof had thus developed an enormous antipathy toward England. He was particularly conflicted about involvement with the International Institute of African Languages and Cultures. In the beginning, the institute promised to live up to its "international" name and satisfy Meinhof.[24] It was touted as a center for "the study of the languages and mental culture of Africa"[25] and called upon Africanists across Europe to join. Both Meinhof and Westermann were invited to be directors of the institute. Westermann accepted and became codirector along with French anthropologist Henri Labouret,[26] while Meinhof declined the post because of his busy schedule.[27] Then, when Meinhof claimed he was unable to attend the institute's foundational meeting, Hanns Vischer, a Swiss-born education reformer and organizing secretary of the institute, refused to take no for an answer.[28] Vischer wrote Meinhof to tell him that because of his stature in the field of African studies his presence was vital, and pleaded with him to come. Eventually, the meeting was rescheduled to suit the schedules of Meinhof and French anthropologist Maurice Delafosse.[29] Meinhof attended and was impressed by the institute's inaugural festivities. He and other Africanists were honored at a breakfast held by the British government, which was represented by colonial secretary L. S. Amery. Meinhof believed that his placement between Amery and Nigerian "founder" Sir Frederick Lugard at the meal demonstrated the British "appreciation for German work" and that "we Germans can be satisfied with the course of the negotiations to now, and through further cooperation must show that we are indispensable to the development of Africa."[30] Meinhof was optimistic about the institute's future and believed that it was committed to reincorporating Germans into the international community of Africanist scholars.

Neither the British policies toward the German mission nor academic evaluations of German scholarship were ever as harsh as Meinhof suggested. German missionaries were allowed to return to the now-English colonies, where they worked alongside Britons. For instance, in Cameroon, which was divided into British and French mandates after World War I, the French were the ones insistent on keeping Germans out of their former mission fields, not the British. While the French handed stations that had been controlled by Basel over to the Paris Mission without chagrin, the English were reluctant to take over German property. With support from British Protestant societies, the Baslers were even permitted to resume their duties in the field in 1925.[31] Further, the International Institute did come through on its promise to continue support of German scholarship, as is reflected in *Africa,* the journal it began to publish in 1928. It included substantial contributions by Germans. In 1929 there were eight articles with German authors, five in 1930, and seven in 1931.[32]

Between 1925 and 1927, when the institute was being established, it therefore seemed that Meinhof would reconcile with the British. When it came to nonlinguistic African education, Germans fell in line with the English and maintained, in contradistinction to the French, that Europeans should not teach Africans to behave like whites. Instead, both believed they should be trained to be "self-aware Negroes, who after many generations would be in the position to manage their own affairs."[33] This made sense, considering that the French preached a policy of direct rule, in which the ultimate goal was to incorporate its African subjects into the French polity as equal citizens who would see themselves as French.[34] By contrast, England and Germany embraced indirect rule and did not believe Africans could become full-fledged English or German citizens. Westermann commented, "The African should be educated for effective life and work within his native environment and on the basis of his own race qualities and genius . . . [so] the aim of education should be to make him a useful member of his own community."[35] Westermann's attitude dovetailed well with the general Protestant missionary conviction that each ethnic group should reach Christianity and civilization in its own unique manner, but needed Western guidance to get there.

As an ardent supporter of German missions Meinhof was also pleased with the British outlook and was briefly an enthusiastic participant in the institute's endeavors.[36] Yet he was also against institute plans to focus mainly on the "practical" aspect of African studies. He urged its members to consider incorporating a more scholarly approach to languages and cultures.[37] This, combined with a perceived slight concerning orthography—not to mention his preexisting deep-seated hostility for England—finally led Meinhof to reject collaboration with the institute, as much as he felt it might be useful to the furtherance of German colonial science. In addition, Meinhof's relationship with Westermann, the other founder of *Afrikanistik,* ended over disagreements regarding the institute; Westermann produced the orthography—known as "Westermann-script"—that the institute adopted, while Meinhof argued that it should remain with Richard Lepsius's nineteenth-century system. Their friendship chilled, and never resumed.[38]

Meinhof's inability to resolve his problems with the English originally deprived him of a setting for his work in the post–World War I world. Shortly after the war, the Hamburg Colonial Institute was dissolved. The changed political climate, in which there were no longer German colonies, meant there was little reason to maintain an academic institution devoted to colonial sciences. Still, Germany did not lose all interest in its colonies and the possibility of their recovery during the 1920s. Colonialism was not at the forefront of official policy, but the "colonial question" lingered throughout the Weimar and Nazi periods. With the exception of the Center and Bavarian People's Parties, which did not especially care one way or the other about the colonies, and the Communists, who were decidedly against them, most German political groups wanted some measure of colonial control returned to their nation.[39] Even so, without "official" colonialism, there was no particular call for a German *Kolonialinstitut* or for *Afrikanistik,* whose main purpose—at least in the highly disputed practical sense—seemed to have evaporated along with Germany's imperial aspirations.

The loss of the institute did herald the beginning of a new academic era in Hamburg. Its demise paved the way for the establishment of a full-fledged university, and its branches reconstituted as departments of the newly minted University of Hamburg in 1919. This meant that Meinhof's seminar and *Zeitschrift* enjoyed a continued, if tense, existence. In a 1923 letter to Frank M. Sanders, director for the Committee of Missionary Preparation in New York City, Meinhof even remarked that ninety-four students had enrolled for classes in either African or Pacific languages during the winter of 1922–23.[40] This was many more than had attended during the institute's first years. Moreover, while the journal was debilitated and its survival threatened by dwindling sources of funding, the publication was somehow kept afloat with library exchanges and financial assistance from the *Notgemeinschaft für deutsche Wissenschaft* (Emergency Foundation for German Scholarship), an organization that helped scholars in need throughout the interwar period.[41]

Even so, there were many unwanted changes awaiting *Afrikanistik* in the interwar era. Meinhof's Seminar for Colonial Languages was rechristened the Seminar for African and Pacific languages, while his *Zeitschrift für Kolonialsprachen* was renamed the *Zeitschrift für Eingeborenensprachen* (Journal of Native Languages). Meinhof also felt betrayed by his employers. There was lip service given to the idea that the University of Hamburg would continue to have a colonial mission and function as Germany's "colonial" university in the new age. Yet in a 1924 letter to shipping magnate Woermann, Meinhof said that there had been no interest "for years" in colonial studies on the part of university leaders, and that *Afrikanistik* had been particularly neglected. He even intimated that the university had "disturbed and hindered" his work.[42] During Weimar, Meinhof's expectations for the success of *Afrikanistik* in Germany were generally low, and necessitated the reluctant turn toward England, other European countries, and South Africa.

Afrikanistik under the Nazis

For Africanists in general and Meinhof in particular, the 1920s were punctuated by disappointments that contributed to a sympathy for the Nazis and subsequent move to join them. There was a renewed—if modest—interest in African colonialism during the 1930s and 1940s, which was accompanied by the Africanist hope that the Nazis might restore Germany's colonies and once again endow their research with greater nationalist purpose.[43] The Nazis encouraged this hope; from 1933 Meinhof headed the University of Hamburg's Committee for Foreign and Colonial Studies,[44] and in 1939 the Colonial Institute was "reestablished" as a branch of the university, complete with its own course listings. This new incarnation of the institute was placed under the direction of historian Adolf Rein, with close collaboration from Ernst Dammann, Meinhof's onetime student.[45] After 1940, both Meinhof and Westermann belonged to the *Kolonialwissenschaftliche Abteilung* (Department of Colonial Sciences) of the National Socialist *Reichsforschungsrat,* which has been termed a "coordinating monopoly for African research in Germany" during the Third Reich.[46]

Colonialism was never among the top foreign policy priorities for the Nazis, however. In March 1938, Hitler rejected Neville Henderson's proposal that the colonies be restored to Germany in exchange for European détente.[47] Amery self-servingly reported in his 1940 *The German Colonial Claim,* "the Nazi leaders are obsessed by the dream of a colonial empire to be won at our expense, and will not lightly abandon it."[48] With respect to Africa, this was likely an exaggeration. Nonetheless, it does appear that the Nazis were intent upon reclaiming the colonies and with them the justice they believed was stolen by the Treaty of Versailles. It was a secondary preoccupation, but one that persisted.

The troubles of the 1920s and renewed optimism of the 1930s were not the only forces motivating Meinhof and his colleagues to support Nazism. There was some ideological basis for Africanist complicity. Meinhof and many of his peers—including August Klingenheben, Bernhard Struck, Ernst Dammann, and Ernst Zylharz—all became members of the Nazi Party. Westermann never did, but he still worked for its *Kolonialwissenschaftliche Abteilung.* Meinhof, who had belonged to the German conservative party through 1919 and then the right-wing *Deutschnationale Volkspartei* (DNVP) until 1931,[49] joined the Nazis relatively early, in May 1933.[50] Moreover, the Africanist fealty to National Socialism is unsurprising in light of the preceding colonial story: The Africanists had a set notion of race, cultivated from the mid- to late nineteenth century and elaborated in the early twentieth, that was predicated on the belief that there were intrinsic cultural, spiritual, and biological differences between peoples—even if they often denied the biological component. Spiritual differences between Europeans and Africans were held to be so deeply ingrained that they manifested themselves in the most obvious expressions of each racial group, that is, their language and its accompanying literature.[51] Such deterministic views dovetailed well with those of the Nazis.

There were other reasons for Africanist collaboration with the Nazis. Meinhof, for one, was a rabid nationalist in the tradition of Büttner or Fabri. During World War I he held three motivational lectures on the importance of supporting the country's military aims.[52] In his *Deutschland und der Preußische Geist* (*Germany and the Prussian Spirit*), Meinhof fiercely defended what he referred to as Germany's "democratic monarchy" and condemned the British and the French, accusing them of having far less freedom than the Germans. "The foreigners have despots," he claimed, "a leadership where only the few are allowed to tell the others what to do, indeed what to think!"[53] Another of his essays, *Sittlichkeit und Krieg* (*Morality and War*), addressed the singularity of Germany's national spirit and how important it was for the nation to fend off "foreign morals." Meinhof said that it "is not as though we meant that the morals of other peoples were bad; they may be good for those people . . . but at any rate our people wishes to live according to its own morals, in its own way, and not to have a foreign morality thrust upon it."[54] Meinhof's passionate insistence on German uniqueness—which was not unlike his opinion that each African ethnicity had its own distinctive characteristics—underscored his nationalistic inclinations. Despite his sometime collaboration with British, French, and other non-German scholars, he remained resolute in his belief that there were intrinsic differences among them that could not be resolved.

At the same time, Meinhof's attitude toward what he considered "lower" or "inferior" races was decidedly paternalistic, favoring a Christian education for Africans, not their forced labor, slavery, or wholesale eradication. His approach toward Africans grew fundamentally out of the Protestant missionary tradition. This tradition endorsed a "separate but equal" credo, whereby different races, white and black, would grow independently into civilization and Christianity, with the former aiding the latter. Meinhof's 1937 article "Europäer und Afrikaner," written deep in the period of Nazi rule, demonstrates this mode of thinking. He began the essay by saying that "the destruction [*Ausrottung*] of the natives would be . . . the biggest economic mistake."[55] He echoed a theme common to much of his earlier work, referring to the native population as Germany's greatest "natural resource" in the colonies.[56] He continued, though, to maintain that he did not advocate African enslavement or believe that economic prosperity was the only tangible benefit Germans could glean from a relationship with natives. Instead, Meinhof envisioned the ideal colony as one where Africans and Europeans would work together to develop the potential of the land that both inhabited. "This is not about the displacement of the natives," he argued, "but rather about cooperation with them."[57]

While Meinhof was certainly a racial determinist, his assessment of peoples whom he considered "inferior" was never as harsh or unforgiving as that of the Nazis. He even praised various aspects of African languages and cultures as *superior* to those of the Germans. For instance, he declared that agglutinative Bantu languages were sometimes more rational than inflecting Indo-European or Semitic ones.[58] In addition, Meinhof's brand of racial stereotyping and classification was contradictory from the start. As we have seen, his Hamitic theory led him directly into loops of circular logic that were impossible to escape. Meinhof insisted that race and language were independent from each other, and that linguistic groupings had nothing to do with racial ones. Still, Meinhof always relied on the anthropological definitions offered by his friend Luschan, and until very late in life he continued to refer to those Africans he had designated "Hamites" in terms of their lighter skin and their supposed historical domination of black groups. Meinhof's opinions on race were often divergent, and he was unable to decide exactly *how* it had influenced the development of language or culture.[59]

Meinhof also did not have a particularly negative opinion of Jews. When he spoke of them at all, it was usually in terms of the Hebrew language. He grouped it with the inflecting Semitic languages, which he categorized among the most sophisticated.[60] As a religion, Meinhof looked favorably on Judaism, because he believed it had provided a strong fundament for Christianity. In his lecture on *Sittlichkeit und Krieg* he praised the ancient Hebrews for their martial success. He exhorted Germans to follow the Hebrew lead and recognize that a nation could be religious and morally just, yet still fight.[61] Meinhof *did* discuss Semites as possible kin to the African Hamites, or even the link between Hamites and Indo-Europeans.[62] However, since he had a relatively positive assessment of Hamitic languages and cultures, this opinion was not derogatory. Finally, Meinhof's personal relationships with Jews were not hostile. In the 1920s he was a founding member of the *Religionswissenschaftliche Gesellschaft* (Religious Studies Society), a group that met to hear and discuss various lectures on religion. The *Gesellschaft* was frequented by prominent Jewish scholars such as philosopher Ernst Cassirer and art historian Aby Warburg. In 1919 the *Gesellschaft* even asked the community's rabbinate to participate in its meetings.[63] Cassirer contributed an article to Meinhof's 1927 *Festschrift,* as did expatriate German Jewish anthropologist Franz Boas.[64]

None of this excuses the complicity of Meinhof or his colleagues with the Nazi regime; nor does it mean that they never harbored destructive, racist sentiments. For instance, Meinhof was thoroughly revolted by the idea of mixed sexual relationships. Unlike Büttner, he believed that white and black should remain sexually separate and that those missionaries who allowed themselves to stray had committed a grave error and should be released from their evangelical duties.[65] In addition, while August Klingenheben, Meinhof's successor as director of the Seminar for African Languages, probably became a member of the National Socialist party in 1936 primarily in order to win his new position, his ideological motives for having done so remain obscure.[66] The reasons that Africanists became members of or worked with the Nazi Party were generally varied, based on self-interest or on personal conviction, rooted both in the racial theories spawned in the late nineteenth and early twentieth centuries, as well as in the dissatisfaction of missionaries and scholars with the turn of events following World War I.

The Move toward South Africa

Many of the ties that German Africanists had with colonial scientists in other countries were severed after the Nazis gained power. The "turn outward" of the 1920s was therefore partially reversed in the 1930s.[67] Even so, *Afrikanistik*'s greatest impact was still on South Africa, since German ideas about language, culture, and race remained influential there during and after the Nazi period. Indeed, while the "turn" necessitated by World War I and the Treaty of Versailles led to a distasteful cooperation with Britain and France, it also offered German Africanists the opportunity to work more closely with South Africa. Helping the British or French was problematic. By contrast, German Africanists embraced and nurtured the relationship with South Africa throughout the 1920s and, to the extent that they could, into the 1930s and 1940s. While Meinhof's ties to the British and French grew more strained, his involvement with South Africa's linguistic and anthropological community intensified and flourished.

Meinhof and his cohort were of course not the first Germans to develop theories on native languages and cultures in South Africa. Wilhelm Bleek, along with a host of German missionaries from the Berlin, Rhenish, and Hermannsburg societies, initiated a long and fruitful collaboration between German and South African scholars of literature, linguistics, and anthropology. Further, while the children of German settlers took on South African citizenship, they often maintained a sense of Germany identity. This was true for Eiselen, the son of a Berlin missionary, as well as for Dorothea Bleek, Wilhelm's daughter and a renowned scholar of San/Bushman culture and language in her own right.

German schools of thought became models for South African scholarship in other ways. Hamburg was the prototype for the School of African Life and Languages that was established in Cape Town in 1920. Robert Gordon has pointed out that it was Hamburg's removal from African "hotspots" that made it a paradigm of objectivity that South Africans would not only respect but duplicate. He commented that when scholars were deciding where to locate their top African studies programs, "the claims of places like the Rand, the Eastern Cape and Natal, which had 'special native problems' in *situ,* were answered by a stress on the need for scientific detachment and calm which could only be obtained at a distance. It was pointed out that the most prominent school of this type was in Hamburg, well away from the field."[68] The metropole offered the best conditions for studying the "native" not only for Germans, but for white South Africans as well.

There were multiple German influences on South African anthropology and linguistics. It was not Meinhof alone who exerted an impact but the general German philological and ethnological thinking that he represented. Before World War I, German ethnology was largely defined by diffusionism, the theory that held that cultural characteristics did not emerge in isolation in each solitary ethnic group but instead "diffused" from one culture "area" to another. Diffusionism was historical in nature, since it postulated cultural development on a diachronic axis. Cultural change was determined not from within but from the outside. Diffusion was not limited to German anthropology; it enjoyed a long history in the Anglophone context.[69] Further, German influence, including Meinhof's, filtered into English anthropology. In particular, C. G. Seligmann's 1930 *Races of Africa* contains ethnological classifications very similar to the ones that Meinhof espoused, if somewhat more differentiated.[70]

Nonetheless, diffusion differed from the kind of anthropology that started to dominate the British school during the 1920s and 1930s, namely, social functionalism as represented by Bronislaw Malinowski and A. R. Radcliffe-Brown. Social functionalism was synchronic and required the deep exploration of individual cultures as units to uncover—as its name implied—the functions of all rituals and objects. While the popularity of social anthropology grew in England, functionalism did not catch on to the same degree in 1920s and 1930s Germany, where older, historical anthropological and linguistic methodology continued to hold sway.[71] In South Africa, functionalism was largely the province of English-speaking scholars such as Isaac Schapera, with Afrikaners like van Warmelo and Eiselen instead attracted to *volkekunde,* a variety of ethnology that was partly reliant on German ideas and, as the similarity between the words suggests, German *Völkerkunde.*

Not all German scholars rejected social anthropology, either; in fact, Westermann embraced it, as he made clear in his book *The African Today and Tomorrow.* He praised the Institute of African Languages and Cultures for taking the practical approach of social anthropology and questioned whether historical and diachronic anthropology was up to the task of helping solve colonial conundrums. Westermann agreed with Malinowski and endorsed the study of present experience through the current political and social organization of African groups.

> Even the representative of historical ethnology will do well not to ignore the problems of modern life. Those phenomena which seem to him to be old and autochthonous, and therefore a worthy object of his study, are in reality the results of innumerable past changes, and it should be of interest to him to watch such changes taking place under his eyes and to see their effect on the life of the people concerned.[72]

This did not mean that Westermann dismissed historical ethnology wholecloth. In *The African Today and Tomorrow* he discussed the racial and linguistic divisions among Africans, including Hamitic ones. People that he referred to as "Ethiopids" had, he said, invaded "Negro countries in Eastern Africa and further South" during the fifteenth century.[73] Westermann's work had become increasingly influenced by social anthropology and what he saw as its practical benefits, but he continued to incorporate older methodological models as well.

While Westermann welcomed social anthropology, German and British schools still had many splits along diachronic and synchronic lines. The cleavage between Afrikaner ethnology and British social anthropology that became so marked during apartheid had, moreover, already begun to widen in the 1920s, with Afrikaners allying themselves much more closely with older German ideas of cultural diffusion than with nascent British functionalism.[74] This was in keeping with Afrikaner ideology and its Calvinist focus on the unique place of each *volk* in the world as preordained by God, which included a special emphasis on the particular role of the Afrikaners themselves as His chosen people.[75] Afrikaner anthropology thus came to focus on the concept of *volk*—the "people" as an ethnic unit or group—and not on the individual as an entity with a life apart from it.[76] J. S. Sharp has argued that Afrikaner studies of culture hinged on the concept of *ethnos,* which was originally applied by the German ethnologist Wilhelm Mühlmann, and meant that each human society was a closed, fixed world unto itself, with its own laws, customs, and unique properties. The mixing of "nations" would therefore have disastrous consequences.[77] Afrikaner concepts of *volk* and its mystical status were, furthermore, very similar to those of the early nineteenth-century German romantics, who believed that the German people were intrinsically bound to the land on which they lived, and that they had a specific national *Geist* unique to them, and to them alone.[78]

German scientists like Westermann, Luschan, and Meinhof also visited South Africa themselves, holding lectures and reporting on their experiences once back in Germany. Westermann went to South Africa in the early 1930s and ended up dedicating his book *The African Today and Tomorrow* to the University of the Witwatersrand. Luschan had traveled to the country at the beginning of the twentieth century and while there reported on both his anthropological conclusions concerning the "Hottentots" and Meinhof's linguistic assessment of the same. Meinhof took his own trip in 1927–28.[79] At the time, his presence was celebrated by South African peers such as Lestrade, who delivered the paper "A Great Africanist" to herald Meinhof's arrival in South Africa. Lestrade, who was born in Amsterdam but spent most of his life in South Africa, was the government ethnologist who established the ethnological section of the Department of Native Affairs in Pretoria in 1925.[80] Although he never studied with Meinhof in Germany, he was among the linguist's most steadfast supporters and even remarked that "the greatest advance in all Bantu philology was the advent of Carl Meinhof."[81] In "A Great Africanist," Lestrade commented in a similar vein that he believed Meinhof's visit might well prove portentous for South Africa and assist it in answering the "Native Question." Lestrade considered Meinhof among the very few who were truly expert in "the mentality of the native" and saw him as an important guide in deciding how to govern and police Africans.[82] He also dismissed as ridiculous the idea that Meinhof was a mere theoretician, not "competent to pronounce on (practical) problems," and said that "practical men of all kinds" were "applying more and more to the students of primitive mentality" for the information they needed to work successfully among Africans.[83]

Lestrade was not the only South African convinced of the importance of German theories to African studies. Meinhof's lecture tour, which took him all over the country to both universities and other venues, was favorably reported in local newspapers such as the Johannesburg *Rand Daily Mail* and Cape Town's *Cape Argus* and *Cape Times.* Meinhof was so pleased with his positive welcome in the press that he held out hope that his visit would "contribute to a closer connection between German and South African science."[84] The media did seem to like him. According to a Mr. Renner of the German consulate in Pretoria, the *Rand Daily Mail* had reported that "in South Africa, Professor Meinhof has a virtually pioneering effect, and national scientists must follow his lead. In particular, his studies with regard to African songs, legends, and sayings are of the greatest importance, as they grant insight on the psyche of the natives."[85] Furthermore, on January 23, 1928, the *Cape Times,* which published articles about each of the several lectures that Meinhof gave at the University of Cape Town, praised the scholar for delving into the "fascinating realm of native myth, legend, and romance" with "authority and humour."[86] The *Times* also commented—as it had in other instances—that Meinhof's audience was enthusiastic about his speech, supplying him with a "hearty" thank you at its conclusion.[87] Finally, in reporting on a speech that Meinhof gave to the University Club in Cape Town, the January 26 issue of the same paper noted that senator F. S. Malan thanked Meinhof "for his presence in this country at the present time, and for his work," which he thought would be helpful in determining the solution to the Native Bills that were then being debated in parliament. These bills were primarily concerned with whether Africans and coloreds living in the Cape should be stripped of their franchise; they were the only nonwhites in South Africa who could vote, and their enfranchisement generated heated discussions.[88]

That Malan was supportive of Meinhof complicates the question of whom he was influencing in South Africa. Afrikaner or not, Malan was neither conservative nor segregationist. A prominent representative of Cape Liberalism, Malan was in favor of maintaining the Cape franchise, not dismantling it. It therefore might not appear that Malan would have been receptive to Meinhof's ideas about cultural particularism. However, as Peter Kallaway has pointed out, Malan's defense of the Cape Franchise and of African rights more generally was limited to a narrow political context. Neither he nor most of his Cape Liberal fellows would have contested the status quo in South Africa or wanted to elevate Africans to the same position as Europeans.[89] This was not inconsistent with Meinhof's thinking; as an ardent supporter of Protestant missions, Meinhof rejected attempts to deny Africans basic human rights or call on arguments of biological inferiority. Instead, Meinhof based his racism on the notion that Africans and Europeans had achieved different stages of civilization, and that the former would continue to develop in its own, unique direction. Both Meinhof and Malan embodied a paternalism that recognized the merits of African culture but did not acknowledge equality between blacks and whites. What Malan's welcome of Meinhof indicates, then, is that Meinhof's ideas appealed to a wide spectrum of South Africans who had differing visions of what sort of relationship blacks and whites should maintain.[90]

While Malan praised Meinhof, Meinhof in turn praised South African scholarship. Indeed, German and South African linguistics and anthropology influenced each other mutually. Meinhof claimed that South Africa had significantly affected his own career. It was in Cape Town, as he remarked in his speech to the University Club, that "the science to which he had devoted his life's work," African linguistics, had been founded by Bleek.[91] For years before he traveled to South Africa, Meinhof had relied heavily on missionary data from the country, and once there he was able to take advantage of interaction with Xhosa, Zulu, and San/Bushmen on a level not available to him in Germany.[92]

An even greater effect on Meinhof, however, may have come from his South African students and their collaboration with him in the 1920s and early 1930s. The first of these to take their degrees in Germany—Eiselen, van Warmelo, and their lesser-known colleagues, linguists B. I. C. van Eeden and J. A. Engelbrecht—arrived during the 1920s, before Meinhof traveled to South Africa himself. When they studied with Meinhof, all were primarily students of linguistics.[93] He held them in very high regard, and considered both van Warmelo and Eiselen for teaching appointments at his seminar.[94] Of Eiselen, Meinhof said, "I know him only as a man of faultless character, who has always done his work conscientiously and thoroughly."[95] Further, Meinhof worked with van Warmelo on the translation of Meinhof's *Grundriss* into English in 1932. While the two men sometimes had opposing opinions on the project and quarreled over whether certain languages were independent tongues or dialects, Meinhof fully valued van Warmelo's contribution. Meinhof even characterized the resulting translation as more van Warmelo's work than his own.[96]

Meinhof and the German linguistic, anthropological, and missionary tradition had a lasting impact on his students, even though the issue of Meinhof's influence has stirred mild controversy. Hammond-Tooke, who was both a South African anthropologist and former student of van Warmelo, dismissed the idea that Meinhof's conservatism had affected Eiselen and challenged the notion that early National Socialism had played a role in Eiselen's education in Germany.[97] Hammond-Tooke instead claimed that Meinhof's only contribution to Eiselen's schooling was linguistic, and so the fact that the German became a Nazi was probably unimportant. This is likely true. It is very dangerous to say that because the teacher was a Nazi, the student must also have been one; further, Meinhof's own reasons for joining the party were unclear, and his understanding of race did not fit neatly into the Nazis' biological/eugenic paradigm.

In other ways, however, Meinhof did shape the thought of his South African students and colleagues. Lestrade considered Meinhof a major force in his academic life. The German linguist's influence is palpable in Lestrade's work, even where the latter does not cite Meinhof directly. In a lecture entitled "The Place of the Bantu Languages among the Language-Families of Africa, and Their Regional-Genealogical Classification," Lestrade warned against conflating race and language when it came to Bantu and other African peoples, saying that "indeed, very often the same languages are spoken by peoples of widely varying physical and cultural types, while people of the same physical and cultural types often speak languages which belong to widely different families." Later in the same talk, however, Lestrade commented that "nevertheless it is true in a general way that the boundaries of linguistic families coincide, on the whole, with the boundaries of racial and cultural classification." He was obviously conflicted, since he continued to comment that "this fact, added to our very scanty knowledge of the racial and cultural complexes of Africa, and compared with our fairly wide knowledge of the linguistic situation, has given rise to a certain tendency to use linguistic criteria and linguistic terms in the racial and cultural classification of the African peoples."[98] Lestrade grappled with the issue of how and whether language, race, and culture were interrelated, a topic that had long obsessed Meinhof.

When it comes to van Warmelo and Eiselen, Meinhof's actual students, the situation is more complicated. Lestrade was a career academic who left the ethnological section for the University of Pretoria in 1930.[99] By contrast, Eiselen and van Warmelo are more remembered for their relationship with the South African government and their impact on apartheid and its segregationist policies. Considering their importance to the development of South African politics and society during the apartheid era, if the teachings of Meinhof, his colleagues, and the Berlin Missionary Society were even slightly influential—and I believe they were much more than that—the implications are significant.

I will turn first to Eiselen. Although he began his career as a professor of ethnology at the Afrikaans-speaking Universities of Stellenbosch and Pretoria, he was best known for being Inspector of Native Education (1937–47), the chair of the Commission on Native Education (also known as the Eiselen Commission) (1949), and finally Secretary for Native Affairs (1949–60).[100] In some circles he was considered a champion of black languages and cultures, which he said he wanted to preserve from dissolution and extinction.[101] Further, as Cynthia Kros has shown, after a short detour Eiselen rejected scientific racism and its theories of inherent African inferiority.[102] However, Eiselen was also strongly in favor of separate development for whites and blacks, which was reflected in his developing belief that the South African school system should be highly segregated.[103] His support of segregated schooling was similar to that of the Berlin Mission, whose members maintained that Africans needed to be educated in a manner most befitting their inherent "national" peculiarities and not recast in the same image as Europeans. Kros has argued that the Berlin missionaries differed from their English-speaking counterparts in this respect, since the latter were in favor of Europeanizing the pupils who attended their schools;[104] this was true in some cases but not others, since again both British and Germans often argued against African assimilation and not for it, like the French.

Eiselen's emphasis on the importance of native-tongue instruction also paralleled Meinhof's. Like his Protestant missionary colleagues and forebears, Meinhof insisted on the importance of native-language education out of a strong conviction that Africans needed to be taught in their mother tongues, not foreign ones that might alienate them from their own cultures.[105] In the "Report of the Commission on Native Education, 1945–1951," Eiselen echoed Meinhof's concerns and recommended the "increased use of mother-tongue instruction" in African schools, especially because 75.2 percent of all Bantu pupils were enrolled in grades one through four and were—presumably—unlikely to have had much exposure to English or Afrikaans.[106] He stressed that there were at root neither physical nor psychological differences between European and African children, but that conditioning over time dictated that they be taught in unique manners befitting of their nationalities.

> The now universally accepted principle of leading the child in his education from the known and familiar to the unknown and the unfamiliar has to be applied equally in the case of the Bantu child as with children of any other social group. But educational practice must recognize that it has to deal with a Bantu child, i.e. a child trained and conditioned in Bantu culture, endowed with a knowledge of a Bantu language and imbued with values, interests, and behaviour patterns learned at the knee of a Bantu mother. These facts must dictate to a very large extent the content and methods of his early education.[107]

Eiselen accentuated the role that culture and language would play in African education and did not consider biological race to be a factor in determining curricula or lesson plans. He did not reject the significance of European languages and believed that African knowledge of them would help in both daily interactions with whites and discourse with the outside world. Nevertheless, Eiselen remained adamant that instruction should come first and foremost in the vernacular.

Westermann's influence on Eiselen is also apparent, and similar to Meinhof's. In *The African Today and Tomorrow,* Westermann spoke at length to the issues of missionary schooling and vernacular language training. He maintained that the missionaries had two basic positions concerning "native" education. For adherents of the first, Christianity and Western civilization were a package deal: Africans could not become Christian unless they were also remade in the European image. Meanwhile, those who espoused the second recognized the inherent value of African culture and did not believe it was incompatible with Christianity. Missionaries with this mind-set welcomed anthropological and linguistic studies, since they would strengthen European knowledge of African society and allow Christianity to be promoted in African languages, not foreign tongues.[108]

Van Warmelo never held a post quite as prominent as Eiselen's. Nevertheless his role in shaping native policy was substantial, since he remained South Africa's chief government ethnologist from 1930 until 1969. In that capacity he directed the work of his country's ethnological section, which was a unit in the Department of Native Affairs. Further, he wrote almost half of the books that the section published during his tenure.[109] This research contributed to shaping South African political geography throughout the apartheid era; for instance, Sekibakiba Peter Lekgoathi has shown that van Warmelo's investigations into Ndebele ethnicity engendered suggestions that, for various reasons, the Ndebele were probably not deserving of their own homeland.[110]

That van Warmelo had learned much of his craft from Meinhof is indisputable, considering the importance he placed on the hierarchization of African peoples, as well as his emphasis on the strong link between language and culture. Van Warmelo essentially wrote the Zulu section of the *Grundriss* when he translated it into English and explained that the Zulu came to be where they were through conquest and suppression of other peoples and the transmission of the Zulu language to them.

> The Zulu language has been carried to distant parts of the southern continent through the migration of several warlike Zulu tribes, and it is now understood far beyond the confines of Natal and Zululand. The Transvaal and Rhodesian Ndebele, the Ngoni of Gasaland and East Africa are all of Zulu stock and speak the Zulu language, though no doubt with a considerable admixture of foreign elements.[111]

Although there were certainly more than enough accounts of Shaka and Zulu expansion in existence, the description here still contains mythical qualities: The idea of a strong, conquering outside "tribe"; the suggestion that race and language overlapped; and the belief that, no matter how thorough the defeat, something of the vanquished culture would persist. All of these themes were hallmarks of Meinhof's thought. The parameters were not exactly the same—Meinhof's conquerors were not the Bantu Zulu, but the near-white "Hamites"—but the general historical trajectory was.

Van Warmelo's 1935 *A Preliminary Survey of the Bantu Tribes of South Africa,* a standard classification of all Bantu-speaking peoples in South Africa, demonstrates that van Warmelo believed all aspects of African life were deeply intertwined, just as Meinhof did. Van Warmelo published the text because he thought that the political and social circumstances of the times demanded a detailed categorization of the Bantu.

Specifically, van Warmelo suggested that there was a need to quantify how many natives led "their tribal life comparatively undisturbed" in contrast to those who "possess[ed] no fixed abode save on the sufferance of a European landlord" and so had "drifted away from tribalism or . . . in the case of many thousands, long since severed their connection with any social group of the old order." Such quantification would give the government some idea of the overall population breakdown and enable it to assess the cultural and economic differences between the two groups, those that were "traditional" and those that had been "detribalized."[112]

Van Warmelo's interest in determining the "tribal" affiliations of South African blacks in the late 1920s and 1930s is not surprising, considering the context. Segregationist philosophy of the period held that the detribalization of Africans in urban settings was contributing to the destabilization of South African society, by bringing people who were not "ready" for the benefits of white civilization into constant contact with it.[113] Establishing fixed boundaries between different ethnic groups acted as a safeguard both against economic and cultural competition and against the consequent potential breakdown of white ethnic specificity in favor of class-based identification.[114] Returning Africans to fictive tribal roots was thus seen as one solution to the perceived threat of African encroachment on white terrain.[115] Fear of this encroachment drove resistance to the Cape Franchise and helped precipitate its demise in 1936.[116] In offering potential scientific proof for differences among groups, disciplines such as anthropology and linguistics helped smooth the way toward removing Africans from white society and returning them to their rightful "homes."

While van Warmelo prized both anthropology and linguistics, he saw the latter as better equipped to trace the complex path of Bantu migration in the region. Throughout the *Preliminary Survey* van Warmelo was wary about depending too much on historical or ethnological factors in his classification. He claimed that these tended to be blurred and unreliable, given the constant influx and movement of Bantu peoples in South Africa. History only stretched back so far and then was lost, while the items of material culture that ethnologists studied were often unavailable. Language, by contrast, was more steadfast. Van Warmelo said that "in the days when many tribes were being broken up, and their culture and all its outward visible signs, such as homesteads and the products of arts and crafts, destroyed, the language survived with its speakers."[117] In words reminiscent of Meinhof and Luschan, who also insisted that language remained far more constant than physical or cultural attributes,[118] van Warmelo maintained that language was among the most critical factors in southern African classification.

Van Warmelo did recognize that linguistic reconstruction was not a perfect tool and remarked "that languages have in some instances fallen into complete oblivion, thereby reducing the value of the language criterion to nil." Language was not perfect—it, too, could be effaced much as could cultural characteristics—but it was tenacious, holding on in circumstances when the rest of a culture was completely eradicated. As van Warmelo also noted, even "where the possibility [of reconstruction] is more remote, a careful comparative analysis of structure and vocabulary will afford a most welcome avenue to deeper insight into origins and relationships."[119] Over the course of the book, van Warmelo continued to document instances in which language had persisted even as other outward cultural differences declined. For example, the Nguni languages, including Xhosa, certain forms of Zulu, Swazi, and Ndebele, were all distinct "dialects" and "mutually unintelligible." Even so, they had also been influenced by "mixing" with the "Hottentots and Bushmen," which had introduced "clicks."[120] Moreover, the language of the Lala population—a group that, van Warmelo maintained, had been largely wiped out and "Zuluised"—was "not as completely extinct as is commonly thought . . . [and] I found it easy to obtain connected text from not too old people who use no other language amongst themselves."[121] Although van Warmelo was unable to say definitively which Zulu "tribes" had once been *amaLala,* through language he considered himself well on the way to uncovering information about them.

Biological race also entered van Warmelo's discussion in the *Preliminary Survey,* even if he, like Meinhof, preferred linguistic and cultural interpretations to racial ones. In the *Survey* and elsewhere, language was obviously used as a marker to appraise ethnicity; however, in some cases it was also employed to make assumptions about biology and race, though this was trickier. For instance, this is how van Warmelo described the Lemba, a group that irked South African scholars because they were so difficult to classify.

> They are beyond doubt Semites (Arabs?) who have gradually drifted thus far to the South. The reasons for thinking they are Semites are briefly the following. In their physiognomy most of the Lemba have something so plainly non-Negro that every layman sees it at once, and one meets individuals with positively startling noses. They practice

> circumcision. They do not intermarry with any non-Lemba. All such they call by the very same Arab word that is contemptuously used by the East Coast Swahili for the "bush niggers" of the interior.[122]

While van Warmelo admitted that Lemba language did not differ appreciably from that of their neighbors—in fact, most of them had adopted the languages of the dominant group in the area, the Venda or Tonga—he still drew on a piece of derogatory vocabulary supposedly utilized by the Lemba and other "Arabicized" groups to demonstrate proof of their Semitic heritage.

Conclusion

The importance of German anthropology and linguistics for the development of parallel disciplines in South Africa cannot be underestimated. The South African students who visited Hamburg and Berlin in the 1920s were not only part of a tradition that had linked Germany and South Africa since the mid-nineteenth century but also conduits through which the latest developments in the German colonial sciences would be carried back to South Africa. The academic discourses that they followed did not, however, correspond one-to-one with Nazi ideas about biology and race. There was indeed overlap between fascist and missionary visions of the African Other. Yet missionaries tended to emphasize the role of cultural difference over genetics. The particularities pertaining to each ethnic group were not necessarily rooted in biological variation; as Meinhof explained in his work on phonetics, the notion that a biological difference in the formation of vocal organs was responsible for clicks and other linguistic peculiarities in certain African languages was nonsensical.[123] Culture—such as the filing of teeth among some East African peoples—was instead responsible.[124]

South African historian Hermann Giliomee has commented that it was not chiefly Nazism—or even Romanticism—that made the chief German contribution to apartheid ideology. Rather, it was missionary Protestantism filtered through the Dutch Reformed Church.[125] This German influence stretched back to the nineteenth century, when missionaries discussed the need for each ethnic group to come to Christianity on its own terms, using its unique language. Protestant philologists like Meinhof and Westermann perfected the classificatory schema that defined African languages in ethnic terms and passed on their knowledge to students such as van Warmelo and Eiselen, who then used their education to make policy at home in South Africa. Ideas about linguistic difference, originally constituted in conversations between missionaries in the field and academics in the German metropole, ultimately had their strongest impact in South Africa where colonialism did not end with World War II but continued into the 1990s.

Conclusion: The Legacy of *Afrikanistik*

The German discourse on African languages and cultures was rooted in the late eighteenth and early nineteenth centuries, when the discipline of comparative philology transformed the way scholars thought about origins and ethnicity. The Protestant missionaries who shaped the discipline of African studies were brought up in a pietist tradition, which held that the gospel could only be communicated in one's mother tongue. The lines dividing academic and missionary rhetoric on language in this period were not rigid; J. G. Herder, whose ideas about language and nationalism were seminal to the construction of concepts like *Volk,* was likewise raised with pietism, and it had a substantial impact on his belief system.[1] Yet German-speaking missionaries were mostly preoccupied with the practical effects of language study, and they learned African languages first and foremost as a pragmatic necessity. Moreover, they were not nationally inclined and worked jointly with Protestants of differing denominations and European nationalities. The main language of their scholarship was English, not German, and it reached a wide audience in Europe, Africa, and North America.

Outside of Namibia, Germany did not have a significant political presence in southern Africa.[2] Still, three German missionary societies—the Berlin, Rhenish, and Hermannsburger—had established roots in the region by the mid- to late nineteenth century, and one, the Moravians of Herrnhut, was in South Africa from 1737.[3] Other German missionaries, such as Zulu linguist Jakob Döhne, began their work with German societies but switched to English-speaking ones. The German linguist Wilhelm Bleek made his mark in South Africa too, first as the librarian to Cape Colony governor Sir George Grey, then as the first to codify Bantu philology and collect Bushman oral literature. Some of the children and later descendants of Bleek, as well as of the German missionaries, also became involved with African studies—both in linguistics and anthropology. Dorothea Bleek followed her father Wilhelm as an expert in Bushman language and culture,[4] while Werner Eiselen was a first-generation South African from a German missionary family; it was his father, Ernst Ludwig Gustav, who arranged for him to study in Hamburg.[5] Further, Eiselen was related to Karl Nauhaus, the missionary who had studied East African languages with Meinhof in the 1890s; his mother Friderike was born a Nauhaus. N. J. van Warmelo was of Dutch descent but married into a German missionary family, the Giesekkes, and spoke fluent German.[6] In addition, the liberal philosopher R. F. A. Hoernlé could claim German missionary roots, although his relatives in the Berlin Missionary Society had labored in India, not Africa. While not allied with thinkers such as Eiselen, Hoernlé nevertheless shared a similar background and, as Paul B. Rich has shown, was very concerned with the intellectual development of the German-inspired Afrikaner *volkekunde*.[7]

In South Africa and beyond, German Protestant missionaries were active throughout the nineteenth century and, early on, maintained an ecumenical world perspective that included close collaboration with colleagues from other countries. Yet as the century progressed, nationalism became an increasingly pertinent issue for German missionaries. Confronted with a newly unified country with colonial ambitions, they had to decide whether to embrace German imperialism or remain loyal to their older, ecumenical tradition. Individuals like Rhenish mission inspector Friedrich Fabri and Carl Büttner were especially strong supporters of the colonial cause, insisting that their fellows assist not only the colonial state but also the German businessmen who worked in it.[8] There were numerous disagreements about the extent to which missionaries should become involved with colonialism,[9] but in the end most German-speaking mission societies did defend German imperialism and turned away from their formerly international attitude.[10] Those who were scholars now often wrote in German, too, and various German journals of African philology emerged.

From the beginning of their involvement with African studies, missionaries employed a cultural and linguistic approach toward research on ethnicity, not a biological one. Language and culture continued to be the primary factors used in constructions of ethnic hierarchies among later nineteenth- and early twentieth-century linguists like Meinhof and Westermann. At the same time, race in the biological sense entered more frequently into discussions of Africa. Meinhof and his anthropologist colleague Luschan were often chastised for conflating language with race. Conflation was especially noticeable in Meinhof's *Sprachen der Hamiten,* which was supposed to be based on purely linguistic information but incorporated photographic images of people meant to represent various races.[11]

As German missionaries became increasingly nationalistic, and ideas about biological race filtered into discourse on African languages and cultures, the central location for studying Africa shifted, moving from the missionary field to the metropolitan university. Once Germany had acquired African and Asian colonies in the 1880s, scholars and government officials believed there was a need for broader training in non-Western languages and mores. The *Seminar für Orientalische Sprachen* opened in the fall of 1887 and originally focused on the so-called *Kultursprachen* of the Middle East, South Asia, and East Asia. African language courses quickly grew popular, however, as Germany's commitment to the African colonies deepened and more civil servants were assigned to work in them. Missionary participation in the institutionalized discipline remained vital; Büttner was the first African language lecturer at the seminar, and Westermann began to work there in the early 1900s. Yet nonmissionaries were becoming more prominent, too, with former colonial officials like Velten and Lippert joining the fray. Moreover, courses at the seminar had different foci than missionary teachings. Both the seminar's founders and missionary linguists valued practicality and the potential of African language knowledge to assist in subduing local populations. Still, despite many overlapping goals, missionaries were obviously most interested in conversion, and colonialists in compelling Africans to work for them.

Practical and academic rationales for studying Africa's languages also conflicted in Meinhof's work. Further, Meinhof's methodologies were often considered too arcane for the classroom; his emphasis on *Urbantu* and learning the grammatical, morphological, and phonetic structures of the Bantu language family was antithetical to the seminar's pragmatic objectives. Indeed its director, Sachau, originally rejected the idea of Meinhof teaching at his institution because he disagreed with Meinhof's pedagogy. In the first years of the twentieth century, however, Meinhof's theories moved to the vanguard of African language and culture studies, and missionaries prized and hoped to imitate his efforts. Sachau thus acquiesced, welcoming Meinhof to the seminar.

The relationship did not last long. Meinhof and Sachau quarreled over whether the former could found a phonetics laboratory in Berlin. As biological factors grew more important to African linguistics, Meinhof attempted to reorient the discipline away from humanistic enterprises and toward the physical sciences. Phonetics was crucial to this shift, because it emphasized how the human body produced speech, not the cultural peculiarities that shaped different languages. Sounds were captured by machine and recorded on cylinders or phonographic discs, technically removing the speaker from the equation. Sachau was not convinced that the African studies section of the seminar needed a special phonetics laboratory. When this became clear, Meinhof left Berlin for Hamburg. Hamburg had recently opened its own Colonial Institute to compete with Berlin, and the new establishment was more than happy to grant Meinhof his request for a laboratory, as well as to create a Department of Colonial Languages to place under his direction.

Meinhof may have hoped to underscore the significance of abstracted speech sounds in his phonetics laboratory, but he could not have denied the impact of his African colleagues—including informants, interpreters, lecturers, assistants, and research subjects—to their scholarly activities. While Germans usually spoke of Africans as "helpmates," not peers, the field of African studies could never have existed without their participation. From the early nineteenth century, Africans worked alongside the Europeans who wanted to learn their languages, collaborating on the construction of dictionaries, grammars, primers, and Bibles. They had the power to subvert European aspirations by withholding linguistic or cultural information, or by acting contrary to Western expectations. In addition, the lecturers who moved to Berlin or Hamburg to assume teaching positions provide an invaluable window on how Africans lived in Germany, what obstacles they encountered, and what advantages they gleaned from their time in the metropole.

Meinhof and other mainly armchair scholars, who rarely ventured away from the metropole, thus relied heavily on African informants and teachers. They also continued to depend on Protestant missionaries still living in Africa, who were themselves indebted to Africans for their knowledge. Both missionaries and those informants who remained in the colonies were now far removed from the academic "centers" of Berlin and Hamburg, and relegated to a scholarly periphery. News from home came in dribs and drabs, and there was little connection among missionaries pursuing linguistic and anthropological research on outlying stations. It was largely for this reason that Meinhof created a new journal, the *Zeitschrift für Kolonialsprachen.* The *Zeitschrift,* which first appeared in 1910, was intended to join missionaries and others who lived in remote regions to their colleagues, apprising them of academic developments back home as well as of what kinds of research their peers in the field were doing. While it did come to serve this function, since the majority of its contributors were missionaries, it was around this period that rifts began to emerge between Meinhof and the Protestant mission establishment. Like Sachau, missionary elders were uncertain that Meinhof's studies had much practical benefit, and although Meinhof was still a frequent guest at missionary conferences and houses, mission leaders no longer had the time to send their candidates to him.

World War I interrupted the growth of *Afrikanistik.* Because many of its most promising young practitioners were called to serve in the German army, scholarship declined between 1914 and 1918. There were notable exceptions; women such as Maria von Tiling and Elise Kootz-Kretschmer, a Moravian missionary stationed in East Africa during the war, entered the discipline.[12] Moreover, von Tiling and others traveled to nearby POW camps to interview African inmates and gather information on their languages and cultures. World War I also initiated two new trends in African studies: First, scholars started to move toward the ivory tower, since there were no longer German colonies that they could practically assist with their research; second, they turned outward to seek new, non-German or nationalist imperial ventures. The latter proved extremely difficult, owing to the animosity between Germany and its former enemies, who were the remaining colonial powers in Africa.

African studies still had its place in post–World War I Germany, even if the discipline had no German Empire to support. In the 1920s, while the German Africanists regrouped and resigned themselves to the fact that their country was no longer a colonial force, scholars like Meinhof refused to relinquish claims of dominance in fields such as African linguistics, instead reluctantly choosing to join the members of other nations in continuing to develop metropolitan spaces for the study of the colonized. That these spaces were no longer in Hamburg or Berlin but London, however, was ultimately too difficult for Meinhof, who cut all ties to the International Institute of African Languages and Cultures when it did not live up to his expectations. At the same time, he was happy to see his methodologies applied in places like Cape Town, Johannesburg, and Pretoria, where he found eager students and a receptive audience. The link between Germany and South Africa that had been nurtured since the nineteenth century remained stable, despite the fact that the Union government had supported the Allies in World War I and Jan Smuts's army had wrested South West Africa away from Germany.[13] However, while white South African academics generally admired Meinhof, it was the Afrikaner contingent more than the British that the German linguist considered his ally. German missionary descendants mostly became Afrikaners—that is, like Eiselen they spoke Afrikaans alongside German as their first language—and often self-identified with the Afrikaans community. Many also continued to support German theories of ethnic particularity; as Brian Du Toit has shown, they drew heavily on ideas of missionary-philosophers like Gustav Warneck, who emphasized the ethnic unit over the individual when considering how to approach new converts to Christianity.[14] This theory was then translated into areas beyond the church, influencing officials such as Eiselen in their interpretation of how Bantu education should be structured, among other things.

In the 1930s German intellectual contact with South Africa diminished but never entirely ended, even though South Africa once again aligned itself with the Allies during World War II. A contingent of Afrikaners did firmly side themselves with the Nazis. Indeed, as T. D. Moodie and, more recently, Patrick Furlong have contended, fascist ideas were seminal to the construction of Afrikaner nationalism in this period and beyond.[15] Yet the connection between German and South African thought was more complicated than this argument suggests.[16] German missionaries and linguists such as Bleek and Meinhof had an impact not because they were fascists but because their philosophy provided a rationale for segregation in a country whose white population feared African urbanization and wanted to solve their "Native Question," especially after the establishment of Union in 1910. The German missionary tradition, which emphasized the significance of language to ethnicity and cultural particularism, may have overlapped with fascist notions of biological race, but it did not correspond one-to-one. Instead, German missionary discourse reflected a pernicious paternalism, which relegated Africans to a prior level of human development but promised eventual parity between white and black—in an extremely distant future. The belief was that Africans should reach "civilization" on their own ethnic terms, not those of Europeans. Simultaneously, however, Africans would require European guidance, since they were not "mature" enough to accomplish civilizational benchmarks on their own. This premise was attractive in a South Africa where whites wanted Africans kept at a distance, but also readily available to serve as laborers. Contact between the races would "edify"

Africans, but segregated neighborhoods would ensure that Africans nurtured their unique cultures in a closed environment. German missionary hypotheses therefore dovetailed well with white desires to implement segregationist social engineering.

While some German Africanists were, like Meinhof, either Nazi Party members or sympathizers who felt that their needs would be better served under the fascist regime than they had been in the Weimar era, they never embraced a crude biologicism. They did see the Nazis as heralding the arrival of a new German empire in Africa and restoring meaning to their work. This should never excuse their collaboration with the National Socialists, only demonstrate the complexity of German racism and multitude of racial theories existing in the country not only in the 1930s and 1940s but from at least the early nineteenth century, if not before.

The legacy of *Afrikanistik* is obviously not confined to Germany. Its disciplinary history played out on an international stage as German Africanists attempted, sometimes successfully and sometimes not, to work with foreign scholars toward the realization of a comprehensive—pragmatic as well as theoretical—program of African studies. Whether the practical aspects of the field were as significant as its philosophical or imaginary ones for Germany itself is debatable. Meinhof and his peers hoped to have some influence on the practical unfolding of German colonialism in the field, but the empire they served collapsed too early for their ideas to have had lasting effects outside of Namibia, which fell under South African control during World War I. Hundreds of students were trained in Zizow, Berlin, and Hamburg between 1887 and the end of World War I, many of whom later embarked on colonial careers in government or military service. A handful of these, many of them missionaries, continued to compile their own dictionaries or grammars once abroad. But for the most part, African studies had a limited role. There is little concrete evidence that Africans were treated differently according to where they fell in the classificatory schemes that Meinhof and others proposed. Further, the goal of seeing Germany's African subjects taught in either their native languages or languages closely related to their own, which Meinhof and the missionaries shared, ran counter to what the *Reichskolonialamt* wanted. In an effort to create a class of low-level civil servants who could act as liaisons between the African and German communities, the governments of individual colonies hoped to disseminate German, not indigenous tongues, through the colonial school system.[17]

More intangibly, the categories and racial divisions that Africanists suggested may have proved more potent. The idea that language, race, and culture were intertwined was forceful, even if confusing, and could apply not only to Europeans but to Africans and sundry "colonial others." In the classrooms and laboratories of Berlin and Hamburg, German scholars produced a knowledge of Africa that emphasized its multiplicity and plasticity. The continent was defined as a region of complex racial and linguistic difference that, far from having remained static or "trapped in the past," was constantly changing with each new influx of migrating peoples. Language formed the basis for understanding Africa's complicated ethnic map, and it showed Europeans how to draw boundaries between groups that might earlier have appeared indistinguishable. Whether or not *Afrikanistik* affected German colonial policy in concrete terms is thus not the most important issue. What is significant is how *Afrikanistik* allowed Africa to be parceled out into discrete, easily definable categories that could then be hierarchically arranged.

German African studies also had international reverberations. In South Africa, where some of its earliest practitioners lived and worked, the discipline provided a tool for tracing the historical movements of Africans and determining where their "ancestral" homelands lay. Moreover, German Africanists were active elsewhere in Europe even after the discipline was institutionalized at the Berlin Seminar in 1887. They contributed essays to non-German journals, collaborated with peers overseas, attended conferences abroad, and served on the boards of foreign organizations such as the British International Institute of African Languages and Cultures. These Africanists maintained links to the United States, too, through sustained contact with scholars such as German émigré Franz Boas or missionaries from various American societies.[18]

What place does *Afrikanistik* have in contemporary Germany? Today there are five departments teaching the subject, in Berlin, Hamburg, Leipzig, Bayreuth, and Cologne. In addition, there are similar African studies programs in Vienna and Basel, and a minor in *Afrikanistik* is offered in Zurich. All such programs remain embedded in philological, linguistic, and literary traditions. There is a strong focus on learning African languages, often Swahili or Hausa. African anthropology and history are of course taught as well, but usually not as part of the discipline called *Afrikanistik*. Faculties of anthropology, which include Africanists, are often housed in *Völkerkunde* museums, while historians are sometimes found in institutes for African studies, and sometimes in history departments.[19] The present definition of *Afrikanistik* is still largely linguistic, as is indicated on the website of the Hamburg *Institut für Afrikanistik und Äthiopistik.*[20] Contemporary professors of *Afrikanistik* trace their academic "lineage" back to either of the two early twentieth-century disciplinary founders, Westermann or Meinhof; for instance, Ludwig Gerhardt, a current professor emeritus in Hamburg, counts himself among Meinhof's academic progeny.[21] The racialist sentiments that shaped the discipline's roots are largely gone, however, and Meinhof, for one, is mostly remembered and revered for his Bantu phonology and grammar. His *Sprachen der Hamiten,* by contrast, is mostly considered a strange artifact based on a wrongheaded idea, representative of the times in which he lived, and not an enduring aspect of the discipline.

The significance of linguistics and the belief in its ties to ethnicity did persist in South Africa after World War II ended and apartheid was instituted in 1948. Indeed, this is when the Afrikaans-speaking students who had trained in Germany enjoyed their greatest impact. Van Warmelo retired from his position as chief government ethnologist in 1969 but continued to be an active scholar through his death twenty years later.[22] Eiselen held his position as Secretary of Native Affairs until 1959 when, as Ivan Evans has explained, he was made "ambassador to the North Tswana National Unit," a post that was mainly ceremonial. This meant that Eiselen's main contributions came during apartheid's early years. Evans has shown that Eiselen was replaced because his ideas about the primacy of ethnic idenity to separate development had been eclipsed by H. F. Verwoerd's more crudely stated belief in *baaskap,* which Evans defines as "outright racial determination."[23] Nonetheless, the influence that Eiselen exerted on the original advancement of group areas planning, homeland policy, and Bantu education was substantial, and it paved the way toward the stricter enforcement of division that appeared once his tenure was over.

The "next generation" of South African linguists and anthropologists drew on hypotheses cultivated not only by van Warmelo, but also by Meinhof, Westermann, and the missionaries. Among them were Ernst Westphal, himself the son of a German missionary in Vendaland, a linguist who trained with English-speaking linguist C. M. Doke in South Africa and then worked for years at the School of Oriental and African Studies in London;[24] Dirk Ziervogel, a contemporary of Westphal who employed theories from both Meinhof and van Warmelo;[25] P. J. Schoeman, an anthropologist who studied under Eiselen while he was at Stellenbosch in the 1930s;[26] and P. J. Coertze, another Eiselen student who in 1949 took over from his mentor and became professor of anthropology at the University of Pretoria.[27] These academics all continued to train others from their university seats. The links joining scholars across the nineteenth and twentieth centuries thus remained strong, even as contexts changed and the religious roots of African studies diminished. Over time, the discipline took on both academic and practical significance in a variety of arenas, both international as well as distinctly German and South African. It shaped European understandings of African identity and ethnicity and, in some instances, colonial policy. From its origins on the mission field through its institutionalization in Germany and application in South Africa, *Afrikanistik* served to harden stereotypes and contribute to classificatory schemes that ultimately had a very destructive effect on Africans, even as its practitioners believed they were saving them.

Notes

INTRODUCTION

1. G. P. Lestrade, "In Memory of Carl Meinhof," *African Studies* (formerly *Bantu Studies*) 5, no. 2 (June 1946): 73.

2. W. D. Hammond-Tooke, *Imperfect Interpreters: South Africa's Anthropologists, 1920–1990* (Johannesburg: University of the Witwatersrand Press, 1997), 65.

3. Werner Eiselen, "In Memory of Carl Meinhof," *African Studies* (formerly *Bantu Studies*) 5, no. 2 (June 1946): 78–79.

4. Carl Meinhof, *Die Sprachen der Hamiten* (Berlin: L. Friedrichsen, 1912), 17.

5. Carl Meinhof, *Die Entstehung flektierender Sprachen* (Berlin: Dietrich Reimer, 1936), 38.

6. Joseph Greenberg, *The Languages of Africa* (Bloomington: Indiana University Press, 1966), 31–33.

7. Although some of his opinions on purely grammatical and morphological issues still have merit; see, for instance, Bernd Heine, Thilo Schadeberg, and Ekkehard Wolff, eds., *Die Sprachen Afrikas: mit zahlreichen Karten und Tabellen* (Hamburg: Buske, 1981), 148.

8. Nancy Leys Stepan, *The Idea of Race in Science: Great Britain, 1800–1960* (Hamden, CT: Archon, 1982), 17, and Saul Dubow, *Scientific Racism in Modern South Africa* (Cambridge: Cambridge University Press, 1995), 80–81, have both commented that pseudoscientific ideas about race, while wholly discredited, can provide tremendous insight because it is evident that racism was a fundament of nineteenth- and twentieth-century Western thought, and that the echoes of pseudoscientific racism, however muted, persist in present-day European and North American culture. African linguistics is, obviously, *not* a pseudoscience. Nonetheless, some of the ideas on the interconnection between race and language promoted by pre–World War II Africanist linguists do fall into a pseudoscientific category, and the study of such ideas can illuminate the trajectories of developing racist thought in such seemingly disparate countries as Germany and South Africa.

9. The idea that Christianity and European civilization could uplift Africa's "benighted" people was not new. Indeed, it was one justification for both the end of the slave trade and the beginning of European colonization. Among many others see A. G. Hopkins, "'The New International Economic Order in the Nineteenth Century': Britain's First Development Plan for Africa," in *From Slave Trade to Le-*

gitimate Commerce: The Commercial Transition in Nineteenth Century West Africa, ed. Robin Law (Cambridge: Cambridge University Press, 1995), 240–64.

10. Thorsten Altena, *"Ein Häuflein Christen mitten in der Heidenwelt des dunklen Erdteils": Zum Selbst- und Fremdverständnis protestantischer Missionare im kolonialen Afrika, 1884–1918* (Münster: Waxmann, 2003), 52.

11. Ferdinand Hestermann, *Die Deutsche Afrikanistik bis 1913: Kritische Darstellungen der neuesten Ansichten über Gruppierungen und Bewegungen der Sprachen und Völker in Afrika* (Vienna: Self-published, 1929; based on *Anthropos* article of 1913); Archives of the Institut für Afrikanistik und Äthiopistik, Hamburg (hereafter referred to as AIAÄ), Übersetzung "Grundriss" und Warmelo allgemein, N. J. van Warmelo to Carl Meinhof, November 26, 1929, concerning a disagreement between Meinhof and van Warmelo over the inclusion of various languages on a language map of Africa.

12. Ali A. Mazrui, "The Re-invention of Africa: Edward Said, V. Y. Mudimbe, and Beyond," *Research in African Literatures* 36, no. 3 (Fall 2005): 68–82.

13. Mahmood Mamdani, *When Victims Become Killers: Colonialism, Nativism, and the Genocide in Rwanda* (Princeton: Princeton University Press, 2002), 85–86, and Philip Gourevitch, *We Wish to Inform You that Tomorrow We Will Be Killed with Our Families: Stories from Rwanda* (New York: Farrar, Straus, and Giroux, 1998), 50ff., are among those who have called attention to the Hamitic hypothesis and its devastating effect in Rwanda, which was once part of German East Africa. However, it is important to note that Belgian priests were largely responsible for the proliferation of the hypothesis in that region after the Germans lost it in World War I. For the case of Burundi, please see Rene Lemarchand with Lee H. Hamilton, *Burundi: Ethnic Conflict and Genocide* (Cambridge: Cambridge University Press, 1996), 50.

14. Gauri Viswanathan, *Masks of Conquest: Literary Study and British Rule in India* (New York: Columbia University Press, 1989), 2.

15. For a comparison with how the concept of the Orient shifted over time see Todd Kontje, *German Orientalisms* (Ann Arbor: University of Michigan Press, 2004), 12ff.

16. Thomas Trautmann, *Aryans and British India* (Berkeley: University of California Press, 1997), 22, after David Ludden, "Orientalist Empiricism: Transformations of Colonial Knowledge," in *Orientalism and the Postcolonial Predicament: Perspectives on South Asia,* ed. Carl Breckenridge and Peter van der Veer (Philadelphia: University of Pennsylvania Press, 1993). Said's own work also drew heavily on Raymond Schwab's *The Oriental Renaissance: Europe's Rediscovery of India and the East, 1680–1880,* trans. Gene Patterson-Black and Victor Reinking (New York: Columbia University Press, 1984). Schwab began his investigation of the European fascination with the Orient with linguistics and moved beyond it to explore how Orientalist ideas permeated other academic disciplines as well as the public imagination.

17. Trautmann, 22–23.

18. Keith Breckenridge, "Verwoerd's Bureau of Proof: Total Information in the Making of Apartheid," *History Workshop Journal,* no. 59 (2005): 83–108.

19. The essays in Ann Laura Stoler and Frederick Cooper's *Tensions of Empire: Colonial Cultures in a Bourgeois World* (Berkeley: University of California Press,

1997) demonstrated that the totality of colonial society—meaning both its metropolitan core as well as its actual colonies—was a hybrid creation, with Europeans and non-Europeans exerting mutual influence on each other and on the development of a uniquely colonial culture. Further to this point see Stoler, "Rethinking Colonial Categories: European Communities and the Boundaries of Rule," in *Colonialism and Culture,* ed. Nicholas B. Dirks (Ann Arbor: University of Michigan Press, 1992), 319–52, and Lynn Zastoupil, "Intimacy and Colonial Knowledge," *Journal of Colonialism and Colonial History* 3, no. 2 (2002): 1–41. Both Stoler and Zastoupil examined colonial society through the lens of sexual intimacy, demonstrating how intimate relationships could lead to the creation of colonial "texts." While most of the relationships between African informants and German missionaries or scholars were not sexual, they shared an intellectual intimacy that spawned the many dictionaries, grammars, and primers that were produced throughout the nineteenth and early twentieth centuries.

20. There have been many recent publications concerning different aspects of German imperialism; among others they include Sara Friedrichsmeyer, Sara Lennox, and Susanne Zantop, eds., *The Imperialist Imagination: German Colonialism and Its Legacy* (Ann Arbor: University of Michigan Press, 1998); Fatima El-Tayeb, *Schwarze deutsche: Der Diskurs um Rasse und nationale Identität 1890–1933* (Frankfurt am Main: Campus Verlag, 2001); Eric Ames, Marcia Klotz, and Lora Wildenthal, eds., *Germany's Colonial Pasts* (Lincoln: University of Nebraska Press, 2005); Sebastian Conrad and Jürgen Osterhammel, eds., *Das Kaiserreich transnational: Deutschland in der Welt 1871–1914* (Göttingen: Vandenhoeck & Ruprecht, 2004); Sebastian Conrad, *Globalisierung und Nation im deutschen Kaiserreich* (Munich: C. H. Beck Verlag, 2006); Birthe Kundrus, ed., *Phantasiereiche: Zur Kulturgeschichte des deutschen Kolonialismus* (Frankfurt am Main: Campus, 2003); Birthe Kundrus, *Moderne Imperialisten: Das Kaiserreich im Spiegel seiner Kolonien* (Cologne: Böhlau, 2003); Jürgen Zimmerer, *Deutsche Herrschaft über Afrikaner* (Berlin: LIT Verlag, 2004); George Steinmetz, *The Devil's Handwriting: Precoloniality and the German Colonial State in Qingdao, Samoa, and Southwest Africa* (Chicago: University of Chicago Press, 2007); Pascal Grosse, *Kolonialismus, Eugenik und bürgerliche Gesellschaft in Deutschland 1850–1918* (Frankfurt am Main: Campus Verlag, 2000); Michael Pesek, *Koloniale Herrschaft in Deutsch-Ostafrika: Expeditionen, Militär und Verwaltung seit 1880* (Frankfurt am Main: Campus Verlag, 2005); Isabel V. Hull, *Absolute Destruction: Military Culture and the Practices of War in Imperial Germany* (Ithaca: Cornell University Press, 2006); Lora Wildenthal, *German Women for Empire, 1894–1945* (Durham: Duke University Press, 2001); Andrew Zimmerman, *Anthropology and Antihumanism in Imperial Germany* (Chicago: University of Chicago Press, 2001); Matti Bunzl and H. Glenn Penny, eds., *Worldly Provincialism: German Anthropology in the Age of Empire* (Ann Arbor: University of Michigan Press, 2003); H. Glenn Penny, *Objects of Culture: Ethnology and Ethnographic Museums in Imperial Germany* (Chapel Hill: University of North Carolina Press, 2002); and Christine Stelzig, *Afrika am Museum für Völkerkunde zu Berlin, 1873–1919* (Herbholzheim: Centaurus, 2005).

21. Susanne Zantop, *Colonial Fantasies: Conquest, Family, and Nation in Precolonial Germany, 1770–1870* (Durham: Duke University Press, 1997).

22. Bagchi, "Orientalism without Colonialism? Three Nineteenth Century German Indologists and India" (PhD diss., Ohio State University, 1996), 40; see also Kontje, *German Orientalisms;* Suzanne Marchand, "German Orientalism and the Decline of the West," *Proceedings of the American Philosophical Society* (December 2001), and Douglas McGetchin, Peter K. J. Park, and Damodar SarDesai, eds., *Sanskrit and "Orientalism": Indology and Comparative Linguistics in Germany, 1750–1958* (New Delhi: Manohar, 2004). To be fair, Said does admit that "any work that seeks to provide an understanding of academic orientalism and pays little attention to scholars like Steinthal, Müller, Becker, Goldziher, Brockelmann, Nöldeke—to mention only a handful—needs to be reproached, and I freely reproach myself." Still, he also said that "the German Orient was almost exclusively a scholarly, or at least a classical, Orient." Said, 17–19.

23. Jennifer Jenkins, "German Orientalism: Introduction," *Comparative Studies of South Asia, Africa, and the Middle East* 24, no. 2 (2004): 97–100.

24. Tuska Benes, "Comparative Linguistics as Ethnology: In Search of Indo-Germans in Central Asia, 1770–1830," *Comparative Studies of South Asia, Africa, and the Middle East* 24, no. 2 (2004): 117–32.

25. Tuska Benes, *In Babel's Shadow: Language, Philology, and the Nation in Nineteenth-Century Germany* (Detroit: Wayne State University Press, 2008), 16; George S. Williamson, *The Longing for Myth in Germany: Religion and Aesthetic Culture from Romanticism to Nietzsche* (Chicago: University of Chicago Press, 2004), 127.

26. Susan Shell, "Kant's Conception of a Human Race," in *The German Invention of Race,* ed. Sara Eigen and Mark Larrimore (Albany: State University of New York Press, 2006), 55–72; Robert Bernasconi, "Kant as an Unfamiliar Source of Racism," in *Philosophers on Race: Critical Essays,* ed. Julie K. Ward and Tommy L. Lott (London: Blackwell, 2002), 145–66; Emmanuel Chukwudi Eze, "The Color of Reason: The Idea of 'Race' in Kant's Anthropology," in *Anthropology and the German Enlightenment: Perspectives on Humanity,* ed. Katherine M. Faull (Lewisburg, PA: Bucknell University Press, 1995), 200–250.

27. Ibid.

28. G. W. F. Hegel, "Geographical Basis of World History," in *Race and the Enlightenment: A Reader,* ed. Emmanuel Chukwudi Eze (Oxford: Blackwell, 1997), 110–49.

29. Andrew Bank, *Bushmen in a Victorian World: The Remarkable Story of the Bleek-Lloyd Collection of Bushman Folklore* (Cape Town: Double Storey, 2006), 158.

30. Carl Meinhof, *Die moderne Sprachforschung in Afrika* (Berlin: Buchhandlung der Berliner evangelischen Missionsgesellschaft, 1910), 1–26.

31. Carl Meinhof, *An Introduction to the Study of African Languages,* trans. Alice Werner (New York: J. M. Dent and Sons, 1915), 156.

32. Zantop, *Colonial Fantasies;* Russell A. Berman, *Enlightenment or Empire: Colonial Discourse in German Culture* (Lincoln: University of Nebraska Press, 1998).

33. Bradley D. Naranch, "Inventing the *Auslandsdeutsche:* Emigration, Colonial Fantasy, and German National Identity, 1848–1871," in *Germany's Colonial Pasts,* ed. Eric Ames, Marcia Klotz, and Lora Wildenthal (Lincoln: University of Nebraska Press, 2005), 21–40.

34. Kontje, *German Orientalisms,* 61–132.

35. Zantop, *Colonial Fantasies;* Harry Liebersohn, *Aristocratic Encounters: European Travelers and North American Indians* (Cambridge: Cambridge University, 1998); Beatrix Heintze, "Ethnographic Appropriations: German Exploration and Fieldwork in West-Central Africa," *History in Africa* 26 (1999): 69–128; Johannes Fabian, *Out of Our Minds: Reason and Madness in the Exploration of Central Africa* (Berkeley: University of California Press, 2000), 11–12.

36. William Kemp Lowther Clarke, *A Short History of S.P.C.K.* (New York: Macmillan, 1919), 15; Eugene Stock, *One Hundred Years: Being the Short History of the Church Missionary Society* (London: Church Missionary Society, 1899), 1–15.

37. William Canton, *A History of the British and Foreign Bible Society,* vol. 2 (London: J. Murray, 1904), 23.

38. Richard Lovett, *The History of the London Missionary Society, 1795–1895,* vol. 1 (London: H. Frowde, 1899), 96, 100.

39. Altena, 83; Karl Rennstich, "Mission—Geschichte der protestantischen Mission in Deutschland," in *Der Pietismus im neunzehnten und zwanstigsten Jahrhundert,* ed. Gustav Adolf Benrath, Martin Sallmann, and Ulrich Gäbler, vol. 3, *Geschichte des Pietismus* (Göttingen: Vandenhoeck & Ruprecht, 2000), 308–20.

40. Penny, *Objects of Culture,* 11–13.

41. Benedict Anderson, *Imagined Communities: Reflections on the Origin and Spread of Nationalism,* rev. ed. (London: Verso, 2006).

42. Bundesarchiv Berlin (hereafter referred to as BAB) R/1001, 4550, *Die Zeitschrift für afrikanische Sprachen,* vol. 1, April 1886–28 Februar 1895, Carl Büttner, correspondent unknown, June 4, 1886.

43. James J. Sheehan, "What Is German History? Reflections on the Role of the Nation in German History and Historiography," *Journal of Modern History* 53, no. 1 (March 1981): 2–23, noted that reading the history of Germany backward as the triumphant march of nationalism culminating in the Bismarckian unification of 1871 is problematic, not least because it is inherently difficult to locate the boundaries of "Germany" or point to any entity that could firmly be identified as such prior to that date. The question of what Germany is, or who is part of it, is salient since it is clear that missionary scholars did not think of themselves in terms of "German" identity before the latter half of the nineteenth century.

44. Daniel Headrick, *The Tentacles of Progress: Technology Transfer in the Age of Imperialism, 1850–1940* (Oxford: Oxford University Press, 1988).

45. Sebastian Conrad, *Globalisierung und Nation im Deutschen Kaiserreich* (Munich: Beck, 2006), 99–101.

46. Marcia Klotz, "Introduction" and "Global Visions from the Colonial to the National Socialist World," *European Studies Journal* 16 (Fall 1999): 1–8, 37–68.

47. Kundrus, *Moderne Imperialisten,* 44ff.

48. Kundrus, *Moderne Imperialisten;* Daniel Walther, *Creating Germans Abroad: Cultural Policies and Settler Identities in Namibia* (Athens: Ohio University Press, 2002); Robbie Aitken, *Exclusion and Inclusion: Gradations of Whiteness and Socio-economic Engineering in German Southwest Africa, 1884–1918* (New York: Peter Lang, 2007).

49. Kristin Kopp, "Constructing Racial Difference in Colonial Poland," in *Germany's Colonial Pasts,* ed. Ames, Klotz, and Wildenthal, 76–96.

50. Altena, 29–32.

51. Pascal Grosse, *Kolonialismus, Eugenik und bürgerliche Gesellschaft in Deutschland 1850–1918* (Frankfurt am Main: Campus Verlag, 2000).

52. Zimmerman, *Anthropology and Antihumanism in Imperial Germany,* 135.

53. Kathrin Roller, "Mission und 'Mischehen,' Erinnerung und Körper—geteiltes Gedächtnis an eine afrikanische Vorfahrin. Über die Familie Schmelen-Kleinschmidt-Hegner," in *Namibia-Deutschland. Eine geteilte Geschichte. Widerstand, Gewalt, Erinnerung,* ed. Larissa Förster, Dag Henrichsen, and Michael Böllig (Publikation zur gleichnamigen Ausstellung im Rautenstrauch-Joest-Museum für Völkerkunde Köln und im Deutschen Historischen Museum Berlin 2004/2005) (Wolfratshausen: Editions Minerva Hermann Farnung, 2004), 194–211, and "Zwischen Rassismus und Frömmigkeit—Biopolitik aus erfahrungsgeschichtlicher Perspektive. Über die Geschwister Hegner, Mathilde Kleinschmidt und Ludwig Baumann als Nachfahren einer deutsch-afrikanischen Missionsfamilie," in *Rassenmischehen—Mischlinge—Rassentrennung: Zur Politik der Rasse im deutschen Kolonialreich,* ed. Frank Becker (Stuttgart: Franz Steiner, 2004), 220–40; Ursula Trüper, *Die Hottentottin. Das kurze Leben der Zara Schmelen (ca. 1793–1831), Missionsgehilfin und Sprachpionerin in Südafrika* (Cologne: Rüdgier Köppe, 2000).

54. Nils Ole Oermann, *Mission, Church, and State Relations in South West Africa under German Rule (1884–1915)* (Stuttgart: Franz Steiner, 1999), 158ff., 195.

55. Lora Wildenthal, *German Women for Empire, 1884–1945* (Durham: Duke University Press, 2001), 88.

56. See Stephen J. Gould, *The Mismeasure of Man,* revised and expanded edition (New York: W. W. Norton, 1996), 74ff., for a discussion of the history of polygeny.

57. P. Hausleiter, "Die Stellung der Mission zur Rassenfrage," *Verhandlungen der XII. Missions=Konferenz zu Bremen vom 6. bis 10 Mai 1909* (Bremen: Kommissionsverlag der Norddeutschen Missions=Gesellschaft, 1909), 22–31.

58. There are, however, many German-language studies of German missionaries, among them Horst Gründer, *Christliche Mission und deutscher Imperialismus: Eine politische Geschichte ihrer Beziehungen während der deutschen Kolonialzeit (1884–1914) unter besonderer Berücksichtigung Afrikas und Chinas* (Paderborn: Schöningh, 1982); Altena, *"Ein Häuflein Christen . . ."*; Ulrich van der Heyden and Holger Stoecker, eds., *Mission und Macht im Wandel politischer Orientierungen: Europäische Missionsgesellschaften in politischen Spannungsfeldern in Afrika und Asien zwischen 1800 und 1945* (Wiesbaden: Franz Steiner Verlag, 2005); and Andrea Schultze, *"In Gottes Namen Hütten bauen." Kirchlicher Landbesitz in Südafrika: die Evangelisch-Lutherische Kirche Südafrikas zwischen 1834 und 2005* (Stuttgart: Franz Steiner Verlag, 2005).

59. Hermann Giliomee, *The Afrikaners: Biography of a People* (Charlottesville: University of Virginia Press, 2003), 447ff.; T. Dunbar Moodie, *The Rise of Afrikanerdom: Power, Apartheid, and the Afrikaner Civil Religion* (Berkeley: University of California Press, 1975), 9.

60. Tina Campt, "Converging Spectres of an Other Within: Race and Gender in Prewar Afro-German History," *Callaloo* 26, no. 2 (Spring 2003): 322–41.

61. Ronald Hyam and Peter Henshaw, *The Lion and the Springbok: Britain and South Africa since the Boer War* (Cambridge: Cambridge University Press, 2003), 102ff.

62. Carl Meinhof, "Aus dem Seelenleben der Eingeborenen," *Jahrbuch über die deutschen Kolonien* 1909, II: 47–52.

63. The *Reichskolonialamt* did sometimes consult on language issues with linguists such as Meinhof and his colleagues Diedrich Westermann and Bernhard Struck, as well as with missionary societies. See, for instance, BAB R 1001/6177, Bd. 1, Erforschung der Sprachen der eingeborenen Völkerschaften Südwestafrikas, Juni 1904–März 1936, letter from Heinrich Vedder, Rhenish Society missionary, to Dr. Conze, Colonial Director, November 13, 1909, concerning studies of click languages that Vedder had undertaken.

64. Wolfgang Werner, "A Brief History of Land Dispossession in Namibia," *Journal of Southern African Studies* 19, no. 1 (March 1993): 135–46; Reinhart Kössler, "From Reserve to Homeland: Local Identities and South African Policy in Southern Namibia," *Journal of Southern African Studies* 26, no. 3 (September 2000): 447–62.

65. N. J. van Warmelo, *A Preliminary Survey of the Bantu Tribes of South Africa,* Union of South Africa, Department of Native Affairs, Ethnological Publications, vol. 5 (Pretoria: Government Printer, 1935), 12ff.

66. W. D. Hammond-Tooke, *Imperfect Interpreters,* 78.

67. Van Warmelo, *A Preliminary Survey,* 36.

68. Altena, 57.

69. Alan Kirkaldy, *Capturing the Soul: The Vhavenda and the Missionaries* (Pretoria: Protea, 2005), and Caroline Jeannerat, "An Ethnography of Faith: Personal Conceptions of Religiosity in the Zoutpansberg, South Africa in the Nineteenth and Twentieth Centuries" (PhD diss., University of Michigan, Ann Arbor, 2007), both cover the history of the Berlin mission among one of these groups, the Venda. Meanwhile Schultze, *"In Gottes Namen Hütten bauen...,"* has looked at the history of the Berlin mission in South Africa over a wider area.

70. Norman Etherington, "Kingdoms of This World and the Next: Christian Beginnings among Zulu and Swazi," in *Christianity in South Africa: A Political, Social, and Cultural History,* ed. Richard Elphick and Rodney Davenport (Berkeley: University of California Press, 1997), 89–106, on the Hermannsburgers, and Elizabeth Elbourne and Robert Ross, "Combating Spiritual and Social Bondage: Early Missions in the Cape Colony," in *Christianity in South Africa,* ed. Elphick and Davenport, 31–50, on the Moravian arrival.

71. Gustav Menzel, *Die Rheinische Mission. Aus 150 Jahren Missionsgeschichte* (Wuppertal: Verlag der Vereinigten Evangelischen Mission, 1978), 230.

72. Carl Meinhof, "Die sprachwissenschaftliche Arbeit Berliner Missionare," *Missionsberichte der Gesellschaft zur Beförderung der evangelischen Missionare unter den Heiden zu Berlin,* 1905: 111–17.

73. Mario A. Di Gregorio, "Reflections of a Nonpolitical Naturalist: Ernst

Haeckel, Wilhelm Bleek, Friedrich Müller, and the Meaning of Language," *Journal of the History of Biology* 35 (2002): 79–109.

74. George Stocking, *After Tylor: British Social Anthropology, 1888–1951* (Madison: University of Wisconsin Press, 1995), 23.

75. J. S. Sharp, "The Roots and Development of Volkekunde in South Africa," *Journal of Southern African Studies* 8, no. 1 (1981): 16–36; Robert Gordon, "Serving the Volk with Volkekunde: On the Rise of South African Anthropology," in *Knowledge and Power in South Africa: Critical Perspectives across the Disciplines,* ed. J. Jansen (Johannesburg: Skotaville, 1991), 79–87.

76. Patrick Furlong, *Between Crown and Swastika: The Impact of the Radical Right on the Afrikaner Nationalist Movement in the Fascist Era* (Hanover, NH: Wesleyan University Press, 1991).

77. Giliomee, *The Afrikaners: Biography of a People,* 350, suggests for instance that while Hendrik Verwoerd did study in Germany during the late 1920s, he was much more influenced by American sociology than by Nazi science.

78. Martin Legassick, "Legislation, Ideology, and Economy in Post-1948 South Africa," *Journal of Southern African Studies* 1, no. 1 (Oct. 1974): 5–35, 21.

79. Geheimes Staatsarchiv Preußischer Kulturbesitz (hereafter referred to as GStaPKB) Rep. 208A, Seminar für Orientalische Sprachen, Geheimes Staatsarchiv, Acta betreffend Dr. Büttner, Nr. 114, Bl. 1–77, correspondence of Carl Büttner, likely to Eduard Sachau, August 1, 1887.

80. Menzel, *C. G. Büttner;* Vereinigte Evangelisches Missionsarchiv, Wuppertal (hereafter referred to as VEM), RMG 1.611b B/c II 38, Büttner, Carl Gotthilf, Band II, correspondence between Büttner and the Rhenish Society Mission Inspector, January 17, 1880.

81. Menzel, *C. G. Büttner,* 103.

82. BAB R 1001 6172, A. W. Schreiber to the Kolonialabteilung des auswärtigen Amtes, Berlin, March 18, 1901.

83. Staatsarchiv Hamburg (hereafter referred to as StaH) 364-7, Professorenrat des Kolonialinstituts AI c Io 1, "Ausbildung von Missionaren und Missionsschülern," J. Spiecker, Mission Inspector of the Missionshaus zu Barmen, to Director Walter Oehler of the Ausschuß der deutschen evang. Missionen, copied to Carl Meinhof, November 5, 1909.

84. Zimmerman, 22.

85. GStaPKB Rep 76Va Sekt. 2 Tit. X, Nr. 124 Bd. VII, Acta betreffend das Seminar für Orientalische Sprachen bei der Universität zu Berlin, vol. I, vom Juli 1907 bis Dezember 1910, correspondence from Eduard Sachau, Berlin, to Kaiserlich Russischen Botschafter in Berlin Graf von der Osten-Sacken, Berlin, April 18, 1908.

86. Nina Berman, *Impossible Missions,* 139–74.

CHAPTER 1

1. Charles Hole, *The Early History of the Church Missionary Society, for Africa and the East, to the end of A.D. 1814* (London: Church Missionary Society, 1896), 115. Georgetown is the city now known as Freetown.

2. Hans-Werner Gensichen, "Jänicke, Johann," in Gerald H. Anderson, *Biographical Dictionary of Christian Missions* (Grand Rapids, MI: Eerdmans, 1999), 328, notes that this seminary was founded by revivalist and pietist Johannes Jänicke in 1800.

3. P. E. H. Hair, "Nyländer, Gustavus Reinhold," in Anderson, *Biographical Dictionary,* 502; Samuel Abraham Walker, *The Church of England Mission in Sierra Leone, including an Introductory Account of That Colony and a Comprehensive Sketch of the Niger Expedition in the Year 1841* (London: Seeley, Burnside, and Seeley, 1847), 251.

4. Wilhelm Bleek, *The Library of His Excellency, Sir George Grey, K.C.B., Philology, Vol. I—Part I, South Africa* (London: Trübner, 1858), 223.

5. *Proceedings of the Church Missionary Society for Africa and the East, Twenty-fifth year, 1824–1825* (London: R. Watts, 1825), xvi; Bleek, *The Library of his Excellency, Sir George Grey,* 224.

6. Walker, 98.

7. Anderson, 502.

8. Tuska Benes, *In Babel's Shadow: Language, Philology, and the Nation in Nineteenth-Century Germany* (Detroit: Wayne State University Press, 2008), 34ff.

9. Jonathan Strom, "Problems and Promises of Pietism Research," *Church History* 71, no. 3 (2002): 536–54.

10. Krista O'Donnell, Renate Bridenthal, and Nancy Reagin, "Introduction," in *The Heimat Abroad: The Boundaries of Germanness,* ed. O'Donnell, Bridenthal, and Reagin (Ann Arbor: University of Michigan Press, 2005), 1–14. The authors argue that the *Kulturnation* was disseminated well beyond the physical boundaries of "Germany." See also Sheehan, "What Is German History?"

11. Eugene Stock and John Henry Kennaway, *The History of the Church Missionary Society: Its Environment, Its Men, and Its Work,* vol. 2 (London: Church Missionary Society, 1899), 72, draw specific attention to the Württemburg origins of the society's German missionaries.

12. Mary Fulbrook, *Piety and Politics: Religion and the Rise of Absolutism in England, Württemburg, and Prussia* (Cambridge: Cambridge University Press, 1983), 6–7.

13. Walter H. Conser, *Church and Confession* (Atlanta: Mercer University Press, 1984), 27–28, has concluded that the main difference between the pietism of the seventeenth and eighteenth centuries and its nineteenth-century, new pietist cousin was the latter's encounter with Romanticism and rejection, with it, of the principles of the Enlightenment and justification by reason in favor of justification by faith.

14. Andrew F. Walls, "The Eighteenth-Century Protestant Missionary Awakening in Its European Context," in *Christian Missions and the Enlightenment,* ed. Brian Stanley (Grand Rapids, MI: Eerdmans, 2001), 22–44.

15. C. Magbaily Fyle, *Historical Dictionary of Sierra Leone* (Lanham, MD: Rowman and Littlefield, 2006), xxxiii–xxxiv.

16. Hole, 115.

17. Pheng Cheah, *Spectral Nationality: Passages of Freedom from Kant to Postcolonial Literatures of Liberation* (New York: Columbia University Press, 2003), 125; Benes, *In Babel's Shadow,* 40, 59.

18. Anderson, 502.

19. Zantop, *Colonial Fantasies.* Zantop also cites Mary Evelyn Townsend, *The Origins of Modern German Colonialism, 1871–1885* (New York: Columbia University Press, 1921), 22, on this point, and see also Zantop, Friedrichsmeyer, and Lennox, "Introduction" to the *Imperialist Imagination,* 3–33; Woodruff Smith, *European Imperialism in the Nineteenth and Twentieth Centuries* (Chicago: Nelson Hall, 1982); Beatrix Heintze, "Ethnographic Appropriations: German Exploration and Fieldwork in West-Central Africa," *History in Africa* 26 (1999): 69–128; Cornelia Essner, *Deutsche Afrikareisende im neunzehnten Jahrhundert: Zur Sozialgeschichte des Reisens* (Stuttgart: Steiner, 1985), 37–42; and Liebersohn, *Aristocratic Encounters,* 115ff.

20. Garland Hampton Cannon, *The Life and Mind of Oriental Jones: Sir William Jones, the Father of Modern Linguistics* (Cambridge: Cambridge University Press, 1990), 241ff.; Trautmann, *Aryans and British India,* 28ff.

21. George S. Williamson, "Gods, Titans, and Monsters: Philhellenism, Race, and Religion in Early-Nineteenth-Century Mythography," in *The German Invention of Race,* ed. Sara Eigen and Mark Joseph Larrimore (Binghamton: SUNY Press, 2006), 147–66.

22. O. H. Spohr, "Biographical Introduction" to *The Natal Diaries of Dr. W. H. I. Bleek* (Cape Town: A. A. Balkema, 1965), 1.

23. Klaus-Pieter Koepping, *Adolf Bastian and the Psychic Unity of Mankind: The Foundations of Anthropology in Nineteenth Century Germany* (St. Lucia: University of Queensland Press, 1983), 13–14.

24. Christina Ernst and Sabine Tischer, "Die Ausstellung der Kolonisierten," in *Andenken an den Kolonialismus,* Ausstellungskataloge der Universität Tübingen 17, ed.Völker Harms (Tübingen: ATTEMPTO, 1984); Lothar Dittrich and Annelore Rieke-Müller, eds., *Carl Hagenbeck (1844–1913): Tierhandel und Schaustellungen im Deutschen Kaiserreich* (New York: Peter Lang, 1998); Sierra Bruckner, "The Tingle-Tangle of Modernity: Popular Anthropology and the Cultural Politics of Identity in Imperial Germany" (diss., University of Iowa, Iowa City, 1999); and Nigel T. Rothfels, *Savages and Beasts: The Birth of the Modern Zoo* (Baltimore: Johns Hopkins University Press, 2002), 81ff.

25. Jon Miller, *Missionary Zeal and Institutional Control: Organizational Contradictions in the Basel Mission on the Gold Coast, 1828–1917* (Grand Rapids, MI: Eerdmans, 2003), x.

26. Hole, 115, 136. Today "Susoo" is known as "Susu."

27. *Proceedings of the Church Missionary Society for Africa and the East, Nineteenth Year, 1818–1819* (London: L. B. Seeley, 1819), 84.

28. Walls, 38. This does not mean that there were no missionary linguists from other national backgrounds; there certainly were, as the English, for instance, produced Robert Needham Cust, who researched languages from across the continent, J. W. Appleyard, a specialist in Xhosa, and Henry Tindall, whose primary research was on Nama. Nonetheless, Germans outnumbered their foreign colleagues in the linguistic field.

29. CMS efforts in East Africa began in Ethiopia, but in 1843 the mission was driven out and forced to settle further south, in Mombasa (Kenya). The society's

other East African fields were founded after German unification and had few German-speaking missionaries. Stock, 68, 120–21.

30. J. F. Ade Ajayi, *Christian Missions in Nigeria, 1841–1891: The Making of a New Elite* (London: Longman, 1965), 127, cited in Walls, 39.

31. George Mosse, *The Crisis of German Ideology: Intellectual Origins of the Third Reich* (New York: Schocken, 1964); Leon Poliakov, *The Aryan Myth: A History of Racist and Nationalist Ideas in Europe* (New York: Barnes and Noble, 1971, 1974), 71ff.; and see also John Toews, *Becoming Historical: Cultural Reformation and Public Memory in Early Nineteenth Century Berlin* (Cambridge: Cambridge University Press, 2004), 30–31.

32. Johann Gottfried Herder, *On World History: An Anthology,* ed. Hans Adler and Ernest A. Menze (Armonk, NY: M. E. Sharpe, 1997), 302–9.

33. Jack Zipes, *The Brothers Grimm: From Enchanted Forests to the Modern World* (New York: Palgrave Macmillan, 2002), 68–69.

34. Williamson, *The Longing for Myth in Germany,* 26–27.

35. Fulbrook, 8; Walls, 30ff.

36. Williamson, 155.

37. Jonathan Sheehan, *The Enlightenment Bible: Translation, Scholarship, Culture* (Princeton: Princeton University Press, 2005), 57ff.

38. Johannes Wallmann, "Was ist Pietismus?" in Andreas Lindt, ed., *Pietismus und Neuzeit XX/1994: Ein Jahrbuch zur Geschichte des neueren Protestantismus* (Göttingen: Vandenhoeck und Ruprecht, 1995), 11–27.

39. Sheehan, 60.

40. Walls, 36, notes that while there were fewer continental Europeans in the LMS than the CMS, they still comprised 13.5 percent of the overall LMS before 1850. See also Gunther Pakendorf, "'For There is no Power but of God': The Berlin Mission and the Challenges of Colonial South Africa," *Missionalia* 25 (1997): 255–73.

41. The first German-speaking missionary with connections to the BFBS was Nyländer, who wrote to the society to request Arabic Bibles for use in western Africa in 1814. See British and Foreign Bible Society Archives (hereafter referred to as BFBSA), Correspondence Book (CB) Volume 7, September 20, 1814, to January 17, 1816, G. R. Nyländer to the BFBS, September 1, 1814, Yongroo, Bullom Shore, West Africa.

42. Adrian Hastings, *The Church in Africa, 1450–1950* (Oxford: Oxford University Press, 1996), 225–26.

43. J. F. Schön, *Grammar of the Hausa Language* (London: Church Missionary House, 1862), xiv, quoting T. F. Buxton, *The African Slave Trade and Its Remedy,* 62.

44. This Berlin Missionary Society (Berliner Missionsgesellschaft) was an offshoot of the Berlin Seminary that sent pupils like Nyländer to the CMS. The seminary was under the direction of the pietist Jänicke, who later established the BMS. See Brian Stanley, "Christian Missions, Antislavery, and the Claims of Humanity, c. 1813–1873," in *World Christianities, c. 1815–1914, The Cambridge History of Christianity,* vol. 8, ed. Sheridan Gilley and Brian Stanley (Cambridge: Cambridge University Press, 2006), 444.

45. Anonymous, *The Missionary Guide-book, Or, A Key to the Protestant Missionary Map of the World: Shewing the Geography, Natural History, Climate, Population, and Government of the Several Countries to which the Missionary Efforts Have Been Directed: with the Moral, Social, and Religious Condition of Their Inhabitants* (London: Seeley, Burnside, and Seeley, 1846), 468.

46. Anonymous, "Proceedings of Other Societies," *Missionary Herald* 47 (1851): 130–31.

47. Miller, x, 5.

48. J. Kofi Agbeti, *West African Church History: Christian Missions and Church Foundations, 1482–1919* (Leiden: Brill Archive, 1986), 80–81.

49. Birgit Meyer, *Translating the Devil: Religion and Modernity among the Ewe in Ghana* (Trenton, NJ: Africa World Press, 1999), 29–30.

50. VEM, RMG 1.583 a B/c II 10, Kolbe, Friedrich, Band 1, 1844–1860, Lebenslauf.

51. VEM, RMG 1.583 a B/c II 10, Kolbe, Friedrich, Band 1, 1844–1860, F. W. Kolbe Brf. an Dep. 10 Januar, 1853.

52. Berliner Missionswerk (hereafter referred to as BMW), Correspondenz mit dem Missionar J. L. Döhne. Wartburg, Natal, 1863–1864, III.7.4, Lebenslauf.

53. BMW, Correspondenz mit dem Missionar J. L. Döhne. Wartburg, Natal, 1863–1864, III.7.4., Döhne to mission inspector Wollmann, April 1, 1859.

54. J. L. Döhne, *A Zulu-Kafir Dictionary, Etymologically Explained, with Copious Illustrations and Examples, Preceded by an Introduction on the Zulu-Kafir Language* (Cape Town: Printed at J. G. Pike's Machine Printing Office, 1857), iii–iv.

55. W. H. I. Bleek, *A Comparative Grammar of South African Languages, Part I, Phonology* (London: Trübner, 1862), 30.

56. Döhne, *A Zulu-Kafir Dictionary,* v. Ironically, Döhne eventually returned to the BMS.

57. Norman Etherington, "Introduction" in Norman Etherington, ed., *Missions and Empire: The Oxford History of the British Empire Companion Series* (Oxford: Oxford University Press, 2005), 1–18; Andrew Porter, "An Overview," same volume, 40–63.

58. Etherington, 17–18.

59. Altena, 29–32.

60. S. W. Koelle, *Polyglotta Africana; Or, a Comparative Vocabulary of Nearly Three Hundred Words and Phrases, in more than 100 Distinct African Languages* (London: Church Mission House, 1854); P. E. H. Hair, *The Early Study of Nigerian Languages: Essays and Bibliographies* (Cambridge: Cambridge University Press, 1967), 2, 7.

61. Sara Pugach, "Koelle, Sigismund Wilhelm (1823–1902)," in *Encyclopedia of Language and Linguistics,* ed. Keith Brown, 2nd ed. (Amsterdam: Elsevier, 2005).

62. A. B. C. Sibthorpe, *The History of Sierra Leone: Revised, Remodeled, and Enlarged,* 3rd ed. (London: Elliot Stock, 1906), 155.

63. Ibid., 128.

64. Rachael Gilmour, "'A Nice Derangement of Epitaphs': Missionary Language Learning in Mid-Nineteenth Century Natal," *Journal of Southern African Studies* 33, no. 3 (September 2007): 521–38.

65. Harold James, *A German Identity, 1770–1990* (London: Weidenfeld & Nicolson, 1989).

66. Indeed, the conservatives united under Prince Klemens von Metternich imposed harsh crackdowns on those agitating for liberal political and social changes.

67. Zipes, 92.

68. Sir William Jones, "The Third Anniversary Discourse, on the Hindus, Delivered 2 February, 1786," in *A Reader in Nineteenth Century Historical Indo-European Linguistics*, ed. Winfred P. Lehmann (Bloomington: Indiana University Press, 1967), 7–20.

69. See, for example, Holger Pedersen, *The Discovery of Language: Linguistic Science in the Nineteenth Century*, trans. John Webster Spargo (Bloomington: Indiana University Press, 1962, 1959); R. H. Robins, *A Short History of Linguistics* (London: Longman, 1967); Hans Aarsleff, *From Locke to Saussure: Essays on the Study of Language and Intellectual History* (Minneapolis: University of Minnesota Press, 1982); Geoffrey Sampson, *Schools of Linguistics: Competition and Evolution* (London: Hutchinson, 1980); and Anna Morpurgo Davies, *History of Linguistics: Nineteenth Century Linguistics*, vol. 4, ed. Giulio Lepschy (London: Longman, 1994), among others, for more detailed discussions of the genesis of comparative philology. Morpurgo Davies for one says that while "comparative" studies of language were carried out prior to the late eighteenth- and early nineteenth-century era, the science of comparative philology was not really institutionalized until then, when chairs for the subject were first established at German universities.

70. See, for instance, Trautmann, 38, after Jones, *The Works of Sir William Jones*, 13 vols., ed. Anna Marian Jones (London: G. G. and J. Robinson, and R. H. Evans, 1807), and Bernard Cohn, "The Command of Language and the Language of Command," in Bernard Cohn, *Colonialism and Its Forms of Knowledge: The British in India* (Princeton: Princeton University Press, 1996).

71. Maurice Olender, *The Languages of Paradise: Race, Religion, and Philology in the Nineteenth Century*, trans. Arthur Goldhammer (Cambridge: Harvard University Press, 1992), 11–12.

72. Friedrich von Schlegel, *Über die Sprache und Weisheit der Inder: Ein Beitrag zur Begründung der Altertumskunde*, new ed., E. F. K. Koerner preparer (Amsterdam: Benjamins, 1977), 147.

73. Olender, 38.

74. F. W. Kolbe, "On the Affinity between the Indo-European and the African Bantu Languages," *Cape Monthly Magazine*, n.s., vol. 3 (1871): 298–303.

75. Olender, 63.

76. Suzanne Marchand, *Down from Olympus: Archaeology and Philhellenism in Germany, 1750–1970* (Princeton: Princeton University Press, 1996), 109.

77. Edwin Bryant, *The Quest for the Origins of Vedic Culture: The Indo-Aryan Migration Debate* (Oxford: Oxford University Press, 2001), 14–15.

78. Trautmann, 74.

79. Benes, 9.

80. Ibid., 95.

81. Andrew F, Walls, *The Cross-cultural Process in Christian History: Studies in*

the Transmission and Appropriation of Faith (London: Continuum International Publishing Group, 2002), 209.

82. F. W. Kolbe, *A Language-Study Based on Bantu; or, An Inquiry into the Laws of Root Formation, the Original Plural, the Sexual Dual, and the Principles of Word-Comparison; with Tables Illustrating the Primitive Pronominal System Restored in the African Bantu Family of Speech* (London: Trubner, 1888), iii.

83. Jakob Grimm, *Deutsche Grammatik* (Göttingen: Dieterichsche Buchhandlung, 1819–37).

84. Marchand; Klaus Berghahn and Beate Pinkerneil, *Am Beispiel Wilhelm Meister: Einführung in die Wissenschaftsgeschichte der Germanistik* (Königstein: Athenäum Verlag, 1980).

85. Benes, 65–66.

86. Martin Litchfield West, *Indo-European Poetry and Myth* (Oxford: Oxford University Press, 2007), 1, citing Konrad Koerner, *Indogermanische Forschungen* 86 (1981): 1–29.

87. Bryant, 20. Bryant also says that while Klaproth popularized the term *Indo-Germanic,* it was Conrad Malte-Brun who actually coined it in 1810.

88. Benes, 66.

89. See, for instance, Stephen Alter, *Darwinism and the Linguistic Image: Language, Race, and Natural Theology in the Nineteenth Century* (Baltimore: Johns Hopkins University Press, 1999), 42.

90. Hermann Jungraithmayr, *Was ist Primitiv? Zum Stand der Sprachgeschichtsforschung in Afrika* (Stuttgart: Franz Steiner Verlag Wiesbaden GMBH, 1987), 191–92. According to Jungraithmayr, this did *not* mean that nineteenth-century philologists considered Chinese more primitive than Bantu or other African languages. Instead, they maintained that when a language had reached the very highest, most complex stages, it once again simplified. In such a case, the simplicity did not denote primitivity but a different kind of sophistication.

91. Carl Meinhof, *Die Christianisierung der Sprachen Afrikas* (Basel: Verlag der Missionsbuchhandlung, 1905), 12.

92. Jungraithmayr, 191–92.

93. Meinhof, *Die Christianisierung der Sprachen Afrikas,* 8–9.

94. Kurt R. Jankowsky, *The Neogrammarians: A Re-evaluation of Their Place in the Development of Linguistic Science* (The Hague: Mouton, 1972).

95. Wilhelm Bleek, "'Grimm's Law' in South Africa; or, Phonetic Changes in the South African Bantu Languages. I.—In the South-Eastern Branch," *Transactions of the Philological Society* (1843–44): 2–23.

96. Carl Meinhof, "Das dalsche Gesetz," *Zeitschrift der deutschen morgenländischen Gesellschaft* (1903): 299–304. Here Meinhof discusses how Edmund Dahl, a Herrnhut missionary, had discovered a sound law applicable to East African Bantu languages.

97. Alter, *Darwinism and the Linguistic Image,* 73–78. Comparative philology did not just borrow from evolutionary biology. Alter also shows that the "linguistic image" was pervasive in the writings of Darwin and his contemporaries, meaning that they had also borrowed from comparative philology.

98. In Konrad Koerner's "Introduction" to the publication of Schleicher's *Die Sprachen Europas in systematischer Übersicht und linguistische Untersuchungen* (Amsterdam: Benjamins, 1983), XXIX, however, Koerner holds that, while Schleicher's work had evolutionary undertones and stressed historical-developmental aspects of language change, since he began writing about linguistic classification in 1848, it is not truly possible to call him an evolutionist in the Darwinian sense.

99. August Schleicher, *Die Sprachen Europas in systematischer Übersicht und linguistische Untersuchungen* (Amsterdam: Benjamins, 1983).

100. Bank, *Bushmen in a Victorian World,* 12.

101. Robert J. Thornton, "'That Dying Out Race': W. H. I. Bleek's Approach to the Languages of Southern Africa," *Social Dynamics* 9, no. 2 (1983): 2, cited in Bank, 16.

102. Jan Knappert, "Origin and Development of the Concept of Hamitic: The First Sixty Years, 1851–1911," *Orientalia Lovaniensia Periodica,* 6–7 (1975–1976): 303–20.

103. Bleek, *A Comparative Grammar,* 19.

104. 43.

105. W. H. I. Bleek, *"Reynard the Fox" in South Africa, or Hottentot Fables and Tales* (London: Trübner, 1864), xii.

106. Bleek, *A Comparative Grammar,* 30.

107. W. H. I. Bleek, *"Reynard the Fox" in South Africa,* xiv.

108. Jungraithmayr, 191; Mario di Gregorio, "Reflections of a Non-Political Naturalist."

109. Meinhof, "Warum studiert man primitive Sprachen?" in *Die Moderne Sprachforschung in Afrika: Hamburgische Vorträge von Carl Meinhof,* ed. Carl Meinhof, 13. Meinhof here says he imagines that his audience is confused by his discussion of African grammar because they believe "But they have no grammar!" However, Wolff, "Die Erforschung der afrikanischen Sprachen," 19–23, shows that there were some attempts to codify grammars for African languages from the sixteenth century on.

110. It should be noted that not all Protestant Missions were the same; there are, indeed, many groups and denominations covered under the blanket term *Protestant.* As S. von Sicard notes in *The Lutheran Church on the Coast of Tanzania, 1887–1914* (Uppsala: Almqvist & Wiksells, 1970), 53, there were three mission societies in Berlin alone, known as Berlin I, II, and III (the one usually mentioned in this study is Berlin III). Even so, as many of these came together for the national Mission Conferences that Meinhof also attended, and because they shared similar concerns when it came to the issue of language study, I have chosen to group them together under the label *Protestant.*

111. J. B. Schlegel, *Schlüssel zur Ewe-Sprache, dargeboten in den grammatischen Grundzügen des Anlo-Dialekts derselben* (Bremen: Bei W. Vallett, 1857), IV.

112. Carl Meinhof, "Die afrikanischen Völker und die Mission," *Mission und Pfarramt* 3 (1910): 91.

113. Such was, for instance, the case with J. Zimmerman's *A Grammatical Sketch of the Akra- or Gã Language, with Some Specimens of It from the Mouth of*

the Natives, and a Vocabulary of the Same, with an Appendix on the Adanme-Dialect (Stuttgart: J. F. Steinkopf, 1858), VII, and Karl Endemann, *Versuch einer Grammatik der Sotho* (Berlin: W. Hertz, 1876).

114. Schön, *Oku Ibo*, 4.

115. Robert Cust, "Dr. Schön," *Church Missionary Gleaner* 16–17 (1889): 36.

116. Howard Temperley, *White Dreams, Black Africa: The British Anti-Slavery Expedition to the River Niger* (New Haven: Yale University Press, 1991).

117. Schön, *Oku Ibo*, 3.

118. "Besprechung" of W. Gründler, "Die Bedeutung gemeinsamer Ausbildungsstätte für die Spezialausbildung der Missionare," in *Verhandlungen der XIII. Kontinentalen Missionskonferenz* (Bremen: Kommissionsverlag der Norddeutsche Missions-gesellschaft, 1913), 43–58.

119. Meyer, 57.

120. James Tanis, "Reformed Pietism and Protestant Missions," *Harvard Theological Review* 67, no. 1 (January 1974): 65–73.

121. M. Louise Pirouet, "The Legacy of Johann Ludwig Krapf," *International Bulletin of Missionary Research* 23, no. 2 (April 1999): 69–75.

122. Hastings, *The Church in Africa, 1450–1950*, 226.

123. Pirouet.

124. BFBSA, Journal of the Reverend J. L. Krapf, August 27, 1839.

125. BFBSA Editorial Correspondence Inwards, No. 1, 1858–1860, Krapf to Mr. H. Knolleke, January 21, 1860.

126. BFBSA ECB 27, 1890–1891, letter of Mr. H. E. Millard in Vienna to the BFBS Secretariat, January 8, 1891, discussing Krapf and Reinisch.

127. BFBSA Editorial Correspondence Inwards No. 6, 1868–1869, Krapf to Knolleke, September 10, 1869.

128. BFBSA Editorial Correspondence Inwards No. 8, 1870–72, Krapf to R. B. Girdlestone, April 3, 1871.

129. BFBSA, loose letter from Christaller to the Assistant Foreign Secretary of the BFBS, May 14, 1864.

130. BFBSA Editorial Correspondence Inwards No. 7, 1869–1870, Krapf to Girdlestone, August 18, 1870.

131. Ibid.

132. Döhne, *A Zulu-Kafir Dictionary*, vii.

133. Ibid.

134. E. S., *The Missionary Career of Dr. Krapf, Missionary of the Church Missionary Society in Abyssinia and East Africa, and Pioneer of Central African Exploration*, reprinted from the Church Missionary Intelligencer, February and March 1882 (London: Church Missionary Society), 4.

135. Catherine Griefenow-Mewis, "J. L. Krapf and His Role in Researching and Describing East African Languages," *AAP* no. 47, *Swahili Forum III* (1996): 161–62. With reference to R. C. Bridges's "Introduction" to J. L. Krapf's *Travels, Researches, and Missionary Labours, during an Eighteen Years' Residence in Eastern Africa; Together with Journeys to Jagga, Usambara, Ukambani, Shoa, Abessinia, and Khartum; and a Coasting Voyage from Mombaz to Cape Delgado* (New York: Johnson Reprint Co., 1860, 1968), 52.

136. J. L. Krapf, *Outline of the Elements of the Kisuáheli Language, with Special Reference to the Kinika Dialect* (Tübingen: Lud. Fried. Fues., 1850), 9–15.

137. Joan Leopold, *The Prix Volney* (New York: Springer, 1999), 107.

138. BFBSA, Krapf to R. B. Girdlestone, Head of the British and Foreign Bible Society translation department, July 20, 1872.

139. BFBSA, loose letter from Christaller to the Assistant Foreign Secretary, November 3, 1866.

140. BFBSA Editorial Correspondence Inwards No. 1, 1858–1860, J. F. Schön to T. W. Meller, December 9, 1859.

141. BFBSA Editorial Correspondence Inwards, No. 2, 1860–62, C. A. Gollmer to H. Knolleke, August 30, 1860.

142. BFBSA Editorial Correspondence Inwards, No. 3, 1863–65, Krapf to S. B. Bergne, September 10, 1863.

143. Bryant, 24, points out that *race* and *nation* were generally used interchangeably in the mid-nineteenth century.

144. BFBSA Editorial Correspondence Inwards No. 1, 1858–1860, Krapf to Knolleke, March 3, 1860.

145. Benoit Massin, "From Virchow to Fischer: Physical Anthropology and 'Modern Race Theories' in Wilhelmine Germany," in *Volksgeist as Method and Ethic: Essays on Boasian Ethnography and the German Anthropological Tradition*, ed. George Stocking (Madison: University of Wisconsin Press, 1996), 79–154.

146. J. L. Krapf, *An Imperfect Outline of the Elements of the Galla Language* (London: Church Missionary Society, 1840), 1.

147. J. L. Krapf, *Vocabulary of the Engútuk Eloikob, or of the Language of the Wakuafi-Nation in the Interior of Equatorial Africa* (Tübingen: Lud. Fries. Fues., 1854), 11, 11fn. Paul Spencer has noted that the people whom Krapf referred to as "Wakuafi" were, in fact, another branch of the Maasai. See Paul Spencer, *Time, Space, and The Unknown: Maasai Configurations of Power and Providence* (New York: Routledge, 2003), 62–63.

148. C. T. Wyrod, "The Light on the Horizon: N'ko Literacy and Formal Schooling in Guinea" (master's thesis, Elliott School of International Affairs of the George Washington University, Washington, DC, 2003).

149. S. W. Koelle, *Outlines of a Grammar of the Vei Language, Together with a Vei-English Vocabulary and an Account of the Discovery and Nature of the Vei Mode of Syllabic Writing* (London: Keegan, Paul, Trench, Trübner & Co., 1851), 4. Koelle has, though, generally been viewed as more sympathetic to Africans than most of his contemporaries; here see Miller, *Missionary Zeal and Institutional Control,* 206.

150. S. W. Koelle, *Grammar of the Bórnu or Kanuri Language* (London: Church Missionary House, 1854), 1.

151. Ibid., 3–7.

152. See Andreas Hofbauer, "Von Rasse zu Identität: Vom Ringen um Paradigmen in der 'Wissenschaft vom anderen,'" *Anthropos* 92 (1997): 569–77.

153. Schön, *Grammar of the Hausa Language,* xii, 13.

154. C. F. Schlenker, *Grammar of the Temne Language* (London: Church Missionary Society, 1864), iv.

155. Krapf, *Vocabulary of the Engútuk Eloikob,* 10.

156. F. W. Kolbe, *A Language-Study Based on Bantu;* Kolbe, "On the Origin of Language," *Cape Monthly Magazine,* n.s., vol. 3 (1871): 93, 95; and Kolbe, "On the Affinity between the Indo-European and the African Bantu Languages," *Cape Monthly Magazine,* n.s., vol. 3 (1871): 303.

157. Benes, 201; Williamson, 212; Bryant, 25.

158. Benes, 65, 84.

159. Kolbe, *A Language-Study Based on Bantu,* 6.

160. Krapf, *An Imperfect Outline of the Elements of the Galla Language,* 2.

161. Kolbe, *A Language-Study Based on Bantu,* iv.

162. Bleek, *A Comparative Grammar of South African Languages, Part I, Phonology,* 125.

163. Bank, 74ff., 232.

164. Ibid., 93.

CHAPTER 2

1. Friedrich Fabri, *Bedarf Deutschland der Kolonien?/Does Germany Need Colonies?* ed. and trans. E. C. M. Breuning and M. E. Chamberlain (New York: Edwin Mellen Press, 1998 [1879]).

2. Peter Duignan and Lewis Henry Gann, *The Rulers of German Africa, 1884–1914* (Stanford: Stanford University Press, 1977), ix.

3. Matthew Fitzpatrick has summarized the various arguments as to why Bismarck decided Germany should become a colonial power. See Fitzpatrick, *Liberal Imperialism in Germany: Expansionism and Nationalism, 1848–1884* (Oxford: Berghahn Books, 2008), 116ff.

4. David Blackbourn and Geoff Eley, *The Peculiarities of German History: Bourgeois Society and Politics in Nineteenth-Century Germany* (Oxford: Oxford University Press, 1984).

5. Geoff Eley, *Reshaping the German Right: Radical Nationalism and Political Change after Bismarck* (Ann Arbor: University of Michigan Press, 1991).

6. Howard Sargent, "Diasporic Citizens: Germans Abroad in the Framing of German Citizenship Law," in *The Heimat Abroad: The Boundaries of Germanness,* ed. Krista O'Donnell, Renate Bridenthal, and Nancy Reagin (Ann Arbor: University of Michigan Press, 2005), 17–39.

7. Jutta Bückendorf, *Schwarz-Weiss-Rot über Ostafrika! Deutsche Kolonialpläne und Afrikanische Realität* (Münster: Lit Verlag, 1997), 318.

8. Ibid.

9. Altena, 28–29.

10. Alexander Merensky, *Wörterverzeichnis zum Gebrauch bei Bearbeitung Afrikanischer Sprachen* (Berlin: Buchhandlung der Berliner evangelischer Gesellschaft, 1891).

11. Altena, 29–30.

12. Ibid.

13. Ibid., 31–32.

14. Friedrich Wilhelm Bautz, "Reinhold Grundemann," in the *Biographisch-*

Bibliographisches Kirchenlexikon, Band II (Herzberg: Verlag Traugott Bautz), 1990.

15. Reinhold Grundemann, *Zur Statistik der Evangelischen Mission* (Gütersloh: Bertelsmann, 1886), cited in BAB R/1001, 4550, *Die Zeitschrift für afrikanische Sprachen,* vol. 1, April 1886–28 Februar 1895, letter from Carl Büttner to the *Reichsamt des Innen,* June 4, 1886.

16. Friedrich Fabri, "Ueber den Ursprung der Sprache," in Friedrich Fabri, *Die Entstehung des Heidenthums und die Aufgabe der Heidenmission* (Barmen [Wuppertal]: W. Langwiesche's Verlagshandlung, 1859).

17. BFBSA Editorial Correspondence Inwards No. 3, 1863–65, Friedrich Fabri to the Reverend S. B. Bergne, Secretary of the BFBS, October 19, 1863.

18. BFBSA Editorial Correspondence Inwards No. 5, 1867–1868, Fabri to Bergne, March 16, 1867.

19. Arne Perras, *Carl Peters and German Imperialism, 1856–1918* (Oxford: Clarendon Press, 2004), 93.

20. GStaPKB Rep. 208A, Seminar für Orientalische Sprachen, Acta betreffend Dr. Büttner, Nr. 114, Bl. 1–77, Lebenslauf, n.d.

21. Gustav Menzel, *Die Rheinische Mission* (Wuppertal: Verlag der Vereinigten Evangelischen Mission, 1978), 52–58.

22. BAB R/1001, 4550, *Die Zeitschrift für afrikanische Sprachen,* vol. 1, April 1886–28 Februar 1895, Carl Büttner, correspondent unknown, June 4, 1886.

23. VEM, RMG 1.611 b B/c II 38, Carl Büttner, Büttner, letter to the Rheinische Mission (likely Fabri), November 7, 1872.

24. Ibid.

25. VEM, RMG 1.611 b B/c II 38, Carl Büttner, "Die ersten Eindrücke von Volk und Land," n.d., ca. April 1873.

26. Büttner, letter to the Rheinische Mission, February 20, 1873.

27. Büttner, letter to the Rheinische Mission, May 3, 1873.

28. Büttner, letter to the Rheinische Mission, February 20, 1873.

29. Rehana Ebr.-Vally, *Kala Pani: Caste and Colour in South Africa* (Colorado Springs: International Academic, 2001), 44–52, provides an excellent description of the category "coloured" as it was defined in both preapartheid and apartheid South Africa.

30. Büttner, letter to the Rheinische Mission, n.d., ca. January 1873.

31. Wildenthal, *German Women for Empire,* 86. The Foreign Office rejected Büttner's advice.

32. Ibid.

33. Arthur de Gobineau, *The Inequality of Human Races,* trans. Adrian Collins (New York: G. P. Putnam, 1915), 25.

34. Massin, "From Virchow to Fischer," 129–30.

35. Büttner, letter to the Rheinische Mission, December 21, 1873.

36. Büttner, letter to the Rheinische Mission, September 3, 1874.

37. Gustav Menzel, *C. G. Büttner, Missionar, Sprachpolitiker und Politiker in der deutschen Kolonialbewegung* (Wuppertal: Verlag der Vereinigten Evangelischen Mission, 1995), 26.

38. Büttner, letter to the Rheinische Mission, December 21, 1873.

39. Pier M. Larson, "'Capacities and Modes of Thinking': Intellectual Engagements and Subaltern Hegemony in the Early History of Malagasy Christianity," *American Historical Review* 102, no. 4 (1997): 969–1002.

40. Büttner, letter to the Rheinische Mission, December 21, 1873.

41. Büttner, letter to the Rheinische Mission, August 29, 1875.

42. Büttner, letter to the Rheinische Mission, January 24, 1874.

43. Zimmerman, *Anthropology and Antihumanism in Imperial Germany,* 67.

44. John M. Efron, *Defenders of the Race: Jewish Doctors and Race Science in Fin-de-Siècle Europe* (New Haven: Yale University Press, 1994), 25.

45. Alan S. Weber, ed., *Nineteenth Century Science: A Selection of Original Texts* (Peterborough, ON: Broadview Press, 2000), 345–46.

46. William Osgood Aydelotte, *Bismarck and British Colonial Policy: The Problem of Southwest Africa, 1883–1885* (New York: Octagon Books, 1974 [1937]).

47. Menzel, *C. G. Büttner,* 69.

48. Ibid., 112–14.

49. Ursula Trüper, "Carl Gotthilf Büttner—Missionar, Kolonialpolitiker und Sprachforscher," in *Kolonialmetropole Berlin: Eine Spurensuche,* ed. Ulrich van der Heyden and Joachim Zeller (Berlin: Berlin Edition, Quintessenz Verlag, 2002), 122–25.

50. Menzel, *Rheinische Mission,* 216–22.

51. Perras, *Carl Peters and German Imperialism, 1856–1918* (Oxford: Clarendon Press, 2004), 81–86. Perras also comments, however, that Peters eventually broke with the *Deutsch-Ostafrikanische Missionsgesellschaft* over the issue of Peters's stance toward Catholic missionization. Peters, an equal-opportunity manipulator, welcomed the Catholics as long as they promised not to interfere with the activity of the *Deutsch-Ostafrikanische Gesellschaft.*

52. Altena, *"Ein Häuflein Christen mitten in der Heidenwelt des dunklen Erdteils,"* 132.

53. GStaPKB Rep. 208A, Seminar für Orientalische Sprachen, Geheimes Staatsarchiv, Acta betreffend Dr. Büttner, Nr. 114, Bl. 1–77, Carl Büttner to Eduard Sachau, director of the Seminar for Oriental Languages, Berlin, January 2, 1889.

54. Altena, 135.

55. It might even be said that the Seminar was a "metropolitan field" and that its students and teachers conducted "fieldwork" at it. But this concept is problematic. It is a double entendre, as *field* here can refer either to a discipline itself or, as would be the case with *fieldwork,* a location of research. The latter definition of *field* is also somewhat anachronistic, as the term *fieldwork* only entered the English language in an anthropological sense with A. C. Haddon around the turn of the twentieth century. Nonetheless, in a limited way Berlin, and later Hamburg, can be understood as "fields" in both senses, since Afrikanistik and *Orientalistik* indeed became metropolitan "fields," or disciplines, as well as concentrated sites for the study of the "Other." For the history of the fieldwork concept, see Akhil Gupta and James Ferguson, "Discipline and Practice: 'The Field' as Site, Method, and Location," in *Anthropological Locations: Boundaries and Grounds of a Field Science* (Berkeley: University of California Press, 1997), 6; Henrika Kucklick, "After Ish-

mael: The Fieldwork Tradition and Its Future," same volume, 47–65; George Stocking, "The Ethnographer's Magic: Fieldwork in British Anthropology from Tylor to Malinowski," in George Stocking, *The Ethnographer's Magic and Other Essays in the History of Anthropology* (Madison: University of Wisconsin Press, 1992), 27; and Henrika Kuklick and Robert E. Kohler, *Science in the Field* (Chicago: University of Chicago Press, 1996), *Osiris*, 2nd series, vol. 11.

56. Roger Chickering, *We Men Who Feel Most German: A Cultural Study of the Pan-German League, 1886–1914* (Boston: George Allen and Unwin, 1984), 33–36; Eley, *Reshaping the German Right*, 44.

57. GStaPKB Rep 76Va Sekt. 2. Tit. 1, Bd. I, Acta betreffend das Seminar für Orientalische Sprachen bei der Universität zu Berlin, vol. I, vom Februar 1885 bis Oktober 1887, Carl Peters, "Begründung des Gesuches betr. Aufnahme der wichtigsten Bantusprachene in den Lehrplan des Orientalischen Seminars." Branches of Peters's society from throughout Germany also sent letters to Bismarck, confirming that their members were in full agreement with Peters and wanted to see Bantu language courses incorporated at the seminar. Moreover, related societies, for example the Central Association for Commercial Geography and the Advancement of German Interests Overseas, dispatched similar requests for the integration of Bantu.

58. Matthew Jefferies, *Contesting the German Empire, 1871–1918* (Oxford: Blackwell, 2008), 175.

59. Jan Rüger, *The Great Naval Game: Britain and Germany in the Age of Empire* (Cambridge: Cambridge University Press, 2007).

60. For instance, Eduard Sachau, "Seminar-Chronik für das Studien-Jahr 1897/1898," *Mittheilungen des Seminars für Orientalische Sprachen* Jg. 1 (1898): III–IV, shows that 222 students were businesspeople studying foreign languages in order to conduct their business abroad. Moreover, Sachau's "Seminar Chronik für die Zeit von Ostern 1898 bis Ostern 1899," *Mittheilungen des Seminars für Orientalische Sprachen* Jg. 2 (1899): I–IV, details the careers its students were to assume once they had left the Seminar, and shows that eight of the students bound for Africa were military officers, while ten would be working as civil servants.

61. Sachau, *Denkschrift*, 12n. Also reported in Wolfgang Morgenroth, "Das Seminar für Orientalische Sprachen in der Wissenschaftstradition der Sektion Asienwissenschaften der HUB," in *Das "Seminar für Orientalische Sprachen" in der Wissenschaftstradition der Sektion Asienwissenschaften der Humboldt-Universität zu Berlin*, ed. Hannelore Bernhardt, Beiträge zur Geschichte der Humboldt-Universität zu Berlin, Nr. 25 (Berlin, 1990), 7–8.

62. GStaPKB, Rep 76Va Sekt. 2 Tit. 1, Nr. 28 Bd. I, Acta betreffend das Seminar für Orientalische Sprachen bei der Universität zu Berlin, letter of Wilhelm Grube to Gustav von Goßler, Minister der Geistlichen-Unterrichts-und Medizinal-Angelegenheiten, December 12, 1884.

63. Ibid., letter of Matzfeldt, Auswärtiges Amt, to von Goßler, August 3, 1885.

64. BAB R 1001 6171, August 1898–28 Februar 1898, Erforschung der Sprachen der eingeborenen Völkerschaften, correspondence between August Seidel and den *Verwaltungsrat der Wohlfahrtslotterie zu Zwecken der deutschen Schutzgebiete, z.N. des stellvertretenden Vorsitzenden*, Herrn Wirklichen Geheimen Rats Sachse, 31/10/98.

65. Where it would be associated with, but also independent of, the university. See Heinrich Pöhl, *Die deutsche Auslandshochschule* (Tübingen: J. C. B. Mohr [Paul Siebeck]), 1913.

66. GStaPKB Rep 76Va Sekt. 2 Tit. 1, Nr. 28 Bd. I, Acta betreffend das Seminar für Orientalische Sprachen bei der Universität zu Berlin, vol. I, vom Februar 1885 bis Oktober 1887, Gustav von Goßler, Minister der Geistlichen-Unterricts-und-Medizinal-Angelegenheiten, to Chancellor Otto von Bismarck, April 8, 1885; and Bismarck to Goßler, April 11, 1885.

67. Denkschrift vom 3. April 1886, contained in Eduard Sachau, *Denkschrift über das Seminar für Orientalische Sprachen an der Königlichen Friedrich-Wilhelms Universität zu Berlin von 1887 bis 1912* (Berlin: Kommissionsverlag von Georg Reimer, 1912), Beilage 1, 45.

68. Kirsten Zirkel, "Military Power in German Colonial Policy: The Schutztruppen and Their Leaders in East and South-West Africa, 1888–1918," in *Guardians of Empire: The Armed Forces of the Colonial Powers, c. 1700–1964,* ed. David Killingray and David Omissi (Manchester: Manchester University Press, 1999), 91–113.

69. Sachau, *Denkschrift,* 15.

70. Goßler to Bismarck, April 8, 1885.

71. Sachau, *Denkschrift,* 12.

72. Verzeichnis der Vorlesungen usw. für Winter 1887/88, in Sachau, *Denkschrift,* Beilage 7, 55.

73. Bernhardt, ed., *Das "Seminar für Orientalische Sprachen" in der Wissenschaftstradition der Sektion Asienwissenschaften der Humboldt-Universität zu Berlin,* Appendix 2a. Herero was followed in rapid succession by Hausa (1898), Duala (1899), Ewe (1899), Kinyamwezi (1902), Fulbe (1903–4), Ethiopian (Ge'ez) (1905–6), Amharic (1905–6), Nama (1907–8), Twi (1908–9), Ovambo (1909–10), and Ewondo (Jaunde) (1910–11).

74. "Verzeichnis derjenigen Offiziere, die im Seminar Kolonialsprachen studiert haben," Beilage 11, in Sachau, *Denkschrift,* 70–74.

75. GStaPKB Rep 76Va Sekt. 2 Tit. 1, Nr. 28 Bd. I, Acta betreffend das Seminar für Orientalische Sprachen bein der Universität zu Berlin, vol. I, vom Februar 1885 bis Oktober 1887, *Promemoria* concerning the possibility of founding a Seminar for Oriental Languages, ca. 1885.

76. Charles E. McClelland, "Professionalization and Higher Education in Germany," in *The Transformation of Higher Learning, 1860–1930,* ed. Konrad Jarausch (Chicago: University of Chicago Press, 1983), 306–20.

77. Marchand, *Down from Olympus,* 137; Gunta Haenicke, *Zur Geschichte der Anglistik an deutschsprachigen Universitäten 1850–1925* (Augsburg: Universität Augsburg, 1979), 272.

78. Haenicke, *Zur Geschichte der Anglistik an deutschsprachigen Universitäten 1850–1925,* 211.

79. Hinrich C. Seeba, "Nationabücher: Zur Kanonisierung nationaler Bildungsmuster in der frühen Germanistik," in *Wissenschaft und Nation: Zur Entstehungsgeschichte der deutschen Literaturwissenschaft,* ed. Jürgen Fohrmann and Wilhelm Vosskamp (Munich: Wilhelm Fink Verlag, 1991), 57–71.

80. BAB R/1001, 4550, *Die Zeitschrift für afrikanische Sprachen,* vol. 1, April 1886–28 Februar 1895, report of Carl Büttner on the need for a journal of African languages, November 13, 1886.

81. Meinhof, "Warum studiert man primitive Sprachen?"

82. GStaPKB Rep. 208A, Seminar für Orientalische Sprachen, Acta betreffend Dr. Büttner, Nr. 114, Bl. 1–77, Sachau memo, n.d., ca. September 1887.

83. BAB R/1001, 4550, *Die Zeitschrift für afrikanische Sprachen,* volume 1, April 1886–28 Februar 1895, Carl Büttner, likely to Eduard Sachau, April 27, 1886.

84. Ibid., report of Büttner to von Goßler, Minister of Culture and Education, March 25, 1889.

85. Ibid., letter from Büttner to von Goßler, March 24, 1888.

86. Ibid., Büttner to von Goßler, 3/25/89.

87. BAB R/1001, 4550, *Die Zeitschrift für afrikanische Sprachen,* volume 3, vom 18. Juli 1897 bis 7. März 1902, letter from Seidel to the AAKA, July 12, 1898.

88. GStaPKB Rep. 208A, Seminar für Orientalische Sprachen, Acta betreffend den Lehrer des Suaheli, Dr. Jur. G. Neuhaus, Bl. 1–91, Nr. 115, various.

89. GStaPKB Rep. 208A, Nr. 116, Akte betreffend Carl Velten, Bd. I, letter of Eduard Sachau to the *Kultusminister,* January 19, 1895.

90. GStaPKB Rep. 208A, Nr. 116, Bd. I, letter of Carl Velten to Eduard Sachau, January 15, 1894.

91. GStaPKB Rep. 208A, Nr. 116, Bd. I, letter of Carl Velten to Eduard Sachau, March 11, 1895; for information on the German war with the Hehe, see Alison Redmayne, "Mkwakwa and the Hehe Wars," *Journal of African History* 9, no. 3 (1968): 409–36.

92. GStaPKB Rep. 208A, Nr. 116, Bd. I, letter of Carl Velten to Eduard Sachau, January 15, 1896.

93. Gerhard Böhm and Mirjana Kutnjak, trans., "Development and Nature of African Linguistics in the Nineteenth Century with Special Reference to German-speaking Countries," in *The Prix Volney: Volume III: Contributions to Comparative Indo-European, African, and Chinese Linguistics,* ed. Joan Leopold (Dordrecht: Kluwer, 2000), 255–302.

94. In the 1890s, the seminar had only eighty-eight students who were headed for "colonial" foreign service, military duty, or postal work in Africa, yet their ranks rose over the course of the decade.

95. Eduard Sachau, "Seminarchronik für die Zeit vom Oktober 1905 bis August 1906," *Mittheilungen des Seminars für Orientalische Sprachen,* Jahrgang 7, 1904: I–VII.

96. Eduard Sachau, "Seminarchronik für die Zeit vom Oktober 1905 bis August 1906," *Mittheilungen des Seminars für Orientalische Sprachen,* Jahrgang 9, 1906: I–VIII.

97. Verzeichnis von Kolonialbeamten, die im Seminar Kolonialsprachen studiert haben, in Sachau, *Denkschrift,* Beilage 12 in Sachau, *Denkschrift,* 75–77.

98. BAB R 1001 6176 Erforschung der Sprachen der eingeborenen Völkerschaften—Ostafrika, December 1901 to June 1938, Correspondence between Governor Adolf von Götzen and the AAKA, 7/2/02, zu K 13168.

99. Peter K. Austin, *One Thousand Languages: Living, Endangered, and Lost* (Berkeley: University of California Press, 2008), 98, 100.

100. Johannes Fabian, *Language and Colonial Power: The Appropriation of Swahili in the Former Belgian Congo, 1880–1938* (Cambridge: Cambridge University Press, 1986), 9, 149.

101. Charles Pike, "History and Imagination: Swahili Literature and Resistance to German Language Imperialism in Tanzania, 1885–1910," *International Journal of African Historical Studies* 19, no. 2 (1986): 201–33.

102. Stumpf, *La politique linguistique au Cameroun de 1884 à 1960,* 112, and Austen and Derrick, *Middlemen of the Cameroons Rivers,* 145.

103. Not realizing that Schön was German, Sachau counted him among the "English" missionaries active in Hausa research.

104. GStaPKB, Rep. 208A, 76, Geheimes Staatsarchiv, Acta betreffend den Lektor der Haussa-Sprache, Mohammed al Boschir, Bl. 1-108, 1896–1901, Eduard Sachau to Dr. Bosse, June 15, 1896, and *Notiz aus Luzar's Oriental List,* vol. VII, 12, 256.

105. GStaPKB, Rep. 208A, 76, Geheimes Staatsarchiv, Acta betreffend den Lektor der Haussa-Sprache, Mohammed al Boschir, Bl. 1-108, 1896–1901, Eduard Sachau to Dr. Bosse, Director of the Ministry for "geistlichen pp. Angelegenheiten," March 4, 1896.

CHAPTER 3

As Meinhof was called by his colleague Lestrade in an essay of the same name; see Lestrade, University of Cape Town Archives (hereafter referred to as UCT) BC 255 B 2 K 3, the Lestrade Papers, G. P. Lestrade, "A Great Africanist," n.d., ca. 1927–28.

1. StaH 361-1 Hochschulwesen, Dozenten- u. Personalakten IV, 673, Meinhof, Carl, 23.7.1857, Carl Meinhof's Biographischer Bogen and Lebenslauf. See also Ludwig Gerhardt, "The Place of Carl Meinhof in African Linguistics," *Afrika und Übersee,* Bd. 78, 1995: 163–75, and Carl Meinhof, "Was ich mit afrikanischen Sprachen erlebte," *Afrika-Rundschau* 10, no. 2–3 (1944): 17–24.

2. Franz Kern, *Ludwig Giesebrecht als Dichter, Gelehrter, und Schulmann* (Stettin: Th. von der Nahmer, 1875), and Walter Menn, ed., *Pommersche Lebensbilder,* Bd. 4 (Cologne, 1966), 292–315.

3. Such as the six-volume *Geschichte der deutschen Kaiserzeit* (Leipzig: Duncker und Humblot, 1877–95).

4. Gustav Friedrich Hertzberg, *August Hermann Francke und sein Hallisches Waisenhaus* (Halle: Verlag der Buchhandlung des Waisenhauses, 1898).

5. Köstlin was the author of *Life of Luther* (Whitefish, MT: Kessinger Publishing's Rare Reprints, 2004), among others.

6. *Confessionalism* refers to the idea that only those who strictly adhered to the doctrinal teachings of a particular church—i.e., without any heterodoxy—could truly belong to it.

7. Claude Welch, *Protestant Thought in the Nineteenth Century, Volume I, 1799–1870* (New Haven: Yale University Press, 1972), 218ff.

8. Paul Tillich, *A History of Christian Thought, from its Judaic and Hellenistic Origins to Existentialism,* ed. Carl E. Braaten (New York: Simon and Schuster, 1972), 506–9.

9. Rudolf von Raumer, *Herr Professor Schleicher in Jena und Die Urverwandschaft der semitischen und indoeuropäischen Sprachen. Ein kritisches Bedenken* (Frankfurt am Main: Heyder & Zimmer, 1864); and *Fortsetzung der Untersuchung über die Urverwandtschaft der semitischen und indoeuropäischen Sprachen* (Frankfurt am Main: Heyder & Zimmer, ca. 1860).

10. Rudolf von Raumer, "Die Urverwandschaft der semitischen und indoeuropäischen Sprachen," in Rudolf von Raumer, *Gesammelte sprachwissenschaftliche Schriften* (Frankfurt am Main: Heyder & Zimmer, 1863), 460–539, and *Sendschreiben an Herrn Professor Whitney, über die Urverwandschaft der semitischen und indogermanischen Sprachen* (Frankfurt am Main: Heyder & Zimmer, 1876), 1–20.

11. Cremer was a Greek lexicographer and biblicist who promoted the theory that there was a difference between profane and sacred Greek. See Adolf Deissman, "Hellenistic Greek," in *The New Schaff-Herzog Encyclopedia of Religious Knowledge,* ed. Samuel Macauley Jackson, vol. 5: 211–15. Accordingly, Cremer was author of the *Biblico-Theological Lexicon of New Testament Greek,* trans. William Urwick (Edinburgh: T. & T. Clark, 1878).

12. Cremer, Harless, and Thomasius all studied under Halle theologian Friedrich August Tholuck and incorporated his teachings on sin and regeneration into their own scholarly work; see Welch, *Protestant Thought in the Nineeteenth Century,* 218, and Gerhard Diekmeyer, *Wort und Gewißheit: Das Schriftprinzip in der Theologie Hermann Cremers* (Witten: R. Brockhaus Verlag, 1999), 74.

13. Carl Meinhof, "Die Aussprache des Hebräischen," in *Neues Jahrbuch für Philosophie und Pädagogik,* ed. Fleckeisen, II.Abt. 1885: 146–57; Review of H. L. Strack, *Hebräische Grammatik, Evangelische Kirchenzeitung* 1885: 1055–56.

14. Meinhof, "Orthographische Briefe an eine Dame," *Plattdütsch Vereens-Blatt* (Leipzig, 1879 Nr. 3–12, 1880 Nr. 2–3).

15. AIAÄ BVIII 14, Intern. Inst. Gründung, Meinhof, Gutachten über Orthogr., Seminar für Afrikanistik.

16. Carl Meinhof, "Vorbemerkungen zu einem vergleichenden Wörterbuch der Bantusprachen," *Zeitschrift für afrikanische und oceanische Sprachen* 1 (1895): 268–81.

17. Carl Meinhof, *Grundriss einer Lautlehre der Bantusprachen nebst Anleitung zur Aufnahme von Bantusprachen,* 2nd ed. (Berlin: Dietrich Reimer [Ernst Vohsen], 1910), 47.

18. BAB R 1001 6171, Carl Meinhof to "Herr Major," 26 April 1898, for Schumann and Nauhaus; A. N. Tucker, "Systems of Tone-Marking African Languages," *Bulletin of the School of Oriental and African Studies, University of London* 27, no. 3 (1964): 594–611, citing Theodor and Paul Schwellnus, "Die Verba des Tsivenda," *Mitteilungen des Seminars für orientalische Sprachen* 6 (1904): 12–31, for the Schwellnuses.

19. BAB R 1001 6172, *Gutachten* of Karl Endemann to the A.A.K.A., March 21, 1901.

20. For a list of both the conferences Meinhof attended and the mission-spon-

sored journals in which he published, please see Emmi Meyer, "Das Werk von Carl Meinhof. Dargestellt in seinen Schriften," *Zeitschrift für Eingeborenen-Sprachen* 34 (1944): 131–72.

21. BAB R 1001 6172, *Gutachten* of Karl Endemann to the A.A.K.A., March 21, 1901.

22. C. Schumann, *Grundriss einer Grammatik der Kondesprache* (Berlin: Mitteilungen des Seminars für Orientalische Sprachen, 1899), Vorwort.

23. Meinhof, *Grundriss*, 47–56. This chapter is titled "Anleitung zur Aufnahme von Bantusprachen [instructions for recording Bantu languages]."

24. Ibid., 47. Meinhof's program entailed discovering which etymological forms existed in each language and how they could be classified according to what was already known about the structure of Bantu. For instance, "*ka* findet man vielleicht als Präf. Kl. 13 oder als Verbalendung der Intransitiva," and so forth. In other words, knowing that *ka* belonged to a specific category in related Bantu languages made it likely that it had a similar meaning in an unknown one.

25. BAB R 1001 6172, Walther Trittelvitz, Berlin, to the Kolonialabteilung des auswärtigen Amtes, Berlin, March 29, 1901.

26. BAB R 1001 6172, Kolonialabteilung des auswärtigen Amtes, Berlin, to Herrn Missionsinspektor Pastor Trittelvitz, Berlin, Herrn Missionsinspektor, Berlin, Der Vorsitzenden der evangelischen Brüder-Unität Dr. C. Buchner, Berthelsdorf bei Herrnhut, and Herrn Missionsinspektor Dr. Schreiber, Barmen, March 15, 1901.

27. BAB R 1001 6172, A. W. Schreiber to the Kolonialabteilung des auswärtigen Amtes, Berlin, March 18, 1901. Schreiber and Meinhof later became good friends.

28. BAB R 1001 6172, Inspektor Wendland, Berlin, to the Kolonialabteilung des auswärtigen Amtes, Berlin, March 22, 1901.

29. Trittelvitz to the A.A.K.A.

30. BAB R 1001 6173, Prussian Minister of Culture to the *Reichskanzler*, April 9, 1902.

31. Altena, 31.

32. Meinhof, *Grundriss*, VI, 57ff., and BAB R 1001 6173, Carl Meinhof to Auswärtigen Amt, Kolonial-Abteilung March 3, 1902.

33. BAB R 1001 6173, Carl Meinhof to Auswärtigen Amt, Kolonial-Abteilung March 3, 1902.

34. BAB R 1001 6173, Auswärtige Abteilung des Reichskolonialamtes to the Reichssekretär des Reichsschatzamtes, January 18, 1902, and the reply, January 31, 1902.

35. BAB R 1001 6173, Carl Meinhof to Auswärtigen Amt, Kolonial-Abteilung March 3, 1902.

36. Ibid. Meinhof claimed that his orthographic system, based on the work of the Egyptologist Lepsius, was already being employed for the Makonde language.

37. Carl Meinhof, "Aus dem Seelenleben der Eingeborenen," *Jahrbuch über die deutschen Kolonien* II (1909): 51–52.

38. Meinhof, *Grundriss*, V.

39. BAB R 1001 6170, Carl Meinhof to the kaiserliche auswärtige Amt, Berlin, December 11, 1897.

40. In Petrus Maria Le Berre, *Grammaire de la langue ponguée* (Paris: Imprimerie S. Raçon et Compagnie, 1873).

41. Meinhof, *Die Christianisierung der Sprachen Afrikas,* 17.

42. Ibid.

43. August Schleicher, *Compendium der vergleichenden Grammatik der indogermanischen Sprachen. Kurzer Abriss einer Laut- und Formenlehre der indogermanischen Ursprache, des Altindischen, Alteranischen, Altgriechischen, Altitalischen, Altkeltischen, Altslawischen, Litauischen und Altdeutschen* (Weimar: H. Böhlau, 1866).

44. J. Haller, *Die Vorbildung unserer Missionare* (Basel: Verlag der Missionsbuchhandlung, 1904); Tobias Eiselen, "Der Missionar und seine Rolle—eine missionsgeschichtliche Untersuchung zur Missionarausbildung und Praxis, dargestellt an Jakob Andreas Spieth (1856–1914)" (master's thesis, University of Hamburg, 1987), 46–49; W. Gründler, "Die Bedeutung gemeinsamer Ausbildungsstätten für die Spezialausbildung der Missionare," 24–30.

45. BMW 1/582, 1856–1908, "Instruktion für den Inspektor des Missions Seminars, der Gesellschaft zur Beförderung der evangelischen Missionen unter den Heiden," Berlin, den 2. August 1833.

46. Ibid., "Zeugnis" for Heinrich Kittlaus, signed by mission inspectors Wangemann, Kratzenstein, and Wendland, February 1, 1890.

47. At Leipzig students began to learn Swahili in their final year of seminary, whereas the younger missionaries of the *Brüdergemeine* usually either worked with their older brethren or went to Berlin or Zizow for African language training.

48. Haller, 28.

49. BMW Acta des Missionszöglings Carl Endemann aus Ruhland, Abt. II, Fach 3, E. No. 2, Tit III, E. No. 22, Vol. 2, Karl Endemann to the Committee of the Berlin Mission Society and its president, Dr. Goetze, March 12, 1875.

50. Meinhof, "Wie treibt ein Missionar am besten die Erlernung der Sprache des Volkes, unter dem er arbeitet?" and commentaries thereto, in *Verhandlungen der elften Kontinentalen-Missions-Konferenz zu Bremen* (Berlin: Buchhandlung der Berliner evangelischen Missionsgesellschaft, 1906), 5–33; "Das missionarische Sprachproblem," *Allgemeine Missionszeitschrift,* Berlin (1906): 256, among others.

51. Richard Lepsius, *Standard Alphabet for Reducing Unwritten Languages and Foreign Graphic Systems to a Uniform Orthography in European Letters* (London: Williams & Norgate, 1863).

52. Carl Meinhof, "The Training of Missionaries in Regard to Language," World Missionary Conference, Edinburgh 1910, 263.

53. BAB R 1001 6170, 6171. Kol. Ausw. Amt to Herr Major (name illegible), May 5, 1898; Carl Meinhof to the Kolonialabteilung des Auswärtigen Amtes zu Berlin, November 3, 1899. At the time, Meinhof had nine children and a meager salary and therefore declared himself to be in desperate financial straits.

54. BAB R 1001 6171. Erforschung der Sprachen der eingeborenen Völkerschaften. Eduard Sachau to the Director of the Kolonial-Abteilung des Auswärtigen Amtes, February 16, 1900.

55. Sachau to the Director of the Kolonial-Abteilung des Auswärtigen Amtes, February 16, 1900.

56. BAB R 1001 6170, Carl Meinhof to the Kolonial-Abteilung des auswärtigen

Amtes, April 26, 1898. This was why Meinhof had such difficulty procuring governmental financing for the publication of the *Grundriss* and had to turn to the *Deutsche morgenländische Gesellschaft* for financial assistance.

57. GStAPKB, Rep. 208A, Seminar für Orientalische Sprachen/25 Carl Meinhof, 1902–1909, Das Seminar für orientalische Sprachen, Sachau to the Minister der geistlichen Unterrichts- und Medicinal-Angelegenheiten, June 29, 1902.

58. GStAPKB Rep. 208A, Seminar für Orientalische Sprachen 25 Carl Meinhof, 1902–1909, Seminar für orientalische Sprachen, Meinhof to Sachau, April 1, 1903.

59. Sachau to the Minister der geistlichen Unterrichts- und Medicinal-Angelegenheiten, 29/6/02.

60. Carl Meinhof, "Ueber den gegenwärtigen Stand der afrikanischen Sprachforschung," *Verhandlungen des deutschen Kolonial Kongresses 1905 zu Berlin* (Berlin: Dietrich Riemer, 1906), 119.

61. BAB R 1001 6171, Carl Meinhof to the Kolonial-Abteilung, April 26, 1898.

62. Siegmund Brauner, "Carl Meinhof und Wilhelm Wundt," 59–69.

63. Meinhof, "Vorbemerkungen zu einem vergleichenden Wörterbuch der Bantusprachen."

64. Diedrich Westermann, *Die Sudansprachen, eine sprachvergleichende Studie* (Hamburg: L. Friedrichsen, 1911).

65. StaH 364-5 Universität I D 110.20.13, Beschwerde von Dr. Heepe gegen Professor Meinhof wegen nicht erfolgter Drucklegung des Jaunde-Wörterbuchs, 1921–1928, Evaluations of Heepe's manuscript by Diedrich Westermann, July 28, 1922, and December 7, 1922.

66. StaH 364-5 I, Universität I, D 110.20.16, Ehrenstreitsfälle von Mitgliedern des Lehrkörpers, Beschwerde von Prof. Meinhof gegen die Philosophische Fakultät, Meinhof to the Universitätssenat, December 13, 1922, Meinhof to the University Rector, January 3, 1923.

67. Ibid., W. Schubring to Rektor Lauffer, January 8, 1923. Schubring's letter indicates that Meinhof may also have mismanaged funds for the *Abhandlungen*, suggesting that he did not want to publish Heepe's manuscript to cover his own financial mishaps.

68. Personal communication with Ludwig Gerhardt, January 1999.

69. AIAÄ BVIII 14, Intern. Inst., Gutachten über Orthogr., Seminar für Afrikanistik, letter from Meinhof to Westermann, May 11, 1927.

70. Ibid.

71. Diedrich H. Westermann and Ida C. Ward, *Practical Phonetics for Students of African Languages* (Oxford: Oxford University Press, 1933), was the book that set the standard for African orthography in this era.

72. Bernhard Struck, "Somatische Typen und Sprachgruppen in Kordofan," *Zeitschrift für Ethnologie* 22, 23 Jg. (1920–21): 129–70.

73. GStaPKB, Rep. 208A, Nr. 121, Blatt 1-173, Lektoren des Suaheli, Bd. I, 1899–1909, Carl Velten to Eduard Sachau, June 16, 1904, and Carl Velten, *Gutachten* (Evaluation) of Mtoro bin Mwenyi Bakari, May 5, 1905.

74. GStaPKB Rep. 208A, Nr. 121, Blatt 1-173, Lektoren des Suaheli, Bd. I, 1899–1909, Report by Meinhof concerning Bakari, May 26, 1905.

75. AIAÄ "Arbeiten von Meinhof," Carl Meinhof, "Uebersicht über die Sprachen Afrikas für die Zwecke der Kolonialverwaltung," unpublished, n.d.

76. Ludger Wimmelbücker, *Mtoro bin Mwinyi Bakari (c. 1869–1927): Swahili Lecturer and Author in Germany* (Oxford: African Books Collective, 2009), 79.

77. The article "Kolonialwissenschaftlicher Ausschuß an der Hansischen Universität," in the *Hamburger Tageblatt*, Nr. 5, January 6, 1937, discussed how Meinhof was leading a committee that addressed issues of "population politics" (*Bevölkerungspolitik*) in the former German colonies.

78. Altena, 144ff.

79. This excludes Semitic languages such as Arabic, which were primarily spoken north of the Sahara.

80. Felix von Luschan, "Hamitische Typen," in Carl Meinhof, *Sprachen der Hamiten* (Berlin: L. Friedrichsen, 1912).

81. Grosse, *Kolonialismus, Eugenik und bürgerliche Gesellschaft in Deutschland 1850–1918.*

82. Hull, *Absolute Destruction*, 132, has commented that "there were countless 'punitive expeditions' in Germany's colonies—between 1891 and 1894 German East Africa recorded 54 of these, for example."

83. Although in the 1920s segregationist laws were only intermittently enforced, and racially mixed neighborhoods persisted. See Alan Mabin, "Comprehensive Segregation: The Origins of the Group Areas Act and Its Planning Apparatuses," *Journal of Southern African Studies* 18, no. 2 (1992): 405–29.

84. Zimmerer, *Deutsche Herrschaft über Afrikaner*, 108–9.

85. From "Das Sterbende und das Neue Afrika," a report on a lecture Meinhof held in Hamburg after returning from South Africa, in the *Hamburger Nachrichten*, Nr. 245, 2July 26, 1928.

86. The Ciskei was an area in the Eastern Cape that eventually became one of two Xhosa homelands.

87. W. W. M. Eiselen, "Natives Urged to Help South African Government with Their Own Development," Native Affairs Fact Paper XIV, based on a speech made in the Ciskei on October 17, 1950, 7.

88. Pierre Hugo, "Transformation: The Changing Context of Academia in Post-Apartheid South Africa," *African Affairs* 97, no. 386 (January 1998): 5–27. Citing Bettina Schmidt, *Creating Order: Culture as Politics in 19th and 20th Century South Africa* (Nijmegen: Third World Centre, 1996), 267, 270.

89. Adam Kuper, *Culture: The Anthropologist's Account* (Cambridge: Harvard University Press, 1999), 1.

90. Although Eiselen was not particularly religious.

CHAPTER 4

1. Staatsbibliothek zu Berlin (hereafter referred to as Stabi), Nachlaß Felix von Luschan, Briefe mit Carl Meinhof, letter from Meinhof to Luschan of September 8, 1904.

2. The word *Anthropologie* in German does not encapsulate several different

branches of the same discipline—physical anthropology, cultural anthropology, social anthropology, etc.—as it does in English. Instead, it refers specifically to physical anthropology, while cultural anthropology can be glossed as *Ethnologie* or even *Völkerkunde.* See Matti Bunzl and H. Glenn Penny, "Introduction: Rethinking German Anthropology, Colonialism, and Race," in *Worldly Provincialism: German Anthropology in the Age of Empire,* ed. Matti Bunzl and H. Glenn Penny (Ann Arbor: University of Michigan Press, 2003), 1–30.

3. Luschan was a physician and had studied under the French physical anthropologist Paul Broca. See Massin, 84.

4. Zimmerman, *Anthropology and Antihumanism in Imperial Germany,* 49.

5. See, for instance, Peter Pels, "The Rise and Fall of the Indian Aborigines: Orientalism, Anglicism, and the Emergence of an Ethnology of India, 1833–1869," in *Colonial Subjects: Essays on the Practical History of Anthropology,* ed. Peter Pels and Oscar Salemink (Ann Arbor: University of Michigan Press, 2000), 82–116. Pels demonstrates that while twentieth-century anthropologists dismissed missionary ethnology as "amateur," the anthropological profession is nonetheless heavily indebted to missionary research.

6. Beatrix Heinze, "Ethnographic Appropriations: German Exploration and Fieldwork in West-Central Africa," *History in Africa* 26 (1999): 69–128.

7. Zimmerman, 5; Penny, *Objects of Culture,* 18.

8. Klaus-Peter Koepping, *Adolf Bastian and the Psychic Unity of Mankind: The Foundations of Anthropology in Nineteenth Century Germany* (St. Lucia: University of Queensland, 1983).

9. Massin, "From Virchow to Fischer," 79–154.

10. Ibid., 86–87.

11. Woodruff Smith, "Anthropology and German Colonialism," in *Germans in the Tropics: Essays in German Colonial History,* ed. Arthur J. Knoll and Lewis H. Gann (New York: Greenwood Press, 1987), 40–51.

12. Zimmerman, 203–5.

13. AIAÄ Ethnogr.-anth. Briefwechsel BV 2 (b) vom 3 Oktober 1920 bis 1. September 1932, Afrikanistik Seminar, letter from Carl Meinhof to a Herr Printz of the Bibliothek der deutschen Morgenländischen Gesellschaft, Halle, December 9, 1931.

14. Ferdinand Hestermann, "Völker und Sprachen in Afrika," *Anthropos* 1912, vii, 219–50, and 1913, vii, 722–60; cited in C. G. Seligmann, "Some Aspects of the Hamitic Problem in the Anglo-Egyptian Sudan," *Journal of the Royal Anthropological Institute of Great Britain and Ireland* 43 (July–December 1913): 42–43.

15. StaH 361-6 Hochschulwesen—Dozenten und Personalakten II 312, Akten betreffend die Vorlesungen des Herrn Dr. Panconcelli-Calzia, notes of a meeting concerning the Hamburg Colonial Institute's chief phonetician, Giulio Panconcelli-Calzia, October 27, 1915; Ferdinand Hestermann, *Kritische Darstellungen der neuesten Ansichten über Gruppierungen und Bewegungen der Sprachen und Völker in Afrika* (Vienna: Self-published, 1929; based on *Anthropos* article of 1913).

16. It may also have had to do with the Austrian Schmidt's staunchly anticolonialist position, which was in sharp contradiction to Meinhof's procolonial zeal; see Suzanne Marchand, "Priests among the Pygmies: Wilhelm Schmidt and the

Counter-Reformation in Austrian Ethnology," in *Worldly Provincialism: German Anthropology in the Age of Empire,* ed. Bunzl and Penny (Ann Arbor: University of Michigan Press, 2003), 283–316.

17. Zimmerman, 203–5.

18. Massin, 97–98.

19. Ibid., 102–4.

20. George Stocking, *After Tylor,* 406–21 passim, was speaking specifically about British social anthropology, but his argument can be extended to anthropology in other colonial contexts.

21. Matti Bunzl and H. Glenn Penny, "Introduction: Rethinking German Anthropology, Colonialism, and Race."

22. Ibid., 14.

23. Penny, *Objects of Culture,* 145.

24. Here see also Rüger, *The Great Naval Game,* 50ff., for how concern for the masses shaped how the navy was marketed in the imperial age.

25. Carl Meinhof, "Die Sprachwissenschaft in Afrika als Hilfswissenschaft," in Carl Meinhof, *Die Moderne Sprachforschung in Afrika* (Berlin: Buchhandlung der Berliner ev. Missionsgesellschaft, 1910), 113.

26. Meinhof, "Aus dem Seelenleben der Eingeborenen," *Jahrbuch über die deutsche Kolonien* v. II, 1909: 47–52.

27. Meinhof, "Aus dem Seelenleben der Eingeborenen," *Jahrbuch über die deutsche Kolonien* v. VI, 1913: 54–58.

28. David Phillippson, *African Archaeology* (Cambridge: Cambridge University Press, 1993), 2. Phillipson stresses the importance of archaeology to the historical enterprise, maintaining that "the archaeologist's interpretation of technological skills or economic practices, particularly hunting, agriculture, and the herding of domestic animals, will generally be far more complete and reliable than those that can be obtained by other types of research"; Kay Williamson, "Linguistic Evidence for the Use of Some Tree and Tube Food Plants in Southern Nigeria," in *The Archaeology of Africa: Food, Metals, and Towns,* ed. Thurstan Shaw, Paul Sinclair, Bassey Andah, and Alex Okpoko (London: Routledge, 1993), 139.

29. David Lee Schoenbrun, *A Green Place, A Good Place: Agrarian Change, Gender, and Social Identity in the Great Lakes Region to the Fifteenth Century* (Portsmouth, NH: Heinemann, 1998), 19.

30. Stabi, Nachlaß Felix von Luschan, Meinhof to Luschan, October 18, 1909, November 8, 1912.

31. Joseph Greenberg, *The Languages of Africa* (Bloomington: Indiana University Press; The Hague: Mouton, 1966), 49.

32. Seligman, *The Races of Africa.*

33. Kay Williamson and Roger Blench, "Niger-Congo," in *African Languages: An Introduction,* ed. Bernd Heine and Derek Nurse (Cambridge: Cambridge University Press, 2000), 12.

34. Christopher Ehret, *Southern Nilotic History: Linguistic Approaches to the Study of the Past* (Evanston: Northwestern University Press, 1971).

35. *Negrito* is one word for those peoples who spoke Sudanic/Nigritic languages.

36. Günther Spannaus, "Historisch-Kritisches zum Hamitenproblem in Afrika," in *In Memoriam: Karl Weule: Beiträge zur Völkerkunde,* ed. Otto Reche (Leipzig: R. Voightländer, 1929), 181.

37. Ibid., 182, 186, 190–91.

38. James Fenton, "A Short History of Anti-Hamitism," Review of Gérard Prunier, *The Rwanda Crisis: History of a Genocide* (New York: Columbia, 1995), *New York Review of Books,* vol. 43, 3 (February 15, 1996): 7–8.

39. On the history of the Hamitic hypothesis see Sanders, "The Hamitic Hypothesis: Its Origins and Functions in Time Perspective," 522–31; Michael Spöttel, *Hamiten: Völkerkunde und Antisemitismus* (Frankfurt am Main, 1996); Jan Knappert, "Origin and Development of the Concept of Hamitic: The First Sixty Years: 1851–1911," *Orientalia Lovaniensia Periodica* 6–7 (1975–76): 303–20; William McKee Evans, "From the Land of Canaan to the Land of Guinea: The Strange Odyssey of the 'Sons of Ham,'" *American Historical Review* 85, no. 1 (February 1980): 15–43; and Saint-Clair Drake, "Detruire de la mythe chamitique, devoir des hommes cultivés," *Presence Africaine,* Numèro Special, 1959: 215–30, among others.

40. Carl Meinhof, *Die Sprachen der Hamiten* (Hamburg: L. Friedrichsen, 1912), VIII.

41. Although as Evans demonstrates in "From the Land of Canaan to the Land of Guinea," at certain points biblical Hamites were indeed imagined as "white" and "red-haired."

42. Meinhof, *Die Sprachen der Hamiten,* VIII.

43. Felix von Luschan, response to "Diskussion über den Vortrag des Hrn. V. Luschan," *Zeitschrift für Ethnologie,* 1906, IV: 913.

44. Karl Heinz Ciz, *Robert Hartmann (1831–1893): Mitbegründer der deutschen Ethnologie* (Gelsenkirchen: Verlag Andreas Müller, 1984), 71–77; Lilias Homburger, *Les langues négro-africaines et les peuples qui les parlent* (Paris: Payot, 1941).

45. Richard Lepsius, *Nubische Grammatik mit einer Einleitung über die Völker und Sprachen Afrikas* (Berlin: W. Hertz, 1880) and *Standard Alphabet for Reducing Unwritten Languages and Foreign Graphic Systems to a Uniform Orthography in European Letters* (London: Seeleys, 1855).

46. Friedrich Müller, whose *Grundriss der Sprachwissenschaft* (Vienna: A. Hölder) was published over the course of many years, from 1876 to 1888, is not to be confused with the eminent philologist Friedrich *Max* Müller, who taught for many years in England; Knappert, "Origin and Development of the Concept of Hamitic: The First Sixty Years, 1851–1911," 308.

47. Carl Meinhof, "Ueber den gegenwärtigen Stand der afrikanischen Sprachforschung," *Verhandlungen des deutschen Kolonial Kongresses 1905 zu Berlin* (Berlin: Dietrich Riemer, 1906), 119.

48. Luschan, "On the Racial Affinities of the Hottentots," in *Addresses and Papers read at the Joint Meeting of the British and South African Associations for the Advancement of Science, held in South Africa, 1905,* vol. 3 (Johannesburg: South African Association for the Advancement of Science, 1905), 115.

49. Ibid., 115.

50. Felix von Luschan, "Anthropological View of Race," in *Select Discussions of Race Problems: A Collection of Papers of Especial Use in Study of Negro American Problems; with the Proceedings of the Twentieth Annual Conference for the*

Study of Negro Problems, ed. John Alvin Bigham (Atlanta: Atlanta University Press), 24–31, cited in W. E. B. Du Bois, "Miscegenation," in *Interracialism: Black-White Intermarriage in American History, Literature, and Law,* ed. Werner Sollors (Oxford: Oxford University Press, 2000), 461–72.

51. Luscan, "On the Racial Affinities of the Hottentots," 111.

52. Carl Meinhof, "The Language of the Hottentots," in *Addresses and Papers read at the Joint Meeting of the British and South African Associations for the Advancement of Science* (Johannesburg: South African Association for the Advancement of Science, 1905), 121.

53. Felix von Luschan, "Sechs Pygmäen aus Ituri," *Zeitschrift für Ethnologie,* Jg. 38 (1906): 718–19.

54. Ibid., 725.

55. Ibid., 725.

56. Ibid., 731. Today, "pygmy" languages are grouped with the Nilo-Saharan language family—the same one that includes the Hamites. See M. Lionel Bender, "Nilo-Saharan," in *African Languages,* ed. Heine and Nurse, 43–73.

57. Carl Meinhof, "Das Ful in seiner Bedeutung für die Sprachen der Hamiten, Semiten und Bantu," *Zeitschrift der Deutschen Morgenländischen Gesellschaft* 65 (1911): 177–200.

58. Meinhof, *Die Sprachen der Hamiten,* 31.

59. Ibid., 2–4.

60. Carl Meinhof, "Über M. Merkers 'Masai,'" *Zeitschrift für Ethnologie* 36 (1904): 738.

61. Ibid., 738. *Alarodic* is a racially charged term for Caucasian.

62. Ibid., 740.

63. Ibid., 739–40.

64. Felix von Luschan, "Hamitische Typen," in Carl Meinhof, *Sprachen der Hamiten* (Berlin: L. Friedrichsen, 1912), 251. While in this instance Luschan did not grapple with Meinhof's hypothesis that the Bantu were the product of a centuries-long intermingling between white Hamites and black speakers of Sudanic languages, he did allow the linguist to insert a footnote to this effect.

65. Theo Vennemann and Terence H. Wilbur, eds., *Schuchardt, the Neogrammarians, and the Transformational Theory of Phonological Change: Four Essays by Hugo Schuchhardt, Theo Vennemann, Terence H. Wilbur* (Linguistische Forschungen, 26) (Frankfurt am Main: Athenäum, 1972).

66. Hugo Schuchardt, Review of "Meinhof, Carl: *Die Sprachen der Hamiten,* nebst einer Beigabe: *Hamitische Typen* Felix von Luschan," *Wiener Zeitschrift für die Kunde des Morgenlandes,* 26 (1912): 407–8.

67. Edward Sapir, "Review of Carl Meinhof, *Die Sprachen der Hamiten,*" *Current Anthropological Literature,* vol. 2 (Lancaster, PA: American Anthropological Association and the American Folklore Society, 1913).

68. Paul Staudinger, "Commentary," on Carl Meinhof, "Ueber den gegenwärtigen Stand der afrikanischen Sprachforschung," *Verhandlungen des deutschen Kolonialkongresses* 1910, 102–3.

69. Carl Meinhof, "Ueber den gegenwärtigen Stand der afrikanischen Sprachforschung," *Verhandlungen des deutschen Kolonialkongresses 1905,* Berlin, 1905, 106.

70. Stabi, Nachlaß Felix von Luschan, Meinhof to Luschan, November 28, 1907.

71. Carl Meinhof, "Sudansprachen und Hamitensprachen," *Zeitschrift für Kolonialsprachen* 1 (1910): 164.

72. GStaPKB, Rep. 208A, 76, Geheimes Staatsarchiv, Acta betreffend den Lektor der Haussa-Sprache, Mohammed al Boschir, Bl. 1-108, 1896–1901, Eduard Sachau to Dr. Bosse, Director of the Ministry for "geistlichen pp. Angelegenheiten," March 4, 1896.

73. The history of the Hausa and Fulbe is interconnected with that of the Sokoto Caliphate, which rose in the early nineteenth century. See Murray Last, *The Sokoto Caliphate* (New York: Humanities Press, 1967).

74. GStaPKB, Rep. 208A, Nr. 77, Haussa-Lektoren 1908–1922, Sachau to Ludwig Holle, Prussian Minister of Culture, July 12, 1909; Sachau to Adam Mischlich, Togo, August 8, 1909.

75. Ibid., Westermann to Sachau, August 9, 1910; Abdullah Adam's contract with the Seminar for Oriental Languages, December 7, 1910.

76. Meinhof also employed his own Fulbe lecturer, a man named Musa bin Adam, at the Hamburg Colonial Institute. Meinhof, *Die Sprachen der Hamiten,* 31.

77. Ibid.

78. Hans Georg-Wolf, *English in Cameroon* (Berlin: Walter de Gruyter, 2001), 8, indeed says, "The conspicuousness of the Fulani was ascribed to Caucasoid origin, believed to be reflected in their language."

79. Williamson and Blench, "Niger-Congo," 15. Meinhof thought that Wolof had been "pervaded by a strong Ful element," but that it was Sudanic, while Fulfulde was essentially Hamitic. See Carl Meinhof, *An Introduction to the Study of African Languages,* trans. Alice Werner (London: J. M. Dent & Sons, 1915), 153.

80. StaH Hochschulwesen Dozenten u. Personalakten IV, 1177. Ergangen 30. Ministerium für Volksbildung, sachbetreff Dr. phil. August Klingenheben, d. 26/1/67, Gotz, Dean of the Philosophical Faculty, Leipzig, to the Ministry for Education, Dresden, March 12, 1930.

81. Ibid., Report Betr. die planmäßige außerordentliche Professur für Neu-Arabisch und hamitische Sprachen Afrikas an d. Universität Leipzig, March 15, 1930.

82. Ibid., Philosophical Faculty, University of Leipzig, to the Ministry for Education, Dresden, April 1, 1930.

83. Bernhard Struck, "Somatische Typen und Sprachgruppen in Kordofan," *Zeitschrift für Ethnologie* 22, 23 Jg. (1920–21): 129–70.

84. AIAÄ, Ethnogr.-anth. Briefwechsel BV 2 (b) vom 3 Oktober 1920 bis 1. September 1932, Carl Meinhof, Hamburg, to Bernhard Struck, Dresden, May 28, 1921.

85. StaH, Philosophical Faculty, Leipzig, to the Ministry of Education, Dresden, April 1, 1930.

CHAPTER 5

1. *Bericht über die Vorlesungen. Wintersemester 1910/11. Die wissenschaftliche Vorlesungen, Ostern 1910–11,* states that after a count of heads 749 participants had been present at eight general lectures on *Die Dichtung der Afrikaner* (African liter-

ature), with an average of 94 in attendance at each meeting. The broad cross-section of listeners, who were required to indicate their profession in a survey printed in the *Bericht,* shows that Meinhof also had a varied public. The attendees at Meinhof's lectures included businessmen, teachers, theologians, and married and unmarried women.

2. Georg Thilenius and Karl Rathgen, "Ruckblick auf die beide ersten Studienjahre," *Reden von Professor Dr. Georg Thilenius und Professor Dr. K. Rathgen bei der Feier der Übergabe des Vorsitzes im Professorenrat* and *Bericht über das zweite Studienjahr, Winter 1909/10, Sommer 1910,* Hamburg, 1910, 10–11, explained that there had been movements to found a university in the city since 1845.

3. Werner von Melle, *Dreißig Jahre Hamburger Wissenschaft, 1891–1921* (Hamburg: Kommissionsverlag von Broschet, 1923), vol. 1, 448 (unless otherwise noted, all cites in von Melle are from volume 1).

4. StAH 364-5 Heft 1, Sem. f. Afr. Spr. IVW Nr. 102 Bd. II, "Verwendung des Suaheliboys von Reg. Rat Zache als Sprachgehilfe im Seminar," 5 June 1912. Specifically, Zache referred to Mtoro as a "Gelehrter."

5. Meyer-Bahlburg and Wolff, *Afrikanische Sprachen in Forschung und Lehre,* 39–40.

6. "Gesetz betr. Errictung eines Kolonial-Instituts in Hamburg, 1908," *Amtsblatt der freien und Hansestadt Hamburg,* Dienstag, den 7. April 1908.

7. *Bericht über das erste Studienjahr,* Hamburg 1909, 9; Dominique Hübler, *Die Zentralstelle des Hamburgischen Kolonialinstituts,* Hausarbeit zur Diplomprüfung, etc., Hamburg, January 1991, 16–17, 22.

8. William O. Henderson, *Studies in German Colonial History,* 2nd ed. (London: Routledge, 1976), 3.

9. Ibid., 45–46, 115. Henderson has shown that in addition to Woermann, various other Hamburg firms, including Hertz and Hansing & Co., had extensive business interests in Zanzibar.

10. George Steinmetz, *The Devil's Handwriting,* 12–13, for instance, says that "Samoa was the site of the first modern German overseas plantation economy, created by the Hamburg firm Godeffroy in the 1860s and 1870s."

11. L. H. Gann, "Economic Development in Germany's African Empire," in *Colonialism in Africa, 1870–1960,* ed. Gann and Peter Duignan (Cambridge: Cambridge University Press, 1975), 213–55.

12. Ibid., 221, 223.

13. Jennifer Jenkins, *Provincial Modernity: Local Culture and Liberal Politics in Fin-de-Siècle Hamburg* (Ithaca: Cornell University Press, 2003), 277, says that Hamburgers saw their city as the German Empire's "gateway to the world."

14. Catherine Hall, *Civilizing Subjects: Colony and Metropole in the English Imagination, 1830–1867* (Chicago: University of Chicago Press, 2002), 274, says, "The men and women of Birmingham learned about the colonial order of things through a multiplicity of forms. Here was no consolidated vision of empire, but rather a cacophony of sounds: abolitionists contending with scientific racists, would-be colonisers competing with the more cautious voices of those who saw empire as an unncessary expense, exhibitors rivalling missionaries in the advertising of their wares."

15. Rüger, *The Great Naval Game,* 98–100.

16. Frederick Cooper and Ann Laura Stoler, "Between Metropole and Colony: Rethinking a Research Agenda," in *Tensions of Empire: Colonial Cultures in a Bourgeois World,* ed. Cooper and Stoler (Berkeley: University of California Press, 1997), 1–58.

17. See chapter 6 for a discussion of how the Colonial Institute tried to restrict African movement in Hamburg.

18. Von Melle, 463–64.

19. Jake W. Spidle, "Colonial Studies in Imperial Germany," *History of Education Quarterly* (Fall 1973): 231–47.

20. Hull, *Absolute Destruction,* 44ff.

21. Spidle; Lora Wildenthal, *German Women for Empire, 1884–1945* (Durham: Duke University Press, 2001), 73, here discusses perhaps the most famous case of colonial "profligacy," that of Carl Peters—who had a servant executed for cavorting with his African concubine, whom he also had put to death.

22. Spidle.

23. *Deutsche Kolonialschule, Lehr- und Anstaltsplan, einschließlich Vorlesungs-Verzeichnis* (Witzenhausen: Chr. Trautvetter, n.d), 5.

24. *Bericht über das erste Studienjahr,* 17.

25. Ibid., 22.

26. The catalog did include lectures on ethnology, physical anthropology, tropical hygiene, geography, colonial administration, law, and even so-called *Kultursprachen* like English and Arabic.

27. Von Melle, 469–70.

28. *Bericht über das erste Studienjahr,* 23.

29. Von Melle, 468.

30. StAH 364-7 A I a 11, Hamburgisches Kolonialinstitut, Auszug aus dem Protokolle des Professorenrats, Hamburg, February 29, 1908.

31. StAH 364-7 EII 9 b, 1, 1b, 11 March 1908, "Heranziehung des Regierungsrats Ludw. Meyer, Steglitz, zu Vorlesungen über Verwaltungspraxis und Kisuaheli," and StAH 364-7 E II 9 b 1, 1a, June 6, 1908, "Beauftragung des Rektors Blank-Tanga mit Suaheli-Unterricht, 1908, 1912."

32. Protestant missionaries also contributed to *Kiongozi,* even though it was a government-sponsored publication. AIAÄ BVII 4, Evangel. Mission, Martin Klamroth to Carl Meinhof, February 25, 1913.

33. StAH 364-7, E II 9 b, 1, 1b, April 8, 1908.

34. Trautmann, *Aryans and British India,* 19, 217–18.

35. Swahili is a Bantu language with a significant number of Arabic loan words, although Derek Nurse and Thomas Spear have argued that these only appeared late in the language's history, in the eighteenth and nineteenth centuries. See Nurse and Spear, *The Swahili: Reconstructing the History and Language of an African Society, 800–1500* (Philadelphia: University of Pennsylvania Press, 1985), 80–81.

36. Emin Pasha, a.k.a. Eduard Schnitzer, was a German doctor, linguist, botanist, ornithologist, and colonial civil servant. General Charles Gordon appointed him Governor of Equatoria, a province in the Sudan, in 1878. See Tim Jeal,

Stanley: The Impossible Life of Africa's Greatest Explorer (New Haven: Yale University Press, 2008), 314–15.

37. StAH 364-7 A I b I 2, "Errichtung des Professur für afrikanische Sprachen 1909," January 25, 1909, February 3, 1909.

38. Ibid., 25 January 1909. Also see Carl Meinhof, "Die Bedeutung des Studiums der Eingeborenen für die Kolonialverwaltung," 354.

39. E. Schwörer, *Kolonial-Deutsch: Vorschläge einer künftigen deutschen Kolonialsprache in systematisch- grammatikalischer Darstellung und Begründung* (Diessen vor München: Jos. C. Hubers Verlag, 1916).

40. "Errichtung des Professur für afrikanische Sprachen 1909," February 3, 1909.

41. StAH 364-7 A I b I, 2, January 25, 1909.

42. StAH 364-7 B IV b 6, Geheim-Akte betreffend Berufung von Professor Meinhof D. Doktor in die Professor für afrikanische Sprachen, 1909, February 3, 1909.

43. Geheim-Akte betreffend Berufung von Professor Meinhof D. Doktor in die Professor für afrikanische Sprachen.

44. Geheim-Akte betreffend Berufung von Professor Meinhof D. Doktor in die Professor für afrikanische Sprachen.

45. StAH 364-7 B IV b 6, Justus Strandes to Carl Becker, January 13, 1909.

46. Carl Meinhof, "Die Laien und ihre Heranziehung zur Mitarbeit an der Mission," *Jahrbuch der sächsischen Missionskonferenz* 1909: 91–98.

47. Carl Meinhof, Berlin, Open Letter (untitled), n.d., ca. 1908–9, 2.

48. Niall Ferguson, *Paper and Iron: Hamburg Business and German Politics in the Era of Inflation, 1897–1927* (Cambridge: Cambridge University Press, 2002), 59.

49. "Letters from the Continent" by "An Old Traveler," *Evangelical Magazine and Missionary Chronicle* 14 (1836): 572.

50. StAH 364-7 B IV b 6, Carl Becker to Justus Strandes, February 3, 1909.

51. Carl Meinhof, "Zweites Korreferat" to the "Zweiter Hauptvortrag" of the conference, W. Gründler's "Die Bedeutung gemeinsamer Ausbildungsstätten für die Spezialausbildung der Missionare," 39, and *Die erziehende Kraft der Mission* (Berlin: Buchhandlung der Berliner evangel. Missionsgesellschaft, 1912), 3–4.

52. StaH Professorenrat des Kolonialinstituts AI c 10 1, "Ausbildung von Missionaren und Missionschülern," Minutes of the Meetings of the *Professorenrat*, June 9 and June 19, 1909.

53. Becker to Strandes, February 3, 1909.

54. Strandes to von Melle, February 18, 1909.

55. StAH 364-7 A I c 10 1, "Ausbildung von Missionaren und Missionschülern."

56. Strandes to von Melle, February 18, 1909.

57. GStAPKB/Rep. 208 A, Seminar für Orientalische Sprachen/25 Carl Meinhof, 1902–1909, "Übersiedlung" of Carl Meinhof from Berlin to Hamburg, ca. 1909.

58. StAH 364-7 IV W 102, I, 1, 17/12/09, *Seminar für afrikanische Sprachen*, December 17, 1909.

59. Ibid., Summer 1910.

60. Carl Meinhof, "Die Bedeutung des Studiums der Eingeborenensprachen für die Kolonialverwaltung."

61. StAH 364-7 A I b 1, 5, "Errichtung eines Lehrstühles für Sudansprachen, 1910–11."

62. Bernd Heine et al., *Die Sprachen Afrikas: mit zahlreichen Karten und Tabellen* (Hamburg: Buske, 1981), 17.

63. Diedrich Westermann, *Die Sudansprachen, eine sprachvergleichende Studie* (Hamburg: L. Friedrichsen, 1911).

64. BAB R 1001 6196, doc. 188, n.d., ca. October 1905.

65. StAH 364-7 A I b 1, 5, Carl Meinhof, Hamburg, "Bericht über Professor Diedrich Westermann," December 21, 1910.

66. Diedrich Westermann, *Die Nutzplflanzen unserer Kolonien und ihre wirtschaftliche Bedeutung für das Mutterland* (Berlin: Dietrich Reimer, 1909).

67. StAH 364-7 A I b 1, 5, "Errichtung eines Lehrstühles für Sudansprachen, 1910–11."

68. StAH 364-7 A 1 b 1, Westermann to Meinhof, 14 December 1910, and Meinhof to Thilenius, December 30, 1910.

69. StAH Akten, Ministerium für Volksbildung, sachbetreff Dr. phil. August Klingenheben, d. 26/1/67/Hochschulwesen Dozenten u. Personalakten IV, 1177, Personalbogen August Klingenheben, c. 1930.

70. StAH 364-7/G II a I d II II 8, Bericht über Fleiß und Leistungen des beamteten Hörer im Suaheli-Kursus des W.-S. 1910/11, S.S. 1911, W.S. 1911/12, S.S. 1912, W.S. 1912/13, S.S. 1913, W.S. 1913/14, S.S. 1914. This report indicates that the following numbers of civil servants took Swahili at the *Seminar für Kolonialsprachen* in these semesters: two in spring 1911, two in fall 1910–11, three in spring 1912, three in fall 1912–13, four in spring 1913, one in fall 1913–14, and three in spring 1914.

71. Spidle, "Colonial Studies in Imperial Germany"; Walter K. H. Hoffmann, *Vom Kolonialexperten zum Experten der Entwicklungszusammenarbeit: acht Fallstudien zur Geschichte der Ausbildung von Fachkräften für Übersee in Deutschland und in der Schweiz* (Saarbrücken: Verlag Breitenbach, 1980), 54.

72. StAH 364-7 A I c 2 4, Kurt Redlich, "Hamburgisches Kolonialinstitut und Allgemeines Vorlesungswesen," n.d., ca. 1914–15, in Sprechsaalartikel des Hörers Kurt Redlich für das "Hamburgische Fremdenblatt" über den Besuch des Kolonialinstituts, 1914.

73. Meinhof, "Der Mythus," in *Die Dichtung der Afrikaner,* 25–27 passim, and "Die Sage," also in *Die Dichtung der Afrikaner,* 43.

74. Meinhof, "Der Mythus," 28. Meinhof follows with a reference to the Masai, and the fact that, among them as well as among their "heathen neighbors," one can witness the origins of a primitive monotheism. Moreover, in "Die Sage," 50–51, he explained that the presence of lighter-skinned, blond gods in African sagas might also be related to the Hamitic invasions.

75. Carl Meinhof, "The Soul of an African Language," *International Review of Missions* 16 (1927): 82.

76. Carl Meinhof, "The Training of Missionaries in Regard to Language," World Missionary Conference, Edinburgh 1910, 263.

77. Carl Meinhof, "Lautforschungen in Afrika und ihre Bedeutung für die allgemeine Phonetik," in Carl Meinhof, *Die Moderne Sprachforschung in Afrika. Hamburgische Vorträge von Carl Meinhof* (Berlin: Buchhandlung der ev. Missionsgesellschaft, 1910), 54.

78. Archiv der evangelischen Missionswerk, Basel (hereafter known as EMW), QK-4, 1, Missionsgesellschaften C. England, III Teil, Konf. Brit. Miss. Gesellsch., J.M.C., C. Zirkulare 1. Teil, Memorandum by the Rev. W. H. T. Gairdner, "Missionary training methods on the Continent," März 1912.

79. Meinhof, "Lautforschungen in Afrika und ihre Bedeutung für die allgemeine Phonetik," 52.

80. Ibid., 51.

81. Ibid., 60. See also G. L. Cleve, "Die Lippenlaute der Bantu und die Negerlippen, mit besonderer Berücksichtigung der Lippenverstümmelungen," *Zeitschrift für Ethnologie* 35 (1903): 681–701 passim.

82. Meinhof, 60; Cleve, 683.

83. Meinhof, 59–60.

84. Carl Meinhof, "Die Urgeschichte im Lichte der afrikanischen Linguistik," *Deutsche Literaturzeitung,* Nr. 37, XXXIII Jg. (September 14, 1912): 2309–17.

85. Mary Louise Pratt, "Scratches on the Face of the Country; or, what Mr. Barrow saw in the Land of the Bushmen," in *"Race," Writing, and Difference,* ed. Henry Louis Gates Jr. (Chicago: University of Chicago Press, 1985, 1986), 199–243, or *Imperial Eyes: Travel Writing and Transculturation* (New York: Routledge, 1992), 176.

86. StAH 361-5, I, I VW 122 1, 3, "Laboratoriumsordnung," n.d., ca. 1910–11, Phonetisches Laboratorium.

87. StAH 361-5 I I VW 122 I, 3, Bernhard Schädel to Max Förster, April 27, 1911, Phonetisches Laboratorium.

88. Anna Morpurgo Davies, *Nineteenth Century Linguistics,* vol. 4 of *History of Linguistics,* ed. Giulio Lepschy, 139. See also *What Is Philology? Proceedings from the Conference "What Is Philology?"* Special Focus Issue of *Comparative Literature Studies* 27, no. 1 (1990): 6, where in the "Introduction" Jan Ziolkowski says that, whatever else the contributors to the volume might have thought about the definition of philology, "At the conference the equation of philology with linguistics was rejected without any objections."

89. Carl Meinhof, "Warum studiert man primitive Sprachen?" 18.

90. Ibid., 14–16.

91. Ibid., 22.

92. Carl Meinhof, "Überblick über die Sprachen und Sprachfamilien in Afrika," in *Die moderne Sprachforschung in Afrika,* 44–45 passim.

93. P. E. H. Hair, *The Early Study of Nigerian Languages,* 36–37.

94. Carl Meinhof, "Die Bedeutung der experimentellen Phonetik für die Erforschung der afrikanischen Sprachen," *Vox* 1 (1913): 22.

95. Ibid., 23.

96. Giulio Panconcelli-Calzia, *Experimentelle Phonetik* (Berlin: Vereinigung wissenschaftlicher Verleger, Walter de Gruyter, 1921), 7.

97. Ibid., 11.

98. Ibid., 12–13.

99. Ibid., 17–18.

100. Personal communication with Karen Landahl, Professor of Linguistics and Phonetics at the University of Chicago, October 1999.

101. Panconcelli-Calzia, *Experimentelle Phonetik,* 22.

102. Ibid., 24–25.

103. As K. Kohler has explained in "Three Trends in Phonetics: The Development of Phonetics as a Discipline in Germany since the Nineteenth Century," in *Towards a History of Phonetics,* ed. R. E. Asher and Eugénie J. A. Henderson (Edinburgh: University Press, 1981), 168–69, these machines were not always as reliable as their defenders claimed them to be.

104. W. J. Hardcastle, "Experimental Studies in Lingual Coarticulation," also in *Towards a History of Phonetics,* ed. Asher and Henderson, 52; Panconcelli-Calzia, "Über die aspirierten und nichtaspirierten Verschlußlaute sowie den Frageton im Suaheli," 311.

105. Sarah Barrows, *Experimental Phonetics as an Aid to the Study of Language* (Columbus: Ohio State University, ca. 1913–14), 66–67.

106. StAH 361-5 I I VW, Nr. 122, Band III, Heft 13, Phonetisches Laboratorium, Giulio Panconcelli-Calzia to the Oberschulbehörde, Sektion für die wissenschaftliche Anstalten, July 8, 1914, Anlage einer Meerschweinchenzüchterei. In order to introduce his students to anatomy of the vocal organs, Panconcelli-Calzia had been using larynxes, likely human ones, supplied by the police. However, while this was not "ausreichend," he requested permission to raise guinea pigs on the laboratory grounds and then use only those that had been "abgetöteten" in his exercises.

107. Panconcelli-Calzia, *Experimentelle Phonetik,* 13.

108. "Erster internationaler Kongreß für experimentelle Phonetik," *Hamburger Fremdenblatt* Nr. 93, April 22, 1914.

109. Barrows, 63.

110. "Ausstellung des Seminars für Kolonialsprachen," *Deutsche Kolonialzeitung, Organ der Deutschen Kolonialgesellschaft,* Nr. 25, Berlin, 22/6/12, 29. Jg.

111. Carl Meinhof, *Eine Studienfahrt nach Kordofan* (Hamburg: L. Friedrichsen, 1916), 13.

CHAPTER 6

1. StaH 361-1 Hochschulwesen, Dozenten- u. Personalakten IV, 673, Meinhof, Carl, 23.7.1857, Carl Meinhof's Biographischer Bogen and Lebenslauf.

2. Ibid., and Carl Meinhof, "Das Verbum in der Isubu-Sprache," *Zeitschrift für afrikanische Sprachen* 3 (1889–90), 206–34; "Ein Märchen aus Kamerun (Duala)," *Zeitschrift für afrikanische Sprachen* 3 (1889–90): 241–46; "Das Zeitwort in der Benga-Sprache," *Zeitschrift für afrikanische Sprachen* 3 (1889–90): 265–84.

Isubu and Benga were both spoken in regions near the Duala and were closely related.

3. Stabi, Nachlaß von Luschan, Briefen von Carl Meinhof, December 18, 1900.

4. See Dittrich and Rieke-Müller, eds., *Carl Hagenbeck*, and Rothfels, *Savages and Beasts.*

5. As a general rule the assistants were called *Lektoren* at the Seminar for Oriental Languages and *Sprachgehilfen* at the Colonial Institute. There is a subtle difference, as being a *Lektor* implied having the status of a lecturer, whereas having the title *Sprachgehilfe* connoted the more subordinate role of "helper."

6. These performers were, of course, likely also very different from how they were "presented" to the public. Z. S. Strother's essay "Display of the Body Hottentot," in *Africans on Stage: Studies in Ethnological Show Business,* ed. Bernth Lindfors (Bloomington: Indiana University Press, 1999), 1–40—along with the rest of the collection—provides a good example of how images of the Africans who visited Europe to participate in exhibitions were created, maintained, and manipulated.

7. There are some works and lectures that have mentioned some of the African and European actors I discuss; these include Katharina Oguntoye, *Eine Afro-Deutsche Geschichte: zur Lebenssituation von Afrikanern und Afro-Deutsche in Deutschland, 1884–1950* (Berlin: Hoho-Verl. Hoffmann, 1997); Paulette Reed-Anderson, *Eine Geschichte von mehr als 100 Jahren: die Anfänge der Afrikanischen Diaspora in Berlin* (Berlin: Ausländerbeauftragte des Senats, 1995); *Metropole, Menschen, Nahaufnahme: Afrikaner in Berlin* (Berlin: Die Ausländerbeauftragte des Senats, 1997); and *Rewriting the Footnotes: Berlin und die Afrikanische Diaspora* (Berlin: Ausländerbeauftragte des Senats, 2000). See also Elisa von Joeden-Forgey, "From 'Territorium Nullius' to 'Personum Nullius': German Colonial Law and the Invention of the 'Eingeborene,'" unpublished conference paper, African Studies Association 44th Annual Meeting, November 2001. None of these, however, address the academic involvement of *Lektoren* and *Sprachgehilfen* in Germany, or how they might have used scholarly participation to better their own positions in the metropole and the colony.

8. Gaurav Desai, *Subject to Colonialism: African Self-Fashioning and the Colonial Library* (Durham: Duke University Press, 2001), 29. There is a rich literature on African participation in European anthropology, linguistics, and other intellectual enterprises; see also Bruce Berman, "Ethnography as Politics, Politics as Ethnography: Kenyatta, Malinowski, and the Making of *Facing Mount Kenya,*" *Canadian Journal of African Studies* 30, no. 2 (1996): 313–44; Roger Sanjek, "Anthropology's Hidden Colonialism: Assistants and Their Ethnographers," *Anthropology Today* 9, no. 2 (April 1993): 16–32; Lyn Schumaker, *Africanizing Anthropology: Fieldwork, Networks, and the Making of Cultural Knowledge in Central Africa* (Durham: Duke University Press, 2001); and Frances Karttunen, *Between Worlds: Interpreters, Guides, and Survivors* (New Brunswick: Rutgers University Press, 1994).

9. GStaPKB Rep. 208A, Nr. 70, Ewe-Lektoren, 1904–1930, March 29, 1913, Sachau to the Minister of Education.

10. Paulette Reed-Anderson, *Metropole, Menschen, Nahaufnahme,* 19; Charles

Tutschek, *A Grammar of the Galla Language,* ed. Lawrence Tutschek, Munich, 1845, xii–xxv.

11. Tutschek, *A Grammar of the Galla Language,* contains letters from two of the assistants. See also Angelika Jacobi, *A Fur Grammar: Phonology, Morphophonology, and Morphology* (Tübingen: Helmut Buske Verlag, 1990), 8.

12. BFBSA Editorial Correspondence Inwards, No. 3, 1863–65, Krapf to S. B. Bergne, September 10, 1863.

13. BFBSA Editorial Correspondence Inwards No. 6, 1868–1869, Krapf to S. B. Bergne, July 3, 1868.

14. BFBSA Editorial Correspondence Inwards No. 8 (ca. 1870–72), n.d., Krapf to Knolleke.

15. Krapf's colleague Schön also hired an African, the Reverend J. C. Taylor, to work with him in Europe. However, by this time Schön was living in New Brompton, England, and probably never traveled to Germany. This underlines the point that even through the mid-nineteenth century German missionaries often worked comfortably with foreign empires and had no particular national loyalties. See BFBSA Editorial Correspondence Inwards 1858–1860, J. F. Schön, New Brompton, to T. W. Meller, December 9, 1859.

16. Reed-Anderson; Bradley D. Naranch, "Return of the Natives: Regulating the African Presence in Imperial Germany, 1884–1907," unpublished paper presented at the 44th Annual African Studies Association Conference, Houston, TX, November 15–18, 2001.

17. In writing out names that are obviously transcribed from Arabic, I am following the most common and frequent spellings for these that were provided in the German texts on the *Lektoren.* This accounts for their odd and incongruous appearance.

18. StAH 361-5, IV W 102, I, Heft 11, *Seminar für afrikanische Sprachen,* Carl Meinhof to Max Förster, 19, May 1911, "Einstellung eines Lektors für Ful und Haussa"; see also Hilke Meyer-Bahlburg and Ekkehard Wolff, *Afrikanische Sprachen in Forschung und Lehre: 75 Jahre Afrikanistik in Hamburg (1909–1984)* (Berlin: Dietrich Reimer, 1986), 87–90 passim.

19. GStaPKB Rep. 208A, 39, Akte betreffend Hassan Taufik (Tewfink), Lektor des Ägyptisch-Arabischen, Contract of Hassan Taufik, 26 July 1887.

20. Hans J. Massaquoi has described the Africans he saw at Hagenbeck's Zoo in Hamburg during the early 1930s as "barefoot and dressed in tattered rags." Massaquoi, whose father was from Liberia and mother from Germany, also commented, "Except for their skin color and hair, the Africans on display looked nothing like my relatives or any of the Africans I had met at my grandfather's house." See Hans J. Massaquoi, *Destined to Witness: Growing Up Black in Nazi Germany* (New York: HarperCollins, 2001), 25.

21. For a similar argument in a different context, see Ann Laura Stoler, "Sexual Affronts and Racial Frontiers: European Identities and the Cultural Politics of Exclusion in Colonial Southeast Asia," in *Tensions of Empire: Colonial Cultures in a Bourgeois World,* ed. Frederick Cooper and Ann Laura Stoler (Berkeley: University of California Press, 1997), 198–237.

22. GStaPKB Rep 76Va Sekt. 2 Tit. X, Nr. 124 Bd. VII, Acta betreffend das

Seminar für Orientalische Sprachen bei der Universität zu Berlin, vol. I, vom Juli 1907 bis Dezember 1910, correspondence from Eduard Sachau, Berlin, to Kaiserlich Russischen Botschafter in Berlin Graf von der Osten-Sacken, Berlin, April 18, 1908.

23. GStaPKB Rep 76Va Sekt. 2 Tit. 1, Nr. 28 Bd. I, Acta betreffend das Seminar für Orientalische Sprachen bei der Universität zu Berlin, vol. I, vom Februar 1885 bis Oktober 1887, Abschrift aus Blocks Dictionnaire de l'administration française, deuxième édition, Paris 1878, Art. Instruction supérieure S. 1152.

24. GStaPKB Rep 76Va Sekt. 2 Tit. 1, Nr. 28 Bd. II, Acta betreffend das Seminar für Orientalische Sprachen bei der Universität zu Berlin, vol. I, vom November 1887 bis Dezember 1892, Eduard Sachau to unknown, February 27, 1891; see also Spidle, "Colonial Studies in Imperial Germany."

25. GStaPKB, Rep. 208A, Acta betreffend Lector Sleman bin Said, Nr. 119, Bl 1-98, 1889–1892, Eduard Sachau to Herr Minister Dr. von Goßler, director of the Ministry for Scholastic, Educational, and Medical Affairs, n.d., ca. July 1889.

26. Ibid., Karl Reinhardt to Eduard Sachau, July 2, 1889.

27. Ibid., Contractual agreement of Suleiman bin Said, signed by Karl Reinhardt, to take work at the Seminar for Oriental Languages, June 4, 1889.

28. GSTaPKB, Rep. 208, Acta betreffend Au Fung Tschii, Lektor des Südchinesischen, Contract between Au Fung Tschii and the Seminar for Oriental Languages, October 14, 1890.

29. GSTaPKB, Rep. 208, Acta betreffend Hsüeh Tschen, Lektor des Nordchinesischen, vol. 1, contract between Hsüeh Tschen and the Seminar for Oriental Languages, July 12, 1890.

30. See John Middleton, *The World of the Swahili: An African Mercantile Civilization* (New Haven: Yale University Press, 1994), 9–11, for a description of the ethnic makeup of this group.

31. Anonymous, "Kunst, Wissenschaft, und Literatur," Beiblatt zu Nr. 14, *National-Zeitung,* April 8, 1891.

32. GStaPKB, Rep. 208A, Acta betreffend Lector Sleman bin Said, Nr. 119, Bl 1-98, 1889–1892, correspondence between Karl Reinhardt and Eduard Sachau, March 4, 1890.

33. GStaPKB Rep. 208A, 39, Geheimes Staatsarchiv, Akte betreffend Hassan Taufik (Tewfink), Lektor des Ägyptisch-Arabischen, Vita Des Herrn Taufik, Lektor des Aegyptisc=Arabischen am Seminar für Orientalischen Sprachen, and correspondence of Sachau to Althoff, August 24, 1892.

34. GStaPKB Rep. 208A, 42, Acta betreffend Mohammed Nassar, Lektor des Aegyptisch-Arabischen, Sachau to Minister Jacob Pascha, Cairo, March 29, 1893.

35. GStaPKB Rep. 208A, 40, Geheimes Staatsarchiv, Akte betreffend Maarbes, Lektor des Syrisch-Arabischen, Notice of the Death of Amin Ma'arbes by Ottilie Ma'arbes, geb. Kaatz, June 3, 1915.

36. GStaPKB, Rep. 208A, Acta betreffend Amir Bin Nasir, Lector des Suaheli, Bl. 1-53, 1891–1895, list of visitors to Amur bin Nasur's office hours, n.d., ca. June 1892.

37. GStaPKB, Rep. 208A, Nr. 121, Blatt 1-173, Lektoren des Suaheli, Bd. I, 1899–1909, Carl Velten to Eduard Sachau, June 16, 1904.

38. Ibid., Carl Velten, *Gutachten* (Evaluation) of Mtoro bin Mwenyi Bakari, May 5, 1905.

39. Ibid., Velten to Sachau, June 16, 1904.

40. GStaPKB Rep. 208A, Nr. 121, Blatt 1-173, Lektoren des Suaheli, Bd. I, 1899–1909, Contract for Swahili teaching assistants, ca. October 1905.

41. StaH 361-5, I VW Nr. 102, Band I, Heft 6, betr. Seminar für afrikanische Sprachen, Max Förster to School Inspector Professor Dr. Ahlburg, Hamburg, 16 November 1910, "Annahme einer Witbooi-Hottentotten als Sprachgehilfen."

42. StAH IV W 102, I, Heft 6, 15/2/11.

43. StAH IV W102, I, Heft 12, 17/1/12.

44. Ibid.

45. Kundrus, *Moderne Imperialisten.*

46. Lora Wildenthal, "Race, Gender, and Citizenship in the German Colonial Empire," in *Tensions of Empire: Colonial Cultures in a Bourgeois World,* ed. Frederick Cooper and Ann Laura Stoler (Berkeley: University of California Press, 1997), 263–83.

47. GStaPKB Rep. 208A, Nr. 121, Blatt 1-173, Lektoren des Suaheli, Bd. I, 1899–1909, Report by Meinhof concerning Bakari, May 26, 1905.

48. BMW 1/584, Das Missions-Seminar, den Unterricht, 1902–1923, Karl Axenfeld to the *Schatzmeister* of the *Gesellschaft zur Beförderung der evangelischen Missionen unter den Heiden zu Berlin,* September 27, 1907; Axenfeld to the *Schatzmeister,* December 12, 1908.

49. Stabi, Nachlaß Felix von Luschan, Meinhof to von Luschan, February 24, 1916. In this letter, Meinhof lavished praise on Toso, commending him for his dependability and letting Luschan know that he had provided abundant assistance to the academic community, both by proofreading missionary A. T. Mohr's *A Dictionary of English-Tshi (Asante)* (Basel: Evangelical Missionary Society) and by supplying German ethnologist Bernhard Ankermann with information on marriage customs in Togo.

50. Martin Heepe, *Jaunde-texte von Karl Atangana und Paul Messi, nebst experimentalphonetischen Untersuchungen über die Tonhöhen im Jaunde und einer Einführung in die Jaundesprache* (Hamburg: L. Friedrichsen, 1919), 3–4, 13–20. On pages 3–4, Heepe describes both apparati in detail.

51. Njo Dibone and Elli Meinhof, *Märchen aus Kamerun* (Strassburg: Heitz und Mündel, 1889).

52. Stabi, Nachlaß von Luschan, Briefen von Carl Meinhof, December 18, 1900.

53. Suleiman (Sleman) bin Said, "Sitte der Sansibarileute," in Carl Büttner, *Lieder und Geschichte der Suaheli, Beiträge zur Volks- und Völkerkunde,* 3rd volume (Berlin: Verlag von Emil Felber, 1894), 144–45, 152–53.

54. Amur bin Nasur, "Leben des Herrn Amur bin Nasur," in Büttner, *Lieder und Geschichte der Suaheli,* 180.

55. Ibid., 184–85.

56. Owing, one would suspect, to the strained relations between Zanzibaris and Comoros Island people during this era.

57. Nasur, 170.

58. GStaPKB, Rep. 208A Nr. 120, Acta betreffend Amir Bin Nasir, Lector des Suaheli, Bl. 1-53, 1891–1895, Amir to Sachau, June 26, 1895.

59. Sara Pugach, "Theories of Language and Race in German Studies of Africa," in *Jan Czekanowski: Africanist Ethnographer and Physical Anthropologist in Early Twentieth Century Germany and Poland,* ed. Adam Jones (University of Leipzig Papers on Africa, History and Culture Series No. 10, Leipzig: Institut für Afrikanistik, 2002), 70–102.

60. Trüper, "Amur bin Nasur ilOmeiri—Lektor der Suahelisprache am Seminar für Orientalische Sprachen."

61. Heepe, 89–90.

62. F. Quinn, "Charles Atangana of Yaoundé," *Journal of African History* 21 (1980): 485–95.

63. Heepe, *Jaunde-Texte,* 88, 107.

64. Ibid., 87–88, 116–18.

65. Ibid., 127.

66. One example of this sort of ethnography can be found in Jakob Spieth, "Die religiöse Veranlagung des Afrikaners," in *Der Afrikaner, seine wirtschaftliche Leistungsfähigkeit, geistige Befähigung, religiöse Veranlagung,* ed. J. K. Vietor, Carl Meinhof, and Jakob Spieth (Bremen: Verlag der Norddeutschen Missionsgesellschaft, 1912), 17–28.

67. See also Sanjek, "Anthropology's Hidden Colonialism," 15, on a similar pattern in the British case.

68. Heepe, *Jaunde-Texte,* 214; in this instance Messi admiringly says that the Germans "fight so, as if death was nothing special."

69. Ibid., 211.

70. Ibid., 212.

71. Ibid., 117.

CHAPTER 7

1. StaH, Staatsverwaltung der Hansestadt Hamburg, Hochschulwesen, Dozenten u.-Personalakten IV, 1177, Personalakte, Klingenheben, Prof. Dr. August, Lebenslauf, Hamburg, April 12, 1911; letter from Meinhof to von Melle describing Klingenheben's military activities, March 16, 1915; letter from Klingenheben to Meinhof, March 31, 1919, informing the latter of his plans to return to work in Hamburg.

2. StaH Dempwolff, Personalakte, Verleihung des Professortitels, Staatsarchiv Hamburg, Hochschulwesen-Personalakten, I 153 Bd. 1, Letter from Meinhof to von Melle, June 6, 1916.

3. StaH 364-7 Professorenrat des Kolonialinstituts, E XVIII 1 b 11, Akte Betreffend: Studienreise des Herrn Heepe nach Deutsch=Ostafrika (Teilungen an der Eröffnungsfeier der Tanganyikabahn in Daressalam, 1914 [1918]), letter of Meinhof to von Melle, January 16, 1914; and anonymous note, August 7, 1918.

4. Hilke Meyer-Bahlburg, "Erinnerung an die erste deutsche Afrikanistin: Maria von Tiling wäre am 13 Februar 100 Jahre alt geworden," *Berichte Meinungen aus der Universität Hamburg* 16, no. 2 (April 1986): 53–54.

5. Wilhelm Czermak, Review of Maria von Tiling, *Somali-Texte und Untersuchungen zur Somali-Lautlehre* (Berlin: Reimer; Hamburg: Boysen, 1925), *Wiener Zeitschrift für die Kunde des Morgenlandes* 33 (1926): 150–56, cited in Meyer-Bahlburg, "Erinnerung ..."

6. StaH Personalakten des Maria Klingenheben, geb. von Tiling, Oberschulbehörde, Sektion für Wissenschaftlichen Anstalten, Hochschulwesen Dozenten und Personalakten, IV 1732, K. 202, letter of Carl Meinhof to the Oberschulbehörde, n.d., ca. December 1918.

7. Alice Werner, Review of Maria von Tiling's *Somali-Texte, Bulletin of the School of Oriental Studies* 4, no. 1 (1926): 189–91.

8. AIAÄ Ethnogr.-anth. Briefwechsel BV 2 (b) vom 3 Oktober 1920 bis 1. September 1932, letter of Meinhof to Professor A König, Schwabach bei Nürnberg, January 7, 1921. Moreover, recordings of POWs from various parts of the world are held at the Berlin-Phonogramm-Archiv. See for instance Thomas Ulbrich, "Historische koreanische Aufnahmen im Lautarchiv der Humboldt-Universität und im Berliner Phonogramm-Archiv," *Baessler-Archiv* 49 (2001): 139–64.

9. GStaPKB Rep. 208 A, Nr. 77, Haussa-Lektoren 1908–1922, letter from Sachau to Kommandentur des Halbmondlagers zu Wunsdorf, December 13, 1916.

10. Andrew Evans, "Anthropology at War: Racial Studies of POWs during World War I," in *Worldly Provincialism: German Anthropology in the Age of Empire,* ed. Matti Bunzl and H. Glenn Penny (Ann Arbor: University of Michigan Press, 2003), 198–229.

11. Poliakov, *The Aryan Myth,* 71–105; Römer, *Sprachwissenschaft und Rassenideologie in Deutschland;* Mosse, *The Crisis of German Ideology.*

12. W. D. Hammond-Tooke, *Imperfect Interpreters: South Africa's Anthropologists, 1920–1990* (Johannesburg: Witwatersrand University Press, 1997), 59–60; and see also Saul Dubow, *Scientific Racism in Modern South Africa* (Cambridge: Cambridge University Press, 1995), 80–81; Cynthia Kros, "Economic, Political, and Intellectual Origins of Bantu Education 1926–1951" (PhD diss., University of the Witwatersrand, Johannesburg, 1996), 121–26; Caroline Jeannerat, "The Classification of Tradition in van Warmelo's Writing," unpublished seminar paper (University of the Witwatersrand, Johannesburg, 1998), 4–8, for other opinions.

13. It was originally to be called the International Bureau of African Languages and Tribal Cultures.

14. See Richard V. Pierard, "Shaking the Foundations: World War I, the Western Allies, and German Protestant Missions," *International Bulletin of Missionary Research* (January 1998): 13–19; H. Debrunner, *A Church between Colonial Powers: A Study of the Church in Togo* (London: Lutterworth Press, 1965), 143–63 passim. Pierard's article provides a thorough historical description of their expulsion from the colonies. The article also shows that German missionaries were not unilaterally forced out of all of Germany's former colonies; in Southwest Africa, which became a South African territory, most were allowed to stay, as authorities feared another uprising by the Herero. On this point see also Lothar Engel, *Kolonialismus und Na-*

tionalismus im deutschen Protestantismus in Namibia 1907 bis 1945 (Herbert Lang: Bern, 1976), 159ff.

15. Roehl's "entarabisiert" Swahili translation of the Bible caused no end of controversy in the 1920s, in which he proposed eradicating Swahili words derived from Arabic. See various correspondence in AIAÄ BVIII 4 b, Evangelische Mission, and also Karl Roehl, "The Linguistic Situation in East Africa," *Africa* 3 (January 1930): 190–202, and G. W. Broomfield, "The Re-Bantuization of the Swahili Language," *Africa* 4 (1931): 77–85.

16. AIAÄ BVIII 4 b, Evangelische Mission, letter of Karl Roehl to Carl Meinhof, 13 September, 1926. The text of article 438 of the Versailles Treaty, to which Roehl refers, reads as follows: "The Allied and Associated Powers agree that where Christian religious missions were being maintained by German societies or persons in territory belonging to them, or of which the government is entrusted to them in accordance with the present Treaty, the property which these missions or missionary societies possessed, including that of trading societies whose profits were devoted to the support of missions, shall continue to be devoted to missionary purposes. In order to ensure the due execution of this undertaking the Allied and Associated Governments will hand over such property to boards of trustees appointed by or approved by the Governments and composed of persons holding the faith of the Mission whose property is involved. The Allied and Associated Governments, while continuing to maintain full control as to the individuals by whom the Missions are conducted, will safeguard the interests of such Missions. Germany, taking note of the above undertaking, agrees to accept all arrangements made or to be made by the Allied or Associated Government concerned for carrying on the work of the said missions or trading societies and waives all claims on their behalf."

17. Julius Richter, *Vor schweren Entscheidungen* (n.p.: Berlin, 1920). Found in AIAÄ BVII 4, Evangel. Mission (reponiert).

18. Ibid. Richter thought that if the Germans did not participate, they would be shutting themselves out of the opportunity to help make decisions about the future of the mission on an international level.

19. Ibid.

20. Carl Meinhof, "Skizzen von der allgemeinen studentischen Missionskonferenz in Liverpool," *Die Evangelische-Mission Illustriertes Familienblatt* 14 (March 1908): 78–81. This unusual article describes Meinhof's first visit to England in 1908, which produced a mixture of sentiments ranging from shock at the country's "primitivity," which reminded him of "ancestral days [*Urvater Tagen*]" in Germany, to admiration for the "modern," "warm-hearted" people who lived there.

21. Meinhof, "The Training of Missionaries in Regard to Language," World Missionary Conference, Edinburgh 1910: 263–69.

22. AIAÄ BVII 4, Evangel Mission (reponiert). Carl Meinhof to Dr. Abernethy, July 20, 1922.

23. Marcia Wright, *German Missions in Tanganyika, 1891–1941*, 73.

24. AIAÄ BVIII 1, Intern. Inst. Gründung. Points for Discussion from the original planning meeting for the "International Bureau for the Study of African Languages and Cultures (what would eventually be named the International Institute of

African Languages and Cultures), September 21–22, 1925. The points for discussion stated, "To fulfil its purpose, the Bureau should be as international as possible, having members in all countries who might possibly form local branches, and obtaining the active co-operation of all the various agencies connected with Africa."

25. Ibid. Among others, all the goals of the Institute appear to have devolved from this one point.

26. Renowned anthropologist Maurice Delafosse was originally chosen as the codirector representing France but fell ill and died before he could assume the position.

27. AIAÄ BVIII 1, Intern. Inst. Gründung. Carl Meinhof to the Hochschulbehörde, Hamburg, July 6, 1926.

28. Vischer was also Secretary of the Colonial Office Advisory Committee on Native Education in British Tropical Africa from 1924 to 1928, and later, between 1929 and 1939, Joint Secretary of the Colonial Office Advisory Committee on Education in the Colonies. See Sonia F. G. Parkinson, "Sir Hanns Vischer, Champion of African Cultures: A Portrait of an Adviser on Colonial Education," in *Colonial Educators: The British Indian and Colonial Education Service, 1858–1953*, ed. Clive Whitehead (London: I. B. Tauris, 2003), 106–48.

29. AIAÄ BVIII 1, Intern. Inst. Gründung. Hanns Vischer to Carl Meinhof, August 12, 1925, August 21, 1925.

30. AIAÄ BVIII I, Intern. Inst. Gründung. Carl Meinhof to the Hochschulbehörde, Hamburg, July 6, 1926.

31. Charles W. Weber, *International Influences and Baptist Mission in West Cameroon: German-American Missionary Endeavors under International Mandate and German Colonialism* (Leiden: E. J. Brill, 1993), 24–25.

32. See *Africa,* vols. 2, 3, and 4, 1929–1931. One of these articles, "The Basis of Bantu Philology," 2 (1929): 57–70, was by Meinhof, who had also contributed "The Soul of an African Language" in 1928.

33. AIAÄ BVIII 1, Intern. Inst. Gründung, Deutsche Botschaft, London, to the Auswärtige Amt, Berlin; letter copied to Carl Meinhof, Hamburg.

34. Although, as both Mahmood Mamdani and Alice Conklin have explained, the French policy of direct rule did shift after World War I, and the French, too, came to support indirect rule. See Mahmood Mamdani, *Citizen and Subject: Contemporary Africa and the Legacy of Late Colonialism* (Princeton: Princeton University Press, 1996), 82–83; Alice Conklin, *A Mission to Civilize: The Republican Idea of Empire in France and West Africa, 1895–1930* (Stanford: Stanford University Press, 2000), 212ff.

35. AIAÄ BVIII 1, Intern. Inst. Gründung, memorandum by Diedrich Westermann, n.d., probably late fall 1925.

36. Ibid.

37. Ibid., Carl Meinhof, untitled commentary on the foundation of the "International Bureau of African Languages and Tribal Cultures," 28 October 1924. The specific, untranslated text referring to the Institute here reads "Diese ganze Arbeit kann nur dann erfolgreich getan werden, wenn Theorie und Praxis sich die Hand reichen.—Wir brauchen hier nicht eine Wissenschaft der weltenfern ihren unfruchtbaren Spekulationen nachhängt, sondern eine solche, die in stetem lebhaften

Verkehr mit den Sprachen und der Literatur Afrikas steht und die Nöte und Erfolge der Praxis mit aufmerksamen Augen verfolgt. Wir brauchen eine Praxis, die bereit ist, fortgesetzt zu lernen, und die nicht eigensinnig bei alten Methoden beharrt, nur weil sie alt sind. Theorie und Praxis müssen dauernd Hand in Hand gehen. Nur so werden wir gute Ergebnisse erzielen."

38. Holger Stoecker, "The Advancement of African Studies in Berlin by the 'Deutsche Forschungsgemeinschaft,'" 75.

39. Andrew Crozier, *Appeasement and Germany's Last Bid for Colonies* (New York: St. Martin's, 1988), 16; see also Wolfe W. Schmokel, *Dream of Empire: German Colonialism, 1919–1945* (New Haven: Yale University Press, 1964), 51.

40. AIAÄ BVII 4, Evangel. Mission (reponiert). Carl Meinhof, Hamburg, to Frank M. Sanders, New York, April 16, 1923. The letter was written in response to a request from Sanders for information about the Colonial Institute and the methods Meinhof employed in teaching African and other "native" languages there.

41. AIAÄ Tauschverkehr des Zeitschrift für Eingeborenensprachen, 1920–1930; Holger Stoecker, "The Advancement of African Studies in Berlin by the 'Deutsche Forschungsgemeinschaft,' 1920–1945," 67–94.

42. AIAÄ BVIII 1, Intern. Inst. Gründung. Carl Meinhof to Eduard Woermann, October 30, 1924.

43. DEMH Nr. 289, Wissenschaftliche Zusammenarbeit Freytag-Meinhof, 1931–1944, Carl Meinhof to Pastor Johannes Reinhard, May 15, 1933.

44. Ibid.

45. Ernst Dammann, *70 Jahre erlebte* Afrikanistik*: Ein Beitrag zur Geschichte der Wissenschaft,* 80–81.

46. Stoecker, 78.

47. Crozier, 1.

48. L. S. Amery, *The German Colonial Claim* (New York: Longmans, Green, 1940), 5.

49. Into which the other had melded.

50. Rainer Hering, "Meinhof, Carl Friedrich Michael," in the *Biographisch-Bibliographisches Kirchenlexikon,* Band XVII (Herzberg, Germany: Verlag Traugott Bautz, 2000), 920–23.

51. Carl Meinhof, "The Soul of an African People," among others.

52. Carl Meinhof, *Deutsche Erziehung,* Deutsche Vorträge Hamburgischer Professoren, Nr. 9, 27 November 1914 (Hamburg: L. Friedrichsen, 1914); *Sittlichkeit und Krieg,* Vortrag gehalten vor Arbeitern im Hamburger Volksheim am 3. Dezbr. 1914 (Hamburg: C. Boysen, 1914); and *Deutschland und der Preußische Geist,* Vortrag gehalten im Hamburger Volksheim am 11. November 1915 (Hamburg: C. Boysen, 1915).

53. Meinhof, *Deutschland und der Preußische Geist,* 4.

54. Meinhof, *Sittlichkeit und Krieg,* 5.

55. Carl Meinhof, "Europäer und Afrikaner." Sonderdurck der *Afrika-Rundschau,* 7 (November 1937): 5–18. He did however say that, in certain situations, it would be necessary to "keep Africans out of areas designated for Europeans."

56. Carl Meinhof, "Aus dem Seelenleben des Eingeborenen," *Jahrbuch über die deutschen Kolonien* 7 (1914): 34–37.

57. Meinhof, "Europäer und Afrikaner."

58. Meinhof, *Die Christianisierung der Sprachen Afrikas,* 14. "Hier wird der Mensch, die Person, scharf von allen anderen Dingen geschieden ... Das alles ist dem Europäer sehr lästig, aber gewiß logischer, als das grammatische Geschlecht [Here the human being, the person, is sharply divided from all other things... this is all very much a bother to the European, but certainly more logical than grammatical gender]."

59. Carl Meinhof, *Die Sprachen der Hamiten,* among others. Meinhof thought that race and language were once united, but that through eons of human history the link had degraded as members of different "races" intermarried and had "mixed" offspring.

60. See Meinhof, *Die Christianisierung der Sprachen Afrikas,* 7.

61. Carl Meinhof, *Sittlichkeit und Krieg,* 15.

62. Meinhof, "Über M. Merkers Masai."

63. AIAÄ Religionswissenschaftliche Gesellschaft, 1916–1922, Protokoll der Sitzung der religionswissenschaftliche Gesellschaft am. 3. Juni 1919. Specifically, point 3 of the *Protokoll* says "Von dem Oberrabbiner Spitzer ist festzustellen, ob er oder ein anderer Rabbiner besonderes Interesse für die Ziele der Gesellschaft hat." And in the *Protokoll* of June 10, 1920, a Rabbi Sonderling is listed as having attended that month's meeting.

64. Ernst Cassirer, "Die Bedeutung des Sprachproblems für die Entstehung der neueren Philosophie" and Franz Boas "Die Ausdrücke für einige religiöse Begriffe der Kwakiutl-Indianer," in *Festschrift Meinhof: Sprachwissenschaftliche und andere Studien* (Hamburg: J. J. Augustin, 1927), 502–14, 386–92. Boas also sat on the committee that prepared the congratulatory manuscript, which included Dempwolff, Panconcelli-Calzia, Alice Werner, and Westermann.

65. Hering, "Meinhof, Carl Friedrich Michael," 923.

66. StAH 361-1 IV, 1177, Personalakte, Klingenheben, Prof. Dr. August. Aktenzeichen: P K. 23. Letter from Prof. Dr. Strothmann, Hansische Universität, Orientalische Seminar, to the British military authorities, 1 December 1945. In this letter, Strothmann claimed that Klingenheben was "induced" to join the NSDAP while in Leipzig and then made to function as a *Blockwart* in Hamburg. Klingenheben's ideological position is, again, uncertain, but the fact that he joined so late may indeed indicate that he did so more for career reasons than out of personal conviction.

67. Even Westermann, a longtime friend of British anthropology, left his post at the Institute for African Languages and Cultures after 1936.

68. Robert Gordon, "Early Social Anthropology in South Africa," *African Studies* 49, no. 1: 18–19.

69. G. Stocking, *After Tylor,* 106, 184ff.

70. Seligman, *Races of Africa,* 86.

71. Stoecker, "The Advancement of African Studies in Berlin by the 'German Research Foundation,' 1920–1945."

72. Diedrich Westermann, *The African Today and Tomorrow,* new rev. ed., published for the International Institute of African Languages and Cultures by the Oxford University Press (London: Humphrey Milford, 1939), 11.

73. Ibid., 20, 24. The classificatory system that Westermann used was more complex and layered than the earlier, Hamitic/Bantu/Sudanic method of categorization. Even so, the tendency to consider Hamites superior to other African populations remained, with Westermann referring to their having "racial superiority."

74. R. Gordon and A. D. Spiegel, "Southern African Revisited," *Annual Review of Anthropology* 22 (1993): 83–105.

75. T. D. Moodie, *The Rise of Afrikanerdom: Power, Apartheid, and the Afrikaner Civil Religion* (Berkeley: University of California Press, 1975), 22–25ff.

76. R. Gordon, "Serving the *Volk* with *Volkekunde,*" in *Knowledge and Power in South Africa,* ed. J. Jansen (Johannesburg: Skotaville, 1991), 8.

77. J. S. Sharp, "The Roots and Development of Volkekunde in South Africa," *Journal of Southern African Studies* 8, no. 1 (1981): 16–36.

78. Poliakov, *The Aryan Myth;* Mosse, *The Crisis of German Ideology;* but see also Aletta J. Norval, *Deconstructing Apartheid Discourse* (London: Verso, 1996), 77–79, for a contrary opinion on the influence of German thought on Afrikaner intellectuals.

79. BAB R 1001/6173, Thielmann, Reichsschatzamt, to das Auswärtige Amt, Kolonial-Abteilung, October 19, 1901.

80. Wilhelm J. G. Möhlig, "Lestrade, Gérard Paul," in *Lexikon der* Afrikanistik*: Afrikanische Sprachen und ihre Erforschung,* ed. Hermann Jungraithmayr and Wilhelm J. G. Möhlig (Berlin: Dietrich Reimer, 1983), 145. See also W. D. Hammond-Tooke, "N. J. van Warmelo and the Ethnological Section: A Memoir," *African Studies* 54, no. 1 (1995): 119, and the same in *Imperfect Interpreters: South Africa's Anthropologists, 1920–1990,* 109.

81. University of Cape Town Archives (hereafter referred to as UCTA) BC 255 A15.1–A15.9, the Lestrade Papers, G. P. Lestrade, "An Introduction to Bantu Philology" (likely lecture notes), n.d.

82. UCTA BC 255 B 2 K 3, the Lestrade Papers, G. P. Lestrade, "A Great Africanist," n.d., ca. 1927–28.

83. Ibid.

84. StAH 361-1 I 290 Bd. 4, Beurlaubungen, Erkrangungen, 1910–1936 (Meinhof), Carl Meinhof to the Hochschulbehörde, Hamburg, March 13, 1928.

85. StAH 361-1, I 290 Bd. 4, Beurlaubungen, Erkrangungen, 1910–1936 (Meinhof), Renner to the auswärtige Amt, Berlin, copied to the Senat, Hamburg, May 6, 1928.

86. "Souls that Return as Snakes: Fascinating Realm of Bantu Folklore, Lecture by Prof. Meinhof," *Cape Times,* Monday, January 23, 1928: 14.

87. Ibid., and see also "Study of Native Languages: Use of Scientific Methods, Lecture by Professor Meinhof," *Cape Times,* Thursday, January 19, 1928: 10.

88. "Study of African Languages: Meinhof on His Life Work," in the *Cape Times,* Thursday, January 26, 1928: 9. On the Native Bills, see Frank Welsh, *South Africa: A Narrative History* (New York: Kodansha International, 1999), 403, 407.

89. P. Kallaway, "F. S. Malan, the Cape Liberal Tradition, and South African Politics, 1908–1924," *Journal of African History* 15, no. 1 (1974): 113–29.

90. In a similar vein, Cynthia Kros has argued that Meinhof and Westermann's theories were actually most appealing to liberal intellectuals such as J. D. Rheinallt

Jones. See Cynthia Kros, "W. W. M. Eiselen: Architect of Apartheid Education," in *The History of Education under Apartheid, 1948–1994,* ed. Peter Kallaway (New York: Peter Lang, 2002), 53–73.

91. Kallaway, "F. S. Malan."

92. StAH 361-1, I 290 Bd. 4, Beurlaubungen, Erkrangungen, 1910–1936 (Meinhof), Carl Meinhof to the Hochschulbehörde, Hamburg, March 13, 1928.

93. For instance, van Warmelo's dissertation under Meinhof was called *Die Gliederung der südafrikanischen Bantusprachen* (Hamburg: J. J. Augustin, 1927), and Eiselen's was entitled *Die Veränderung Konsonanten durch ein vorgehendes "i" in den Bantusprachen* (Berlin: Reimer, 1924).

94. AIAÄ BII 1, Übersetzung "Grundriss" und Warmelo allgemein, Nicholas van Warmelo to Carl Meinhof, April 16, 1929, June 4, 1929, Carl Meinhof to Nicholas van Warmelo, July 2, 1929, among others. On Eiselen, AIAÄ untitled file, Preliminary report concerning the appointment of a Professor for African Languages, July 20, 1935. Meinhof practically begged Warmelo to come back to Hamburg after Klingenheben left for Leipzig in 1930, an offer Warmelo declined. Then in 1935 Meinhof briefly mentioned Eiselen in a report discussing who might assume the directorship of the Seminar for African Studies upon his retirement, but Eiselen was also quickly dismissed as more of an ethnologist than a linguist.

95. London School of Economics Archive, Papers of the International African Institute, file 1/19. Confidential report of Carl Meinhof on Dr. Werner Eiselen, April 14, 1934.

96. AIAÄ BII 1, Übersetzung "Grundriss" und Warmelo allgemein, Carl Meinhof to Mr. Brookes, editor at Oxford University Press, December 31, 1928. Meinhof told Brookes that he thought of van Warmelo and not himself as the "Verfasser" (author) of the translation.

97. W. D. Hammond-Tooke, *Imperfect Interpreters,* 66; Cynthia Kros, *Eiselen: Idealists and Idealism Revisited,* unpublished seminar paper presented to SACHES, Scottburgh, October 1993, quoted in Hammond-Tooke.

98. UCTA BC 255 A151, the Lestrade Papers, "The Place of the Bantu Languages among the language-families of Africa, and their regional-genealogical classification."

99. Möhlig, "Lestrade, G. P.," 145, *Lexikon der Afrikanistik.*

100. Hammond-Tooke, *Imperfect Interpreters,* 68.

101. T. Dunbar Moodie, *The Rise of Afrikanerdom: Power, Apartheid, and the Afrikaner Civil Religion,* 273–74, 293–94, and Gordon, "Serving the *Volk* with *Volkekunde,*" in Hammond-Tooke, *Imperfect Interpreters,* 65–66; Cynthia Kros, "W. W. M. Eiselen: Architect of Apartheid Education."

102. Kros, "W. W. M. Eiselen: Architect of Apartheid Education," 55–56.

103. Kros, *Economic, Political, and Intellectual Origins of Bantu Education, 1926–1951.*

104. Kros, "W. W. M. Eiselen: Architect of Apartheid Education," 57.

105. Carl Meinhof, "Die afrikanischen Völker und die Mission," *Mission und Pfarramt* 3 (1910): 91.

106. Excerpt from W. W. M. Eiselen, *Report of the Commission on Native Education, 1945–1951,* in Edgar H. Brookes, ed. *Apartheid: A Documentary Study of Modern South Africa* (London: Routledge and Kegan Paul, 1968), 44.

107. Ibid., 45.

108. Westermann, *The African Today and Tomorrow,* 222ff.

109. Van Warmelo wrote twenty out of forty-four volumes.

110. Sekibakiba Peter Lekgoathi, "Chiefs, Migrants, and North Ndebele Ethnicity in the Context of Surrounding Homeland Politics, 1965–1978," *African Studies* 62, no. 1 (July 2003): 53–77. Of course, as Lekgoathi explains, ethnological recommendations only went so far—economic and other political considerations also helped mold homeland boundaries.

111. C. Meinhof, *Introduction to the Phonology of the Bantu Languages,* trans. N. J. van Warmelo (Berlin: Dietrich Reimer/Ernst Vohsen, 1932), 82.

112. N. J. van Warmelo, *A Preliminary Survey of the Bantu Tribes of South Africa,* Union of South Africa, Department of Native Affairs, Ethnological Publications, vol. 5 (Pretoria: Government Printer, 1935), 5.

113. P. Cocks, "Max Gluckman and the Critique of Segregation in South African Anthropology, 1921–1940," *Journal of Southern African Studies* 27, no. 4 (December 2001): 739–56.

114. H. Giliomee, "The Growth of Afrikaner Identity," in *Segregation and Apartheid in Twentieth-Century South Africa,* ed. W. Beinart and S. Dubow (London: Routledge, 1995), 189–205.

115. J. Peires, "Ethnicity and Pseudo-Ethnicity in the Ciskei," in *Segregation and Apartheid in Twentieth-Century South Africa,* ed. W. Beinart and S. Dubow (London: Routledge, 1995), 256–84.

116. N. Worden, *The Making of Modern South Africa,* 3rd ed. (Oxford: Blackwell, 2000), 85.

117. Van Warmelo, *A Preliminary Survey,* 7.

118. Luschan, "Beigabe, Hamitische Typen" to Carl Meinhof, *Die Sprachen der Hamiten.*

119. Van Warmelo, *A Preliminary Survey of the Bantu Tribes of South Africa,* 7.

120. Ibid., 59.

121. Ibid., 70.

122. Ibid., 122.

123. Meinhof, "Die Bedeutung der experimentellen Phonetik für die Erforschung der afrikanischen Sprachen," *Vox* (1913).

124. As in Cleve, "Die Lippenlaute der Bantu und die Negerlippen, mit besonderer Berücksichtigung der Lippenverstümmelungen."

125. Hermann Giliomee, "The Making of the Apartheid Plan, 1928–1948," *Journal of Southern African Studies* 29, no. 2 (June 2003): 373–92.

CONCLUSION

1. Ioannis D. Evrigenis and Daniel Pellerin, "Introduction," to J. G. Herder, *Another Philosophy of History and Selected Political Writings* (Indianapolis: Hackett, 2004), xix.

2. Although Germany was interested in collaborating with the Boer Republics against the British in the era leading up to the Anglo-Boer War of 1899–1902 and in establishing a stronger foothold in the region. The British were es-

pecially worried about Germany's attraction to Amatongaland. See Seligmann, *Rivalry in Southern Africa,* 17.

3. Brian M. Du Toit, "Missionaries, Anthropologists, and the Policies of the Dutch Reformed Church," *Journal of Modern African Studies* 22, no. 4 (December 1984): 617–32.

4. See among others Dorothea Bleek, *The Naron: A Bushman Tribe of the Central Kalahari* (Cambridge: Cambridge University Press, 1928). The younger Bleek maintained ties to German scholars, for example, contributing to Meinhof's *Festschrift* with "The Distribution of the Bantu Languages in South Africa," in Meinhof's *Festschrift,* 55–64.

5. Du Toit, 625. Moreover, as Du Toit points out, Eiselen was far from the only German missionary child or grandchild to grow up and become an influential South African academic.

6. BMW 1/3155, 1927–1945, Berliner Missionsgesellschaft, Giesekke, Ludwig [Missionar], Band III, Trauanzeige Gerda Giesekke und N. J. van Warmelo, January 2, 1934.

7. Paul B. Rich, *Hope and Despair: English-Speaking Intellectuals and South African Politics, 1896–1976* (London: British Academic Press, 1993), 41, 49.

8. Gustav Menzel, *Aus 150 Jahre Missionsgeschichte—Die Rheinische Mission,* 293.

9. Dieter Becker and Andreas Feldtkeller, *Es begann in Halle,* 47.

10. Altena, 51.

11. Von Luschan, "Hamitische Typen."

12. Marcia Wright, *Strategies of Slaves and Women: Life-Stories from East/Central Africa* (New York: Lilian Barber, 1993), 180ff., discusses how Kootz-Kretschmer chronicled the biographies of African women through World War I. See also S. Augustin, "Elise Kootz-Kretschmer: Missionarsfrau und Ethnographin der Safwa in Ostafrika," *Unitas Fratrum* 45–46 (1999): 153–63.

13. Ronald Hyam and Peter Henshaw, *The Lion and the Springbok,* 27.

14. Du Toit, 622.

15. Moodie, *The Rise of Afrikanerdom,* 130; Furlong, *Between Crown and Swastika,* 140.

16. Norval, *Deconstructing Apartheid Discourse,* 77–78, also demonstrates that the specific South African context shaped the reception of German romanticism in the country. Fervent Afrikaner nationalists like Piet Meyer and Nico Diedrichs, who were not involved in the linguistic and anthropological discourses discussed in this book, sought to transpose German theories of culture onto an exclusively Afrikaner understanding of *volk,* the Afrikaans word, not *Volk,* its German counterpart.

17. Stumpf, *La politique linguistique au Cameroun de 1884 à 1960,* 17.

18. Meinhof received many letters from American missionaries. For instance, Stanley White of the Board of Foreign Missions of the Presbyterian Church of the United States wrote Meinhof in 1915 to ask for information on his method of incorporating phonetics into African language research. See AIAÄ BVII 4, Evangel. Mission (reponiert), Stanley White to Carl Meinhof, November 29, 1915.

19. Hamburg's longtime historian of Africa, Leonhard Harding, was in the his-

tory department, not the *Institut für Afrikanistik und Äthiopistik;* the same was true of his successor, Andreas Eckert. In Berlin, historians do indeed belong to the *Institut für Asien- und Afrikawissenschaften,* but the department is still dominated by those whose main fields are linguistics and literature, with eight linguists and four literary specialists, but only four historians.

20. Der Geschäftsführende Direktor des Institut für Afrikanistik und Äthiopistik, "Institut für Afrikanistik und Äthiopistik," http://www.uni-hamburg.de/Wiss/FB/10/AfrikaS/index.html#start (accessed July 10, 2000).

21. Personal communication with Ludwig Gerhardt, November 1998.

22. For instance, van Warmelo collaborated on an article with E. M. Shaw in 1988, one year before he died. See E. M. Shaw and N. J. van Warmelo, "The Material Culture of the Cape Nguni: Part 4 Personal and General," *Annals of the South African Museum* 58, no. 4 (1988): 2–8.

23. Ivan Evans, *Bureaucracy and Race: Native Administration in South Africa* (Berkeley: University of California Press, 1997), 273.

24. David Rycroft, "Professor Ernst Oswald Johannes Westphal, 1919–1990," *African Languages and Cultures* 5, no. 1 (1992): 91–95.

25. Dirk Ziervogel, *The Eastern Sotho: A Tribal, Historical, and Linguistic Survey (with Ethnographic Notes) of the Pai, Kutswe, and Pulana Bantu Tribes of the Pilgrim's Rest District of the Transvaal Province, Union of South Africa* (Pretoria: Van Schaik, 1954).

26. Robert Gordon, "Apartheid's Anthropologists," *American Ethnologist* 15, no. 3 (August 1988): 535–53.

27. Du Toit, 625.

Bibliography

ARCHIVAL SOURCES CONSULTED

AEM Archiv der evangelischen Missionswerk, Basel QK-4, 1

AIAÄ Archive of the Institut für Afrikanistik und Äthiopistik
"Arbeiten von Meinhof"
Ethnogr.-anth. Briefwechsel BV 2 (b) vom 3 Oktober 1920 bis 1. September 1932
Ethnogr.-anth. Briefwechsel BV 2 (c) vom 1 Sept. 1932
BVII 4, Evangel. Mission (reponiert)
B VIII 4 (b) Evangelische Mission
BVIII 1 Intern. Inst.Gründung
BVIII 14, Intern. Inst. Gutachten über Orthogr.
BII 1, Übersetzung "Grundriss" und Warmelo allgemein
Religionswissenschaftliche Gesellschaft, 1916–1922
Tauschverkehr des Zeitschrift für Eingeborenensprachen, 1920–1930
Zeitschrift für Kolonialsprachen, 1908–1911, B IV
Zeitschrift für Kolonialsprachen, 1911–1913, B IV
Zeitschrift für Kolonialsprachen, 1917–1919 BIV (c)

BAB Bundesarchiv Berlin
R 313 Akten betreffend die Schreibweise der geographnamen in D. Ostafrika, vom Juni 1892 bis Januar 1932. Bd. 1
R 1001 4550, Die Zeitschrift für afrikanische Sprachen, Volume 1, April 1886–28 Februar 1895
R 1001 6165–6176, Erforschung der Sprachen der Eingeborenen Völkerschaften
R 1001/6177, Bd. 1, Erforschung der Sprachen der eingeborenen Völkerschaften Südwestafrikas, Juni 1904–März 1936
R 1001 6196, Seminar für Orientalische Sprachen

BFBSA British and Foreign Bible Society Archives
Correspondence Book (CB) Volume 7, 20 September 1814 to 17 January 1816
ECB 27, 1890–1891
Editorial Correspondence Inwards, No. 1, 1858–60
Editorial Correspondence Inwards, No. 2, 1860–62

Editorial Correspondence Inwards, No. 3, 1863–65
Editorial Correspondence Inwards, No. 5, 1867–68
Editorial Correspondence Inwards, No. 6, 1868–69
Editorial Correspondence Inwards, No. 7, 1869–70
Editorial Correspondence Inwards, No. 8, 1870–72
Journal of the Reverend J. L. Krapf

BMW Berlin evangelisches Missionswerk Archive
1/582, 1856–1908
1/584, Das Missions-Seminar, den Unterricht, 1902–1923 1/3155, 1927–1945, Berliner Missionsgesellschaft, Giesekke, Ludwig [Missionar], Band III
Acta der Gesellschaft zur Beförderung der evangelischen Missionen untern den Heiden zu Berlin betreffend die Missions-Station Lupembe, Abthl. III, Fach 9, Nr. 1, Angefangen 1898, Beendigt 1914
Acta des Missionszöglings Carl [*sic*] Endemann aus Ruhland
Correspondenz mit dem Missionar J. L. Döhne, Wartburg, Natal, 1863–1864, III.7.

GStaPKB Geheimes Staatsarchiv Berlin
Heinrich-Schnee-Archiv
Rep 76Va Sekt. 2 Tit. X, Nr. 124 Bd. VII, Acta betreffend das Seminar für Orientalische Sprachen bei der Universität zu Berlin, vol. I, vom Juli 1907 bis Dezember 1910
Rep. 208A, Seminar für Orientalische Sprachen

JSG J. S. Gericke Library Archive, Stellenbosch
J. A. Engelbrecht Papers

Stabi Staatsbibliothek zu Berlin
Nachlaß Felix von Luschan

StaH Staatsarchiv Hamburg
361-1 Hochschulwesen, Dozenten- und Personalakten
364-5 Universitäten
364-6 Kolonialinstitut
364-7 Professorenrat des Kolonialinstituts

UCTA University of Cape Town Library Archive
Wilhelm Bleek Papers
G. P. Lestrade Papers

VEM Vereinigte Evangelisches Missionsarchiv, Wuppertal
RMG 1.583 a B/c II 10, Kolbe, Friedrich, Band 1, 1844–1860
RMG 1.611b B/c II 38, Büttner, Carl Gotthilf, Band II

PRIMARY SOURCES

Adametz, Leopold. *Herkunft und Wanderungen der Hamiten erschlossen aus ihren Haustierrassen.* Vienna: Verlag des Forschungsinstitutes für Osten und Orient, 1920.

Adelung, J. C. *Mithridates oder allgemeine Sprachenkunde mit dem Vater Unser als*

Sprachprobe in bey nahe fünfhundert Sprachen und Mundarten. 1806 (I); 1809 (II); 1812 (III/1,2); 1816 (III/3); 1817 (IV). Berlin: Vossische Buchhandlung, 1806, 1809, 1812, 1816, 1817.

Amery, L. S. *The German Colonial Claim.* New York: Longmans, Green, 1940.

Andersson, Charles J. A. "Explorations in South Africa, with Route from Walfisch Bay to Lake Ngami, and Ascent of the Tioge River." *Royal Geographical Society, Proceedings.* 1855.

Barrows, Sarah T. "Experimental Phonetics as an Aid to the Study of Language." *The Pedagogical Seminary: A Quarterly,* vol. xxiii (1916): 63–95.

Bent, J. T. *The Ruined Cities of Mashonaland.* 3rd ed. London, 1896.

Bleek, Dorothea. *The Naron: A Bushman Tribe of the Central Kalahari.* Cambridge: Cambridge University Press, 1928.

Bleek, Wilhelm. *A Brief Account of Bushman Folk-Lore and Other Texts.* London, 1875.

Bleek, Wilhelm. *A Comparative Grammar of South African Languages.* London: Trübner, 1869.

Bleek, Wilhelm. "'Grimm's Law' in South Africa; or, Phonetic Changes in the South African Bantu Languages. I.—In the South-Eastern Branch." *Transactions of the Philological Society,* 1843–44.

Bleek, Wilhelm. *The Library of His Excellency, Sir George Grey, K.C.B., Philology,* vol. 1, part 1, *South Africa.* London: Trübner, 1858.

Bleek, Wilhelm. *The Natal Diaries of Dr. W. H. I. Bleek.* Edited by O. H. Spohr. Cape Town: A. A. Balkema, 1965.

Bleek, Wilhelm. *"Reynard the Fox" in South Africa, or Hottentot Fables and Tales.* London: Trübner, 1864.

Boas, Franz. "Die Ausdrücke für einige religiöse Begriffe der Kwakiutl-Indianer." In *Festschrift Meinhof: Sprachwissenschaftliche und andere Studien,* 386–92. Hamburg: J. J. Augustin, 1927.

Boas, Franz. *Race, Language, and Culture.* Chicago: University of Chicago Press, 1982. First published 1940.

Boas, Franz. "The Study of Geography." *Science* 9.210 (November 2, 1887): 137–41.

Bodenstein, Bernhard. *Die Beschäftigung ausländischer Arbeiter in der Industrie.* Leipzig: Baedeker, 1908.

Böhner, H., and J. G. Christaller. *Übungen in der Akra- oder Ga-Sprache.* Basel: Gedruckt für die Basler Mission auf der Goldküste, West-Afrika, Verlag der Missionsbuchhandlung, 1890.

Bourquin, Walther. *Neue Ur-Bantu Wortstämme: nebst einem Beitrag zur Erforschung der Bantu-Wurzeln.* Beiheft of the *Zeitschrift für Eingeborenensprachen.* Berlin: Dietrich Reimer, 1923.

Bourquin, Walther, Clement Doke, Werner Eiselen, G. P. Lestrade, and B. I. C. van Eeden. "Meinhof's Contributions to Our Knowledge of African Languages." *African Studies* 5 (1946): 73–77.

Brauer, Erich. *Züge aus der Religion der Herero, ein Beitrag zur Hamitenfrage.* Leipzig: R. Voigtländer, 1925.

Bremer, Otto. Review of Carl Meinhof, *Grundriss einer Lautlehre der Bantusprachen. Wiener Zeitschrift für die Kunde des Morgenlandes,* 14 (1900).

Brookes, Edgar H., ed. *Apartheid: A Documentary Study of Modern South Africa.* London: Routledge and Kegan Paul, 1968.

Broomfield, G. W. "The Re-Bantuization of the Swahili Language." *Africa* 4 (1931): 77–85.

Büttner, Carl. *Anthologie aus der Suaheli-Literatur (Gedichte und Geschichten der Suaheli), Erster Theil.* Berlin: Verlag von Emil Felber, 1894.

Büttner, Carl. *Lieder und Geschichte der Suaheli, Beiträge zur Volks- und Völkerkunde.* 3rd vol. Berlin: Verlag von Emil Felber, 1894.

Cassirer, Ernst. "Die Bedeutung des Sprachproblems für die Entstehung der neueren Philosophie." In *Festschrift Meinhof: Sprachwissenschaftliche und andere Studien,* 502–14. Hamburg: J. J. Augustin, 1927.

Christaller, J. G. *A Grammar of the Asante and Fante Language called Tshi (Chwee, Twi): based on the Akuapem dialect with reference to the other (Akan and Fante) dialects.* Basel: printed for the Basel Evang. Missionary Society, 1875.

Claus, Dr. "Die Wangómwia: Mit Bemerkungen zu den Sprachproben von K. Meinhof [*sic*], Hamburg." *Zeitschrift für Ethnologie,* Jg. 42 (1910): 489.

Cleve, G. L. "Die Lippenlaute der Bantu und die Negerlippen, mit besonderer Berücksichtigung der Lippenverstümmelungen." *Zeitschrift für Ethnologie* 35 (1903): 681–701.

Cremer, Hermann. *Biblico-Theological Lexicon of New Testament Greek.* Translated by William Urwick. Edinburgh: T. & T. Clark, 1878.

Cust, Robert. "Dr. Schön." *Church Missionary Gleaner* 16–17 (1889): 36.

Czermak, Wilhelm. Review of Maria von Tiling, *Somali-Texte und Untersuchungen zur Somali-Lautlehre. Wiener Zeitschrift für die Kunde des Morgenlandes* 33 (1926): 150–56.

Dempwolff, Otto. "Sprechapparate beim Unterricht in der Namasprache." *Vox: Internationales Zentralblatt für Experimentelle Phonetik* (1913). Heft 5, 251.

Dempwolff, Otto. "Über aussterbende Völker." *Zeitschrift für Ethnologie* (1904): 384–415.

Deutsche Kolonialschule, Lehr- und Anstaltsplan, einschließlich Vorlesungs-Verzeichnis. Witzenhausen: Chr. Trautvetter, n.d.

Dibone, Njo, and Elli Meinhof. *Märchen aus Kamerun.* Strassburg: J. H. Ed. Heitz (Heitz und Mündel), 1889.

Döhne, J. L. *A Zulu-Kafir Dictionary, Etymologically Explained, with Copious Illustrations and Examples, Preceded by an Introduction on the Zulu-Kafir Language.* Cape Town: Printed at J. G. Pike's Machine Printing Office, 1857.

Du Bois, W. E. B. "Miscegenation." In *Interracialism: Black-White Intermarriage in American History, Literature, and Law,* edited by Werner Sollors, 461–72. Oxford: Oxford University Press, 2000.

Duisberg, Adolf von. *Grundriss der Kanuri-Sprache in Bornu.* Vol. 15, *Archiv für das Studium deutscher Kolonialsprachen.* Berlin: G. Reimer, 1913.

Eiselen, W. W. M. "Natives Urged to Help South African Government with their own Development." Native Affairs Fact Paper XIV. Based on a speech made in the Ciskei on October 17, 1950.

Eiselen, W. W. M. *Report of the Commission on Native Education, 1945–1951.* Excerpt in *Apartheid: A Documentary Study of Modern South Africa,* edited by Edgar H. Brookes, 44–45. London: Routledge and Kegan Paul, 1968.

Endemann, Karl. *Versuch einer Grammatik der Sotho-Sprache.* Berlin: W. Hertz, 1876.

Fabri, Friedrich. *Bedarf Deutschland der Kolonien?/Does Germany Need Colonies?* Edited and translated by E. C. M. Breuning and M. E. Chamberlain. New York: Edwin Mellen Press, 1998. First published 1879.

Fabri, Friedrich. *Die Entstehung des Heidenthums und die Aufgabe der Heidenmission.* Barmen (Wuppertal): W. Langwiesche's Verlagshandlung, 1859.

Frobenius, Leo. *Und Afrika sprach. . . . Wissenschaftlich erweiterte Ausgabe des Berichts über den Verlauf der dritten Reiseperiode der Deutschen Inner-Afrikanischen Forschungs-Expedition in den Jahren 1910 bis 1912.* 3 Bände. Berlin: Vita, Deutsches Verlagshaus, 1912–13.

Giesebrecht, Ludwig. *Wendische Geschichte aus den Jahren 780 bis 1182.* Berlin: Gaertner, 1843.

Giesebrecht, Wilhelm. *Geschichte der deutschen Kaiserzeit.* Six vols. Leipzig: Duncker und Humblot, 1877–95.

Gill, David. "Annual Address to the South African Philosophical Society." *Transactions of the South African Philosophical Society* 2, part 3, 1880–81.

Gleiss, Franz, and O. Rösler. *Schambala-grammatik, mit Übungssätzen nebst einer Sammlung von Redensarten in Gesprächsform.* Archiv für das Studium deutscher Kolonialsprachen, vol. 13. Berlin: Georg Reimer, 1912.

Gobineau, Arthur D. *The Inequality of Human Races.* Trans. Adrian Collins. New York: G. P. Putnam, 1915.

Grundemann, Reinhold. *Zur Statistik der Evangelischen Mission.* Gütersloh: Bertelsmann, 1886.

Gründler, W. "Die Bedeutung gemeinsamer Ausbildungsstätte für die Spezialausbildung der Missionare." In *Verhandlungen der XIII. Kontinentalen Missionskonferenz,* 24–30. Bremen: Kommissionsverlag der Norddeutsche Missionsgesellschaft, 1913.

Hahn, C. Hugo. *Grundzüge einer Grammatik des Herero (im westlichen Afrika) nebst einem Wörterbuche.* Berlin: Wilhelm Hertz, 1857.

Hahn, Theophilus. "Ein Racenkampf im nordwestlichen Theile der Cap-Region." *Globus,* 14 (1869): 270–71.

Haller, J. *Die Vorbildung unserer Missionare.* Basel: Verlag der Missionsbuchhandlung, 1904.

Hambruch, Paul. "Sprachaufnahmen mit einem Knabe aus Neu-Mecklenburg." *Vox Internationales Zentralblatt für Experimentelle Phonetik,* 5–6 (1914): 271–75.

Hausleiter, D. G. "Die Stellung der Mission zur Rassenfrage." *Verhandlungen der XII. Missions=Konferenz zu Bremen vom 6. bis 10 Mai 1909,* 22–31. Bremen: Kommissionsverlag der Norddeutschen Missions=Gesellschaft, 1909.

Heepe, Martin. *Probleme der Bantusprachforschung in geschichtlichem Überblick.* Leipzig: F. A. Brockhaus, 1920.

Herder, Johann Gottfried. *Another Philosophy of History and Selected Political Writings.* Indianapolis: Hackett, 2004.

Herder, Johann Gottfried. *On World History: An Anthology.* Edited by Hans Adler and Ernest A. Menze. Armonk, NY: M. E. Sharpe, 1997.

Hertzberg, Gustav Friedrich. *August Hermann Francke und sein Hallisches Waisenhaus.* Halle: Verlag der Buchhandlung des Waisenhauses, 1898.

Hestermann, Ferdinand. *Die Deutsche Afrikanistik bis 1913: kritische Darstellung der neuesten Ansichten über Gruppierungen und Bewegungen der Sprachen und Völker in Afrika.* Vienna: Mechitharisten-Kongregations-Buchdruckerei, 1929.

Hestermann, Ferdinand. "Völker und Sprachen in Afrika." *Anthropos* 7 (1912): 219–50, and 7 (1913): 722–60.

Hollis, A. C. *The Masai: Their Language and Folklore.* Westport, CT: Negro Universities Press, 1970, 1905.

Humboldt, Wilhelm von. *On Language: The Diversity of Human Language-Structure and Its Influence on the Mental Development of Mankind.* Cambridge: Cambridge University Press, 1988, 1836.

Isenberg, C. W. "A Few Remarks concerning the Nation of the Gallas, and an Evangelical Mission among them." In J. L. Krapf, *An Imperfect Outline of the Elements of the Galla Language,* III–XIV. London: Church Missionary Society, 1840.

Jones, Anna Marian, ed. *The Works of Sir William Jones.* 13 vols. London: G. G. and J. Robinson, and R. H. Evans, 1807.

Jones, Daniel, and Sol Tshekisho Plaatje. *A Sechuana Reader in International Phonetic Orthography (with English Translations).* London: University of London Press, 1916.

Jones, Sir William. "The Third Anniversary Discourse, on the Hindus, Delivered 2 February, 1786." In *A Reader in Nineteenth Century Historical Indo-European Linguistics,* edited by Winfred P. Lehmann, 7–20. Bloomington: Indiana University Press, 1967.

Koelle, S. W. *Outlines of a Grammar of the Vei Language, Together with a Vei-English Vocabulary and an Account of the Discovery and Nature of the Vei Mode of Syllabic Writing.* London: Keegan, Paul, 1851.

Kolbe, F. W. *A Language-Study Based on Bantu; or, An Inquiry into the Laws of Root-Formation, the Original Plural, the Sexual Dual, and the Principles of Word-Comparison; with Tables Illustrating the Primitive Pronominal System Restored in the African Bantu Family of Speech.* London: Trubner, 1888.

Kolbe, F. W. "On the Affinity between the Indo-European and the African Bantu Languages." *Cape Monthly Magazine,* n.s., vol. 3 (1871): 298–303.

Kolbe, F. W. "On the Origin of Language." *Cape Monthly Magazine,* n.s., vol. 3 (1871): 93–97.

Köstlin, Julius. *Life of Luther.* Whitefish, MT: Kessinger Publishing's Rare Reprints, 2004.

Krapf, J. L. *An Imperfect Outline of the Elements of the Galla Language.* London: Church Missionary Society, 1840.

Krapf, J. L. *Outline of the Elements of the Kisuáheli Language, with Special Reference to the Kinika Dialect.* Tübingen: L. F. Fues, 1850.

Krapf, J. L. *Travels, Researches, and Missionary Labours, during an Eighteen Years' Residence in Eastern Africa; Together with Journeys to Jagga, Usambara, Ukambani, Shoa, Abessinia, and Khartum; and a Coasting Voyage from Mombaz to*

Cape Delgado. With an Introduction by Roy C. Bridges. New York: Johnson Reprint Co., 1860, 1968.

Krapf, J. L. *Vocabulary of the Engútuk Eloikob, or of the Language of the Wakuafi-Nation in the Interior of Equatorial Africa.* Tübingen: Lud. Fried. Fues., 1854.

Kropf, Albert. *A Kaffir-English Dictionary.* 2nd ed. Lovedale, S. Africa: Lovedale Mission Press, 1915.

Lange, Rudolf. *Lehrbuch der Japanischen Umgangssprache.* Stuttgart: W. Spemann, 1890.

Le Berre, Petrus Maria. *Grammaire de la langue ponguée.* Paris: Imprimerie S. Raçon, 1873.

Lepsius, Richard. *Nubische Grammatik, mit einer Einleitung über die Völker und Sprachen Afrikas.* Berlin: W. Hertz, 1880.

Lepsius, Richard. *Standard Alphabet for Reducing Unwritten Languages and Foreign Graphic Systems to a Uniform Orthography in European Letters.* London: Williams & Norgate, 1863.

Luschan, Felix von. "Anthropological View of Race." In *Select Discussions of Race Problems: A Collection of Papers of Especial Use in Study of Negro American Problems; with the Proceedings of the Twentieth Annual Conference for the Study of Negro Problems,* edited by John Alvin Bigham, 24–31. Atlanta: Atlanta University Press, 1916.

Luschan, Felix von. "Bericht über eine Reise in Südafrika." *Zeitschrift für Ethnologie* 38, no. 14 (1906): 863.

Luschan, Felix von. "On the Racial Affinities of the Hottentots." In *Addresses and Papers read at the Joint Meeting of the British and South African Associations for the Advancement of Science, held in South Africa, 1905,* vol. 3, 111–18. Johannesburg: South African Association for the Advancement of Science, 1905.

Luschan, Felix von. "Sechs Pygmäen aus Ituri." *Zeitschrift für Ethnologie* 38 (1906): 717–29.

Luschan, Felix von. *Völker, Rassen, Sprachen: Anthropologische Betrachtungen.* Berlin: Deutsche Buch-Gemeinschaft, 1927.

Mead, Margaret. *Coming of Age in Samoa: A Psychological Study of Primitive Youth for Western Civilisation.* New York: Blue Ribbon Books, 1928.

Meinhof, Carl. *Afrikanische Märchen.* Diedrichs Märchen der Weltliteratur. Reinbek bei Hamburg: Rohwolt, 1993, 1991, 1917.

Meinhof, Carl. "Afrikanische Poesien." *Globus,* Bd. 62, Nr. 7, 1892: 97–100, 124–26.

Meinhof, Carl. "Die afrikanischen Völker und die Mission." *Mission und Pfarramt* 3 (1910): 83–95.

Meinhof, Carl. *Afrikanische Religionen: Hamburgische Vorträge.* Berlin: Buchhandlung der Berliner evangelischen Mission, 1912.

Meinhof, Carl. "Aus dem Seelenleben der Eingeborenen." *Jahrbuch über die deutschen Kolonien* 1909, II, 47–52; 1910, III, 84–100; 1912, V, 39–41; 1913, VI, 54–58; 1914, VII, 54–58.

Meinhof, Carl. "The Basis of Bantu Philology: Lecture Delivered at Capetown in January 1928." *Africa* 2 (1929): 39–56.

Meinhof, Carl. "Die Bedeutung der experimentellen Phonetik für die Erforschung der afrikanischen Sprachen." *Vox* (1913).

Meinhof, Carl. "Die Bedeutung des Studiums der Eingeborenensprachen für die

Kolonialverwaltung." *Verhandlungen des deutschen Kolonialkongresses* (1910): 343–59.

Meinhof, Carl. *Die Christianisierung der Sprachen Afrikas.* Basel: Verlag der Missionsbuchhandlung, 1905.

Meinhof, Carl. "Das dalsche Gesetz." *Zeitschrift der deutschen morgenländischen Gesellschaft* (1903): 299–304.

Meinhof, Carl. *Die Dichtung der Afrikaner: Hamburgische Vorträge.* Berlin: Buchhandlung der Berliner evangelischen Gesellschaft, 1911.

Meinhof, Carl. "Dr. C. G. Büttner und die afrikanische Sprachforschung." *Zeitschrift für afrikanische und oceanische Sprachen* 1(1895): 329–33.

Meinhof, Carl. "Einwirkung der Beschäftigung auf die Sprache bei den Bantustämmen Afrikas." *Globus: Illustrierte Zeitschrift für Länder- und Völkerkunde,* Bd. 75, Nr. 23, 17/6/1899: 361–64.

Meinhof, Carl. *Die Entstehung flektierender Sprachen.* Berlin: Dietrich Reimer, 1936.

Meinhof, Carl. *Die Erziehende Kraft der Mission.* Berlin: Buchhandlung der Berliner evangelischen Missionsgesellschaft, 1912.

Meinhof, Carl. "Europäer und Afrikaner." Sonderdruck aus der *Afrika-Rundschau* Nr. 7 (November 1937): 5–18.

Meinhof, Carl. "Das Ful in seiner Bedeutung für die Sprachen der Hamiten, Semiten und Bantu." *Zeitschrift der Deutschen Morgenländischen Gesellschaft* 65 (1911): 177–200.

Meinhof, Carl. *Grundriss einer Lautlehre der Bantusprachen nebst Anleitung zur Aufnahme von Bantusprachen.* 2nd ed. Berlin: Dietrich Reimer (Ernst Vohsen), 1910.

Meinhof, Carl. *Grundzüge einer vergleichenden Grammatik der Bantusprachen.* Berlin: D. Reimer, E. Vohsen, 1906.

Meinhof, Carl. *An Introduction to the Study of African Languages.* Translated by Alice Werner. New York: J. M. Dent and Sons, 1915.

Meinhof, Carl. "Karl Endemann †." *Vox* 29, 1919: 33–34.

Meinhof, Carl. "Die Laien und ihre Heranziehung zur Mitarbeit an der Mission." *Jahrbuch der sächsischen Missionskonferenz* (1909): 91–98.

Meinhof, Carl. "The Language of the Hottentots." In *Addresses and Papers read at the Joint Meeting of the British and South African Associations for the Advancement of Science,* 111–18. Johannesburg: South African Association for the Advancement of Science, 1905.

Meinhof, Carl. "Ein Märchen aus Kamerun." *Zeitschrift für afrikanische Sprachen* 3 (1889–90): 241–46.

Meinhof, Carl. "Das missionarische Sprachproblem." *Allgemeine Missionszeitschrift,* Berlin (1906): 251–61.

Meinhof, Carl. *Die Moderne Sprachforschung in Afrika.* Berlin: Buchhandlung der Berliner evangelischen Missionsgesellschaft, 1910.

Meinhof, Carl. "Die mohammedanische Gefahr in Afrika und die Einheitssprache," Vortrag auf der lutherischen Konferenz zu Mölle im September 1908. *Evangelisches Missions-Magazin N.F.* 53 (1909): 49–65.

Meinhof, Carl. "Nachruf für Professor Endemann." *Zeitschrift für Kolonialsprachen* 9 (1918–19): 65.

Meinhof, Carl. "Orthographische Briefe an Eine Dame." *Plattdütsch Vereens-Blatt.* Leipzig, 1879, Nr. 3–12; 1880, Nr. 2–3. Written under the pen name "Mai."

Meinhof, Carl. "Die praktische Bedeutung der Einheitssprachen für die Kolonien." *Verhandlungen des deutschen Kolonialkongresses* (1910): 733–39.

Meinhof, Carl. *Der Religion der Afrikaner in ihrem Zusammenhang mit dem Wirtschaftsleben.* Oslo: H. Aschenhoug, 1926.

Meinhof, Carl. "Semitische Spuren in Südafrika: Ndalama = Geld." *Globus,* Bd. 62 (1892): 203–5.

Meinhof, Carl. "Skizzen von der allgemeinen studentischen Missionskonferenz in Liverpool." *Die Evangelische-Mission Illustriertes Familienblatt* 14 (March 1908): 78–81.

Meinhof, Carl. *Die Sprachen der Hamiten.* Berlin: L. Friedrichsen, 1912.

Meinhof, Carl. "Die sprachwissenschaftliche Arbeit Berliner Missionare." *Missionsberichte der Gesellschaft zur Beförderung der evangelischen Missionare unter den Heiden zu Berlin* (1905): 111–17.

Meinhof, Carl. *Eine Studienfahrt nach Kordofan.* Hamburg: L. Friedrichsen, 1916.

Meinhof, Carl. "Sudansprachen und Hamitensprachen." *Zeitschrift für Kolonialsprachen* 1 (1910): 164.

Meinhof, Carl. "The Training of Missionaries in Regard to Language." World Missionary Conference, Report of Commission V. Edinburgh-London 1910: 263–69, 332–33.

Meinhof, Carl. "Über M. Merkers 'Masai.'" *Zeitschrift für Ethnologie* 36 (1904): 735–44.

Meinhof, Carl. "Ueber den gegenwärtigen Stand der afrikanischen Sprachforschung." *Verhandlungen des deutschen Kolonialkongresses* (1905): 115–27.

Meinhof, Carl. "Über den gegenwärtigen Stand der afrikanischen Sprachforschung." *Verhandlungen des deutschen Kolonialkongresses* (1910): 93–106.

Meinhof, Carl. "Über die Notwendigkeit des Sprechenlernens für den Missionsarzt." Unpublished, Hamburg, ca. 1911.

Meinhof, Carl. "Untersuchung der Pygmäensprachen." *Zeitschrift für Ethnologie,* Jg. 38 (1906): 729–31.

Meinhof, Carl. "Die Urgeschichte im Lichte der afrikanischen Linguistik." *Deutsche Literaturzeitung,* Nr. 37, 33 Jg. (September 14, 1912): 2309–17.

Meinhof, Carl. "Vorbemerkungen zu einem vergleichenden Wörterbuch der Bantusprachen." *Zeitschrift für afrikanische und oceanische Sprachen* 1 (1895): 268–81.

Meinhof, Carl. "Wie treibt ein Missionar am besten die Erlernung der Sprache des Volkes, unter dem er arbeitet?," and commentaries thereto. In *Verhandlungen der elften Kontinentalen-Missions-Konferenz zu Bremen.* Berlin: Buchhandlung der Berliner evangelischen Missionsgesellschaft (1906): 5–33.

Meinhof, Carl. "Das Zeitwort in der Duallasprache." *Zeitschrift für afrikanische Sprachen* 2 (1889): 1–34.

Meinhof, Carl. "Zum Gedächtnis an Dr. C. G. Büttner." *Pommerscher Hausfreund* 1 (1894): 2–3.

Meinhof, Carl. "Zur Erinnerung an Dr. Carl Gotthilf Büttner." *Kreuzzeitung* 607 (1893).

Meinhof, Carl. "Zur Erinnerung an Dr. C. G. Büttner, gest. 1893." *Allgemeine evangelisch-lutherische Kirchenzeitung* (1893): 1276.

Meinhof, Carl. "Zweites Korreferat" to W. Gründler, "Die Bedeutung gemeinsamer Ausbildungsstätte für die Spezialausbildung der Missionare." In *Verhandlungen der XIII. Kontinentalen Missionskonferenz,* 38–42. Bremen: Kommissionsverlag der Norddeutsche Missions-gesellschaft, 1913.

Melle, Werner von. *Dreißig Jahre Hamburger Wissenschaft, 1891–1921.* 2 vols. Hamburg: Kommissionsverlag von Broschet, 1923.

Merensky, Alexander. *Mein Missionsleben in Transvaal: Erinnerungen des Berliner Missionars in Südafrika von 1859 bis 1882.* Ulrich Van der Heyden, introduction and editor. Berlin: Edition Ost, 1996. First published 1899.

Merensky, Alexander. *Wörterverzeichnis zum Gebrauch bei Bearbeitung Afrikanischer Sprachen.* Berlin: Buchhandlung der Berliner evangelischer Gesellschaft, 1891.

Merker, M. *Die Masai.* Berlin: Dietrich Reimer, 1904.

The Missionary Guide-book, Or, A Key to the Protestant Missionary Map of the World: Shewing the Geography, Natural History, Climate, Population, and Government of the Several Countries to which the Missionary Efforts Have Been Directed: with the Moral, Social, and Religious Condition of Their Inhabitants. London: Seeley, Burnside, and Seeley, 1846.

Mohr, A. T. *A Dictionary of English-Tshi (Asante).* Basel: Evangelical Missionary Society, 1909.

Müller, Friedrich. *Grundriss der Sprachwissenschaft.* 1876.

Nyländer, Gustavus Reinhold. *Grammar and Vocabulary of the Bullom Language.* London: Church Missionary Society, Ellerton and Henderson, 1814.

Nyländer, Gustavus Reinhold. *Select Portions of the Book of Common Prayer, according to the use of the United Church of England and Ireland.* London: Church Missionary Society, Ellerton and Henderson, 1816.

Nyländer, Gustavus Reinhold. *A Spelling-Book of the Bullom Language: With a Dialogue and Scripture Exercise.* London: Church Missionary Society, Ellerton and Henderson, 1814.

Panconcelli-Calzia, Giulio. *Experimentelle Phonetik.* Berlin: Vereinigung wissenschaftlicher Verleger, Walter de Gruyter, 1921.

Panconcelli-Calzia, Giulio. "Über die aspirierten und nichtaspirierten Verschlußlaute sowie den Frageton im Suaheli." *Zeitschrift für Kolonialsprachen* 1 (1910–11): 305.

Paudler, Fritz. *Die hellfarbigen Rassen und ihre Sprachstämme, Kulturen und Urheimaten: Ein neues Bild vom heutigen und urzeitlichen Europa.* Heidelberg: Carl Winter, 1924.

Pöhl, H. *Deutsche Auslandshochschule.* Tübingen: J. C. B. Mohr (Paul Siebeck), 1913.

Proceedings of the Church Missionary Society for Africa and the East, Nineteenth Year, 1818–1819. London: L. B. Seeley, 1819.

Proceedings of the Church Missionary Society for Africa and the East, Twenty-fifth year, 1824–1825. London: R. Watts, 1825.

"Proceedings of Other Societies." *Missionary Herald* 47 (1851): 130–31.

Rathgen, Karl, and Georg Thilenius. "Ruckblick auf die beide ersten Studienjahre." *Reden von Professor Dr. Georg Thilenius und Professor Dr. K. Rathgen bei der Feier der Übergabe des Vorsitzes im Professorenrat* and *Bericht über das zweite Studienjahr, Winter 1909/10, Sommer 1910.* Hamburg, 1910.

Raum, J. *Versuch einer Grammatik der Dschagga-Sprache (Moschi Dialekt).* Vol. 11 of the Archiv für das Studium deutscher Kolonialsprachen. Berlin: G. Reimer, 1909.

Raumer, Rudolf von. *Fortsetzung der Untersuchung über die Urverwandtschaft der semitischen und indoeuropäischen Sprachen.* Frankfurt am Main: Heyder & Zimmer, ca. 1860.

Raumer, Rudolf von. *Herr Professor Schleicher in Jena und Die Urverwandschaft der semitischen und indoeuropäischen Sprachen. Ein kritisches Bedenken.* Frankfurt am Main: Heyder & Zimmer, 1864.

Raumer, Rudolf von. *Sendschreiben an Herrn Professor Whitney, über die Urverwandschaft der semitischen und indogermanischen Sprachen.* Frankfurt am Main: Heyder & Zimmer, 1876.

Raumer, Rudolf von. "Die Urverwandschaft der semitischen und indoeuropäischen Sprachen." In Rudolf von Raumer, *Gesammelte sprachwissenschaftliche Schriften.* Frankfurt am Main: Heyder & Zimmer, 1863.

Reche, Otto, ed. *In Memoriam: Karl Weule: Beiträge zur Völkerkunde.* Leipzig: R. Voightländer, 1929.

Rehse, Hermann. *Kiziba: Land und Leute. Mit einem Vorwort von Professor Dr. von Luschan.* Stuttgart: Strecker & Schröder, 1910.

Roehl, Karl. "The Linguistic Situation in East Africa." *Africa* 3 (January 1930): 190–202.

Roehl, Karl. *Versuch einer systematischen Grammatik der Schambalasprache.* Hamburg: L. Friedrichsen, 1911.

S., E. *The Missionary Career of Dr. Krapf, Missionary of the Church Missionary Society in Abyssinia and East Africa, and Pioneer of Central African Exploration.* Reprinted from the Church Missionary Intelligencer, February and March, 1882. London: Church Missionary Society, 1882.

Sachau, Eduard. *Denkschrift über das Seminar für orientalische Sprachen an der K. Friedrich-Wilhelm Universität.* Berlin, 1912.

Sachau, Eduard. "Seminar-Chronik für das Studien-Jahr 1897/1898." *Mittheilungen des Seminars für Orientalische Sprachen* Jg. 1 (1898): III–IV.

Sachau, Eduard. "Seminarchronik für die Zeit vom Oktober 1903 bis August 1904." *Mittheilungen des Seminars für Orientalische Sprachen,* Jahrgang 7, 1904: I–VII.

Sachau, Eduard. "Seminarchronik für die Zeit vom Oktober 1905 bis August 1906." *Mittheilungen des Seminars für Orientalische Sprachen,* Jahrgang 9, 1906: I–VIII.

Sachau, Eduard. "Seminar-Chronik für die Zeit von Ostern 1898 bis Ostern 1899." *Mittheilungen des Seminars für Orientalische Sprachen* Jg. 2 (1899): I–IV.

Sachau, Eduard. "Vorwort." In Rudolf Lange, *Lehrbuch der Japanischen Umgangsprache,* V–VI. Stuttgart: W. Spemann, 1890.

Sapir, Edward. *Language: An Introduction to the Study of Speech.* New York: Harcourt Brace, 1921.

Sapir, Edward. "Review of Carl Meinhof, *Die Sprachen der Hamiten.*" *Current Anthropological Literature,* vol. 2. Lancaster, PA: American Anthropological Association and the American Folklore Society, 1913.

Schilde, Willi. "Beiträge zur Hamitenfrage." *Sonderabdruck aus den Tagungsberichten der Deutschen Anthropologischen Gesellschaft,* 1925.

Schlegel, J. B. *Schlüssel zur Ewe-Sprache, dargeboten in den grammatischen Grundzügen des Anlo-Dialekts dersselben, mit Wörtersammlung nebst einer Sammlung von Sprüchwörtern und einigen Fablen der Eingebornen.* Bremen: W. Vallet.

Schleicher, Adolf Walter. *Afrikanische petrefakten; ein versuch die grammatischen bildungen und formwurzeln der afrikanischen sprachen durch sprachvergleichug festzustellen.* Berlin: T. Frölich, 1891.

Schleicher, August. *Compendium der vergleichenden Grammatik der indogermanischen Sprachen. Kurzer Abriss einer Laut- und Formenlehre der indogermanischen Ursprache, des Altindischen, Alteranischen, Altgriechischen, Altitalischen, Altkeltischen, Altslawischen, Litauischen und Altdeutschen.* Weimar: H. Böhlau, 1866.

Schleicher, August. *Die Sprachen Europas in systematischer Übersicht und linguistische Untersuchungen.* Amsterdam: Benjamins, 1983, XXIX.

Schlenker, C. F. *Grammar of the Temne Language.* London: Church Missionary Society, 1864.

Schlunk, Martin. "Die Rassenfrage in Südafrika." *Allgemeine Missions-Zeitschrift* 46 (1914): 305–19.

Schlunk, Martin. *Die schulen für Eingeborene in den deutschen Schutzgebieten am 1. Juni 1911; auf Grund einer statistischen Erhebung der Zentralstelle des Hamburgischen Kolonialinstituts dargestellt von Martin Schlunk.* Hamburg: L. Friedrichsen, 1914.

Schmidt, Wilhelm. "L'Origine de l'Idee de Dieu." *Anthropos* 4 (1909).

Schön, J. F. *Oku Ibo. Grammatical Elements of the Ibo Language.* London, 1861.

Schuchardt, Hugo. Review, "Meinhof, Carl: *Die Sprachen der Hamiten,* nebst einer Beigabe: *Hamitische Typen* von Felix von Luschan. Mit 33 Abbildungen auf 11 Tafeln und 1 Karte. Hamburg: L. Friedrichsen, 1912. Großoktav, 256 S." *Wiener Zeitschrift für die Kunde des Morgenlandes,* 26 (1912): 407–8.

Schuchardt, Hugo, Theo Vennemann, and Terence H. Wilbur, eds. *Schuchardt, the Neogrammarians, and the Transformational Theory of Phonological Change: Four Essays.* Frankfurt am Main: Athenäum Verlag, 1972.

Schumann, C. *Grundriss einer Grammatik der Kondesprache.* Berlin: Mitteilungen des Seminars für Orientalische Sprachen, 1899.

Schwellnus, Theodor, and Paul Schwellnus. "Die Verba des Tsivenda." *Mitteilungen des Seminars für orientalische Sprachen* 6 (1904): 12–31.

Schwörer, E. *Kolonial-Deutsch: Vorschläge einer künftigen deutschen Kolonialsprache in systematisch-grammatikalischer Darstellung und Begründung.* Diessen vor München: Jos. C. Hubers Verlag, 1916.

Seidel, August. "J. G. Christaller und die afrikanische Sprachwissenschaft." *Zeitschrift für afrikanische und oceanische Sprachen* 2:267–70.

Seligman, C. G. *Races of Africa.* London: Thornton Butterworth, 1930.

Seligman, C. G. "Some Aspects of the Hamitic Problem in the Anglo-Egyptian Sudan." *Journal of the Royal Anthropological Institute of Great Britain and Ireland* 43 (July–December 1913): 42–49.

Shaw, E. M., and N. J. van Warmelo. "The Material Culture of the Cape Nguni: Part 4 Personal and General." *Annals of the South African Museum* 58, no. 4 (1988): 2–8.

Spannaus, Günther. "Historisch-Kritisches zum Hamitenproblem in Afrika." In *In Memoriam: Karl Weule: Beiträge zur Völkerkunde,* edited by Otto Reche. Leipzig: R. Voightländer, 1929.

Spieth, Jakob. *Die Religion der Eweer in Süd-Togo.* Göttingen: Vandenhoeck & Ruprecht, 1911.

Spieth, Jakob. "Die religiöse Veranlagung des Afrikaners." In *Der Afrikaner, seine wirtschaftliche Leistungsfähigkeit, geistige Befähigung, religiöse Veranlagung,* 17–28. Bremen: Verlag der Norddeutschen Missions=Gesellschaft, 1912.

Staudinger, Paul. "Commentary," on Carl Meinhof, "Über den gegenwärtigen Stand der afrikanischen Sprachforschung." *Verhandlungen des deutschen Kolonialkongresses* (1910): 102–3.

Staudinger, Paul. *In the Heart of the Hausa States.* Vols. 1–2. Translated by Johanna E. Moody. Foreword by Paul Lovejoy. Athens: Ohio University Center for International Studies, 1990. African Series Number 56.

Steane, Karl. *Kleine Fullah-Grammatik.* Vol. 7, Archiv für das Studium deutscher Kolonialsprachen. Berlin: G. Reimer, 1909.

Steinthal, Heymann. *Die mande-neger-sprachen, psychologisch und phonetisch betrachtet.* Berlin: F. Dümmler, 1867.

Stormont, D. D. "On the Word, Bantu." *Blythswood Review* (October 1930): 111–12.

Struck, Bernhard. "Begleitworte zur Uebersichtskarte der Hauptsprachfamilie in Afrika." In *Die Moderne Sprachforschung in Afrika,* edited by Carl Meinhof. Berlin: Buchhandlung der Berliner evang. Missionsgesellschaft, 1910.

Struck, Bernhard. "Die Sprachverhältnisse im 'Moyen Congo.'" Sonderabdruck. *Koloniale Rundschau* 4:204–25.

Tucker, A. N. "Systems of Tone-Marking African Languages." *Bulletin of the School of Oriental and African Studies, University of London* 27, no. 3 (1964): 594–611.

Tutschek, Charles. *A Grammar of the Galla Language.* Edited by Lawrence Tutschek. Munich, 1845.

Vedder, Heinrich. *Semitische Lehnworte in der Namasprache.* Mimeographed. Swakopmund, Namibia, 1909.

Vedder, Heinrich. *Versuch einer Grammatik der Namasprache.* Mimeographed. Swakopmund, Namibia, 1909.

Vedder, Heinrich. *Die Wortbildungsgesetze der Namasprache: ein Versuch.* Mimeographed. Swakopmund, Namibia, 1909.

Velten, Carl. *Suaheli-Sprachführer für Postbeamte.* Berlin: Im Selbstverlag, 1910.

Warmelo, N. J. van. *Die Gliederung der südafrikanischen Bantusprachen.* Hamburg: J. J. Augustin, 1927.

Warmelo, N. J. van. *A Preliminary Survey of the Bantu Tribes of South Africa.* Union of South Africa, Department of Native Affairs, Ethnological Publications, Vol. 5. Pretoria: Government Printer, 1935.

Weber, Alan S., ed. *Nineteenth Century Science: A Selection of Original Texts.* Peterborough, ON: Broadview Press, 2000.

Werner, Alice. Review of Maria von Tiling's *Somali-Texte und Untersuchungen zur Somali-Lautlehre. Bulletin of the School of Oriental Studies* 4, no. 1 (1926): 189–91.

Westermann, Diedrich. *The African To-day and Tomorrow.* New rev. ed. Published for the International Institute of African Languages and Cultures by the Oxford University Press. London: Humphrey Milford, 1939.

Westermann, Diedrich. *Erzählungen in Fulfulde, Nidergeschrieben von Abdallah Adam.* Berlin: Georg Reimer, 1913.

Westermann, Diedrich. *Die Nutzplflanzen unserer Kolonien und ihre wirtschaftliche Bedeutung für das Mutterland.* Berlin: Dietrich Reimer, 1909.

Westermann, Diedrich. *The Shilluk People: Their Language and Folklore.* Berlin: Dietrich Reimer (Ernst Vohsen), 1912.

Westermann, Diedrich. *Die Sudansprachen, eine sprachvergleichende Studie.* Hamburg: L. Friedrichsen, 1911.

Westermann, Diedrich, Otto Dempwolff, Franz Boas, Giulio Panconcelli-Calzia, and Alice Werner. *Festschrift Meinhof: Sprachwissenschaftliche und andere Studien.* Hamburg: J. J. Augustin, 1927.

Westermann, Diedrich H., and Ida C. Ward. *Practical Phonetics for Students of African Languages.* Oxford: Oxford University Press, 1933.

Wirth, A. "Entwicklung der Bantu." *Zeitschrift für afrikanische und oceanische Sprachen* 1 (1895): 270–81.

Wulff, K. Review of *Anthropos, Internationale Zeitschrift für Völker- und Sprachenkunde,* Band I–IV. *Zeitschrift der deutschen morgenländischen Gesellschaft* 65 (1911): 589–99.

Wundt, Wilhelm. *Probleme der Völkerpsychologie.* Leipzig: Ernst Wiegandt, 1911.

Zimmermann, J. *A Grammatical Sketch of the Gã-Language and Some Specimens of It from the Mouth of the Natives.* Stuttgart: J. F. Steinkopf for the Basel Missionary Society, 1858.

SECONDARY SOURCES

Aarsleff, Hans. *From Locke to Saussure: Essays on the Study of Language and Intellectual History.* Minneapolis: University of Minnesota Press, 1982.

Aarsleff, Hans. "Introduction" to Wilhelm von Humboldt, *On Language: The Diversity of Human Language-Structure and Its Influence on the Development of Mankind.* Cambridge: Cambridge University Press, 1988.

Ade Ajayi, J. F. *Christian Missions in Nigeria, 1841–1891: The Making of a New Elite.* London: Longman, 1965.

Adhikari, Mohamed. "The Sons of Ham: Slavery and the Making of Coloured Identity." *South African Historical Journal* 27 (1992): 95–112.

Afigbo, A. E. "Colonial Historiography." In *African Historiography: Essays in Honor of Jacob Ade Ajayi,* edited by Toyin Falola, 39–51. Essex: Longman, 1993.

Agbeti, J. Kofi. *West African Church History: Christian Missions and Church Foundations, 1482–1919.* Leiden: Brill Archive, 1986.

Aitken, Robbie. *Exclusion and Inclusion: Gradations of Whiteness and Socio-economic Engineering in German Southwest Africa, 1884–1918.* New York: Peter Lang, 2007.

Altena, Thorsten. *Ein Häuflein Christen mitten in der Heidenwelt des dunklen Erdteils: Zum Selbst- und Fremdverständnis protestantischer Missionare im kolonialen Afrika, 1884–1918.* Münster: Waxmann, 2003.

Alter, Stephen. *Darwinism and the Linguistic Image: Language, Race, and Natural Theology in the Nineteenth Century.* Baltimore: Johns Hopkins University Press, 1999.

Ames, Eric, Marcia Klotz, and Lora Wildenthal, eds. *Germany's Colonial Pasts.* Lincoln: University of Nebraska Press, 2005.

Anderson, Benedict. *Imagined Communities: Reflections on the Origin and Spread of Nationalism.* London: Verso, 1991.

Anderson, Gerald H. *Biographical Dictionary of Christian Missions.* Grand Rapids, MI: Eerdmans, 1999.

Apter, Andrew. "*Que Faire?* Reconsidering Inventions of Africa." *Critical Inquiry* 19 (Autumn 1992): 87–104.

Asad, Talal, ed. *Anthropology and the Colonial Encounter.* Atlantic Highlands, NJ: Humanities Press, 1975.

Asher, R. E., and Eugénie J. A. Henderson, eds. *Towards a History of Phonetics.* Edinburgh: University Press, 1981.

Augustin, S. "Elise Kootz-Kretschmer: Missionarsfrau und Ethnographin der Safwa in Ostafrika." *Unitas Fratrum* 45–46 (1999): 153–63.

Austen, Ralph A. "Africans Speak, Colonialism Writes: The Transcription and Translation of Oral Literature before World War II." *Cahiers de Littérature Orale* 28 (1990): 29–53.

Austen, Ralph A. "The Colonial in the Attic: Imperialism, the Victorian Domestic Novel and Gentlemanly Capitalism." Manuscript. University of Chicago.

Austen, Ralph A., ed. *In Search of Sunjata: The Mande Oral Epic as History, Literature, and Performance.* Bloomington: Indiana University Press, 1999.

Austen, Ralph A. *Northwest Tanzania under German and British Rule: Colonial Policy and Tribal Politics, 1889–1939.* New Haven: Yale University Press, 1968.

Austen, Ralph A., and Jonathan Derrick. *Middlemen of the Cameroons Rivers: The Duala and Their Hinterland, c. 1600–c. 1960.* Cambridge: Cambridge University Press, 1999.

Austin, Peter K. *One Thousand Languages: Living, Endangered, and Lost.* Berkeley: University of California Press, 2008.

Aydelotte, William Osgood. *Bismarck and British Colonial Policy: The Problem of Southwest Africa, 1883–1885.* New York: Octagon Books, 1974. First published 1937.

Bade, Klaus J., ed. *Imperialismus und Kolonialmission: Kaiserliches Deutschland und koloniales Imperium,* 2nd ed. Stuttgart: Steiner, 1984.

Bagchi, Kaushik. "Orientalism without Colonialism? Three Nineteenth Century

German Indologists and India." PhD diss., Ohio State University, Columbus, 1996.

Bank, Andrew. *Bushmen in a Victorian World: The Remarkable Story of the Bleek-Lloyd Collection of Bushman Folklore.* Cape Town: Double Storey, 2006.

Bautz, Friedrich Wilhelm. "Reinhold Grundemann." In the *Biographisch-Bibliographisches Kirchenlexikon,* Band II. Herzberg: Verlag Traugott Bautz, 1990.

Becker, Dieter, and Andreas Feldtkeller, eds. *Es begann in Halle . . . : Missionswissenschaft von Gustav Warneck bis Heute.* Erlangen: Verlag der Ev.-Luth. Mission, 1997.

Beidelmann, T. O. *Colonial Evangelism: A Socio-historical Study of an East African Mission at the Grass Roots.* Bloomington: Indiana University Press, 1982.

Beinart, W., and S. Dubow, eds. *Segregation and Apartheid in Twentieth-Century South Africa.* London: Routledge, 1995.

Benes, Tuska E. *In Babel's Shadow: Language, Philology, and the Nation in Nineteenth-Century Germany.* Detroit: Wayne State University Press, 2008.

Berger, Heinrich. *Mission und Kolonialpolitik: die katholische Mission in Kamerun während der deutschen Kolonialzeit.* Immensee: Neue Zeitschrift für Missionswissenschaft, 1978.

Berghahn, Klaus, and Beate Pinkerneil. *Am Beispiel Wilhelm Meister: Einführung in die Wissenschaftsgeschichte der Germanistik.* Königstein: Athenäum Verlag, 1980.

Berman, Bruce. "Ethnography as Politics, Politics as Ethnography: Kenyatta, Malinowski, and the Making of *Facing Mount Kenya.*" *Canadian Journal of African Studies* 30, no. 2 (1996): 313–44.

Berman, Nina. *Impossible Missions? German Economic, Military, and Humanitarian Efforts in Africa.* Lincoln: University of Nebraska Press, 2004.

Berman, Nina. "Orientalism, Imperialism, and Nationalism: Karl May's *Orientzyklus.*" In *The Imperialist Imagination: German Colonialism and Its Legacy,* edited by Sara Friedrichsmeyer, Sara Lennox, and Susanne Zantop. Ann Arbor: University of Michigan Press, 1998.

Berman, Russell A. *Enlightenment or Empire? Colonial Discourse in German Culture.* Lincoln: University of Nebraska Press, 1998.

Bernhardt, Hannelore, ed. *Beiträge zur Geschichte der Humboldt-Universität zu Berlin.* Berlin: Der Rektor, Humboldt-Universität zu Berlin, 1990.

Bhabha, Homi K. *The Location of Culture.* London: Routledge, 1994.

Bieder, Robert E. *Science Encounters the Indian, 1820–1880: The Early Years of American Ethnology.* Norman: University of Oklahoma Press, 1986.

Blackbourn, David, and Geoff Eley. *The Peculiarities of German History: Bourgeois Society and Politics in Nineteenth-Century Germany.* Oxford: Oxford University Press, 1984.

Blackburn, Robin. *The Making of New World Slavery: From the Baroque to the Modern, 1492–1800.* London: Verso, 1997.

Böhm, Gerhard, with Mirjana Kutnjak, trans. "Development and Nature of African Linguistics in the Nineteenth Century with Special Reference to German-speaking Countries." In *The Prix Volney,* vol. 3, *Contributions to Comparative Indo-European, African, and Chinese Linguistics,* edited by Joan Leopold, 255–302. Dordrecht: Kluwer, 2000.

Bonsen, Ronald, Hans Marks, and Jelle Miedema, eds. *The Ambiguity of Rapprochement: Reflections of Anthropologists on Their Controversial Relationship with Missionaries.* Nijmegen, the Netherlands: Focaal, 1990.

Bornemann, Fritz. *P. Wilhelm Schmidt S.V.D.* Rome: Apud Collegium Verbi Divini, 1982.

Brandewie, Ernest. "Ethnology and Missionaries: The Case of the Anthropos Institute and Wilhelm Schmidt." In Darrell L. Whiteman, ed., *Missionaries, Anthropologists, and Cultural Change: Studies in Third World Societies* 25 (September 1983): 369–86.

Braude, Benjamin. "The Sons of Noah and the Construction of Ethnic and Geographical Identities in the Medieval and Early Modern Period." *William and Mary Quarterly,* 3rd ser., 54, no. 1 (January 1997): 103–42.

Brauner, Siegmund. "Carl Meinhof und Wilhelm Wundt." In *Sprachkulturelle und historische Forschungen in Afrika: Beiträge zum 11. Afrikanistentag, Köln. 19.–21. September 1994,* edited by Axel Fleisch and Dirk Otten, 59–69. Cologne: Rüdiger Köppe Verlag, 1995.

Breckenridge, Carl, and Peter van der Veer, eds. *Orientalism and the Postcolonial Predicament: Perspectives on South Asia.* Philadelphia: University of Pennsylvania Press, 1993.

Breckenridge, Keith. "Verwoerd's Bureau of Proof: Total Information in the Making of Apartheid." *History Workshop Journal,* no. 59 (2005): 83–108.

Bruch, Rüdiger vom, Friedrich Wilhelm Graf, and Gangolf Hübinger, eds. *Kultur und Kulturwissenschaften um 1900: Krise der Moderne und Glaube an die Wissenschaft.* Stuttgart: Franz Steiner Verlag Wiesbaden GmbH, 1989.

Bruckner, Sierra. "The Tingle-Tangle of Modernity: Popular Anthropology and the Cultural Politics of Identity in Imperial Germany." PhD Diss., University of Iowa, Iowa City, 1999.

Bryant, Edwin. *The Quest for the Origins of Vedic Culture: The Indo-Aryan Migration Debate.* Oxford: Oxford University Press, 2001.

Bückendorf, Jutta. *Schwarz-Weiss-Rot über Ostafrika! Deutsche Kolonialpläne und Afrikanische Realität.* Münster: Lit Verlag, 1997.

Bulman, Stephen. "Sunjata as Written Literature: The Role of the Literary Mediator in the Dissemination of the Sunjata Epic." In *In Search of Sunjata: The Mande Oral Epic as History, Literature, and Performance,* edited by Ralph A. Austen. Bloomington: Indiana University Press, 1999.

Bunzl, Matti, and H. Glenn Penny, eds. *Worldly Provincialism: German Anthropology in the Age of Empire.* Ann Arbor: University of Michigan Press, 2003.

Campt, Tina M. "Converging Spectres of an Other Within: Race and Gender in Prewar Afro-German History." *Callaloo* 26, no. 2 (Spring 2003): 322–41.

Cannon, Garland Hampton. *The Life and Mind of Oriental Jones: Sir William Jones, the Father of Modern Linguistics.* Cambridge: Cambridge University Press, 1990.

Canton, William. *A History of the British and Foreign Bible Society.* Vol. 2. London: J. Murray, 1904.

Cheah, Pheng. *Spectral Nationality: Passages of Freedom from Kant to Postcolonial Literatures of Liberation.* New York: Columbia University Press, 2003.

Chickering, Roger. *We Men Who Feel Most German: A Cultural Study of the Pan-German League, 1886–1914.* Boston: George Allen and Unwin, 1984.

Chidester, David. *Savage Systems: Colonialism and Comparative Religion in Southern Africa.* Charlottesville: University of Virginia, 1996.

Christy, Craig. "Uniformitarianism in Nineteenth Century Linguistics: Implications for a Reassessment of the Neogrammarian Sound-Law Doctrine." In *Progress in Linguistic Historiography,* edited by Konrad Koerner, Studies in the History of Linguistic Science III, Studies in the History of Linguistics 20, 249–56. Amsterdam: John Benjamins, 1980.

Ciz, Karl Heinz. *Robert Hartmann (1831–1893): Mitbegründer der deutschen Ethnologie.* Gelsenkirchen: Verlag Andreas Müller, 1984.

Clarke, William Kemp Lowther. *A Short History of S.P.C.K.* New York: Macmillan, 1919.

Clifford, James. *The Predicament of Culture.* Cambridge: Harvard University Press, 1988.

Cocks, Geoffrey, and Konrad Jarausch, eds. *German Professions, 1800–1950.* Oxford: Oxford University Press, 1990.

Cocks, P. "Max Gluckman and the Critique of Segregation in South African Anthropology, 1921–1940." *Journal of Southern African Studies* 27, no. 4 (December 2001): 739–56.

Cohn, Bernard. *Colonialism and Its Forms of Knowledge: The British in India.* Princeton: Princeton University Press, 1996.

Comaroff, Jean, and John Comaroff. *Ethnography and the Historical Imagination.* Boulder: Westview Press, 1992.

Comaroff, Jean, and John Comaroff. *Of Revelation and Revolution: Christianity, Colonialism, and Consciousness in South Africa.* Vol. 1. Chicago: University of Chicago Press, 1991.

Comaroff, Jean, and John Comaroff. *Of Revelation and Revolution: The Dialectics of Modernity on a South African Frontier.* Vol. 2. Chicago: University of Chicago Press, 1995.

Conklin, Alice. *A Mission to Civilize: The Republican Idea of Empire in France and West Africa, 1895–1930.* Stanford: Stanford University Press, 2000.

Conrad, Sebastian. *Globalisierung und Nation im deutschen Kaiserreich.* Munich: C. H. Beck Verlag, 2006.

Conrad, Sebastian, and Jürgen Osterhammel. *Das Kaiserreich transnational: Deutschland in der Welt 1871–1914.* Göttingen: Vandenhoeck & Ruprecht, 2004.

Conser, Walter H. *Church and Confession.* Atlanta: Mercer University Press, 1984.

Cooper, Frederick, and Ann Laura Stoler, eds. *Tensions of Empire: Colonial Cultures in a Bourgeois World.* Berkeley: University of California Press, 1997.

Cram, David, Andrew Linn, and Elke Nowak, eds. *History of Linguistics 1996: Selected Papers from the Seventh International Conference on the History of the Language Sciences* (ICHOLS VII). Vol. 1: Traditions in Linguistics Worldwide. Philadelphia: John Benjamins, 1999.

Crozier, Andrew. *Appeasement and Germany's Last Bid for Colonies.* New York: St. Martin's, 1988.

Curtin, Philip. *The Image of Africa: British Ideas and Action, 1780–1850.* Madison: University of Wisconsin, 1964.

Dammann, Ernst. *70 Jahre erlebte Afrikanistik: ein Beitrag zur Wissenschaftsgeschichte.* Berlin: D. Reimer, 1999.

Dammann, Ernst. "A Tentative Philological Typology of Some African High Deities." *Journal of Religion in Africa* 2 (1969): 81–95.

Dammann, Ernst. "Ein Wichtiges Jubiläum." *Afrika Heute* 24 (1967): 377–88.

Danziger, Kurt. *Constructing the Subject: Historical Origins of Psychological Research.* Cambridge: Cambridge University Press, 1990.

Das Gupta, Tapan Kumar. *Von Kant zu Bastian: Ein Beitrag zum Verständnis des wissenschaftliche Konzepts von Adolf Bastian, mit vier kleinen Schriften von demselben.* Hamburg: Im Selbstverlag, 1990.

Davies, Anna Morpurgo. *History of Linguistics: Nineteenth Century Linguistics.* Vol. 4. Edited by Giulio Lepschy. London: Longman, 1994.

Debrunner, H. *A Church between Colonial Powers: A Study of the Church in Togo.* London: Lutterworth Press, 1965.

Dedering, Tilman. *Hate the Old and Follow the New: Khoekhoe and Missionaries in Early Nineteenth Century Namibia.* Stuttgart: Franz Steiner Verlag, 1997.

Deissman, Adolf. "Hellenistic Greek." In *The New Schaff-Herzog Encyclopedia of Religious Knowledge,* Volume 5, edited by Johann Jakob Herzug, Philip Schaft, and Albert Hauck, 211–15. New York: Funk and Wagnalls, 1909.

Delius, Peter. *The Land Belongs to Us: The Pedi Polity, the Boers, and the British in the Nineteenth Century Transvaal.* Berkeley: University of California Press, 1984.

Desai, Gaurav. *Subject to Colonialism: African Self-Fashioning and the Colonial Library.* Durham: Duke University Press, 2001.

Diekmeyer, Gerhard. *Wort und Gewißheit: Das Schriftprinzip in der Theologie Hermann Cremers.* Witten: R. Brockhaus Verlag, 1999.

Di Gregorio, Mario A. "Reflections of a Nonpolitical Naturalist: Ernst Haeckel, Wilhelm Bleek, Friedrich Müller, and the Meaning of Language." *Journal of the History of Biology* 35 (2002): 79–109.

Dirks, Nicholas B., ed. *Colonialism and Culture.* Ann Arbor: University of Michigan Press, 1992.

Dittrich, Lothar, and Annelore Rieke-Müller, eds. *Carl Hagenbeck (1844–1913): Tierhandel und Schaustellungen im Deutschen Kaiserreich.* New York: Peter Lang, 1998.

Doke, Clement. "The Growth of Comparative Bantu Philology." *African Studies* 2, no. 1 (1943): 41–64.

Drake, Saint-Clair. "Detruire de la mythe chamitique, devoir des hommes cultivés." *Presence Africaine,* Numèro Special (1959): 215–30.

Dubow, Saul. "Afrikaner Nationalism, Apartheid, and the Conceptualization of 'Race.'" *Journal of African History* 33 (1992): 209–37.

Dubow, Saul. *Scientific Racism in Modern South Africa.* Cambridge: Cambridge University Press, 1995.

Duignan, Peter, and Lewis Henry Gann. *The Rulers of German Africa, 1884–1914.* Stanford: Stanford University Press, 1977.

Durham, Clinton DeWitt. "Leo Frobenius and the Reorientation of German Ethnology, 1890–1930." PhD diss., Stanford, CA, 1985.

Du Toit, Brian M. "Missionaries, Anthropologists, and the Policies of the Dutch Reformed Church." *Journal of Modern African Studies* 22, no. 4 (December 1984): 617–32.

Ebr.-Vally, Rehana. *Kala Pani: Caste and Colour in South Africa.* Colorado Springs: International Academic Publishers, 2001.

Efron, John M. *Defenders of the Race: Jewish Doctors and Race Science in Fin-de-Siècle Europe.* New Haven: Yale University Press, 1994.

Eggert, Johanna. *Missionsschule und sozialer Wandel in Ostafrika; der Beitrag der deutschen evangelischen Missionsgesellschaften zur Entwicklung des Schulwesens in Tanganyika 1891–1939.* Bielefeld: Bertelsmann, 1970.

Ehret, Christopher. *Southern Nilotic History: Linguistic Approaches to the Study of the Past.* Evanston: Northwestern University Press, 1971.

Eigen, Sara, and Mark Joseph Larrimore, eds. *The German Invention of Race.* Binghamton: SUNY Press, 2006.

Eiselen, Tobias. "Der Missionar und seine Rolle: evangelische missionsgeschichtliche Untersuchung zur Missionarsausbildung und Praxis, dargestellt an Jakob Andreas Spieth (1856–1914)." Hamburg Univ., Mag.-Schr., 1987.

Elbourne, Elizabeth, and Robert Ross. "Combating Spiritual and Social Bondage: Early Missions in the Cape Colony." In *Christianity in South Africa: A Political, Social, and Cultural History,* edited by Richard Elphick and Rodney Davenport. Berkeley: University of California Press, 1997.

Eley, Geoff. *Reshaping the German Right: Radical Nationalism and Political Change after Bismarck.* Ann Arbor: University of Michigan Press, 1991.

Eley, Geoff, and James N. Retallack, eds. *Wilhelminism and Its Legacies: German Modernities, Imperialism, and the Meanings of Reform, 1890–1930; Essays for Hartmut Pogge von Strandmann.* Oxford: Berghahn Books, 2003.

Elphick, Richard, and Rodney Davenport, eds. *Christianity in South Africa: A Political, Social, and Cultural History.* Berkeley: University of California Press, 1997.

El-Tayeb, Fatima. *Schwarze deutsche.: Der Diskurs um Rasse und nationale Identität 1890–1933.* Frankfurt am Main: Campus Verlag, 2001.

Engel, Lothar. *Kolonialismus und Nationalismus im deutschen Protestantismus in Namibia 1907 bis 1945.* Beiträge zur deutschen evangelischen Mission und Kirche im ehemaligen Kolonial- und Mandatsgebiet Südwestafrika. Frankfurt am Main: Peter Lang, 1976.

Ernst, Christina, and Sabine Tischer. "Die Ausstellung der Kolonisierten." In *Andenken an den Kolonialismus,* edited by Völker Harms, Ausstellungskataloge der Universität Tübingen 17. Tübingen: ATTEMPTO, 1984.

Essner, Cornelia. *Deutsche Afrikareisende im neunzehnten Jahrhundert: Zur Sozialgeschichte des Reisens.* Stuttgart: Steiner, 1985.

Etherington, Norman. "Kingdoms of This World and the Next: Christian Beginnings among Zulu and Swazi." In *Christianity in South Africa: A Political, Social, and Cultural History,* edited by Richard Elphick and Rodney Davenport, 89–106. Berkeley: University of California Press, 1997.

Etherington, Norman, ed. *Missions and Empire: The Oxford History of the British Empire Companion Series.* Oxford: Oxford University Press, 2005.

Evans, Andrew. "Anthropology at War: Racial Studies of POWs during World War I." In *Worldly Provincialism: German Anthropology in the Age of Empire,* edited by Matti Bunzl and H. Glenn Penny, 198–229. Ann Arbor: University of Michigan Press, 2003.

Evans, Ivan. *Bureaucracy and Race: Native Administration in South Africa.* Berkeley: University of California Press, 1997.

Evans, William McKee. "From the Land of Canaan to the Land of Guinea: The Strange Odyssey of the 'Sons of Ham.'" *American Historical Review* 85, no. 1 (February 1980): 15–43.

Evrigenis, Ioannis D., and Daniel Pellerin, eds. "Introduction." In J. G. Herder, *Another Philosophy of History and Selected Political Writings,* ix–xxxix. Indianapolis: Hackett, 2004.

Fabian, Johannes. *Language and Colonial Power.* Berkeley: University of California Press, 1986.

Fabian, Johannes. *Out of Our Minds: Reason and Madness in the Exploration of Central Africa.* Berkeley: University of California Press, 2000.

Fabian, Johannes. *Time and the Other: How Anthropology Makes Its Object.* New York: Columbia University Press, 1983.

Fabian, Johannes. *Time and the Work of Anthropology: Critical Essays, 1971–1991.* Amsterdam: Harwood Academic Publishers, 1996. First published 1991.

Fenton, James. "A Short History of Anti-Hamitism." Review of Gérard Prunier, *The Rwanda Crisis: History of a Genocide* (New York: Columbia, 1995). *New York Review of Books* 43, no. 3 (February 15, 1996): 7–8.

Ferguson, Niall. *Paper and Iron: Hamburg Business and German Politics in the Era of Inflation, 1897–1927.* Cambridge: Cambridge University Press, 2002.

Fiedler, Klaus. *Christianity and African Culture: Conservative German Protestant Missionaries in Tanzania, 1909–1940.* Leiden: E. J. Brill, 1996.

Fitzpatrick, Matthew. *Liberal Imperialism in Germany: Expansionism and Nationalism, 1848–1884.* Oxford: Berghahn Books, 2008.

Foucault, Michel. *The Archaeology of Knowledge and the Discourse on Language.* New York: Pantheon, 1982.

Foucault, Michel. *Discipline and Punish: The Birth of the Prison.* Reprint ed. New York: Vintage, 1995.

Frankl, P. J. L. "The Word for God in Swahili." *Journal of Religion in Africa* 20, no. 3 (1990): 269–75.

Friedrichsmeyer, Sara, Sara Lennox, and Susanne Zantop, eds. *The Imperialist Imagination: German Colonialism and Its Legacy.* Ann Arbor: University of Michigan Press, 1998.

Fulbrook, Mary. *Piety and Politics: Religion and the Rise of Absolutism in England, Württemburg, and Prussia.* Cambridge: Cambridge University Press, 1983.

Funcke, E. W. "Schwarze Märchen—Weiße Feder: Weiße Sammler des Erzählgutes der schwarzen Gemeinschaften im südlichen Afrika." *South African Journal of Cultural History* 6, no. 1 (1992): 1–12.

Fyle, C. Magbaily. *Historical Dictionary of Sierra Leone.* Lanham, MD: Rowman and Littlefield, 2006.

Gann, L. H. "Economic Development in Germany's African Empire." In *Colonialism in Africa, 1870–1960,* edited by L. H. Gann and Peter Duignan, 213–55. Cambridge: Cambridge University Press, 1975.

Gates, Henry Louis, Jr., ed. *"Race," Writing, and Difference.* Chicago: University of Chicago Press, 1986.

Geisenhainer, Katja. *"Rasse ist Schicksal": Otto Reche (1879–1966)—ein Leben als Anthropologe und Volkerkundler.* Leipzig: Evangelische Verlagsanstalt, 2002.

Gensichen, Hans-Werner. "German Protestant Missions." In *Missionary Ideologies in the Imperialist Era, 1880–1920,* edited by Torben Christensen and William R. Hutchison, 181–90. Aarhus, Denmark: Aros, 1982.

Gensichen, Hans-Werner. "Jänicke, Johann." In *Biographical Dictionary of Christian Missions,* edited by Gerald H.Anderson. Grand Rapids, MI: Eerdmans, 1999.

Gerhardt, Ludwig. "The Place of Carl Meinhof in African Linguistics." *Afrika und Übersee* 78 (1995): 163–75.

Giliomee, Hermann. *The Afrikaners: Biography of a People.* Charlottesville: University of Virgina Press, 2003.

Giliomee, Hermann. "The Growth of Afrikaner Identity." In *Segregation and Apartheid in Twentieth-Century South Africa,* edited by W. Beinart and S. Dubow, 189–205. London: Routledge, 1995.

Giliomee, Hermann. "The Making of the Apartheid Plan, 1929–1948." *Journal of Southern African Studies* 29, no. 2 (2003): 373–92.

Gilmour, Rachael. "'A Nice Derangement of Epitaphs': Missionary Language Learning in mid-Nineteenth Century Natal." *Journal of Southern African Studies* 33, no. 3 (September 2007): 521–38.

Gordon, Robert. *The Bushman Myth: The Making of a Namibian Underclass.* Boulder: Westview, 1992.

Gordon, Robert. "Early Social Anthropology in South Africa." *African Studies* 49, no. 1 (1990): 15–48.

Gordon, Robert. "Serving the *Volk* with *Volkekunde:* On the Rise of South African Antropology." In *Knowledge and Power in South Africa,* edited by J. Jansen. Johannesburg: Skotaville, 1991.

Gordon, R., and A. D. Spiegel. "Southern Africa Revisited." *Annual Review of Anthropology* 22 (1993): 83–105.

Gothsch, Manfred. *Die deutsche Völkerkunde und ihr Verhältnis zum Kolonialismus.* Baden-Baden: Nomos Verlagsgesellschaft, 1983.

Gould, Stephen J. *The Mismeasure of Man.* Revised and expanded edition. New York: W. W. Norton, 1996.

Gourevitch, Philip. *We Wish to Inform You that Tomorrow We Will Be Killed with Our Families: Stories from Rwanda.* New York: Picador, 1998.

Greenberg, Joseph. *The Languages of Africa.* Bloomington: Indiana University Press, 1966.

Greenblatt, Stephen. *Marvelous Possessions: The Wonder of the New World.* Chicago: University of Chicago Press, 1991.

Griefenow-Mewis, Catherine. "J. L. Krapf and His Role in Researching and Describing East African Languages." In *Swahili: Forum III (Afrikanische Arbeitspapiere, No. 47)*, edited by Rose Marie Beck, Thomas Geider, and Werner Graebner, 157–64. Cologne: Institut für Afrikanische, Universitäat Köln, 1996.

Grimm, Hans. "Felix von Luschan als Anthropologe: Von der Kraniologie zur Humanbiologie." *Ethnographische.-Archäologische Zeitschrift* 27 (1986): 415–25.

Grosse, Pascal. *Kolonialismus, Eugenik und bürgerliche Gesellschaft in Deutschland 1850–1918.* Frankfurt am Main: Campus Verlag, 2000.

Gründer, Horst. *Christliche Mission und deutscher Imperialismus: eine politische Geschichte ihrer Beziehungen während der deutschen Kolonialzeit (1884–1914) unter besonderer Berücksichtigung Afrikas und Chinas.* Paderborn: Schöningh, 1982.

Guha, Ranit, and Gayatri Chakrvorty Spivak, eds. *Selected Subaltern Studies.* New York: Oxford University Press, 1988.

Gupta, Akhil, and James Ferguson. *Anthropological Locations: Boundaries and Grounds of a Field Science.* Berkeley: University of California Press, 1997.

Haeberlin, Herman K. "The Theoretical Foundations of Wundt's Folk Psychology." In *Wilhelm Wundt and the Making of a Scientific Psychology,* edited by Arthur L. Blumenthal, Kurt Danziger, Solomon Diamond, and R. W. Rieber, 229–49. New York: Plenum Press, 1980. First published 1916.

Haenicke, Gunta. *Zur Geschichte der Anglistik an deutschsprachigen Universitäten 1850–1925.* Augsburg: Universität Augsburg, 1979.

Hair, P. E. H. *The Early Study of Nigerian Languages: Essays and Bibliographies.* Cambridge: Cambridge University Press, 1967.

Hall, Catherine. *Civilizing Subjects: Colony and Metropole in the English Imagination, 1830–1867.* Chicago: University of Chicago Press, 2002.

Hammond-Tooke, W. D. *Imperfect Interpreters: South Africa's Anthropologists, 1920–1990.* Johannesburg: Witwatersrand University Press, 1997.

Hammond-Tooke, W. D. "N. J. van Warmelo and the Ethnological Section: A Memoir." *African Studies* 54 (January 1995): 119–28.

Hardcastle, W. J. "Experimental Studies in Lingual Coarticulation." In *Towards a History of Phonetics,* edited by R. E. Asher and Eugénie J. A. Henderson. Edinburgh: University Press, 1981.

Harms, Volker, ed. *Andenken an den Kolonialismus: Eine Ausstellung des Völkerkundlichen Instituts der Universität Tübingen.* Tübingen: Attempto Verlag, 1984.

Harries, Patrick. *Butterflies and Barbarians: Swiss Missionaries and Systems of Knowledge in South-East Africa.* Johannesburg: Witwatersrand University Press, 2007.

Harries, Patrick. "The Roots of Ethnicity: Discourse and the Politics of Language Construction in South-East Africa." *African Affairs: Journal of the Royal African Society* 87, no. 346 (1988): 25–52.

Hassing, Per. "German Missionaries and the Maji Maji Rising." *African Studies Review* 3, no. 2 (1970): 373–89.

Hastings, Adrian. *The Church in Africa, 1450–1950.* Oxford: Oxford University Press, 1996.

Headrick, Daniel. *The Tentacles of Progress: Technology Transfer in the Age of Imperialism, 1850–1940.* Oxford: Oxford University Press, 1988.

Heine, Bernd, Thilo C. Schadeberg, and Ekkehard Wolff, eds. *Die Sprachen Afrikas: mit zahlreichen Karten und Tabellen.* Hamburg: Buske, 1981.

Heintze, Beatrix. "Ethnographic Appropriations: German Exploration and Fieldwork in West-Central Africa." *History in Africa* 26 (1999): 69–128.

Henderson, William O. *Studies in German Colonial History.* 2nd ed. London: Routledge, 1976.

Hering, Rainer. "Meinhof, Carl Friedrich Michael." In the *Biographisch-Bibliographisches Kirchenlexikon,* Band XVII. Herzberg: Verlag Traugott Bautz, 2000.

Hillebrecht, Werner, and Henning Melber. "Von den deutschen verschleppt: Spurensicherung." In *Ein Land, Eine Zukunft: Namibia auf dem Weg in die Unabhängigkeit,* 132–51. Wuppertal: Peter Hammer Verlag, 1988.

Hofbauer, Andreas. "Von Rasse zu Identität: Vom Ringen um Paradigmen in der 'Wissenschaft vom anderen.'" *Anthropos* 92 (1997): 569–77.

Hoffmann, Walter K. H. *Vom Kolonialexperten zum Experten der Entwicklungszusammenarbeit: acht Fallstudien zur Geschichte der Ausbildung von Fachkräften für Übersee in Deutschland und in der Schweiz.* Saarbrücken: Verlag Breitenbach, 1980.

Hofmeyr, Isabel. *"We Spend Our Years as a Tale that Is Told": Oral Historical Narrative in a South African Chiefdom.* Portsmouth, NH: Heinemann, 1993.

Hole, Charles. *The Early History of the Church Missionary Society, for Africa and the East, to the End of A.D. 1814.* London: Church Missionary Society, 1896.

Hopkins, A. G. "'The New International Economic Order in the Nineteenth Century': Britain's First Development Plan for Africa." In *From Slave Trade to Legitimate Commerce: The Commercial Transition in Nineteenth Century West Africa,* edited by Robin Law, 240–64. Cambridge: Cambridge University Press, 1995.

Hoyt, David L., and Karen Oslund, eds. *The Study of Language and the Politics of Community in Global Context.* Lanham, MD: Lexington Books, 2006.

Hübler, Dominique. *Die Zentralstelle des Hamburgischen Kolonialinstituts.* Hausarbeit zur Diplomprüfung. Hamburg, January 1991.

Hugo, Pierre. "Transformation: The Changing Context of Academia in Post-Apartheid South Africa." *African Affairs* 97, no. 386 (January 1998): 5–27.

Hull, Isabel V. *Absolute Destruction: Military Culture and the Practices of War in Imperial Germany.* Ithaca: Cornell University Press, 2006.

Hyam, Ronald, and Peter Henshaw, eds. *The Lion and the Springbok: Britain and South Africa since the Boer War.* Cambridge: Cambridge University Press, 2003.

Iliffe, John. *A Modern History of Tanganyika.* Cambridge: Cambridge University Press, 1979.

Irvine, Judith T. "Mastering African Languages: The Politics of Linguistics in Nineteenth-Century Senegal." *Social Analysis* 33 (September 1993): 27–46.

Isichei, Elizabeth. *A History of Christianity in Africa: From Antiquity to the Present.* Grand Rapids, MI: William B. Eerdmans, 1995.

Jacobi, Angelika. *A Fur Grammar: Phonology, Morphophonology, and Morphology.* Tübingen: Helmut Buske Verlag, 1990.

James, Harold. *A German Identity, 1770–1990*. London: Weidenfeld & Nicolson, 1989.

Jankowsky, Kurt. *The Neogrammarians: A Re-evaluation of Their Place in the Development of Linguistic Science*. Pre-publication edition. Washington, DC: Georgetown University, 1968.

Jarausch, Konrad H., ed. *The Transformation of Higher Learning, 1860–1930*. Chicago: University of Chicago Press, 1983.

Jarausch, Konrad H., ed. *The Unfree Professions: German Lawyers, Teachers, and Engineers, 1800–1950*. New York: Oxford University Press, 1990.

Jeal, Tim. *Stanley: The Impossible Life of Africa's Greatest Explorer*. New Haven: Yale University Press, 2008.

Jeannerat, Caroline. *The Classification of Tradition in van Warmelo's Writing*. Unpublished seminar paper, University of the Witwatersrand, Johannesburg, 1998.

Jeannerat, Caroline. "An Ethnography of Faith: Personal Conceptions of Religiosity in the Zoutpansberg, South Africa in the Nineteenth and Twentieth Centuries." PhD diss., University of Michigan, Ann Arbor, 2007.

Jefferies, Matthew. *Contesting the German Empire, 1871–1918*. Oxford: Blackwell, 2008.

Jeffreys, M. D. W. "The Batwa: Who Are They?" *Africa* 23, no. 1 (January 1953): 45–54.

Jenkins, Jennifer. "German Orientalism: Introduction." *Comparative Studies of South Asia, Africa, and the Middle East* 24, no. 2 (2004): 97–100.

Jenkins, Jennifer. *Provincial Modernity: Local Culture and Liberal Politics in Fin-de-Siècle Hamburg*. Ithaca: Cornell University Press, 2003.

Jenkins, Paul. "The Church Missionary Society and the Basel Mission: An Early Experiment in Inter-European Cooperation." In *The Church Mission Society and World Christianity, 1799–1999*, edited by Kevin Ward and Brian Stanley. Grand Rapids, MI: William B. Eerdmans, 2000.

Julien, Charles-André, ed. *Les Africains*. Paris: Éditions J.A., 1977.

Jungraithmayr, Hermann. *Was ist Primitiv? Zum Stand der Sprachgeschichtsforschung in Afrika*. Stuttgart: Franz Steiner Verlag Wiesbaden GMBH, 1987.

Jungraithmayr, Hermann, and Wilhelm G. Möhlig, eds. *Lexikon der Afrikanistik: Afrikanische Sprachen und ihre Erforschung*. Berlin: Dietrich Reimer, 1983.

Kallaway, P. "F. S. Malan, the Cape Liberal Tradition, and South African Politics, 1908–1924." *Journal of African History* 15, no. 1 (1974): 113–29.

Karttunen, Francis. *Between Worlds: Interpreters, Guides, and Survivors*. New Brunswick: Rutgers University, 1994.

Katz, Jacob. *The Darker Side of Genius: Richard Wagner's Anti-Semitism*. Waltham, MA: Brandeis University Press, 1986.

Kern, Franz. *Ludwig Giesebrecht als Dichter, Gelehrter, und Schulmann*. Stettin: Th. von der Nahmer, 1875.

Kirkaldy, Alan. *Capturing the Soul: The Vhavenda and the Missionaries*. Pretoria: Protea, 2005.

Klotz, Marcia. "Introduction" and "Global Visions from the Colonial to the National Socialist World." *European Studies Journal* 16 (Fall 1999): 1–8, 37–68.

Knappert, Jan. "Origin and Development of the Concept of Hamitic: The First Sixty Years: 1851–1911." *Orientalia Lovaniensia Periodica* 6–7 (1975–76): 303–20.

Koepping, Klaus-Peter. *Adolf Bastian and the Psychic Unity of Mankind: The Foundations of Anthropology in Nineteenth Century Germany.* St. Lucia: University of Queensland, 1983.

Koepping, Klaus-Peter. "Enlightenment and Romanticism in the Work of Adolf Bastian: The Historical Roots of Anthropology in the Nineteenth Century." In *Fieldwork and Footnotes: Studies in the History of European Anthropology,* edited by Arturo Alvarez Roldán and Hans F. Vermeulen. London: Routledge, 1995.

Koerner, Konrad. "Introduction" to August Schleicher, *Die Sprachen Europas in systematischer Übersicht und linguistische Untersuchungen,* XXIX. Amsterdam: Benjamins Publishing Company, 1983.

Kohler, K. "Three Trends in Phonetics: The Development of Phonetics as a Discipline in Germany since the Nineteenth Century." In *Towards a History of Phonetics,* edited by R. E. Asher and Eugénie J. A. Henderson. Edinburgh: University Press, 1981.

Kontje, Todd. *German Orientalisms.* Ann Arbor: University of Michigan Press, 2004.

Kopp, Kristin. "Constructing Racial Difference in Colonial Poland." In *Germany's Colonial Pasts,* edited by Eric Ames, Marcia Klotz, and Lora Wildenthal. Lincoln: University of Nebraska Press, 2005.

Kössler, Reinhart. "From Reserve to Homeland: Local Identities and South African Policy in Southern Namibia." *Journal of Southern African Studies* 26, no. 3 (September 2000): 447–62.

Kros, Cynthia. *Economic, Political, and Intellectual Origins of Bantu Education.* PhD diss., University of the Wiwatersrand, Johannesburg, 1996.

Kros, Cynthia. *Eiselen: Idealists and Idealism Revisited.* Unpublished seminar paper presented to SACHES. Scottburgh, October 1993.

Kros, Cynthia. "W. W. M. Eiselen: Architect of Apartheid Education." In *The History of Education under Apartheid, 1948–1994,* edited by Peter Kallaway, 53–73. New York: Peter Lang, 2002.

Kuklick, Henrika. "After Ishmael: The Fieldwork Tradition and Its Future." In *Anthropological Locations: Boundaries and Grounds of a Field Science,* edited by Akhil Gupta and James Ferguson. Berkeley: University of California Press, 1997.

Kuklick, Henrika. "Contested Monuments: The Politics of Archaeology in Southern Africa." In *Colonial Situations: Essays on the Contextualization of Ethnographic Knowledge,* edited by George Stocking. Madison: University of Wisconsin Press, 1991.

Kuklick, Henrika. *The Savage Within: The Social History of British Anthropology, 1885–1945.* Cambridge: Cambridge University Press, 1991.

Kuklick, Henrika, and Robert E. Kohler. *Science in the Field.* Chicago: University of Chicago Press, 1996. *Osiris,* 2nd series, vol. 11.

Kundrus, Birthe. *Moderne Imperialisten: Das Kaiserreich im Spiegel seiner Kolonien.* Cologne: Böhlau, 2003.

Kundrus, Birthe, ed. *Phantasiereiche: Zur Kulturgeschichte des deutschen Kolonialismus.* Frankfurt am Main: Campus, 2003.

Kuper, Adam. *Anthropology and Anthropologists: The Modern British School.* 3rd ed. London: Routledge, 1996, 1973.

Kuper, Adam. *Culture: The Anthropologist's Account.* Cambridge: Harvard University Press, 1999.

Larson, Pier M. "'Capacities and Modes of Thinking': Intellectual Engagements and Subaltern Hegemony in the Early History of Malagasy Christianity." *American Historical Review* 102, no. 4 (1997): 969–1002.

Last, Murray. *The Sokoto Caliphate.* New York: Humanities Press, 1967.

Latour, Bruno, and Steve Woolgar. *Laboratory Life: The Construction of Scientific Facts.* Princeton: Princeton University Press, 1986. First published 1979.

Lau, Brigitte. "Conflict and Power in Nineteenth Century Namibia." *Journal of African History* 27, no. 1 (1986): 29–39.

Laue, Theodor H. von. "R. S. Rattray among the Ashanti." *African Affairs* 75 (1976): 33–54.

Legassick, Martin. "Legislation, Ideology, and Economy in Post-1948 South Africa." *Journal of Southern African Studies* 1, no. 1 (October 1974): 5–35.

Lekgoathi, Sekibakiba Peter. "Chiefs, Migrants and North Ndebele Ethnicity in the Context of Surrounding Homeland Politics, 1965–1978." *African Studies* 62, no. 1 (July 2003): 53–77.

Lemarchand, Rene, with Lee H. Hamilton. *Burundi: Ethnic Conflict and Genocide.* Cambridge: Cambridge University Press, 1996.

Leopold, Joan. *The Prix Volney.* New York: Springer, 1999.

Liebersohn, Harry. *Aristocratic Encounters: European Travelers and North American Indians.* Cambridge: Cambridge University Press, 1998.

Lindfors, Bernth. *Africans on Stage: Studies in Ethnological Show Business.* Bloomington: Indiana University Press, 1999.

Liss, Julia. "German Culture and German Science in the *Bildung* of Franz Boas." In Volksgeist *as Method and Ethic: Essays on Boasian Ethnography and the German Anthropological Tradition,* edited by George Stocking, 185–214. Madison: University of Wisconsin Press, 1996.

Ludden, David. "Orientalist Empiricism: Transformations of Colonial Knowledge." In *Orientalism and the Postcolonial Predicament: Perspectives on South Asia,* edited by Carl Breckenridge and Peter van der Veer. Philadelphia: University of Pennsylvania Press, 1993.

Lukas, Johannes, Ernst Dammann, and Dieter Schröder. *Afrikanische Sprachen und Kulturen—der Hamburger Beitrag zu ihrer Erforschung.* Special edition of the *Mitteilungen der Geographischen Gesellschaft in Hamburg.* Band 56 (1965): 151–79.

Mabin, Alan. "Comprehensive Segregation: The Origins of the Group Areas Act and Its Planning Apparatuses." *Journal of Southern African Studies* 18, no. 2 (1992): 405–29.

Mamdani, Mahmood. *Citizen and Subject: Contemporary Africa and the Legacy of Late Colonialism.* Princeton: Princeton University Press, 1996.

Mamdani, Mahmood. *When Victims Become Killers: Colonialism, Nativism, and the Genocide in Rwanda.* Princeton: Princeton University Press, 2001.

Mannheim, Bruce. *The Language of the Inka Since the European Invasion.* Austin: University of Texas, 1991.

Marchand, Suzanne. *Down from Olympus: Archaeology and Philhellenism in Germany, 1750–1970*. Princeton: Princeton University Press, 1996.

Marchand, Suzanne. "German Orientalism and the Decline of the West." *Proceedings of the American Philosophical Society,* December 2001.

Marchand, Suzanne. "Leo Frobenius and the Revolt Against the West." *Journal of Contemporary History* 32, no. 2 (1997): 153–70.

Marchand, Suzanne. "Priests among the Pygmies: Wilhelm Schmidt and the Counter-Reformation in Austrian Ethnology." In *Worldly Provincialism: German Anthropology in the Age of Empire,* edited by Matti Bunzl and H. Glenn Penny. Ann Arbor: University of Michigan Press, 2003.

Martin, Roger. "Anglicans and Baptists in Conflict: The Bible Society, Bengal, and the Baptizo Controversy." *Journal of Ecclesiastical History* 49, no. 2 (1998): 293–316.

Marx, Christoph. *Völker ohne Schrift und Geschichte: zur historischen Erfassung des vorkolonialen Schwarzafrika in der deutschen Forschung des 19. und frühen 20. Jahrhunderts.* Stuttgart: F. Steiner Verlag, 1988.

Massaquoi, Hans J. *Destined to Witness: Growing Up Black in Nazi Germany.* New York: HarperCollins, 2001.

Massin, Benoit. "From Virchow to Fischer: Physical Anthropology and 'Modern Race Theories' in Wilhelmine Germany." In Volksgeist *as Method and Ethic: Essays on Boasian Ethnography and the German Anthropological Tradition,* edited by George Stocking, 79–154. Madison: University of Wisconsin Press, 1996.

Mazrui, Ali A. "The Re-invention of Africa: Edward Said, V. Y. Mudimbe, and Beyond." *Research in African Literatures* 36, no. 3 (Fall 2005): 68–82.

McClelland, Charles E. "Professionalization and Higher Education in Germany." In *The Transformation of Higher Learning, 1860–1930,* edited by Konrad H. Jarausch, 306–20. Chicago: University of Chicago Press, 1983.

McGetchin, Douglas, Peter K. J. Park, and Damodar SarDesai, eds. *Sanskrit and "Orientalism": Indology and Comparative Linguistics in Germany, 1750–1958.* New Delhi: Manohar, 2004.

Meier, Wilma. *Diedrich Westermann: Erforscher afrikanischer Sprachen und Kulturen.* Bremen: W. Meier, 1994.

Meinert, Wolfgang. "The Language Question in the Colonial Policy of German Imperialism." In *African Studies-Afrika Studien,* edited by Thea Büttner and Gerhard Brehme. Berlin: Akademie Verlag, 1973.

Menn, Walter, ed. *Pommersche Lebensbilder.* Bd. 4. Cologne, 1966.

Menzel, Gustav. *C. G. Büttner: Missionar, Sprachforscher und Politiker in der deutschen Kolonialbewegung.* Wuppertal: Verlag der Vereinigten Evangelischen Mission, 1995.

Menzel, Gustav. *Die Rheinische Mission. Aus 150 Jahren Missionsgeschichte.* Wuppertal: Verlag der Vereinigten Evangelischen Mission, 1978.

Mesthrie, Rajend. *Language in South Africa.* Cambridge: Cambridge University Press, 2002.

Mesthrie, Rajend. "Words Across Worlds: Aspects of Language Contact and Language Learning in the Eastern Cape, 1800–1850." *African Studies* 57, no. 1 (July 1998): 5–26.

Meyer, Birgit. *Translating the Devil: Religion and Modernity among the Ewe in Ghana.* Trenton, NJ: Africa World Press, 1999.

Meyer, Emmi. "Das Werk von Carl Meinhof. Dargestellt in seinen Schriften." *Zeitschrift für Eingeborenen-Sprachen* 34 (1944): 131–72.

Meyer-Bahlburg, Hilke, and Ekkehard Wolff, eds. *Afrikanische Sprachen in Forschung und Lehre: 75 Jahre Afrikanistik in Hamburg (1909–1984).* Berlin: Dietrich Reimer, 1986.

Michalove, Peter, Stefan Georg, and Alexis Manaster Rames. "Current Issues in Linguistic Taxonomy." *Annual Review of Anthropology* 27 (October 1998): 451–72.

Middleton, John. *The World of the Swahili: An African Mercantile Civilization.* New Haven: Yale University Press, 1994.

Miehe, Gudrun. "Historical Relations between African Language Studies and General Linguistics." *Paideuma: Mitteilungen zur Kulturkunde* 42 (1996).

Miller, Christopher. *Theories of Africans: Francophone Literature and Anthropology in Africa.* Chicago: University of Chicago Press, 1990.

Miller, Jon. *Missionary Zeal and Institutional Control: Organizational Contradictions in the Basel Mission on the Gold Coast, 1828–1917.* London: Routledge/Curzon, 2003.

Mitchell, Timothy. *Colonising Egypt.* Cambridge: Cambridge University Press, 1988.

Möhle, Heiko. *Branntwein, Bibeln, und Bananen: der deutsche Kolonialismus—eine Spurensuche (in Hamburg).* Hamburg: Libertäre Assoz., 1999.

Moodie, T. Dunbar. *The Rise of Afrikanerdom: Power, Apartheid, and the Afrikaner Civil Religion.* Berkeley: University of California Press, 1975.

Morgenroth, Wolfgang. "Das Seminar für Orientalische Sprachen in der Wissenschaftstradition der Sektion Asienwissenschaften der HUB." In *Das "Seminar für Orientalische Sprachen" in der Wissenschaftstradition der Sektion Asienwissenschaften der Humboldt-Universität zu Berlin,* edited by Hannelore Bernhardt. Berlin: Beiträge zur Geschichte der Humboldt-Universität zu Berlin, Nr. 25, 1990.

Mosse, George. *The Crisis of German Ideology: Intellectual Origins of the Third Reich.* New York: Schocken, 1964.

Mudimbe, V. Y. *The Invention of Africa: Gnosis, Philosophy, and the Order of Knowledge.* Bloomington: Indiana University Press, 1988.

Naipaul, V. S. *The Mimic Men.* Penguin Books: London, 1967.

Naranch, Bradley D. "Return of the Natives: Regulating the African Presence in Imperial Germany, 1884–1907." Unpublished conference paper, African Studies Association 44th Annual Meeting, Houston, November 2001.

Norval, Aletta J. *Deconstructing Apartheid Discourse.* London: Verso, 1996.

Nurse, Derek, and Thomas Spear. *The Swahili: Reconstructing the History and Language of an African Society, 800–1500.* Philadelphia: University of Pennsylvania Press, 1985.

O'Donnell, Krista, Renate Bridenthal, and Nancy Ruth Reagin, eds. *The Heimat Abroad: The Boundaries of Germanness.* Ann Arbor: University of Michigan Press, 2005.

Oermann, Nils Ole. *Mission, Church, and State Relations in South West Africa under German Rule (1884–1915)*. Stuttgart: Franz Steiner, 1999.

Oguntoye, Katharina. *Eine Afro-Deutsche Geschichte: zur Lebenssituation von Afrikanern und Afro-Deutsche in Deutschland, 1884–1950*. Berlin: Hoho-Verl. Hoffmann, 1997.

Olender, Maurice. *The Languages of Paradise: Race, Religion, and Philology in the Nineteenth Century*. Translated by Arthur Goldhammer. Cambridge: Harvard University Press, 1992.

Pakendorf, Gunther. "'For There is no Power but of God': The Berlin Mission and the Challenges of Colonial South Africa." *Missionalia* 25 (1997): 255–73.

Pakendorf, Gunther. "Wort, Schrift, Kultur: Überlegungen zu Christianisierung und Verschriftlichung am Beispiel der Berliner Mission in Südafrika." *Zeitschrift für Germanistik*, Neue Folge 3 (1998): 590–99.

Parkinson, Sonia F. G. "Sir Hanns Vischer, Champion of African Cultures: A Portrait of an Adviser on Colonial Education." In *Colonial Educators: The British Indian and Colonial Education Service, 1858–1953*, edited by Clive Whitehead, 106–48. London: I. B. Tauris, 2003.

Pedersen, Holger. *The Discovery of Language: Linguistic Science in the Nineteenth Century*. Translated by John Webster Spargo. Bloomington: Indiana University Press, 1962. First published 1959.

Peires, J. "Ethnicity and Pseudo-Ethnicity in the Ciskei." In *Segregation and Apartheid in Twentieth-Century South Africa*, edited by W. Beinart and S. Dubow, 256–84. London: Routledge, 1995.

Pels, Peter. "Anthropology and Mission: Towards a Historical Analysis of Professional Identity." In *The Ambiguity of Rapprochement: Reflections of Anthropologists on Their Controversial Relationship with Missionaries*, edited by Ronald Bonsen, Hans Marks, and Jelle Miedema. Nijmegen, the Netherlands: Focaal, 1990.

Pels, Peter, and Oscar Salemink, eds. *Colonial Subjects: Essays on the Practical History of Anthropology*. Ann Arbor: University of Michigan Press, 1999.

Penny, H. Glenn. *Objects of Culture: Ethnology and Ethnographic Museums in Imperial Germany*. Chapel Hill: University of North Carolina Press, 2002.

Perras, Arne. *Carl Peters and German Imperialism, 1856–1918: A Political Biography*. Oxford: Clarendon Press, 2004.

Pesek, Michael. *Koloniale Herrschaft in Deutsch-Ostafrika: Expeditionen, Militär und Verwaltung seit 1880*. Frankfurt am Main: Campus Verlag, 2005.

Peterson, Derek. "Translating the Word: Dialogism and Debate in Two Gikuyu Dictionaries." *Journal of Religious History* 23, no. 1 (1999): 31–51.

Phillippson, David. *African Archaeology*. Cambridge: Cambridge University Press, 1993.

Pierard, Richard V. "Shaking the Foundations: World War I, the Western Allies, and German Protestant Missions." *International Bulletin of Missionary Research* (January 1998): 13–19.

Pike, Charles. "History and Imagination: Swahili Literature and Resistance to German Language Imperialism in Tanzania, 1885–1910." *International Journal of African Historical Studies* 19, no. 2 (1986): 201–33.

Pirouet, M. Louise. "The Legacy of Johann Ludwig Krapf." *International Bulletin of Missionary Research* (April 1999): 69–75.

Poliakov, Leon. *The Aryan Myth: A History of Racist and Nationalist Ideas in Europe.* New York: Barnes and Noble, 1971, 1974.

Posel, Deborah. *The Making of Apartheid, 1948–1961: Conflict and Compromise.* London: Clarendon, 1991.

Posel, Deborah. "The Meaning of Apartheid before 1948: Conflicting Forces and Interests within the Afrikaner Nationalist Alliance." *Journal of Southern African Studies* 14, no. 1 (October 1987).

Pratt, Mary Louise. *Imperial Eyes: Travel Writing and Transculturation.* New York: Routledge, 1992.

Pratt, Mary Louise. "Scratches on the Face of the Country; or, what Mr. Barrow saw in the Land of the Bushmen." In *"Race," Writing, and Difference,* edited by Henry Louis Gates Jr. Chicago: University of Chicago Press, 1985, 1986.

Prein, Philipp. "Einleitung des Bearbeiters." In Joseph Busse, *Die Nyakyusa: Religion und Magie.* Monographien zur Völkerkunde, Herausgegeben vom Hamburgischen Museum für Völkerkunde, ca. 1998.

Proctor, Robert. "From Anthropologie to Rassenkunde in the German Anthropological Tradition." In *Bones, Bodies, Behavior: Essays on Biological Anthropology,* edited by George Stocking, 138–79. Madison: University of Wisconsin Press, 1985.

Pugach, Sara. "'Christianize'and Conquer: Carl Meinhof, German Evangelical Missionaries, and the Debate over African Languages, 1905–1910." In *Mission und Gewalt: Der Umgang christlicher Missionen mit Gewalt und die Ausbreitung des Christentums in Afrika und Asien in der Zeit von 1792 bis 1918/1919,* edited by Ulrich van der Heyden and Jürgen Becher, 509–24. Stuttgart: Franz Steiner Verlag, 2000.

Pugach, Sara. "Koelle, Sigismund Wilhelm (1823–1902)." In *Encyclopedia of Language and Linguistics,* edited by Keith Brown, 2nd ed. Amsterdam: Elsevier, 2005.

Pugach, Sara. "Theories of Language and Race in German Studies of Africa." In *Jan Czekanowski: Africanist Ethnographer and Physical Anthropologist in Early Twentieth Century Germany and Poland,* edited by Adam Jones, University of Leipzig Papers on Africa, History, and Culture Series No. 10, 70–102. Leipzig: Institut für Afrikanistik, 2002.

Quinn, F. "Charles Atangana of Yaoundé." *Journal of African History* 21 (1980): 485–95.

Ranger, Terence. "Concluding Comments." In *Ethnicity and Nationalism in Africa: Constructivist Reflections and Contemporary Politics,* edited by Paris Yeros, 133–43. New York: Saint Martin's Press, 1999.

Redmayne, Alison. "Mkwakwa and the Hehe Wars." *Journal of African History* 9, no. 3 (1968): 409–36.

Reed-Anderson, Paulette. *Eine Geschichte von mehr als 100 Jahren: die Anfänge der Afrikanischen Diaspora in Berlin.* Berlin: Ausländerbeauftragte des Senats, 1995.

Reed-Anderson, Paulette. *Metropole, Menschen, Nahaufnahme: Afrikaner in Berlin.* Berlin: Die Ausländerbeauftragte des Senats, 1997.

Reed-Anderson, Paulette. *Rewriting the Footnotes: Berlin und die Afrikanische Diaspora.* Berlin: Ausländerbeauftragte des Senats, 2000.

Reineke, Brigitte. "Afrikanische Sprachen am Seminar für Orientalische Sprachen." In *Beiträge zur Geschichte der Humboldt-Universität zu Berlin,* edited by Hannelore Bernhardt, 64–73. Berlin: Der Rektor, Humboldt-Universität zu Berlin, 1990.

Reineke, Brigitte, and Wolfgang Dodt. "Sprache und Kultur im Werk von Carl Meinhof." *Ethnographische-Archäologische Zeitschrift* 27 (1986): 455–71.

Rekdal, Ole Bjørn. "When Hypothesis Becomes Myth: The Iraqi Origin of the Iraqw." *Ethnology: An International Journal of Cultural and Social Anthropology* 37, no. 1 (Winter 1998): 17–38.

Rennstich, Karl. "Mission—Geschichte der protestantischen Mission in Deutschland." In *Der Pietismus im neunzehnten und zwanstigsten Jahrhundert,* vol. 3, *Geschichte des Pietismus,* edited by Gustav Adolf Benrath, Martin Sallmann, and Ulrich Gäbler, 308–20. Göttingen: Vandenhoeck & Ruprecht, 2000.

Rich, Paul B. *Hope and Despair: English-Speaking Intellectuals and South African Politics, 1896–1976.* London: British Academic Press, 1993.

Ringer, Fritz K. *The Decline of the German Mandarins: The German Academic Community, 1890–1933.* Cambridge: Harvard University Press, 1969.

Rizzo, Lorena. "N. J. van Warmelo: Anthropology and the Making of a Reserve." In *New Notes on Kaoko: The Northern Kunene Region (Namibia) in Texts and Photographs,* edited by G. Miescher and D. Henrichsen, 189–206. Basel: Basler Afrika Bibliographien, 2000.

Robert, Dana Lee, ed. *Converting Colonialism: Visions and Realities in Mission History.* Grand Rapids, MI: Eerdmans, 2008.

Robins, R. H. *A Short History of Linguistics.* London: Longman, 1967.

Roldán, Arturo Alvarez, and Hans F. Vermeulen, eds. *Fieldwork and Footnotes: Studies in the History of European Anthropology.* London: Routledge, 1995.

Roller, Kathrin. "Mission und 'Mischehen,' Erinnerung und Körper—geteiltes Gedächtnis an eine afrikanische Vorfahrin. Über die Familie Schmelen-Kleinschmidt-Hegner." In *Namibia-Deutschland. Eine geteilte Geschichte. Widerstand, Gewalt, Erinnerung,* edited by Larissa Förster, Dag Henrichsen, and Michael Böllig, 194–211. Wolfratshausen: Editions Minerva Hermann Farnung, 2004.

Roller, Kathrin. "Zwischen Rassismus und Frömmigkeit—Biopolitik aus erfahrungsgeschichtlicher Perspektive. Über die Geschwister Hegner, Mathilde Kleinschmidt und Ludwig Baumann als Nachfahren einer deutsch-afrikanischen Missionsfamilie." In *Rassenmischehen—Mischlinge—Rassentrennung: Zur Politik der Rasse im deutschen Kolonialreich,* edited by Frank Becker, 220–40. Stuttgart: Franz Steiner, 2004.

Römer, Ruth. *Sprachwissenschaft und Rassenideologie in Deutschland.* Munich: W. Fink, 1985.

Rothfels, Nigel T. *Savages and Beasts: The Birth of the Modern Zoo.* Baltimore: Johns Hopkins University Press, 2002.

Rüger, Jan. *The Great Naval Game: Britain and Germany in the Age of Empire.* Cambridge: Cambridge University Press, 2007.

Rusch, Walter. "Der Beitrag Felix von Luschans für die Ethnographie." *Ethnographisch.-Archäologische Zeitschrift* 27 (1986): 439–53.

Rycroft, David. "Professor Ernst Oswald Johannes Westphal, 1919–1990." *African Languages and Cultures* 5, no. 1 (1992): 91–95.

Said, Edward. *Orientalism.* New York: Vintage Books, 1979.

Sampson, Geoffrey. *Schools of Linguistics: Competition and Evolution.* London: Hutchinson, 1980.

Sanders, Edith R. "The Hamitic Hypothesis: Its Origins and Functions in Time Perspective." *Journal of African History* 10, no. 4 (1969).

Sargent, Howard. "Diasporic Citizens: Germans Abroad in the Framing of German Citizenship Law." In *The Heimat Abroad: The Boundaries of Germanness,* edited by Krista O'Donnell, Renate Bridenthal, and Nancy Reagin. Ann Arbor: University of Michigan Press, 2005.

Schmidt, Bettina. *Creating Order: Culture as Politics in Nineteenth and Twentieth Century South Africa.* The Hague: Cip-Gegevens Koninkije Bibliotheek, 1996.

Schmokel, Wolfe W. *Dream of Empire: German Colonialism, 1919–1945.* New Haven: Yale University Press, 1964.

Schoenbrun, David Lee. *A Green Place, A Good Place: Agrarian Change, Gender, and Social Identity in the Great Lakes Region to the Fifteenth Century.* Portsmouth, NH: Heinemann, 1998.

Schultze, Andrea. *"In Gottes Namen Hütten bauen." Kirchlicher Landbesitz in Südafrika: die Evangelisch-Lutherische Kirche Südafrikas zwischen 1834 und 2005.* Stuttgart: Franz Steiner Verlag, 2005.

Schumaker, Lyn. *Africanizing Anthropology: Fieldwork, Networks, and the Making of Cultural Knowledge in Central Africa.* Durham: Duke University Press, 2001.

Schwab, Raymond. *The Oriental Renaissance: Europe's Rediscovery of India and the East, 1680–1880.* Translated by Gene Patterson-Black and Victor Reinking. New York: Columbia University Press, 1984.

Seeba, Hinrich C. "Nationalbücher: Zur Kanonisierung nationaler Bildungsmuster in der frühen Germanistik." In *Wissenschaft und Nation: Zur Entstehungsgeschichte der deutschen Literaturwissenschaft,* edited by Jürgen Fohrmann and Wilhelm Vosskamp, 57–71. Munich: Wilhelm Fink Verlag, 1991.

Seligmann, Matthew. *Rivalry in Southern Africa, 1893–1899: The Transformation of German Colonial Policy.* London: Palgrave, 1998.

Sharp, J. S. "The Roots and Development of volkekunde in South Africa." *Journal of Southern African Studies* 8, no. 1 (1981): 16–36.

Sheehan, James J. "What Is German History? Reflections on the Role of the Nation in German History and Historiography." *Journal of Modern History* 53, no. 1 (March 1981): 2–23.

Sheehan, Jonathan. *The Enlightenment Bible: Translation, Scholarship, Culture.* Princeton: Princeton University Press, 2005.

Sheldon, Kathleen. "'Rats Fell from the Ceiling and Pestered Me': Phrase Books as Sources for Colonial Mozambican History." *History in Africa* 25 (1998): 341–60.

Sibthorpe, A. B. C. *The History of Sierra Leone: Revised, Remodeled, and Enlarged.* 3rd ed. London: Elliot Stock, 1906.

Sicard, S. von. *The Lutheran Church on the Coast of Tanzania, 1887–1914, with Spe-*

cial Reference to the Evangelical Lutheran Church in Tanzania, Synod of Uzaramo-Ulunguru. Uppsala: Almqvist and Wiksells, 1970.

Smith, Helmut Walser. "The Talk of Genocide, the Rhetoric of Miscegenation: Notes on Debates in the German Reichstag Concerning Southwest Africa, 1904–1914." In *The Imperialist Imagination: German Colonialism and Its Legacy,* edited by Sara Friedrichsmeyer, Sara Lennox, and Susanne Zantop. Ann Arbor: University of Michigan Press, 1998.

Smith, Woodruff. "Anthropology and German Colonialism." In *Germans in the Tropics: Essays in German Colonial History,* edited by Lewis H. Gann and Arthur J. Knoll, 40–51. New York: Greenwood Press, 1987.

Smith, Woodruff. *European Imperialism in the Nineteenth and Twentieth Centuries.* Chicago: Nelson Hall, 1982.

Smith, Woodruff. *Politics and the Sciences of Culture in Germany.* New York: Oxford University Press, 1991.

Spear, Thomas, and Richard Waller, eds. *Being Maasai: Ethnicity and Identity in East Africa.* London: James Currey, 1993.

Spencer, Paul. *Time, Space, and the Unknown: Maasai Configurations of Power and Providence.* New York: Routledge, 2003.

Spidle, Jake W. "Colonial Studies in Imperial Germany." *History of Education Quarterly* (Fall 1973): 231–47.

Spivak, Gayatri Chakravorty. "Three Women's Texts and a Critique of Imperialism." In *"Race," Writing, and Difference,* edited by Henry Louis Gates Jr., 262–80. Chicago: University of Chicago Press, 1986.

Spöttel, Michael. *Hamiten: Völkerkunde und Antisemitismus.* Frankfurt am Main, 1996.

Stanley, Brian. "Christian Missions, Antislavery, and the Claims of Humanity, c. 1813–1873." In *World Christianities, c. 1815–1914. The Cambridge History of Christianity,* edited by Sheridan Gilley and Brian Stanley, vol. 8, 443–57. Cambridge: Cambridge University Press, 2006.

Steinmetz, George. *The Devil's Handwriting: Precoloniality and the German Colonial State in Qingdao, Samoa, and Southwest Africa.* Chicago: University of Chicago Press, 2007.

Stelzig, Christine. *Afrika am Museum für Völkerkunde zu Berlin, 1873–1919.* Herbholzheim: Centaurus, 2005.

Stepan, Nancy Leys. *The Idea of Race in Science: Great Britain, 1800–1960.* Hamden, CT: Archon, 1982.

Stock, Eugene. *One Hundred Years: Being the Short History of the Church Missionary Society.* London: Church Missionary Society, 1899.

Stock, Eugene, and John Henry Kennaway. *The History of the Church Missionary Society: Its Environment, Its Men, and Its Work.* Vol. 2. London: Church Missionary Society, 1899.

Stocking, George. *After Tylor: British Social Anthropology, 1888–1951.* Madison: University of Wisconsin Press, 1995.

Stocking, George. *The Ethnographer's Magic and Other Essays in the History of Anthropology.* Madison: University of Wisconsin Press, 1992.

Stocking, George. *Victorian Anthropology.* New York: Free Press, 1987.

Stocking, George, ed. Volksgeist *as Method and Ethic: Essays on Boasian Ethnography and the German Anthropological Tradition.* Madison: University of Wisconsin Press, 1996.

Stoecker, Helmuth, ed. *German Imperialism in Africa: From the Beginnings until the Second World War.* 2nd ed. London: C. Hurst, 1986.

Stoecker, Holger. "The Advancement of African Studies by the German Research Foundation (GRF), 1920–1945." In *Ordering Africa: Anthropology, European Imperialism, and the Politics of Knowledge,* edited by Helen Tilley, with Robert J. Gordon, 67–94. Manchester: Manchester University Press, 2007.

Stoecker, Holger. *Afrikawissenschaften in Berlin von 1919 bis 1945. Zur Geschichte und Topographie eines wissenschaftlichen Netzwerkes.* Stuttgart: Franz Steiner Verlag, 2008.

Stoler, Ann Laura. "Rethinking Colonial Categories: European Communities and the Boundaries of Rule." In *Colonialism and Culture,* edited by Nicholas B. Dirks, 319–52. Ann Arbor: University of Michigan Press, 1992.

Strom, Jonathan. "Problems and Promises of Pietism Research." *Church History* 71, no. 3 (2002): 536–54.

Strother, Z. S. "Display of the Body Hottentot." In *Africans on Stage: Studies in Ethnological Show Business,* edited by Bernth Lindfors, 1–40. Bloomington: Indiana University Press, 1999.

Stumpf, Rudolf. *La politique linguistique au Cameroun de 1884 à 1960: Comparaison entre les administrations coloniales allemande, française, et britannique et du rôle joué par les sociétés missionnaires.* Bern: Peter Lang, 1979.

Tanis, James. "Reformed Pietism and Protestant Missions." *Harvard Theological Review* 67, no. 1 (January 1974): 65–73.

Temperley, Howard. *White Dreams, Black Africa: The British Anti-Slavery Expedition to the River Niger.* New Haven: Yale University Press, 1991.

Thomas, Nicholas. *Colonialism's Culture: Anthropology, Travel, and Government.* Princeton: Princeton University Press, 1994.

Thornton, Robert J. "'That Dying Out Race': W. H. I. Bleek's Approach to the Languages of Southern Africa." *Social Dynamics* 9, no. 2 (1983): 2.

Tilley, Helen, ed., with Robert J. Gordon. *Ordering Africa: Anthropology, European Imperialism, and the Politics of Knowledge.* Manchester: Manchester University Press, 2007.

Tillich, Paul. *A History of Christian Thought, from Its Judaic and Hellenistic Origins to Existentialism.* Edited by Carl E. Braaten. New York: Simon and Schuster, 1972.

Toews, John. *Becoming Historical: Cultural Reformation and Public Memory in Early Nineteenth Century Berlin.* Cambridge: Cambridge University Press, 2004.

Townsend, Mary E. *Origins of Modern German Colonialism, 1871–1885.* New York: Columbia University Press, 1921.

Townsend, Mary E. *The Rise and Fall of Germany's Colonial Empire, 1884–1918.* New York: Macmillan, 1930.

Trautmann, Thomas. *Aryans and British India.* Berkeley: University of California Press, 1997.

Triebel, Johannes, ed. *Der Missionar als Forscher: Beiträge christlicher Missionare Zur Erforschung fremder Kulturen und Religionen.* Gütersloh: Gerd Mohn, 1988.

Trüper, Ursula. "Carl Gotthilf Büttner—Missionar, Kolonialpolitiker und Sprachforscher." In *Kolonialmetropole Berlin: Eine Spurensuche,* edited by Ulrich van der Heyden and Joachim Zeller, 122–25. Berlin: Berlin Edition, Quintessenz Verlag, 2002.

Trüper, Ursula. *Die Hottentottin. Das kurze Leben der Zara Schmelen (ca. 1793–1831), Missionsgehilfin und Sprachpionerin in Südafrika.* Cologne: Rüdgier Köppe, 2000.

Ulbrich, Thomas. "Historische koreanische Aufnahmen im Lautarchiv der Humboldt-Universität und im Berliner Phonogramm-Archiv." *Baessler-Archiv* 49 (2001): 139–64.

Ustorf, Werner. *Sailing on the Next Tide: Missions, Missiology, and the Third Reich.* Frankfurt am Main: Peter Lang, 2000.

Van der Heyden, Ulrich. *Diplomasie en Politiek: die pers, die Boererepublieke en Duitsland tydens die Anglo-Boereoorlog.* Pretoria: Protea Boekehuis, 2002.

Van der Heyden, Ulrich, and Jürgen Becher, eds. *Mission und Gewalt: Der Umgang christlicher Missionen mit Gewalt und die Ausbreitung des Christentums in Afrika und Asien in der Zeit von 1792 bis 1918/1919.* Stuttgart: Franz Steiner Verlag, 2000.

Van der Heyden, Ulrich, and Heike Liebau, eds. *Missionsgeschichte, Kirchengeschichte, Weltgeschichte: Christliche Missionen im Kontext nationaler Entwicklungen in Afrika, Asien und Ozeanien.* Stuttgart: Franz Steiner Verlag, 1996.

Van der Heyden, Ulrich, and Holger Stoecker, eds. *Mission und Macht Im Wandel politischer Orientierungen: Europäische Missionsgesellschaften in politische Spannungsfeldern in Afrika und Asien zwischen 1800 und 1945.* Stuttgart: Franz Steiner Verlag, 2005.

Van der Heyden, Ulrich, and Joachim Zeller, eds. *Kolonialmetropole Berlin: Eine Spurensuche.* 122–25. Berlin: Berlin Edition, Quintessenz Verlag, 2002.

Vansina, Jan. "Bantu in the Crystal Ball, I." *History in Africa* 6 (1979).

Vansina, Jan. "New Linguistic Evidence and the 'Bantu Expansion.'" *Journal of African History* 36, no. 2 (1995): 173–95.

Vansina, Jan. *Paths in the Rainforests: Toward a History of Political Tradition in Equatorial Africa.* Madison: University of Wisconsin, 1990.

Vermeulen, Hans F. "Origins and Institutionalization of Ethnography and Ethnology in Europe and the USA, 1771–1845." In *Fieldwork and Footnotes: Studies in the History of European Anthropology,* edited by Arturo Alvarez Roldán and Hans F. Vermeulen. London: Routledge, 1995.

Viswanathan, Gauri. *Masks of Conquest: Literary Study and British Rule in India.* New York: Columbia University Press, 1989.

Von Joeden-Forgey, Elisa. "From 'Territorium Nullius' to 'Personum Nullius': German Colonial Law and the Invention of the 'Eingeborene.'" Unpublished conference paper, African Studies Association 44th Annual Meeting, Houston, November 2001.

Walker, Samuel Abraham. *The Church of England Mission in Sierra Leone, includ-*

ing an Introductory Account of that Colony and a Comprehensive Sketch of the Niger Expedition in the Year 1841. London: Seeley, Burnside, and Seeley, 1847.

Wallmann, Johannes. "Was ist Pietismus?" In *Pietismus und Neuzeit XX/1994: Ein Jahrbuch zur Geschichte des neueren Protestantismus,* edited by Andreas Lindt, 11–27. Göttingen: Vandenhoeck und Ruprecht, 1995.

Walls, Andrew F. *The Cross-cultural Process in Christian History: Studies in the Transmission and Appropriation of Faith.* London: Continuum International Publishing Group, 2002.

Walls, Andrew F. "The Eighteenth-Century Protestant Missionary Awakening in Its European Context." In *Christian Missions and the Enlightenment,* edited by Brian Stanley. Grand Rapids, MI: Eerdmans, 2001.

Weber, Charles. *International Influences and Baptist Mission in West Cameroon: German-American Missionary Endeavor under International Mandate and British Colonialism.* Leiden: E. J. Brill, 1993.

Weber, Eugen. *Peasants into Frenchmen.* Stanford: Stanford University Press, 1976.

Weindling, Paul. "Weimar Eugenics: The Kaiser Wilhelm Institute for Anthropology, Human Heredity, and Eugenics in Social Context." *Annals of Science* 42, no. 3 (May 1985): 303–18.

Weingart, Paul. "German Eugenics between Science and Politics." *Osiris,* 2nd ser., 5 (1989): 260–82.

Weiss, Holger. "German Images of Islam in West Africa." *Sudanic Africa* 11 (2000): 53–93.

Welch, Claude. *Protestant Thought in the Nineteenth Century.* Vol. 1, *1799–1870.* New Haven: Yale University Press, 1972.

Welsh, Frank. *South Africa: A Narrative History.* New York: Kodansha International, 1999.

Werner, Wolfgang. "A Brief History of Land Dispossession in Namibia." *Journal of Southern African Studies* 19, no. 1 (March 1993): 135–46.

West, Martin Litchfield. *Indo-European Poetry and Myth.* Oxford: Oxford University Press, 2007.

Whitman, James. "From Philology to Anthropology in Mid-Nineteenth Century Germany." In *Functionalism Historicized: Essays on British Social Anthropology,* edited by George Stocking, vol. 2, 214–29. Madison: University of Wisconsin Press, 1983.

Wildenthal, Lora. *German Women for Empire, 1894–1945.* Durham: Duke University Press, 2001.

Wildenthal, Lora. "Race, Gender and Citizenship in the German Colonial Empire." In *Tensions of Empire: Colonial Cultures in a Bourgeois World,* edited by Frederick Cooper and Ann Laura Stoler, 263–86. Berkeley: University of California Press, 1997.

Williams, Elizabeth A. "Ethnology as Myth: A Century of French Writing on the Peuls of West Africa." *Journal of the History of the Behavioral Sciences* 24, no. 4 (October 1988): 363–77.

Williamson, George S. "Gods, Titans, and Monsters: Philhellenism, Race, and Religion in Early-Nineteenth-Century Mythography." In *The German Invention of*

Race, edited by Sara Eigen and Mark Joseph Larrimore, 147–66. Binghamton: SUNY Press, 2006.

Williamson, George S. *The Longing for Myth in Germany: Religion and Aesthetic Culture from Romanticism to Nietzsche.* Chicago: University of Chicago Press, 2004.

Williamson, Kay. "Linguistic Evidence for the Use of Some Tree and Tube Food Plants in Southern Nigeria." In *The Archaeology of Africa: Food, Metals, and Towns,* edited by Thurstan Shaw, Paul Sinclair, Bassey Andah, and Alex Okpoko. London: Routledge, 1993.

Williamson, Kay, and Roger Blench. "Niger-Congo." In *African Languages: An Introduction,* edited by Bernd Heine and Derek Nurse, 11–42. Cambridge: Cambridge University Press, 2000.

Wimmelbücker, Ludger. *Mtoro bin Mwinyi Bakari (c. 1869–1927): Swahili Lecturer and Author in Germany.* Oxford: African Books Collective, 2009.

Wolf, Hans-Georg. *English in Cameroon.* Berlin: Walter de Gruyter, 2001.

Wolzogen, Christopher von. *Zur Geschichte des Dietrich Reimer Verlages, 1845–1985.* Berlin: Dietrich Reimer, 1985.

Worden, Nigel. *The Making of Modern South Africa.* 3rd ed. Oxford: Blackwell, 2000.

Wright, Marcia. *German Missions in Tanganyika, 1891–1941: Lutherans and Moravians in the Southern Highlands.* Oxford: Clarendon Press, 1971.

Wright, Marcia. *Strategies of Slaves and Women: Life-Stories from East/Central Africa.* New York: Lilian Barber, 1993.

Wyrod, C. T. "The Light on the Horizon: N'ko Literacy and Formal Schooling in Guinea." Master's thesis, Elliott School of International Affairs of the George Washington University, Washington, DC, 2003.

Yates, Timothy. *Christian Mission in the Twentieth Century.* Cambridge: Cambridge University Press, 1995.

Zachernuk, Philip. "Of Origins and Colonial Order: Southern Nigerian Historians and the 'Hamitic Hypothesis' c. 1870–1980." *Journal of African History* 35 (1994): 427–55.

Zantop, Susanne. *Colonial Fantasies: Conquest, Family, and Nation in Precolonial Germany, 1770–1870.* Durham: Duke University Press, 1997.

Zastoupil, Lynn. "Intimacy and Colonial Knowledge." *Journal of Colonialism and Colonial History* 3, no. 2 (2002): 1–41.

Zimmerer, Jürgen. *Deutsche Herrschaft über Afrikaner.* Berlin: LIT Verlag, 2004.

Zimmerman, Andrew. *Anthropology and Antihumanism in Imperial Germany.* Chicago: University of Chicago Press, 2001.

Zipes, Jack. *The Brothers Grimm: From Enchanted Forests to the Modern World.* New York: Palgrave Macmillan, 2002.

Zirkel, Kirsten. "Military Power in German Colonial Policy: The Schutztruppen and Their Leaders in East and South-West Africa, 1888–1918." In *Guardians of Empire: The Armed Forces of the Colonial Powers, c. 1700–1964,* edited by David Killingray and David Omissi, 91–113. Manchester: Manchester University Press, 1999.

Zwernemann, Jürgen. *Culture History and Anthropology: A Century of Research in Germany and Austria.* Uppsala: Ubsaliensis Academiae, 1983.

WEBSITE CONSULTED

http://www.unihamburg.de/Wiss/FB/10/AfrikaS/index.html#start, 10 July 2000

Index